FUNDAMENTALS OF COMMUNICATION

2nd edition

John R. Bittner

The University of North Carolina at Chapel Hill

Prentice Hall, Englewood Cliffs, New Jersey 07632

Library of Congress Cataloging-in-Publication Data

Bittner, John R.
    Fundamentals of communication.
    Bibliography.
    Includes index.
    1. Communication.   I. Title.
P90.B514   1988   001.51   87-15917
ISBN 0-13-335282-X

for

Denise, John, Donald, and Stormy

Editorial/production supervision
    and interior design: Virginia L. McCarthy
Cover design: Wanda Lubelska Design
Manufacturing buyer: Ed O'Doughtery

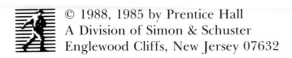 © 1988, 1985 by Prentice Hall
A Division of Simon & Schuster
Englewood Cliffs, New Jersey 07632

Printed in the United States of America

10 9 8 7 6 5 4 3 2 1

ISBN 0-13-335282-X 01

Prentice-Hall International (UK) Limited, *London*
Prentice-Hall of Australia Pty. Limited, *Sydney*
Prentice-Hall Canada Inc., *Toronto*
Prentice-Hall Hispanoamericana, S.A., *Mexico*
Prentice-Hall of India Private Limited, *New Delhi*
Prentice-Hall of Japan, Inc., *Tokyo*
Prentice-Hall of Southeast Asia Pte. Ltd., *Singapore*
Editora Prentice-Hall do Brasil, Ltda., *Rio de Janeiro*

CONTENTS

Part One
FACTORS IN HUMAN COMMUNICATION

2 UNDERSTANDING OURSELVES
Self-Concept and Self-Disclosure   26

3 LANGUAGE   54

4 NONVERBAL COMMUNICATION   78

5 LISTENING   103

Part Two
INTERPERSONAL RELATIONSHIPS AND SMALL GROUPS

6 INTERPERSONAL COMMUNICATION   121

Part Three
PUBLIC SPEAKING AND PERSUASION

9 ANALYZING THE AUDIENCE 184

10 SPEECH ORGANIZATION AND SUPPORT 198

11 RESEARCHING THE SPEECH 219

15   INTERVIEWING   285

16   COMMUNICATION IN THE FAMILY   313

PREFACE

The second edition of *Fundamentals of Communication* retains the features that readers said were the strengths of the previous edition. The text continues to be a complete overview of the discipline that balances the art and science of human communication and also contains a major section on public speaking. New features include:

- **An expanded chapter on small groups that stresses strong leadership and participant skills.**

- **An expanded chapter on listening skills with a step-by-step guide to good listening behavior.**

- **A new section on avoiding sexist language.**

In addition, other features include:

- **Strong emphasis on communication skills of life long value based on a solid foundation of key concepts.**

- **Heavy emphasis on applied examples from a broad range of real-life settings.**

- **Treatment of communication apprehension in the public speaking section.**

- **Sensitivity to the expanding professional role of women and minorities with appropriate examples highlighting the text.**

The second edition of *Fundamentals of Communication* is approached from a background of more than ten years' experience teaching the basic course. It remains the goal of the text to provide readers with critical oral communication skills that will not deteriorate as soon as the basic course ends. Moreover, the text is approached from the premise that students should leave the basic course with more than a quick-fix prescription but rather a strong, lasting understanding of communication concepts. This understanding is central to a well educated person and the basis of success in every facet of our lives.

A comprehensive instructor's manual accompanies the text and is available from Prentice-Hall. In addition to the instructor's manual, the second edition of *Fundamentals of Communication* also contains **detailed speech outlines,** the text of a **sample speech** with questions for analysis and discussion, **questions for review and discussion** at the end of each chapter, **learning exercises** at the end of each chapter, a **classroom exercise** on negotiating a labor contract, **preview objectives, chapter summaries,** a **glossary,** and **diagrams and photographs** to clarify ideas.

ACKNOWLEDGMENTS

Many people deserve my appreciation for the second edition of the text. Users of the previous edition provided suggestions and advice. At the risk of missing someone, a blanket "thank you" is included here as an expression of my deep gratitude.

The sales, marketing, production and editorial staffs of Prentice-Hall continue to be the best in the business.

Former colleagues and teachers including Charles J. Stewart, W. Charles Redding, Bruce Kendall, J. Robert Kibler, Larry Barker, Gus Friedrich, and others deserve mention.

My students at Purdue University, The University of Oregon, DePauw University, and The University of North Carolina at Chapel Hill are thanked.

A special acknowledgement is made to Nancy C. Arnett who authored some of the learning exercises and also the instructor's manual.

No one deserves more credit than Denise.

J.R.B.
Chapel Hill

1

THE PROCESS
OF COMMUNICATION
An Overview

OBJECTIVES

After completing this chapter, you should be able to

- Better understand the importance of speech communication
- Discuss the early forms of human communication
- Define communication
- Apply the definition of communication
- Explain a model of communication
- Describe the process of intrapersonal communication, including perception and noise
- Identify some practical applications of intrapersonal communication
- Discuss the process of interpersonal communication, including noise and fields of experience
- Explain the process of mass communication
- Realize the relationships between intrapersonal, interpersonal, small-group, public, and mass communication.

White frothing water cascades down through a gorge wedged between towering granite cliffs. Bubbling foam from thousands of gallons of surging Salmon River splashes a deceiving harmlessness over the jagged hidden rocks that can rip a rubber raft and a body apart. In less time than it takes to yell "help!", the foolhardy, the uninitiated, and the disrespectful can be lost. Indians, frontier explorers, and early settlers all knew the power of the river and respected it. Today, it is the city dweller, the urban cowboy, and the weekend adventurer who ride the rafts clinging to the safety of life jackets and commercial guides.

We started our river adventure with two other families. The sun's rays were beginning to penetrate the base of the canyon, warming the nip of the early morning river mist. With a bit of apprehension, some excitement, and lots of anticipation, we waited for our guide, Dave, to give us our first instructions.

Dave could only be described as unique. In his mid-30s, he had a rugged complexion that matched the mountains through which he was about to guide us. A one-time Texas cowboy who had worked the cattle herds of the Southwest, he had tried other jobs but settled on the outdoors, tried marriage and stopped trying, tried being a guide and didn't have to try. For Dave, the outdoors was where he belonged. The mountains were all neighbors, the river an intimate friend.

As we listened to Dave's instructions, I knew he had one quality in addition to his reputed skills as a river runner. Dave was an excellent communicator. He said little but commanded our every thought. Sensing an audience both eager and apprehensive, he looked at the young children with an assurance that calmed us all. First, in a casual, almost disinterested way, he told us how to strap on the life jackets. His voice was soft, his sentences were broken, his eye contact shy, but he had every single one of us in the palm of his hand.

"Just stick your arm through here and pull on the strap," Dave said.

The life jackets were a bit awkward, even a bit frightening. This created a conflicting feeling between wanting to be safe and wanting to be as free as possible to swim for dear life.

Dave looked at each of us. No shyness now; this was serious business. When he had checked each clasp, made sure we were comfortable, and gave us the assuring smile and twinkle of an eye, he reached up to adjust his old western felt hat and said, "Let's go."

The raft loaded and moved into the swiftly flowing water. Within an instant, the eerie feeling of knowing we were now under the power of the river and that our destiny lay in Dave's skill with the oars crept over us. Before long, we looked ahead and realized the river had disappeared. The relatively smooth water that had buoyed our confidence was no longer there. With only the words "Hang on!" and a quick glance at each of us, Dave plunged the right oar into the water as the raft suddenly dropped into the rapids before us. Screams of excitement erupted as the white water sprayed over the bow, giving us our first taste of the river's fury and pleasure.

Then, just as quickly as it plunged into the rapids, the raft leveled off. As an audience of passengers, we sat with our eyes glued to our guide to gauge how he fared in negotiating the rapids.

"Everybody okay back there?" Dave asked.

"Great," we replied in false bravado.

"Good. We've got some bigger ones ahead," he acknowledged.

By now, conversations among people who had never met before that morning began to pick up. Relationships form fast when everyone is experiencing the same thing. They form even faster when shared moments of excitement come in quick succession. Small talk began with questions such as: "How are you hanging on?" "Did your camera get wet?" "I'll share some pictures with you if yours don't turn out." "How far is the next rapid?"

For the father and daughter on the trip, it was obvious to us that a special family bond was developing. The young girl was more used to being with her mother, who had stayed behind to take care of other children, than with her father. They sit close together now in the rear of the raft. This is their first trip to this rugged Northwest area. We realize when the trip ends, the father and daughter will become the center of family stories for years to come about the time they ran the river together. You can almost hear the tales of the ride, the luring sight of the upcoming rapids, the thrill of accomplishment, and the ability to tell friends, "We did it!"

Through more rapids, more canyons, past mountains and under bridges, the raft continues its watery journey down the river. A stop for lunch gives everyone a chance to get to know each other better and to share more experiences about family, backgrounds, and friends. We're realizing that not only is this river experience giving us the chance to learn about others but also the chance to learn about ourselves.

When lunch is finished, everyone crawls back in the raft for the second half of our journey. A bend in the river soon brings us to a long, straight canyon. The river is calm. The water is chilly, but in the heat of the noonday sun, the temptation to jump in is too much to resist. With Dave's permission, we are all in the water, floating in our life jackets alongside the raft. While Dave handles the oars, we seem to split into two groups, one on each side of the raft, and carry on a group discussion. Almost deliberately playing on the relaxing day and the calm water, we casually discuss any topic that comes to mind. We are comfortable with each other, and the discussion flows easily. People who would be less forward or less talkative in other social situations are conversing as if they had known each other for years. Gradually a new rapid approaches, and it is time for everyone to climb back into the raft for the last charging ride of the day.

By 5:00 P.M., the van that will carry us back to town can be seen along the highway that borders the river's bank. A hot dinner that awaits us when we reach our docking point is being prepared by the guide service. After an all-you-can-eat feast of pork chops, mashed potatoes, corn, salad, iced tea, and homemade pie, we collapse into the van for the ride back to civilization.

The memories of the day on the river vividly came to mind as I began to plan the content and organization of this book. If everyone who reads this text or takes a course in speech communication could communicate as well as everyone did on that delightful summer day, the world would be a much better place in which to live. Although all of us on the river trip were simply adapting to the situation, to the conversation, and to the people with whom we were sharing our river experience, we were responsible for some of the most important concepts in the process of communication.

Few public speakers can hold the attention of an audience the way Dave did when he gave us his river instructions. And if everyone who ever heard a speech listened as attentively as we did to Dave, the speaker would enjoy a sizable measure of success in getting a point across, and the audience would hear much more information than typically is communicated in a public presentation.

If relationships could develop and be nurtured as quickly and success-fully as ours were on the river, friendships might be richer and enemies fewer. If those same people could share with each other the things we shared, then the silence that permeates many marriages and the distance that separates many parents and children would be replaced by meaningful sharing of information, and by rewarding talk rather than quiet despair.

If we could overcome apprehension, learn as much about ourselves, and gain self-confidence as quickly as we all did on the river, then our ability to function as senders of communication would be greatly enhanced. Strong inter-personal communication, the substance of good relationships, would emerge and blossom. Whether we were participating in a group discussion, appearing for a job interview, interacting with a boss in a large corporation, or sitting at the dinner table with family members, we would be a meaningful contributor to conversation and the exchange of information.

Occasionally we will return to the river as we venture through our study of speech communication. We'll remember Dave's speech, the father and his daughter, the close relationships, and the group discussions by the raft. We will also learn about the importance of nonverbal communication and the impor-tance of language.

As you navigate the rapids we all face in life, I hope the things you learn from this book will not only increase your skill and appreciation of good human communication but also sensitize you to the rewards and satisfaction that come from being a responsible, skilled communicator.

OUR COMMUNICATION ENVIRONMENT

James D. Robinson, III, while serving as chairman of the American Express Corporation, addressed the American Advertising Federation on the paradox of communication. He said that we operate in a media environment where things are packaged in 30-second commercials. We expect other types of communica-tion to take place in the same way. Robinson told his audience, we are consuming more and more information with less and less time to absorb it. "We are becom-ing 'fast-fact junkies' and are masters at using the buzzword. That is not com-munication; it is monologue. Effective communication runs in both directions. We must improve the ways in which we *listen* to our publics, and then respond to what we hear."[1]

James Carey, serving as Dean of the College of Communications at the University of Illinois, observed that the price of error in communication is very high. He noted, "Through worldwide technological communication, we have very much expanded the scale—and the consequences—of our failures to communicate effectively and to understand."[2] Sometimes as students it is hard to realize the importance of communication beyond the classrooms of a college or university. For older students, however, or those who have had experience in business, the importance of good communication is rarely underestimated. At a respected business school, the daytime M.B.A. class thought a course in communication held little value. The executive M.B.A. class, made up of older individuals who had returned to earn their degree at night, viewed the communication course as being of vital importance.

We need to keep in mind that in both our professional and personal lives we will be competing constantly with people who are skilled communicators. In fact, our success as communicators may determine our position in life. Strong communication skills and the ability to interact interpersonally with others may impress those people who can influence promotion within an organization. In our personal lives the ability to make another person feel comfortable through our conversation may encourage a strong friendship and lasting relationship.

The paradox that James Robinson discusses, Dean Carey's sensitivity to communication errors, the older business school students who appreciate good communication skills, the personal relationships we make—all point to the importance of communication in our lives.

THE IMPORTANCE OF EFFECTIVE ORAL COMMUNICATION

As one example, many companies and organizations are placing renewed emphasis on oral communication skills. The ability to interact positively with co-workers is not only critical to success of the individual but is also critical to the success of the organization. A sales manager who cannot instill motivation in the sales staff or the co-worker who irritates others and is uncooperative disrupt not only the lives of individuals but also production and profits.

Public speaking, for example, is a vital quality for upward mobility in any corporate setting. Many students who avoid such courses in school later see peers with more effective oral communication skills being promoted over them. Public presentations are routine and expected at meetings of boards of directors. Junior executives who make presentations at these gatherings are on center stage, in full view of the people who make decisions about promotions, transfers, and advancement. The ability to present information effectively to such groups can be a key opportunity in a professional career.

Many companies also are reexamining such factors as interpersonal communication in their marketing strategies. Instead of hiring models to lure prospective customers into its exhibit booths at trade conventions, a Michigan tool manufacturer decided instead to improve its salespersons' skills in speech communication. The salespersons were required to give two-minute speeches that were videotaped and later analyzed. The importance of holding eye contact with customers, of proper greetings, of knowing what words to avoid, of body language, and the ability to talk with hostile prospects were all included in the training. Even the basics of standing with feet 12 inches apart and hands relaxed at the side were included, for a nervous salesperson at a convention booth frightens people away.

While the training is basic, the return on those training dollars spent by the firm is anything but basic. The company reported a 50 percent jump in sales at a trade convention from the previous year before the training program was instituted. Graduates of the training program reported that working the trade show after having had the training was like going from the minor leagues to the major league. They also said it was easy to spot competitors making serious errors and losing business.[3]

Company recruiters on college campuses know the importance of good speech communication. Conducting thousands of job interviews, recruiters can quickly separate those they want to interview further from those they courte-ously dismiss. What qualities do they look for most? A survey published in a publication for company personnel directors lists, in order of importance, the top five characteristics employers look for in students: (1) oral communication, (2) motivation, (3) initiative, (4) assertiveness, and (5) loyalty.[4]

Another survey asked industry advisors to community colleges what communication competencies community college students should possess for immediate entry into the work force.[5] Listening skills were reported as "abso-lutely essential" by a majority of respondents, and the ability to understand directions ranked first. The ability to work cooperatively in groups was also important, as was the ability to use language effectively, specifically words that are understood by others. Listening, group discussion, and language are all subjects we will explore further in later chapters.

Echoing these sentiments was a report by the College Board listing skills a student should possess to be successful in college. The report told students that *before* they even entered college, they should have

> The ability to engage in discussion as both a speaker and listener—interpreting, analyzing, and summarizing
>
> The ability to contribute to classroom discussions in a way that is readily under-stood by listeners—that is, succinct and to the point
>
> The ability to present an opinion persuasively
>
> The ability to recognize the intention of a speaker and to be aware of the techniques a speaker is using to affect an audience
>
> The ability to recognize and take notes on important points in lectures and discussions
>
> The ability to question inconsistency in logic and to separate fact from opinion.[6]

Human communication through speech is universal. It is interwoven into psychology, sociology, history, political science, law, literature, economics, even biology and zoology. It is this diversity of disciplines, all tied together by the knot of the communication process, that makes the study of human communication exciting and productive. When you have finished this book, I hope you will take with you not only an appreciation of the importance of human communication in our lives but also many of the *skills* necessary to practice good speech communication. Let us begin, now, with a look at the history of communication.

EARLY FORMS OF HUMAN COMMUNICATION

Our ancient ancestors did not communicate with the same clarity that we enjoy today with our well-developed language systems. Approximately 100,000 years ago, the fundamentals of language began to emerge (Fig. 1–1). Around 9,000 years ago, *pictographs*—writings on the insides of caves and on animal skins— further aided spoken communication. About 6,000 years ago, those pictographs became stylized, much like symbols. Those symbols later developed into alphabets.

We now know that as a society develops, communication is a key factor in the rapid growth of learning. Through communication, people can exchange symbols and thus promote learning at a much faster rate. Along with a system of production to create goods and services, a system of defense to protect against intruders, and a method of member replacement sufficient to counteract disease and other elements, a system of communication develops social control and maintains order in society.

Figure 1-1 Early forms of communication included drawings called "pictographs," which were the forerunners of alphabets and later recorded language.

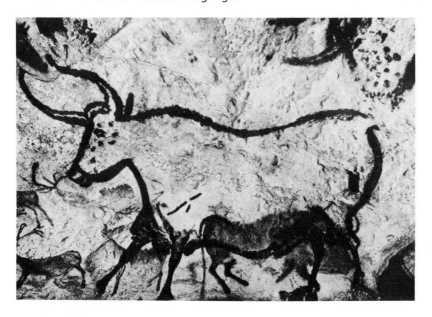

DEFINING COMMUNICATION

How do we define the term *communication?* Although slightly different in their exact wordings, most dictionaries include the following three words somewhere in their definitions: transmit, transfer, and transact. By dissecting these words, we will be closer to our own definition of communication.

Consider the word *transmit.* If we transmit something, are we communicating? What about the person who stands on a hilltop and shouts across the valley to hear the echo? Is that person communicating? What about the baseball player who comes out of the dugout to yell at an umpire? Certainly the player is transmitting information. But is the player communicating? What about the mother who tells her daughter to clean up her room? She has transmitted information; but two days later, the room remains a mess. Again, people are all transmitting information. But did communication take place?

Now consider the word *transfer.* Is the person who stands on the hilltop shouting across the valley to hear the echo transferring information? Certainly that person is transmitting, but does transfer take place if no one hears the shouting? What occurs if someone on the other side of the hilltop shouts back with an answer? Does communication take place? Now let's consider the daughter. What if she heard her mother's request but was too busy to clean up her room and did not respond? Was information transferred? Did communication take place? And what about the baseball player? What if the umpire refuses to change the call after the player charges from the dugout? A transfer of information took place, but did communication take place? What about a person who delivers a speech? After a great deal of preparation and practice, the person steps up to the podium and delivers the address. Certainly information has been transmitted and transferred to the audience, but has communication taken place?

Let us examine the word *transact.* What happens during transaction? Transaction means not only that information has been sent and received, but that some additional information has been *sent back* as a form of *feedback.* For example, we might suggest that if the person yelling across the valley heard a reply, then decided to yell back again, transaction had taken place. If the daughter had at least acknowledged she heard her mother's request to clean up the room, even though she didn't clean it, is that a transaction? And what if the umpire refuses to change the call but nevertheless has a healthy argument with the player? Is this a transaction? Returning to our example of the speaker, has communication taken place if the audience applauds loudly? What if the audience does not applaud?

APPLYING THE DEFINITION

How do we answer all of the above questions? To gain a clearer understanding, let us return to our original source, the dictionary, for its definitions of communication:

Com·mu·ni·ca·tion

1. To make known; impart; transmit. 2. To have an interchange, as of thoughts or ideas. 3. Something communicated. 4. A system of sending and receiving messages, as by telephone, television, or computer. 5. A connection. 6. A channel or conduit for information. 7. Movement of messages from sender to receiver.

The first definition, "To make known; impart; transmit," involved all of our examples. The person shouting from the hilltop, the mother, the umpire, and the speaker made known, imparted, and transmitted information. The next definition, "To have an interchange, as of thoughts or ideas," relates to the word *transaction* and certainly *transfer* (Fig. 1–2). If you're talking with your boss about a production problem you're probably having an interchange of thoughts or ideas. If you're participating in a class discussion, you're having an interchange of thoughts or ideas. An executive delivering a speech, if effective, is having an interchange with the audience. The audience may not be talking or applauding, but if the executive is alert and skilled in the art and science of communication, then the executive is still receiving feedback from the audience. Moreover, the executive is constantly *adapting to feedback*. Questions from the audience are an obvious form of feedback. Reading nonverbal cues sent by members of the audience is a more subtle way the executive can receive and adapt to feedback. Being attuned to eye contact, facial expressions, and posture can all help the executive adapt, both the content and the way the speech is delivered, and to communicate more effectively "with," not "to," the audience.

By now we see that communication is a dynamic process. It is constantly in motion, constantly changing, and constantly being adapted by both the sender (encoder) and receiver (decoder) of communication. Other words in addition to transmit, transfer, and transact frequently creep into definitions of communication. Among those words are: codes, ideas, intentions, conscious, unconscious, face to face, words, meaning, passage, sender, symbols, interactive, messages, channel, connection, receiver, information, irreversible, and interact.

Figure 1-2
Effective communication between individuals involves an "exchange" of information resulting in communication transmission, transfer, and transaction. The sensitivity of both individuals to the feedback being generated by the other person is a prerequisite for success as a communicator. (Ken Karp)

For the purposes of arriving at a simple but easily applied definition, we shall define communication in this book as *the act of sharing symbols*. We will see later that symbols can be verbal or nonverbal and are the components that comprise the "messages" of the communication process. We will also examine the important "sharing" quality of communication. You should keep in mind, however, that if you are assigned to write your own definition or read definitions of communication in other texts, your definition or those of others may be no less applicable to the understanding or study of communication.

A MODEL OF COMMUNICATION

Because the process of communication is so dynamic, it is easier to understand that process if we stop it long enough to study it. For that purpose, we will need a model of communication. Many different models have been advanced over the years; some have come from the study of communication, while others have come from mathematics, psychology, and sociology. The easiest way to view a *communication model* is to consider it as *a stop-action picture of the communication process*. Essentially, it maps the terrain over which communication flows. Different models may also look at different portions of the communication process, much like a road map views the terrain differently from an aerial map.[7]

For this text, we will use the communication model found in Fig. 1–3. The sender in our model transmits a message (represented by the dotted lines), which is sent through a channel (the human voice in face-to-face communication) to another person (represented by the receiver).

Our model also shows a dotted line returning to the sender. This dotted line represents feedback. In face-to-face communication, feedback is instantaneous. It is also necessary for good communication to take place. Earlier in this chapter, it was "feedback" that brought the term *transaction* into our original discussion of the definition of communication. If we apply our own definition of communication, which is "the act of sharing symbols," we can see that for symbols to be shared, feedback must take place. A responsible sender of communication must evaluate constantly the feedback of the receiver. If a manager talks to an employee, the reaction of the employee is feedback. If the employee begins to look disinterested, you may need to respond to that feedback and adjust what you say and how you say it.

In essence, a communication model *sensitizes* us to the communication situations we encounter in everyday life. Being sensitive to those communication situations is the first step toward improving communication.

A communication model also helps us to *analyze* communication situations, for it can show us where things may go wrong or where misunderstandings may occur. This knowledge can help us take the first step in *solving* communication problems. Thus, a communication model can serve three important purposes: *sensitize, analyze,* and *solve.*

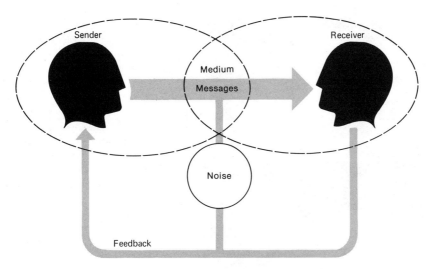

Figure 1-3   A model of communication is a stop-action picture of the communication process. The elements of the model include the sender of communication who encodes information and sends a message through a channel or medium to a receiver who in turn decodes the information and sends feedback to the sender. Noise can create barriers to communication. In mass communication (see Chapter 17), the model acquires the added element of a gatekeeper(s), who controls the flow of information between sender and receiver.

We will use our communication model to help us understand four broad types of communication: intrapersonal, interpersonal, public, and mass communication. As we study them, we will also expand our model.

INTRAPERSONAL COMMUNICATION

Intrapersonal communication is defined as communication within oneself (Fig. 1–4). Applying intrapersonal communication to our communication model, the senders of communication are our senses. The messages are neurological impulses to our brain, which processes those messages and feeds back information to our senses. Perception, understanding, emotions, empathy, and other ways in which we react within ourselves are all forms of intrapersonal communication. Sometimes the messages we receive are stored in our brain, much like a computer stores information. We may use that information later when we engage in a conversation. Other times, the processing and feedback of information is immediate, such as jerking away our hand after touching a hot stove.

Figure 1-4
Intrapersonal communication is communication within ourselves. In this example, the woman's eyes are picking up information from the page of the book, and the brain and central nervous system receive, process, and store the information. Electrochemical impulses feedback messages to the eyes, which re-read a portion of the text or read faster. Intrapersonal communication is the basis of all other types of communication. (Laimute E. Druskis photo)

The Brain and Nervous System

Intrapersonal communication is the basis of all other types of communication, and the brain with its central nervous system is a complex, fascinating part of that communication process. Because the communication model is a stop-action picture of the communication process, let us imagine that we put a microscopic lens on our camera and peer into the depths of the brain. There we will see an enormous communication system consisting of tiny *neurons*.[8] Neurons are specialized cells that send and receive information. We have between 100 billion and 200 billion neurons in our brain, each with tiny fibers reaching out to communicate with other cells.

When a neuron or cell sends a message, a single long fibrous extension called an *axon,* carries the message away from the cell body toward *terminal branches,* which send the message to other cells. The axon is composed of a chemical substance that helps the message move to the terminal branches. Science has discovered that our body actually contains millions of these chemical transmitters that help the process of intrapersonal communication, whether it involves thinking to ourselves or forming the thoughts that become speech.

Moving Intrapersonal Messages

On the receiving end, short fibrous branches called *dendrites* receive messages from surrounding cells. The neurons coordinate this receiving and sending of messages with an on/off code, which forms the basis of the "language" of our nervous system. When an impulse moves down an axon, it is called an *axonal transmission*. Again, we see the word "transmit" creeping into our understanding of human communication.

When we zoom back with our imaginary camera and take a wide-angle view of our body, we can see that our senses act as senders of communication to our brain. Our eyes see an image of light and transmit that image to our brain. The *retina* of the eye thus becomes a sender of communication through the *optic nerve*, which acts as a channel of communication to the brain. When our ears hear something, a similar process occurs. The *eardrum* sends sound waves through the *auditory nerve*, which is the channel linking the ear with the brain. The brain is the receiver of this intrapersonal communication.

PERCEPTION AND INTRAPERSONAL COMMUNICATION

An important function of our brain is *perception*. Perception, as we will discover later in this text, influences how we receive and react to communication (Fig. 1–5). At the most basic level of intrapersonal communication, perception is concerned with the way in which we use our senses to receive messages, such as light images from our eyes.

Figure 1-5   Our perception of the illustration will alter what we see. Looking at the illustration one way we see the head of a duck with the duck's bill on the left. Looking at the illustration still another way, we see instead the head of a rabbit with the rabbit's ear to the left. We filter communication much in the same way. In any communication setting, perception is operating as a form of intrapersonal communication and determines what messages we receive and how we interpret those messages. The illustration was used in early experiments in psychology.

Psychologists have found that we organize what we see based on certain laws. For instance, the *law of nearness or proximity* says that we group symbols that are close together. The *law of similarity* says we also group together things that look alike. The *law of good continuation* says we group together line segments that form straight or smoothly curved lines. If a circle is imposed on top of a square and all of the lines are drawn on white paper, the result will appear as a circle and a square. However, if those same objects are colored solid and of different shades, they will be perceived by us as a cube and a cylinder.

Still another law says that we tend to fill in lines that are broken, making solid lines seem to appear where none exist. This is called the *law of closure.* These four laws were advanced in the 1920s by a group of German psychologists known as the Gestalt school. The important thing to remember is that our senses cause us to perceive things differently. They even can play tricks on our ability to see things as they actually are. Thus, they can interfere with our ability to communicate clearly, both within ourselves and with others.

When perceptual distortion exists, it is called an *illusion.* Illusions happen more frequently than we may realize. Reportedly, 16 percent of all airplane accidents are caused by illusions. Some of the most familiar of these are geometric illusions. Line drawings of an arrow and a feather will appear to be of different lengths even though they are the same size—a geometric illusion. Stationary light against a dark object may tend to move, to dart, or to swoop. This illusion, called the *autokinetic effect,* is responsible for many UFO sightings.

Sound is also linked to perception. If we were watching an auto race, as the race cars approached us, their engines would have a high-pitched sound. As they moved past us and away, the sound from their engines would drop to a low pitch. This phenomenon is called the *Doppler effect.* Sound waves compress as they approach us and expand as they move away, causing the difference in pitch. The way in which sound travels and the way in which we hear sound waves affect what we perceive when we listen to a speech. The size of the auditorium, the use of the sound equipment or audio aids to illustrate the speech, the location of the speaker in relation to the audience, and the acoustics of the room all influence the message the audience hears.

Our model of communication included the component of *noise,* which can interrupt the communication process. Noise can occur in all types of communication. In intrapersonal communication, noise can be either internal or external. *Internal noise* refers to a malfunction of the body. A headache affecting our concentration on our homework is an example of internal noise interrupting intrapersonal communication. An example of *external noise* blocking the intrapersonal communication process is the ring of the telephone disrupting our concentration on a game of chess.

SOME PRACTICAL APPLICATIONS OF INTRAPERSONAL COMMUNICATION

So far we have studied some of the theory of intrapersonal communication. Now let us apply that theory to discover how intrapersonal communication forms our ability to interact with our environment and with others.

Adapting to Our Environment

Each of us adapts biologically to our environment. Cave dwellers may have awakened on a rainy morning, blinked at the downpour, touched the cold drops of moisture on a stone, and felt the chilly breeze against their faces. If it snowed, they sought warmth. If the sun shone, they ventured out of their caves. If it became too hot, they went back inside the cave and cooled off. This process of daylight entering the eye and communicating brightness to a central nervous system,[9] the tactile sense organs of the skin detecting cold moisture on a rock or a chilly breeze, and the decision to stay inside the cave to seek shelter were all forms of communication taking place within the individuals.

Today, although we may make these same decisions while adapting to our environment, we do not make them in a vacuum or away from the concerns of other people. For example, suppose each Saturday morning that our neighbor goes outside to pick the newspaper off the front walk where the delivery girl always deposits it—under the limb of a large pine tree. Each Saturday morning, half awake, our neighbor invariably stands up and hits that tree limb. Connecting one's head with a tree limb sends an immediate impulse to the brain, which is encoded. Intrapersonal communication takes place.

Our neighbor has a number of ways to adapt to the environment and avoid colliding with the pine tree. The person might ask the delivery girl to place the paper on the porch. But that request could delay her schedule perhaps two minutes. It could also prompt the rest of her customers to request the same kind of service. So that idea is discarded for a more realistic one: cutting the limb off the pine tree. Yet all of the other neighbors have commented on how beautiful the street looks. Finally, our neighbor decides simply to be more careful. But that decision was made with full consideration of other people and other relationships. In other words, we integrate our biological functions with those of others in order to survive in our environment.

Adapting to Stress

Stress can be one of the most damaging influences on the biological makeup of the body and can affect greatly our ability to communicate interpersonally. You may have had a stressful day at work. Perhaps a co-worker and you had a disagreement over job responsibilities. The result was a stressful encounter and a resulting stress-filled environment. Stress is a stimulus just as hitting one's head on a pine tree is a stimulus. Any stimulus produces one or more biological reactions. We may develop a headache or sweat profusely when under extreme stress. You may decide to overeat, remembering that a full stomach is a comforting feeling. Yet overeating may not produce that comforting feeling, especially if a stress-prone digestive system can't handle that much food. We may also lie awake with a case of insomnia and pay for that wakefulness the next day. These negative biological adaptations can cause more stress, not less.

Finding positive ways to handle stress is a much better alternative. Physical exercise tends to prepare the body for stressful situations and creates in some people a tension-relieving mechanism. Under a doctor's care, you might develop a jogging regimen or an aerobics exercise program. Some form of relaxation may also help to alleviate stress. Reading a good book in pleasant surroundings or going for a walk in the park or on the beach are ways of alleviating stress. Cutting down on the amount one eats may also help handle stress. All of the solutions are biological adaptations to our environment using our own personal encoding system.

But we must not forget an equally important solution, which is using good interpersonal communication skills to talk to the other person and discuss the problem.

Memory

Memory is a practical application of intrapersonal communication. It involves retrieving and encoding information stored in our brains. Remembering not to bump into the tree limb is an example of our memory helping us to biologically adapt to our environment. Remembering to hold onto the side of the raft while riding the river rapids is another example.

When we are trying to remember something, we know that associating it with something else can help us increase our memory potential. As an example, let us assume we go to a party and meet someone whose name we would very much like to remember. We would like either to ask that person for a date or be asked for a date by that person at some future time. We have decided that remembering that individual's name is the first step in being able to strike up a conversation. Suppose the person's name is Manuel. Perhaps at some other time we've either met or know of another person named Manuel. Stop for a moment and mentally compare the qualities of that Manuel with the Manuel we just met. There may be many or no similarities, but we are forming an *association* with previous information. In short, we are "hanging" new information on old information. The new information is then stored, and the recall is aided by our earlier acquaintance.

Adapting to Individuals

In addition to helping us adapt to our environment, intrapersonal communication helps us adapt to other people. Overcoming the disagreement at work is a good example. We process all kinds of stimuli when we communicate with other people. Using that intrapersonal processing to communicate interpersonally is one of the most important functions of our internal message-processing system. Many psychologists even feel that to manage worry, stress, and anxiety successfully, we must share our problems and communicate with others. Other research suggests that the least damage from stressful situations is done to people who dilute their anxieties through interpersonal relations.[10] Perhaps the co-worker with whom we disagreed about the job responsibility will eventually become a friend we can confide in and help us dilute our own anxieties.

Adapting to Groups

Intrapersonal communication helps us adapt to group relationships, again by using the same internal message-processing system. Suppose you are sitting around at lunch talking with your co-workers about a particular job assignment. As you sit there, you are constantly processing information you receive from others. You are listening, making judgments, and sorting out the various bits of communications being sent to you.

Perhaps you are at a party and there is a bowl of candy. You would very much like to have the last handful remaining in the bowl. Yet you wonder how the other members of the group might feel if they saw you grabbing that last morsel. By wondering, you are using intrapersonal communication to adapt to the group.

When you live with roommates, your behavior adapts to the group, and things you say and do are in a different context from what they would be if you lived alone. Joining in late-night discussions, sharing cleaning chores, and keeping your stereo down low are all forms of adapting to the sociocultural group of which you are a part.

Listening

Even though we are engaged in conversation with another person, we use intrapersonal communication to process information and participate in the listening process.[11] The ability to adapt to messages and to react intelligently and effectively by providing feedback to the other person demands concentration that involves using our brain and thought processes. Effective listening is an art. It necessitates our empathizing with another individual, taking an active part in the communicative process, and possessing good communication skills that will enhance, not detract from the exchange of information.

To summarize, we should remember that intrapersonal communication is the most basic form of communication; it is communication within ourselves. Essentially, it processes information from our environment and helps us adapt to that environment, whether it be biological, physical, interpersonal, or sociocultural. It is a vital part of all other kinds of communication. In fact, interpersonal and mass communication cannot exist without it.

INTERPERSONAL COMMUNICATION

Applying interpersonal communication to our communication model, we find the sender and receiver of communication in interpersonal communication are individuals. The medium of communication is the human voice. *Interpersonal communication* is, therefore, communication in a face-to-face situation.

Processing Information

To better understand this application, let us follow Tom as he walks to class. Coming toward him is someone he would like to ask to a party. He begins to think (intrapersonal communication): *How will I start this conversation? What will I say to get her to stop and talk to me? What will her response be? Will I be embarrassed? Will she say yes or no? What do I do if she says yes?* Finally, when they are close enough, Tom slows down his pace and says to her, "Stephanie, do you have a second?" Stephanie replies, "Sure, Tom. How are you?"

At this point, interpersonal communication has occurred. Tom has *encoded* information, communicated it through the medium of the human voice to Stephanie, and Stephanie has replied. Stephanie has also *decoded* information. She may have been thinking, *Gee, there's Tom. I wonder if he'll stop and talk? He looks great wearing that sweater.*

With Stephanie's response to Tom's question, we see another component of our communication model—feedback. We also have seen a reversal of our original communication model, because when Stephanie spoke to Tom, she became the sender while he became the receiver.

Once again we see that human communication is a very dynamic process. Each person participating in a conversation switches roles back and forth between being the sender and the receiver, continually providing feedback to the other person.

Another component of our communication model that we discussed in relation to intrapersonal communication is noise. In interpersonal communication we can divide noise into *physical* and *semantic* noise.

Physical noise is concerned with audible sounds that may interrupt the communication process. If a loud truck goes by when Stephanie and Tom are speaking and they do not hear each other, their communication would be interrupted by physical noise. Perhaps it starts to rain and they need to interrupt their conversation to take cover. This, too, would be physical noise.

On the other hand, Stephanie may say something that Tom does not understand, something in which the meanings of words become confused. In that instance, semantic noise has interrupted their communication.

At this point, because we are talking about bases for understanding, we want to add an additional component to interpersonal communication and to our communication model—the field of experience.

Fields of Experience

Fields of experience or, more importantly, merging fields of experience, are necessary before effective interpersonal communication can take place. For example, if Stephanie did not know about the Saturday night party, Tom would have had to inform her. In this case, Tom's field of experience would not have overlapped with Stephanie's. Yet they could still communicate effectively because they had other things in common. They had obviously met someplace before. Perhaps they even had taken a class together. These experiences would be common references that would aid them in processing both intrapersonal and interpersonal communication.

Overlapping fields of experience are called *homophily,* and we will discuss this in greater detail in the chapter on interpersonal communication. When such fields of experience overlap, effective interpersonal communication has a better chance of occurring. (Fig. 1–6).

The next time you are having trouble talking with another person or developing a conversation, ask some questions about the other person's interests. As that person replies, expand your questions and continue to probe—with sincere interest—that person's opinions, skills, ideas, likes, and dislikes. When you receive this new information, you can begin to react and emphathize with—share the feelings of—the other person.

SMALL-GROUP COMMUNICATION

With small-group communication we continue to participate in interpersonal communication but we add more people to the conversation. For example, perhaps Stephanie and Tom stop by the campus lunch counter and meet two additional friends. Now the communication has moved from a one-to-one setting to four people. The communication of one person is received by three other people, and each of these people is able to provide the speaker with feedback.

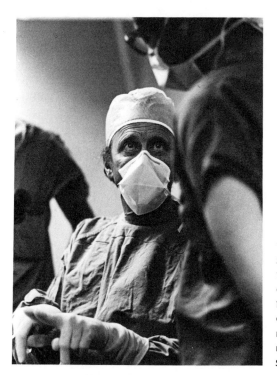

Figure 1-6
Effective interpersonal communication involves sharing fields of experience to create homophily. For example, effective interpersonal communication between two surgeons is critical to the success of the operation. Not only must they share fields of experience and generate homophily, but the messages they exchange must be precise and accurate. Effective interpersonal communication is a foundation for success in many facets of our personal and professional lives. (Laimute Druskis photo)

The encoding and decoding of information becomes more complex as the possible combinations of sender and receiver are increased. All people in the group can react to everyone else in the group.

Participants in small-group communication encounter many more fields of experience. Fields of experience will overlap to create collective homophily in which all members of the group are able to share (Fig. 1–7). Additional relationships will affect the communication process because of liaisons made during the group discussion or because of friendships and acquaintances made before the group meets. Because of experiences between some group members but not others, alliances may develop. In very casual informal groups these alliances will have little effect on communication which takes place. In other settings, such as a negotiation, they will be critical in determining the outcome.

Depending on the type of group, the communication can be affected by the presence of a group leader. This might not be the case with Stephanie, Tom, and their two friends but would become a factor in a sensitive negotiation, a corporate board meeting, a campus organization meeting, and other more formal groups where specific, directed outcomes are expected. Small-group communication is an extension of interpersonal communication, and all of the factors which can affect interpersonal communication can also affect small-group communication.

PUBLIC COMMUNICATION

Public communication involves face-to-face communication to large numbers of people (Fig. 1–8). The politician addressing a rally, a school principal speaking to an assembly, a student delivering a speech to a class are all examples of public

Figure 1-7 Small group communication results in a collective interaction between individuals. Fields of experience overlap, creating understandings through which different members of the group can relate. Additional liaisons can result from friendships and acquaintances made before the group meets. Leaders within the group can affect the interaction that takes place between the participants.

Figure 1-8   Public communication involves communication to large numbers of people. In some settings, such as the General Assembly of the United Nations, sophisticated sound systems carry the speaker's voice to all sections of the assembly hall. (United Nations/M. Grant)

communication. The term *public communication* is many times used synonymously with public speaking. When we study the various ways that a speaker analyzes an audience, the manner in which a speech is researched and delivered, we are studying public communication.

When placing public speaking and public communication in the context of our model of communication, we see that the speaker becomes the sender of communication and the audience the receivers. Because the audience is large, the speaker is less able to respond to individual feedback from each member of the audience. Moreover, the ability to acquire homophily with every member of the audience is lessened because in a public speaking setting the speaker cannot usually interact with the audience the way one interacts in a one-on-one, face-to-face setting. At the same time, however, greater responsibility may be placed on the speaker because of the larger number of people who will be exposed to the message.

Whereas communication in interpersonal and small-group settings tends to be more spontaneous, public communication is many times more structured. Audience analysis becomes critical since the speaker must attempt to determine basic facts about an audience prior to the speech. Their ages, educational level, and motivation for hearing the speech are just three examples. The ability to question another person about his or her feelings and the ability to receive clarification about a point from a member of a small group often is not possible during public communication. Because the opportunity for interaction is limited, close developing relationships between the speaker and the audience are generally not possible.

MASS COMMUNICATION

The fourth type of human communication is *mass communication*. Five factors differentiate mass communication from other types of communication: the presence of a mass medium, delayed feedback, a gatekeeper, physical distance, and limited sensory channels.[12] Our communication model helps to illustrate our discussion of these distinguishing features.

First, the presence of a mass medium helps carry the message between a sender and a receiver. Assume that you are running for student body president. Campaigning interpersonally, you will meet and speak face to face with other students you would like to have vote for you. But the election is fast approaching, and you realize you don't have enough time left to meet enough prospective voters. Or do you? You may not have enough time to communicate with enough students interpersonally, but you may have the time to communicate with them through a mass medium, such as the student newspaper. This time, instead of your voice carrying your message, the newspaper carries it.

The advantage of mass communication is that you can reach a larger number of people. The disadvantage is that you cannot react immediately to feedback and thus alter your message if necessary. If you say the wrong thing, you may not be able to correct your message until the next edition of the newspaper. In mass communication, feedback is usually delayed. This delayed feedback is another factor distinguishing mass communication from other types of communication.

The third distinguishing factor between mass communication and interpersonal communication is the presence of a gatekeeper. A *gatekeeper is anyone who controls the flow of information via a mass medium.* A newspaper editor is one example of a gatekeeper. The gatekeeper most likely is not in the physical proximity of either the sender or the receiver, so it is important for that gatekeeper to have some sense of the receiver's and sender's experiences in order that the flow of information can be controlled effectively and the message properly conveyed. At the same time, it is important for the sender to know about the gatekeeper's experiences in order to ensure that the message is transferred to the receiver. The politician who wants to get a story into the news must have some idea of the type of story the editor wants, so that the politician, or the politician's public relations expert, can tailor his or her message accordingly.

Another factor distinguishing mass communication from interpersonal and intrapersonal communication is physical distance. During interpersonal communication, the people conversing are in direct proximity to each other. However, thousands of miles can separate sender and receiver when mass communication is taking place.

This lack of direct proximity leads us to still another factor distinguishing the types of human communication: limited numbers of sensory channels. When people speak face to face, or interpersonally, they can use all of their senses. Suppose Frank meets Joyce at a party. They might shake hands (touch), smile at each other (sight), detect each other's perfume or after-shave lotion (smell), listen to each other talk (hear), and if they happen to kiss each other hello, even use taste in the sensory process. A major cosmetic manufacturer created an advertising campaign for fruit-scented lipsticks, capitalizing on the role taste plays in a relationship. Yet with mass communication, Frank is only able to see and hear Joyce on television. He cannot use smell, taste, and touch as sensory indicators in the communication linking the two of them together.

RELATIONSHIPS BETWEEN TYPES OF COMMUNICATION

As we stated earlier, interpersonal communication is the foundation of all human communication. We process information through our central nervous systems and then verbalize our intended messages to other people, using our voices or a mass medium. Imagine an ad on TV for a popular recording artist's newest tape. You think about buying the tape but don't know whether you will like all of the songs and thus question whether it is worth the money. To help you decide, you seek the advice of a friend or an *opinion leader,* someone who influences your decisions, attitudes, and behavior. Perhaps your friend collects tapes and keeps up with the latest releases. Or perhaps you and your friend enjoy the same kind of music, and you therefore trust his or her judgment. Your friend tells you the first song on the tape is great but the others are terrible. Based on this advice, you decide not to buy the tape. Your decision involved three types of communication—intrapersonal, as you saw and thought about the commercial; mass communication, because you received the advertisement's message through a mass medium; and interpersonal, because you sought an opinion from your friend.[13]

SUMMARY

We began our discussion of communication by borrowing pages from human history. We learned that skills in oral communication are ranked high in priority for success in our society. Even though technology has changed the ways we use and receive communication, we still see the importance of face-to-face communication.

We defined communication as "The act of sharing symbols," and the words *transmit, transfer,* and *transaction* were used to fine-tune this definition.

To better understand the processes of communication, we used a communication model, which is a pictorial representation of the communication process. Communication models sensitize us to communication situations, help us both to analyze those situations and to solve communication problems.

The basis of all other forms of human communication is intrapersonal communication, or communication within ourselves. Incorporating our senses and our central nervous system, intrapersonal communication starts when special brain cells, called neurons, communicate with other cells. Light and sound are just two of the intrapersonal messages communicated to the brain via the optic and auditory nerves. Noise, both internal and external, can both interfere with and aid intrapersonal communication. Intrapersonal communication helps us adapt to our environment, to stress, to individuals, to groups, and is responsible for our memory and listening, among other functions.

Interpersonal communication is communication in a face-to-face situation. Both physical and semantic noise can interfere with it, while people's fields of experience, when they overlap to create homophily, assist it.

Small-group communication involves groups of three to five people. The same factors that affect communication in an interpersonal setting also affect small-group communication.

Public communication involves direct communication with a large number of people. Many speeches are forms of public communication. Audience analysis and good speaking skills are important to effective public communication.

Mass communication is distinguished from other types of communication by a mass medium, a gatekeeper, physical distance, limited sensory channels, and delayed feedback.

QUESTIONS FOR REVIEW AND DISCUSSION

1. Has the development of mass media both limited and expanded our ability to communicate? Explain.

2. What four laws relating to perception were advanced by German psychologists in the 1920s?

3. What distinguishes intrapersonal communication from interpersonal communication?

4. What are the physical components of the human brain that affect our ability to process information?

5. Intrapersonal communication allows us to process information from the "environment." What are some types of "environment"?

6. What are fields of experience and how do they relate to homophily?

7. What are the five factors that differentiate mass communication from intrapersonal or interpersonal communication?

LEARNING EXERCISES

1. Using the concepts discussed in the chapter, develop your own communication model.

2. Keep a communication diary for one week. Every day record experiences you have had in the five levels of communication: intrapersonal, interpersonal, small-group, public, and mass communication. For example: intrapersonal communication—deciding what to wear; interpersonal communication—borrowing the keys to a friend's car.

ADDITIONAL READINGS

DANCE, F. E.   *Human Communication Theory: Comparative Essays.* New York: Harper & Row, Pub., 1982.
DURDEN-SMITH, J. and D. DESIMONE   *Sex and the Brain.* New York: Arbor House, 1983.
FRISBY, J.   *Seeing: Illusion, Brain and Mind.* Oxford: Oxford University Press, 1979.
GREEN, E., and A. GREEN   *Beyond Biofeedback.* New York: Delacorte Press, 1977.
GRUNEBERG, M. M., and P. MORRIS, eds.   *Aspects of Memory.* London: Methuen and Co., Ltd., 1978.
HAYAKAWA, S. I.   *Through the Communication Barrier: On Speaking, Listening, Understanding.* New York: Harper & Row, Pub., 1979.
WONDER, J. and P. DONOVAN   *Whole Brain Thinking.* New York: William Morrow, 1984.

2

UNDERSTANDING OURSELVES
Self-Concept and Self-Disclosure

OBJECTIVES

After completing this chapter, you should be able to

- Understand the basic human needs toward self-actualization
- Distinguish between values, attitudes, and beliefs
- Know how to maintain our self-concept in the face of challenges
- Compare and contrast the adult, parent, and child ego states
- Manage our different "selves"
- Discuss the forces that affect our self-concept
- Be aware of how we present our self-concept to others
- Explain the concept of self-disclosure.

We started this book with a trip down the river rapids, skillfully ferried by our guide, Dave. Dave had a positive self-concept. He had tried many different things in life and had reached a point where he was content with himself and his surroundings. Some of his experiences had been on the back of a horse on a Texas cattle ranch. Others had been with a hunting party as he guided it in stalking big game. Still others had been on a raft navigating the white waters of the rivers of the Northwest.

Dave was also satisfied with his relationships with others, even with the depth of the relationships he wanted to encounter at this stage in his life. His friends were the people he lived with and worked for, the people who owned the outdoor adventure business and the people he met on the river runs. Dave didn't say much, but when he did, it was positive. He exhibited a calm that we will see shortly is indicative of a positive self-concept. His qualities made him easy to deal with and easy to talk to. As we learned at the start of this book, Dave was a good communicator.

SELF-CONCEPT AND GOOD COMMUNICATION

Self-concept is an important key to good human communication as it determines how we will send communication. As senders of communication, we are continually transmitting messages to others. Sometimes our messages appear on our faces; sometimes we speak them; other times we communicate by what we wear. Although we may consciously send these messages for a specific reason, often the messages we communicate are unintentional. We may communicate them because we cannot help ourselves. Sometimes these messages may reflect positively on us, such as our good attitudes contagiously rubbing off on everyone around us. Other times we may be pessimistic and negative in our feelings. At these times, people want to avoid us and our communication.

The messages we communicate, intentionally or unintentionally, are directly connected to the way we feel about ourselves. The way we intrapersonally process the answer to "Who am I?" can influence how we present ourselves to others.

Psychologist Carl Rogers stresses the importance of self-concept in determining how we perceive our world and how we behave in relation to others.[1] But self-concept is also a complex phenomenon. We are continually affected by society's rules telling us how we should and should not act. Another way to view self-concept is to understand it as perceiving in ourselves what we perceive others perceive us to be. That is not doubletalk. Eleanor Roosevelt said it best when she declared, "No one can make you feel inferior without your consent." Sociologist Erving Goffman referred to a process of impression management in which we "manage" the way we present ourselves to others. For some, it is a process of continually "playing," if you will, "the game." For others who cannot separate the game from what they perceive their true selves to be, there is no playing. The act of constantly monitoring this impression *is* their self-concept. These individuals are referred to as *self-monitors*.

UNDERSTANDING OUR NEEDS

Psychologist Abraham Maslow dealt with the subject of self-concept when he developed his theory of a *needs hierarchy.*[2] Maslow stated that we must satisfy certain basic needs before we can begin to develop our self-concept by satisfying more complex needs. He identified our basic needs, which he termed *physiological,* as those that support life: food, water, and air to breathe. Once those are satisfied, we move on to satisfy the next important needs of safety and security and shelter to protect us from harm.

If we are able to meet these needs successfully, we can then look toward fulfilling other human needs, such as belonging to groups, finding love and affection, and forming friendships. We can even work toward those achievements in other areas of our life that fulfill our need for self-esteem. Finally, we can work toward fulfilling our need for what we call self-actualization.

TOWARD SELF-ACTUALIZATION

Maslow's highest level of human need is that of achieving creativity, meeting challenges, being in harmony with our environment—self-actualization. When we fulfill self-actualization, we are achieving our full potential. Maslow also identified what are called *peak experiences,* the natural highs of life. Sometimes we experience these in our job, in our relationships with others, or in sports.

We can often identify people who have achieved self-actualization by the way they communicate with others. Their communication is upbeat and positive. They are enthusiastic. In business and elsewhere, personal development training programs often use communication as a way to achieve self-actualization and hold on to it. Placing emphasis on using positive language, the programs incorporate such words and phrases as: "That's great," "I'm proud of you," "Super!" and "Way to go." Try inserting positive phrases into your own communication.

Other people who have achieved self-actualization, like our river guide, Dave, may exhibit a calm, self-assurance. Their communication patterns are reflected in a natural ability to listen, for they do not have to psychologically dominate a conversation to obtain their self-esteem. Their communication is not self-centered. The insecure desire to attract continual attention to oneself is replaced by the secure ability to be empathetic to the other person and speak with supportive phrases and sentences.

THE BASIS OF SELF-CONCEPT

Our self-concept is composed of different building blocks that join together to form the way we feel about ourselves. Imagine that the building blocks are held together by clay. Every day we face challenges to our self-concept. These challenges can be viewed as rain. In really heavy rainstorms, the clay gets so wet that it shakes the foundation of our self-concept.

As an example, perhaps you are proud of the way you accomplish a task at work. One day a supervisor comes in and strongly criticizes you. Like rain hitting the building blocks of self-concept, the foundation moves and you become shaken and unsure of yourself. On the other hand, the supervisor may compliment your work and you then feel positive about yourself. The supervisor's positive criticism helped harden the clay and strengthen your self-concept. Life is not all positive criticism, but the small psychological showers we face can help us grow and in the long run make us feel better about ourselves.

To understand better the basis of our self-concept, we will examine the "building blocks" and then discuss everyday challenges. We will be working toward answering the question: "Who am I?"

Values

Values are defined as broad-based qualities of the individual self that are important and affect behavior.[3] Different scholars have categorized our values into those of aesthetic, humanitarian, intellectual, material, power, and religious.[4] What the categories are is not as important as is the importance individuals place on them.

We assign them importance by arranging them in a *value hierarchy*.[5] Consider which of the values just listed that you place high in your life. People who place aesthetic values high tend to see the world in terms of beauty. They may be interested in ballet and poetry, for example. If this value is especially high in their personal value hierarchy, they might even be professional ballerinas or poets. A person who views humanitarian values as especially important would be "people-oriented." The love of people and caring for them would be very significant to this individual. When making a career choice based on such a value structure, this person might become a social worker or consider working in a medically related field.

Material values stress the acquisition and use of material things. For people who focus on material things, their personal income might be the most important aspect of their job. This type of individual might choose a less desirable job that pays more rather than a job that would serve society but pays less.

Different values may operate within the same individual at the same time. Let's suppose that you want to own your own business. You also enjoy making enough money to be comfortable and to give a family member or person close to you nice material things. You also enjoy art, spending much of your free time painting and volunteering your time for the benefit of a local art museum.

Attitudes and Beliefs

Another aspect of our self-concept is our attitudes. An *attitude* is defined as a state of mind or accumulation of opinions about a subject. In essence, attitudes are "support mechanisms" for our values because they often reflect those values. The latter is especially true when we begin to interact with other people.

You might support a particular political candidate because he or she favors a hands-off policy toward big business (a material value). A friend challenges your position because the same candidate neglects the welfare of minorities (a humanitarian value). Your discussions reflect your values and the attitudes that support those values.

A *belief* is the mental process of placing trust in something. Beliefs are closely related to attitudes.[6] In fact, some people argue that trying to separate the two for purposes of discussion merely creates confusion and artificial divisions that do not exist or are not necessary.[7] Nevertheless, a separate discussion of them will help us understand how our own beliefs fit into and support our self-concept. Beliefs, like attitudes and values, have a hierarchy of importance to us, and we hold some to be stronger than others.

Basic Beliefs

Some of our most closely held beliefs are those we acquired as we were growing up. Our family played a large role in developing many of those beliefs. Some of these may be: "My family is very supportive of me," or "I believe the small town in which I grew up was a good place to raise children." Other basic beliefs might include: "I believe my mother was a strong woman," or "I believe my father was a kind man." In each case, the belief is central to our own sense of being. We do not seek continual confirmation of the belief; it is not easily changed; and it has been positively reinforced over time.

How we relate to other people during interpersonal communication can depend very heavily on our beliefs. The fact that our parents were very supportive might give us a sense of self-confidence and an ability to meet others with a positive sense of well-being. Perhaps we have a close friend or loved one who provides us with an "inner strength." Communicating with this person is easy and "supportive." The basic beliefs we hold are part of the answer to the question, "Who am I?" Of all our beliefs, these are the most central to our lives. Even if we did not live in a small town (or never want to), the fact that we once held certain beliefs close to us means they play a part in our self-concept and our relationships with others.

Yet these basic beliefs *can* be changed. An unhappy childhood can be "sorted out" within oneself, and corresponding behavior adjusted to compensate for current relationships with others.

Peripheral Beliefs

Offshoots of our basic beliefs are *peripheral beliefs*. The dividing line between the two is hazy. If you believe strongly that your brother or sister would help you in a time of need, you may have no doubt in your mind that this belief is absolute. It is basic. You cannot imagine anything that would make you believe differently. On the other hand, if you believe you dislike lemon pie, you may be less willing to say that particular belief is absolute. A good piece of pie may be the only thing standing in the way of your changing your mind. This type of belief would be peripheral.

Remember, we have separated values, attitudes, and beliefs in order to gain a clearer understanding of our self-concept. The distinctions between the three can lie in the degree of commitment we have to them and the role that each plays in a given communicative encounter.

Challenges to Values, Attitudes, and Beliefs

At one time or another during our lives, we will have our values, attitudes, and beliefs challenged, altered, or, in some cases, changed drastically. Few people have ideas exactly like ours. We meet people who argue with us, who both intentionally and unintentionally deceive us, and who simply do not see all things the way we do. Some of these challenges to our basic ways of thinking can be very healthy. Other challenges may cause considerable internal strife and make us stop and consider our own worth or our abilities to work or reason.

Holding a positive self-concept is especially difficult when we encounter challenges to values, attitudes, and beliefs about ourselves. The beliefs we hold about religion, social issues, and even other people can be challenged without too much internal damage. But when answers to "Who am I?" are challenged, we face a crisis in self-concept. We also face a crisis in our ability to communicate, because how we identify our self-concept affects how we interact with others. Because no values, attitudes, or beliefs are held closer than the ones we hold about ourselves, we need to understand more about how they affect our lives.

MAINTAINING OUR SELF-CONCEPT

When our self-concept is challenged, our interactions with other people change considerably. The next time you are watching a sports event, watch carefully the way in which winning and losing coaches and winning and losing players interact with the television interviewer. Some coaches and players have learned to live with winning and losing and can handle such matters in a professional manner. In others is a tendency to "cry the blues." They might not directly express those feelings, but if you are sensitive to the way in which they interact with the TV interviewer, you can pick up verbal and nonverbal differences. Eye contact with the interviewer or with the camera may be less for those on the losing end. One's tone of voice, facial expression, or rate of speech can change under those circumstances.

We can maintain a healthy, positive self-concept, which then helps us interact in a healthy and positive way with others, regardless of what challenges or experiences we may face. Consider the life of a famous baseball player. When Yogi Berra first approached the gate of Yankee Stadium in 1947, he must have been awed about the challenges before him. He certainly didn't look like an athlete. Short and squatty, he was anything but the picture of the famous major league hitters of the day. Around the American League, the bench jockeys would laugh at his walk. When Berra threw the ball, it was anyone's guess where it would end up. Once he hit a second-base umpire in the head with a wild throw. Another wild throw landed in the chest of the pitcher. For Yogi, however, the laughs, the mistakes, and the disgusted looks from players and coaches didn't stop his determination to be good at baseball. Instead, he studied the competition, watched the rival batters, and spent extra hours in the batting cage until he knew his and their every weakness. When his career ended, he had played with 14 pennant-winning teams, had hit 358 home runs, had set 18 World Series records, and was voted the American League's most valuable player.[8]

Unquestionably, if Yogi Berra had not accepted his limitations and worked within them, he would have never achieved success. His self-concept when he hit the umpire and pitcher with wild throws was undoubtedly different from when he logged pennant-winning games and most-valuable-player awards. He had not let the challenges facing him alter his positive self-concept. In fact, he had called upon his self-concept to conquer the challenges.

UNDERSTANDING AND CONQUERING CHALLENGES

As we indicated earlier, life is a series of challenges to our values, attitudes, and beliefs. Once we accept this fact, we can deal with these challenges better (Fig. 2–1). Would we be surprised if someone disagreed with us about politics? Not really. It is natural to disagree about politics. The challenge to our self-concept comes in the way in which people disagree with us. For instance, a polite friend may temper his or her comments with statements such as:

> "That's interesting, and I see what you mean. But what would happen if . . . ?"
> "That's a good point; however, maybe we should begin to . . . ."

Neither of these comments is particularly threatening or would bother us very much. The other person was a sensitive sender of communication and respected our self-concept. Our political beliefs may not have been held as being rigid and inflexible, either.

Now consider how we might react if the comments were less polite. What if the other person had said:

> "Your theory doesn't show much common sense."
> "I can't believe you could think that."
> "A view like that could get you arrested tomorrow."

The comments now become more personal. They not only refute political beliefs but also imply a deficiency in one's worth. Comments such as these are not uncommon; we all have met people who are extremely candid and forthright regardless of how their comments are taken. They may not be particularly sensitive senders of communication.

Now we are faced with realigning our thoughts either to agree and change our self-concept, or to disagree and attempt to protect our self-concept, perhaps losing a friend in the process. When we develop intimate relationships with others, we are much more likely to encounter communication dealing with

Don't Be Afraid To Fail

You've failed
many times,
although you may not
remember.
You fell down
the first time
you tried to walk.
You almost drowned
the first time
you tried to
swim, didn't you?
Did you hit the
ball the first time
you swung a bat?
Heavy hitters,
the ones who hit the
most home runs,
also strike
out a lot.
R. H. Macy
failed seven
times before his
store in New York
caught on.
English novelist
John Creasey got
753 rejection slips
before he published
564 books.
Babe Ruth struck out
1,330 times,
but he also hit
714 home runs.
Don't worry about
failure.
Worry about the
chances you miss
when you don't
even try.

Figure 2-1   (United Technologies Corporation)

highly personal topics. When serious dilemmas exist, we might decide that instead of changing our values, attitudes, or beliefs, especially about ourselves, we will draw away from the person, end a relationship, undergo counseling, or take a host of other actions to protect and maintain our self-concept.[9]

STROKING

Why are we concerned about maintaining our self-concept? We are concerned because support for our actions and egos is a necessary part of life. Moreover, this support is the foundation of positive relationships and communication with other people. Support for our egos actually starts from the day we are born. At that time, the support is almost entirely one of touch, that of baby to parent. Later, as we begin to develop the ability to use language, we seek support through interpersonal communication using symbols. Our childhood smiles, words, phrases, and sentences all form models of support. Psychologists refer to this supportive process as *stroking*.[10]

Stroking occurs when we exchange messages with other people. It is the product of interpersonal communication and can involve both verbal and non-verbal messages. A pat on the shoulder accompanied by supportive words are both examples of stroking. Many of us seek stroking to confirm what we say and do.[11] Because we have a need to be stroked, we tend to exchange interpersonal messages that will "pay off" in strokes. We may choose our friends and acquaintances because they are supportive of our attitudes, values, and beliefs and thus stroke our self-concept.

Stroking determines not only how we feel about ourselves but also how we relate to other people. One way to categorize these perceptions of ourselves and others is to use what psychologists refer to as the "I'm OK, you're OK" relationships.

A positive relationship is one in which the sender of communication has a positive self-concept and perceives the same about the receiver of that communication. In this instance, both communicators will stroke each other positively. Each communicator is "OK," and even disagreement is rational.

An alternative relationship is for one person to have been stroked negatively to the point that he or she forms an "I'm *not* OK" self-concept. When this occurs, human communication may become difficult and hindered. The person then begins to say things that reflect how she or he feels about oneself. The person tends to put himself or herself down all the time. Sometimes this can take the form of continually making excuses for oneself. An individual with whom the author is familiar had an "I'm *not* OK" self-concept at work. Part of this self-concept had developed from a previous job because her boss thought she could never do anything right. As a result, any time she received criticism in her new job, her old "I'm *not* OK" self would surface, and she would inevitably say, "Oh, I'm such a jerk." After being made aware of the habit, she stopped making negative comments about herself and both her work and self-concept improved.

Because both communicators can have an "I'm OK" or "I'm *not* OK" self-concept, the possible combinations of message exchanges can include:

I'm OK, you're OK.	I'm OK, you're not OK.
I'm not OK, you're OK.	I'm not OK, you're not OK.

Of these four combinations, the first is the healthiest while the last is the least healthy. Even within the same conversation, depending on the topic, we can fluctuate among different postures about ourselves and other people. For the most part, however, our most consistent posture will determine how we interact with other people.

Because we need to interact with other people, it is important to consider our own self-concept. In what areas of our lives can we say that "I'm OK"? In what areas do we say, "I'm *not* OK"? What about our friends and acquaintances? Do we perceive them as being OK or not OK? Are our preceptions justified? Can we provide stroking to other people that will improve their own self-concept?

ADULT, PARENT, AND CHILD EGO STATES

Another approach to understanding self-concept and how it affects human interaction is to look at psychiatrist Eric Berne's approach with what he calls *ego states*.[12] Three ego states—adult, parent, and child—affect how we interact with others and ultimately how we feel about ourselves.

The ideal state is the *adult state*, which we possess when we are acting in a normal fashion and conducting normal interactions with other people. This is the ego state of the well-adjusted person, the rational thinker. Our self-concept needs to be in the adult state in order for us to make rational choices about our daily lives. Every day we encounter situations that require an adult approach. If a teacher hands back an exam with an F, we might want to just sit down and cry. The rational, adult decision would be to go see the instructor during office hours, listen to explanations of why we answered the questions incorrectly, and learn how to prepare for the next exam. For the meeting to be productive, both parties need to function as rational adults.

The second of Berne's ego states is the *parent state*. Here our communication is more directive, much like a parent talking to a child. "Don't do this" or "Do this" are examples of the parent state. If we are on the receiving end of parent-type communication, especially when we do not perceive ourselves as being in a child state, it can be unnatural, unpleasant, and affect our self-concept. We are having a child-state forced upon us when we perceive ourselves as being in an adult state.

Some situations naturally fall into parent-state communication. The obvious is a parent talking to a child. Superior-subordinate relationships in the workplace, expecially when directions or reprimands occur, can fall into a parent-state type of communication. A skilled administrator, however, can interact with others by many times operating in the adult state (Fig. 2–2). Consider the building inspector—a person of authority—examining the structural framework of a new office tower:

INSPECTOR: We must solve the problem of getting over to the next set of offices while making the passageway meet the building-code standards.

CONTRACTOR: Do you have any suggestions?

INSPECTOR: I'm not sure; perhaps we could run steel beams under the floor system.

CONTRACTOR: I'll need to put wood over the steel because it must match the wood trim on the office walls. Will the wood trim pass the fire code?

INSPECTOR: It will if you treat the wood with fire retardant.

CONTRACTOR: OK, if I make the beam out of 2-inch steel and use treated wood with another layer of untreated wood trim to match the wood trim of the office, will it pass inspection?

INSPECTOR: I don't see any problem with that; go ahead.

Figure 2-2
Skilled administrators interact with subordinates in an adult state. Although other states are sometimes necessary, such as using communication from a parental state when performance falls below expectations and an employee does not respond to other communication, these instances should be rare. Most normal people respond best to adult-state communication when a cooperative relationship is necessary to complete a task.

The conversation between the building inspector and the contractor was one of a superior figure talking to a subordinate because contractors must have their work inspected before a building can be occupied. Both individuals interacted in the adult state and neither challenged the authority, intelligence, or self-concept of the other. If the building inspector had adopted the parent state and said: "That won't work and I won't approve it," the contractor might have become defensive because her own worth and self-concept would have been challenged.

Sitting down and crying when we received the F on the exam is indicative of being in the *child state*. Although the child state is most prevalent in early childhood, we carry some of this child ego state with us into our adult lives. Some of us carry more of our child state into adulthood than others. Again, this is not necessarily a negative quality. If we never acted silly, childlike, or just "let ourselves go" and had fun, life might be rather dull. But to cling to the child state when a rational, adult state would be more beneficial is self-defeating.

EVERYDAY FORCES THAT AFFECT OUR SELF-CONCEPT

How do the events we face in life affect our self-concept? Sometimes these events can cause us to perceive ourselves as being "not OK" when actually we are. They can also prompt us to react as parents or children when we can function quite capably as adults. As you read the examples that follow, ask yourself how the events you face every day might affect your self-concept. Realizing how you feel about yourself and why you feel the way you do is the first step toward effective human communication.

Moving

The things that are part of our daily routine support our self-concept. When we leave familiar surroundings and move to a new town, arrive at college, or even visit a foreign country, we are stripped of much of the "clay" that holds the building blocks of our self-concept together. We know, for example, that our good reputation may not have followed us to a new town. We will need to build that all over again. We must also renegotiate the geography. Our self-confidence in being able to find familiar places must be rebuilt. We do not know where the little delicatessen is, the location of the bookstore, or the coffee shop where we can get away and relax. In foreign country, these situations are compounded because of the added cultural obstacles that play havoc with our self-concept. Navigating through a new town can be hard enough when we cannot read the road signs, but devastating when we do not know the language well enough to even ask for directions.

A New School

Attending a new school can create similar challenges to our self-concept. Going there, we leave behind our friends, our family, and the people who we know respect us and want to be with us. Although we all talk about college as being exciting and a place to meet new friends, inside we feel a tremendous amount of self-doubt: "Will I like my dormmates?" "Will I be able to find the room where my class meets?" "Will my clothes fit in?" All of these self-doubts usually resolve themselves soon after classes begin, but during our early adjustment period, our self-concept may be buffeted.

Deans and counselors point out that another rough time for our self-concept occurs if we decide to go through the procedure of pledging a fraternity or sorority. Called "rushing," the normally weeklong period challenges self-concepts to the core. There are documented cases of suicide directly linked to a rejection from a desired fraternity or sorority. This is especially true during times when a society or school places great importance on joining these institutions, and a person is not "in" if he or she does not pledge. It takes an extremely strong and healthy self-concept to overcome such peer challenges.

Some schools compound this inherent jolt by scheduling rush for either the first week of school or the week before school starts. We are in a new environment; we don't know our way around or how we will fit in. We don't know anyone or we know only a very few people. The support of family and friends is not there. People don't know us. The reputation we worked hard to build back home didn't follow us. We are reduced from being perhaps the star of high school to being just another face in the college crowd. Because we feel so alone, our need for *inclusion,* or our need *to belong, to participate, and to be acknowledged,* is tremendous.

Along comes a method of inclusion—belonging to a sorority or fraternity. But first we must, figuratively speaking, pass inspection before total strangers who give us approximately 15 minutes to prove ourselves worthy. The inspection is not entirely one-sided, however, because we are also deciding whether or not we would like to become a member. As rush week progresses, the inspection periods lengthen, and both we and our prospective sororities or fraternities narrow down our membership choices. Finally, we are either included or rejected. Whatever the outcome, it has been an enormous challenge to our self-concept.

Grades

College presents ample opportunities to evaluate our ability to learn. It also presents us with opportunities to evaluate our positive self-concept, that part of us which perceives us as being intelligent and "above average." Keeping a strong self-concept in the face of constant intellectual challenges can be difficult. We may find ourselves feeling not so intelligent and "below average" at times.

One of the first challenges occurs early in the first term when we face our first quiz or exam. In highly selective schools, the entering students may have been ranked in the top of their high school classes and were accustomed to achieving A's and B's. However, everyone else on campus is also accustomed to achieving A's and B's; the competition for these grades becomes tougher. Unfortunately, we all can't receive A's and B's. Thus, students who perceived themselves as being A-students may suddenly score well below the class average. The self-concept of being above average changes and the illusion of the high school grades and the support they provided disappears.

Achievement Tests

Achievement tests can give us an indication of where we stand in relation to other people, *based on the results of the test.* It is the test, not ourselves or other people, that gauges our competence. Yet many students sink into depression after learning their scores on the Scholastic Aptitude Test (SAT), the Law School Admissions Test (LSAT), or the Graduate Management Admissions Test (GMAT). There on the official-looking computer printout, neatly tucked inside the computerized envelope, comes the news that we are AVERAGE! But how can we be average? Actually, we may excel in many areas of our lives that are not reflected in achievement tests.

A New Job

A new job can be even more challenging than a new school. Our self-concept faces the demands of performing a task well in addition to being respected and getting along with co-workers and management. If we know someone who also works at the same place we have an "anchor" to help hold our self-concept in place. At least we won't start by having to make *all* new friends. Much like a new school, just finding our way around the building, knowing where the restrooms, water fountains, and supplies are, can be harrowing. At lunch we may find ourselves asked to join a group of people, none of whom we know. Again, we are responsible for making positive first impressions.

One way to tackle the first day's work is to understand that everyone before you went through the same experience. Many of your co-workers will understand how your feel, even if they don't outwardly express it. Don't be afraid to admit it is your first day at work or that you are new on the job. Others will understand any shortcomings you might display. Also, try to relax and keep a sense of humor.

Management Evaluations

Getting evaluated by one's supervisor or manager is always stressful. Some companies have instituted performance review and appraisal (PR&A) programs. Employees set goals in consultation with managers and then periodically meet—usually annually or every six months—to review progress toward the goals. Unfortunately, some managers are inept at handling PR&A meetings. Keep in mind that such behavior may reflect their own negative experience with *their* managers, and although this should not become a part of your evaluation, it often does. Also remember that they may feel as uneasy about such meetings as you do, feeling much more comfortable with daily interactions as opposed to periodic formal appraisal meetings. Approach such meetings with the attitude that you will learn from the experience; here is a chance to get across your opinions—assuming your supervisor is receptive to your opinions—and to set some goals for the next meeting. Regardless of what occurs, think about the future, not about the past. Concentrate on your own positive qualities and realize your contributions to the organization.

DEALING WITH LONELINESS

Being alone in an empty apartment, knowing about a party we did not attend, or being excluded from a particular group can all lower our self-esteem. When we are not included, we grope for an explanation. We challenge our perceptions of ourselves and others. We read hidden and inaccurate messages into other people's actions. Too many times we equate being alone with being disliked. And the more we avoid being included, the more we are excluded. The vicious circle continues. An important thing to remember when we're feeling lonely is that our basic desire for inclusion may be artificially inflating our loneliness and the lack of self-confidence it instills.

Effects of Loneliness on Interpersonal Interaction

Loneliness can also influence the way we communicate with others; specifically, it may inhibit communication and make us more withdrawn, especially during our first meetings with another person and at the early stages of a relationship.[13] As such we find it hard to listen attentively and to remember with clarity what someone else is saying. This makes it more difficult to share information with the other person and contributes to interpersonal distance, thus adding to our loneliness. We have less to talk about, which makes it even more difficult to build bridges with others. Consequently, we have less to share with others and have fewer things in common. Our communication skills suffer and we are not effective in expanding on the comments of others during interpersonal interaction. All of this makes it difficult to build relationships with others and this in turn contributes to loneliness. The vicious circle starts up once again.

Overcoming Loneliness

To help overcome loneliness we first need to understand the difference between being alone and being lonely. One does not necessarily mean the presence of the other. Being alone can actually be beneficial. It provides us with the time to approach what Maslow called *self-actualization*. It gives us the time, as Carl Rogers said, to look inside ourselves. On the other hand, we must recognize that loneliness may be contributing to withdrawal and that we must take positive action to seek out other people. Not all encounters will be positive. Those that are take time to develop at their own pace. But these beginning friendships are a big step toward inhibiting more loneliness and will make us feel better about ourselves. And the better we feel about ourselves the more we will engage in positive interactions with others.

PRESENTING OURSELVES TO OTHERS

In 1890, psychologist William James wrote in his book *The Principles of Psychology:*

> A man has as many social selves as there are individuals who recognize him and carry an image of him in their mind. . . . But as the individuals who carry the images form naturally into classes, we may practically say that he has as many different social selves as there are distinct groups of persons about whose opinions he cares. He generally shows a different side of himself to each of these different groups. Many a youth who is demure enough before his parents and teachers swears and swaggers like a pirate among his "tough" young friends. We do not show ourselves to our children as to our club companions, to our masters and employers as to our intimate friends. From this there results what practically is a division of the man into several selves; and this may be a discordant splitting, as where one is afraid to let one set of his acquaintances know him as he is elsewhere; or it may be a perfectly harmonious division of labor, as where one tender to his children is stern to the soldiers or prisoners under his command. (Courtesy: *Psychology Today*)

Impression Management

The writings of William James are as important today as they were a century ago. Today we call this *impression management.*

Sociologist Erving Goffman offered an interesting perspective on how we interact with others.[14] Think about the last play that you attended where you watched the actors fulfilling their different roles. Have you ever stopped to consider that we, too, may fulfill "roles" as we interact with other people? Goffman believed we do and he offered the theater as an analogy to human interaction.

If we accept Goffman's approach to understanding human communication, we can readily see how we present a certain self and maintain a certain impression for many different types of interpersonal encounters. Sometimes we do this by managing what we wear. For example, a corporate executive may want to maintain an image of authority or credibility with employees (Fig. 2–3). To do this, the executive has acquired a substantial wardrobe of business suits and wears them to work. On weekends, she wears jeans. One Saturday while working in the garden, and without taking the time to change, she makes a quick trip to the store where she runs into one of her employees. The employee comments on how unusual it is to see the executive wearing jeans. The executive, trying to maintain her image, enters immediately into impression management by saying, "I've been working in the garden this morning and ran out of seeds." Instead of simply admitting to the employee that she likes to relax on Saturdays, she felt self-conscious about being in jeans. She wanted to maintain her "managed impression" to that employee.

Impression management, whether self-imposed or imposed by others, involves not only the way we present ourselves to others but also the impressions we maintain for ourselves. Certain law-enforcement agencies have conducted research on how police officers' uniforms affect the officers' self-image. In one

Figure 2-3 Our clothes are carefully chosen for certain occasions as part of our practice of impression management. Certain "executive" attire is important for both success and self-confidence in many corporate settings. As important as how one's attire is perceived by others is how it makes the wearer feel. (Laimute E. Druskis photo)

community, the traditional police uniform was changed to gray slacks, blue blazers, white shirts, and blue ties. Immediately, the public saw the officers as easier to approach and more receptive to their concerns. What was not anticipated was the change in self-image the new uniforms created for the officers. They felt less effective and in some cases even fearful of dealing with the public without the traditional police uniform.

The Self-Monitors

Some people are more skillful at impression management than others. Goffman termed such people *self-monitors*. A self-monitor's self-concept is derived not from one central self, but rather from the combination of all the different selves that a person presents to others. Self-monitoring is not to be confused with a dual personality but rather with the ability to adapt to many different situations. High self-monitors have a large repertoire of responses to another person's communication.[15] A self-monitor may be one who does impression management for a living, such as an actor or actress. These people often become so immersed in their various roles that they find themselves unconsciously acting out those parts in real-life situations. Some politicians are so adept at impression management that they become actors (and some actors become politicians), but to a different audience. Meeting different constituencies, they may find they need to adapt to the mannerisms of the different people from whom they seek a vote. Former Mayor Fiorello LaGuardia of New York was said to be so adept at impression management that it was possible to watch silent films of his speeches and determine to what ethnic group he was appealing.

SHYNESS

One Saturday afternoon when I was trying to find a parking space to watch a local football rivalry, the parking lot attendant ushered us into an alleyway that, as it turned out, not only did not have a parking space, but the turnaround area was also filled with three families enjoying their pregame smorgasbord spread out on portable tables. As I started to back out of the alleyway, one of the celebrants called out, "No, wait!" Put your car right there next to the back of mine and have lunch with us!" At first we politely refused, but their insistence and good-natured invitation, accompanied by the fact that backing out of the alleyway and finding another parking space would be extremely difficult, made us decide to stay.

As it turned out, the organizer of the pregame party was an industrial psychologist whose specialization was helping people develop their full potential and overcome shyness. We shared some sandwiches and struck up a conversation about our mutual interest in human development. Our discussion turned to shyness. He pointed out a technique he uses to demonstrate to shy people that in general, people are friendly. He stood right in the middle of the sidewalk that was filled with people and began introducing himself. Not one person turned away. Virtually everyone shook hands with him, and some even started up a conversation. He said he used this technique as a sensitivity crash course against shyness.

Shyness and Interpersonal Relationships

Sometimes shyness is caused by a poor self-concept. For some people, talking to anyone is a painful experience. A shy person may be withdrawn and not enjoy seeking out others. As a result, they are often excluded from the social relationships others enjoy. Sometimes this shyness is learned through negative reinforcement, a case of having been painfully rebuked when dealing with others.

In some ways everyone is shy. All of us don't plunge head-on into every relationship. Testing the waters of a relationship by gradually disclosing facts and feelings about ourselves is a form of shyness. We do not want to bare our inner self immediately and risk being shunned.

Problems arise when our hesitancy to interact with others reaches abnormality. We may avoid other people to the point where shyness becomes a phobia. We may feel inferior to other people and reason that if we interact with others, they will only confirm our inferiority. In other cases, we may simply lack the conversational skills necessary to feel confident about interacting with other people.

Overcoming Shyness

Overcoming shyness is not always easy, but it can be accomplished. There are a number of approaches we can take to increase our self-confidence in interpersonal encounters. Some people need to work on developing good listening skills. Because much of our communication efforts are involved with listening to the other person, the shy person who learns to listen attentively has at least half of the communicative process under control and can accurately respond to the other person's conversation, and the other person can accurately respond back. When people do not listen carefully, their response to the conversation may be incorrect. That incorrect response may result in misunderstandings. For the shy person, this silence is the same as disapproval, which may have caused the person's shy behavior in the first place. Failure to get a response may actually reinforce shyness.

Adjusting our nonverbal communication also can help us overcome shyness. We can change our posture from round-shouldered, withering slumps to alert, straight-shouldered stances. Instead of standing with our arms crossed and nonverbally "blocking" communication, we can let them fall more openly by our sides, inviting communication. Moving closer to the person we are speaking to can express more intimate communicative styles. One research study examined the actual distance people stand from each other while carrying on a conversation.[16] Using a test to measure shyness, they split a group into two parts: very shy and less shy. They found that the very shy people preferred to be approximately eight inches farther away from the person to whom they were talking than did the less shy people. When the opposite sex was involved, this distance increased to 12 inches. Developing our other nonverbal communication skills of eye contact, touch, and gestures can all help alter our shy communicative behavior. As we practice these skills, we will come to redefine our self-concept from being shy to being people-oriented.

The next time we feel ourselves becoming shy, simply ask, "What are we afraid of?" When we cannot come up with an answer, or when we do and successfully realize what hinders our conversation and deal with it, we are on the road to more open and responsive communication.

ASSERTIVENESS

Society has placed greater emphasis in recent years on our ability to be more assertive in our daily relations with other people. Some of this has come about because of the increased professional status of women who, especially in the male-dominated corporate atmosphere, have been perceived as less effective and competent than males simply because they weren't as assertive. In some cases, women have had to learn assertive behavior in order to achieve their deserved recognition and rewards in the competitive working world. The assertiveness movement has also uncovered many men who experience similar reluctance at making their needs and desires known. As a result, both men and women in professional atmospheres, in family life, and in everyday situations are realizing the value of developing an assertive personality.

Assertive, Not Abrasive

It is important to understand that assertive behavior is not aggressive, abrasive, or agitating behavior. In fact, many people who have learned to be assertive report less of a need to be aggressive and pushy. Much like a safety valve, assertive behavior releases discomfort and pressure before it can rise to the level of anger and conflict. Suppose you find that the car you just bought has a knocking sound in the engine. Feeling sheepish that you didn't notice the noise before you bought it, you decide to drive it anyway. A month later you change your mind and decide to return the car. The salesperson at the dealership suggests you have driven the car too long for you to receive a refund. You are upset and enter into a heated discussion with the salesperson, who finally refers you to the manager. Another heated exchange occurs because the manager feels obligated to support the salesperson's decision. Had you clearly stated you were unhappy with the car and returned it when you first noticed the knocking sound, your assertive behavior would have avoided the heated exchange with the salesperson.

Naturally, there is a thin line between being assertive and being aggressive. It takes diplomacy and tact not to cross over the line. When we have achieved the ability to say what we want and state our requests clearly, we can avoid crossing that line because we can avoid misunderstandings. Otherwise, we will only build up frustration, which eventually may be released in an unpleasant way.

Being Assertive by Avoiding Bypass Statements

When the lack of rain caused concern, one newspaper printed the wisdom of a retired professor of law. The professor called the readers' attention to a story that had been told to him back during the drought of 1920. It seems that a local preacher decided that the drought had lasted long enough, and he wasn't going to mix words. He got down on his knees in front of his congregation, lifted his arms, and began to pray:

> Lord, send us rain. The ground is dry and hot and burns the bare feet walking over it. The tobacco leaves next to it are curling up. The cotton plants are wilting in the sun. The corn stalks are already stunted in their growth, the fodder leaves

are withering, there won't be anything but nubbins, and Lord thou knowest I hate worse than hell to shuck nubbins. So Lord, send us rain. Don't send us any flimsy flamsy drizzle drazzle. Send us a gully washer and a trash mover.[17]

Sure enough, the sky opened up on the congregation as it went home. The fields were so wet that the farmers couldn't get in to tend the crops. The creeks were flooding, and still it rained. The preacher decided it was time to pray again. He wasn't any more shy the second time:

Lord, it is true that we didst ask for rain. And it is true that we didst ask for no flimsy flamsy drizzle but for a gully washer and a trash mover. But Lord, this is ridiculous![18]

The rain stopped.

We can speculate on what might have happened to the weather if the preacher had decided to use less direct language. Indirect or "bypass language" is one of the things that keeps us shy because it does not let us express clearly our wished behavior. The preacher wished that it would start and then stop raining, and he did not mince words. He certainly did not use bypass language, which is composed of words that conceal true emotions. Many people use bypass language, especially shy people. Usually they don't get what they want; their interpersonal encounter is unsatisfactory and generates unsatisfactory results.

Avoiding bypass language does not mean that you should spill your feelings all over the place just to prove that you are unintimidated. That is being abrasive and, in a sense, rude to other people. But at the same time, do not be vague. Many parents become extremely frustrated in disciplining their children because they fail to state precisely what behavior they wish. Instead, they participate in word bypass, or deceptive behavior we talked about earlier. Look at the following bypass statements, and then see what behavior is really desired. The problem is that the desired behavior is not verbalized:

Bypass Statement	Wished Behavior
"Perhaps we shouldn't play with the video games so much."	The parent wants the child to stop playing the video games because the noise is giving the parent a headache.
"How do you think Amy's parents feel about the two of you seeing each other so much?"	The parent wishes the son would see someone other than Amy.
"Well, we'll certainly be glad to meet all the girls you date at college. I'll bet you really play the field. That's the way to enjoy college!"	The parent does not want an unwanted pregnancy in the family.

We are all guilty of hiding our true feelings from others. Consider the following examples, this time from a working situation:

Bypass Statement	Wished Behavior
"These orders will be a snap to get out."	The supervisor expects the orders to be filled in no later than 30 minutes.
"We have a lot of territories that are doing quite well this year: Portland, San Diego, Austin, Madison, St. Louis, Savannah, and Philadelphia."	The supervisor is dissatisfied with the account executive's progress and expects a specific dollar amount of the improvement by the end of the month.
"We had an employee in our Oklahoma City store who was fired because he was continually late for work."	If you do not stop being late for work, you will be fired.

How could the supervisor have more clearly expressed his or her feelings in each of these situations? Sooner or later, we may all be in a position in which other employees work for us. How we state our desires will have a direct effect on the level of performance we receive from those employees.

Assertiveness as Protection from Negative Stroking

One of the main benefits of assertive behavior is the ability to protect ourselves from negative stroking. We have learned how negative stroking can lower our self-concept. We can counteract that negative stroking with assertive rebuttals. Let's look at some examples of negative stroking and possible assertive replies:

Negative Stroking	Assertive Reply
"Do you honestly think you have any chance of making the team?"	"I certainly do or I wouldn't be going out for practice."
"If I were you, I wouldn't go out with Jim. I can't stand him."	"You're not me, and I will not choose my dates based upon yours."
"Do you really feel comfortable wearing that bikini?"	"Yes, I do. After all, when you've got it, flaunt it!"
"There you go again."	"No, there *you* go again."
"That is a dumb idea."	"Few ideas are actually dumb. The people who do not understand them are."

These examples are clearly more direct than we encounter in everyday conversation. But negative stroking can take on a more subtle form. Moreover, depending on our self-concept, what is negative stroking for one person may not be negative stroking for another. You know when you have been negatively stroked because you feel intimidated, hurt, and uncomfortable. Right at that moment is when to make an assertive reply to restore your self-esteem within the conversation.

SELF-DISCLOSURE

An important part of communicating and presenting our self-concepts to others lies with how much information we should divulge and how much we should withhold. Called *self-disclosure*, it is a significant part of human communication.[19] For instance, two people waiting in line at the post office may comment on the postal workers' progress. One may say, "They sure are slow," and the other person may agree by saying, "They sure are." With these statements, both have disclosed to each other that neither likes waiting in line. Neither has revealed intimate details of his or her life, but both have participated in self-disclosure. If and when they become closer friends, they will disclose more about themselves. Two lovers, a married couple, or two close friends participate in a great deal of self-disclosure.

Self-Disclosure as Support for Our Self-Concept

Our need for positive reinforcement (stroking) in order for our self-concept to grow and strengthen is well established. By disclosing information about ourselves, especially the things we hold dear—our values, attitudes, and beliefs—we are seeing how other people react to our self-concept. The more we disclose about ourselves, the more we can be supported by others. After all, how can people support us if they don't know us? Disclosing very intimate things about ourselves and having those things reinforced can have a powerful influence on our self-concept.

A relationship in which self-disclosure can occur in an unthreatened environment benefits the self-concepts of all involved. Psychologist Carl Rogers offers a prescription for effective human communication when he defines the characteristics of this "helping relationship":

1. The communicators are perceived by one another as trustworthy, as consistently dependable.
2. They express their separate selves unambiguously.
3. They possess positive attitudes and warmth and caring for the other.
4. A partner in a helping relationship keeps his (her) own separate identity.
5. A partner permits the other to do the same.
6. The helping relationship is marked by empathy. (The communicator attempts to understand the feelings of the other.)
7. The helper accepts the various facets of the other's experience as communicated by the other.
8. The partners in a relationship respond with sufficient sensitivity to allay threat.
9. They are able to free themselves from the threat of evaluation from the other.
10. Each communicator recognizes that the other is changing and is flexible enough to permit the other to change.[20]

Rogers' 10 characteristics are the ideal, and not every relationship or every interpersonal encounter can meet all of them or even some of them. Nevertheless, these characteristics are solid foundations upon which to base improvement of our skills at interacting with each other.

Self-Withholding

Self-disclosure also carries with it a risk. It is the risk that instead of having our self-concept reinforced, we will have it shot down. The more we reveal about ourselves, the more we can be hurt if our qualities are not accepted positively.[21] An old song laments, "We always hurt the ones we love." There is more truth in those words than we realize, because two people in love frequently disclose a great deal of information about themselves. Each is thus vulnerable to the other's discretion of either positively or negatively judging that disclosure.

During our infancy, our life was filled with positive reinforcement. As we grew, we began to receive negative reinforcement in the form of scolding for doing or saying things that did not correspond to the kind of people our parents expected us to be. We may have altered our behavior and, consequently, ourselves because of this scolding. We adjusted to the fact that we were not supposed to say bad words at dinner nor throw temper tantrums at bedtime. Yet while we were adjusting to these incidents in our lives, we suppressed other feelings, allowing them to remain a part of ourselves but not disclosing them to anyone for fear of reprisal. We still may not reveal such things as secret fears, fantasies, or other highly personal feelings to anyone, regardless of how close they are to us.

Another reason for avoiding self-disclosure is the fear of revealing ourself to ourself. Some of us try to keep our real self-concept hidden from ourselves as hard as we try to keep it hidden from others. Few experiences can be more jolting than to examine our true characteristics. Psychiatric therapy sessions in which we delve deeply into our true "selves" sometimes referred to as primal therapy, are often necessary to begin healing certain mentally ill individuals. On a less serious note, we can all be guilty of simply not admitting the truth to ourselves about ourselves.

Sometimes our stereotyped impressions of ourselves and others can contribute to our tendency to avoid self-disclosure. Because of the stereotyped image of the male as a dominant figure in a relationship, some men avoid self-disclosure because they feel it would be an act of weakness and would thus make them lose control over the relationship.[22] Similarly, the stereotyped image of the female as being an unequal figure in a relationship causes some women to avoid self-disclosure in order to avoid weakness.[23]

When Do We Self-Disclose?

Research has taught us that we tend to disclose things about ourselves at different points in a relationship, as that relationship develops.[24] We may disclose our views about the latest movie on the first date, but we would probably not disclose the painful details of our parents' divorce. Such disclosures would occur much later in a relationship, if at all. Moreover, we tend to disclose nega-

tive things about ourselves, if at all, much later. Part of our reason for withhold-
ing negative information is impression management. We want to be liked, respected, and to make a positive impression when we first meet people. Thus, we
stress our positive qualities. As a relationship develops into what Carl Rogers
calls a "helping relationship," we may feel less threatened by disclosing negative
information. Looking at it another way, the relationship must be at the appropriate stage for certain types of self-disclosure to take place.[25]

REASONS FOR SELF-DISCLOSURE

A number of reasons exist for self-disclosing communication. One is *relationship
maintenance*.[26] Imagine a friendship where one person decides not to tell the
other person anything more about oneself. The sharing of information would
stop and it would not be long until the friendship deteriorated. Along with
maintaining the relationship, self-disclosure permits us to *enhance the relationship*.
For example, if we meet someone at work our early conversations might deal
with such mundane things as the weather, working conditions, other co-workers,
where to eat lunch, and similar nonthreatening information. As we get to know
and like the person better we move beyond relationship maintenance to *relationship enhancement*. Perhaps we begin to talk about personal matters such as our
friends, family, children, likes and dislikes about people, political opinions—
things that can tell the other person more about us. We also expect the other
person to enhance the relationship by disclosing more personal concerns as well.
     Mutual trust and a supportive positive communication atmosphere must
exist for the degree and amount of self-disclosure to continue to increase and the
relationship to be enhanced. This expectation of returned self-disclosure—
called *reciprocity*—is still another reason for self-disclosure. In short, when we
give something of ourselves in communication we expect something in return.
Reciprocity is especially important when we meet strangers. It helps to uncover
commonalities that can lead to more communication and a building of the relationship. Another important reason for self-disclosure, especially among strangers or new acquaintances, is *impression formation*. We want to put our best foot
forward so we self-disclose positive things about ourselves. We may also self-
disclose as a means of *self-clarification*. The disclosure helps us to clarify how we
feel about ourselves, or as Carl Rogers noted, to support our self-concept. To get
an accurate answer to the question "Who am I?" we need to talk about ourselves
to another person. In most cases it is a friend in whom we trust. In other more
complex situations the "friend" may be a counselor or psychiatrist.

BECOMING AWARE OF OUR SELF-DISCLOSURE

A responsible communicator is aware of one's own and other people's self-
disclosure. One way to do this is to monitor our *intentions* for self-disclosing
information about ourselves.[27] This starts by remembering the reasons we just
discussed and then monitoring these in our own interactions with others.

We must also be aware of the *amount* of self-disclosure. From time to time we all monopolize a conversation. But where self-disclosure is involved, monopolizing a conversation can leave the impression of being self-centered or insensitive to the rules of a relationship that demand appropriate self-disclosure at different stages of the relationship.

Being aware of the *value* of self-disclosure helps us monitor the impressions we present to others. The old saying "misery loves company" is not necessarily true. People who are continually saying negative things about themselves can leave the impression that they possess a low self-concept and are incompetent.

The *depth* of our self-disclosure is closely related to how far advanced a relationship is. Jane and Harry worked in the manufacturing division of a large corporation. One day Harry began confiding (self-disclosing) to Jane about being overworked. Soon thereafter he began telling Jane intimate details of his failing marriage. Jane began to feel uncomfortable, and eventually she asked for and was granted a transfer to another division. What went wrong? Harry, for whatever reason, was not sensitive to the effect his self-disclosure was having on Jane, with whom he had a professional but not a personal relationship.

Finally, we need to monitor the *accuracy* of our self-disclosure. The self-clarification we discussed earlier demands accuracy. More importantly, being sincere and truthful is necessary for mutual trust in a relationship.

SUMMARY

Self-concept and self-disclosure are key components in the process of human communication. How we perceive ourselves intrapersonally reflects directly on the image we project to others and our ability to engage in interpersonal communication. How much we disclose about ourselves determines the common ground with which we pursue further communication.

Psychologist Carl Rogers points out that our self-concept develops as a result of many different experiences, all affected by the rules of our complex society. Another psychologist, Abraham Maslow, states that before we can fulfill our self-concepts, we first must fulfill a hierarchy of human needs. These include the basics of food, water, and air to breathe; safety and security; love and affection; achievement; and self-actualization.

The basis of our self-concept can be found in our values, attitudes, and beliefs. Values are defined as important, broad-based qualities of an individual that affect one's behavior. Attitudes are support mechanisms for values, and are states of mind or accumulations of opinions about a subject. Beliefs, which include basic and peripheral beliefs, consist of mental processes that place trust in something.

Positive stroking reinforces our self-concept, whereas negative stroking lessens it. How we are stroked early in life determines how our self-concept will develop later in life.

Much of our interaction with others is influenced by whether we communicate as a child, a parent, or an adult. We may also camouflage these different ego states. Although it is a form of deceptive communication, the act of camouflage may not be intentional.

Forces in our everyday lives that challenge our self-concept include where we live, moving, entering college, participating in fraternity or sorority rush, grades, achievement tests, and our ability to communicate. One of the strongest challenges to our self-concept is loneliness. Understanding what causes loneliness, as well as understanding some of the benefits of being alone, can help us deal with this challenge.

Our discussion of impression management centered on how we take on different "roles" to adapt to and "play out" different situations. In essence, we "manage" different impressions of ourselves to different people in order to protect our self-concept. Self-monitors are those people who constantly engage in impression management. Self-concept is the accumulation of all the different impressions that the individual manages.

Shyness is often attributed to a low self-esteem. When we avoid communicating with others, we deprive ourselves of the opportunity for positive reinforcement, which actually lessens a tendency toward shyness.

Becoming more assertive can alleviate shyness, but we must not confuse being assertive with being aggressive or abrasive. Avoiding bypass statements and effectively handling negative stroking are two important steps toward overcoming shyness.

An important part of human communication revolves around how much information we should divulge to others and how much we should withhold. Participating in self-disclosure can open the door for other people to support us. It can also open the door of vulnerability with the risk of negative stroking. The intent, amount, value, depth, and accuracy of our self-disclosure can greatly affect our relationships.

QUESTIONS FOR REVIEW AND DISCUSSION

1. What is Maslow's hierarchy of needs?
2. What are the results of challenges to our values, attitudes, or beliefs?
3. How is "stroking" related to self-concept?
4. How does self-concept affect communication?
5. According to Eric Berne, what are the three types of ego states present in individuals?
6. What is deceptive communication?
7. What are the benefits/pitfalls of managing our ego states and thus our communication?
8. What is impression management?
9. What does it mean to use bypass language?

10. What functions does self-disclosure fulfill?

11. What are the reasons for self-disclosure?

12. What factors must we monitor to be fully aware of our self-disclosure?

LEARNING EXERCISES

1. Stop and consider your own beliefs. List them on a sheet of paper and then think back to determine what influenced your beliefs and how strongly you adhere to your beliefs.

2. List the things you possess, not including such things as cars and furniture, that you would take with you if you went to live in a foreign country for a year. Which items would contribute to your self-concept support system?

ADDITIONAL READINGS

BOOKER, D. D., *Making Friends with Yourself and Other Strangers.* New York: Julian Messner, 1982.
ELGIN, S. H., *The Gentle Art of Verbal Self Defense.* Englewood Cliffs, N.J.: Prentice-Hall, 1980.
FENSTERHEIM, H., and J. BAER *Stop Running Scared!* New York: Rawson-Wade Pubs., Inc., 1977.
MAY, R. *The Meaning of Anxiety.* New York: W. W. Norton & Co., Inc., 1977.
ROGERS, C. *Carl Rogers on Personal Power.* New York: Delacorte Press, 1977.
SHAFFER, M., *Life After Stress.* New York: Plenum, 1982.
SLAIKEU, K. and S. LAWHEAD *The Phoenix Factor.* Boston: Houghton Mifflin, 1985.
TIGER, L. *Optimism: The Biology of Hope.* New York: Simon & Schuster, 1979.
TUAN, Y. *Landscapes of Fear.* New York: Pantheon, 1979.
ZIMBARDO, P.G. *Shyness.* Reading, MA: Addison-Wesley, 1977.

3

LANGUAGE

OBJECTIVES

After completing this chapter, you should be able to

- Trace the beginnings of language
- Realize that language is constantly in a state of transition
- Explain how infants and young children develop language skills
- Describe the four primary functions of language use for children
- Discuss the ways in which adults use language
- Understand that different situations call for different kinds of language behavior
- Talk about the language of commitment
- Explain how symbols, referents, grammar, connotation, and denotation affect the meaning of language
- Discuss the language variables of complexity, intensity, immediacy, abstraction, concreteness, and vocabulary
- Identify different language styles and patterns
- Learn how to avoid using sexist language.

Some years ago while living in the Midwest, I greatly enjoyed the fall afternoons when the leaves began to change; the crisp air would twinge the nostrils, and the antique season would begin. Now for serious collectors, there is no such thing as an antique *season*. But for me, the once-in-a-while furniture refinisher, who would visit every garage sale in sight and travel a hundred miles just to peruse some dusty books in the back of an old barn, the fall was truly the antique season.

The antique season also called forth another phenomenon of antique culture—the auctioneer. I heard my first auctioneer as a child. The auctioneer had just started the bidding on an antique sleigh and a corner cupboard. The next thing I knew, my father and I were loading both the sleigh and the cupboard into the back of our pickup truck and heading home. It happened so fast, and my father had not said one word. The auctioneer had done all the talking, and his command of language was superb. Although speaking extremely fast and in partial syllables, he controlled the crowd with the tongue of a master salesperson.

Few people who read this book will need to control language with the skill of an auctioneer. Yet we may all find ourselves in situations where language determines the outcome of a sale, a marriage proposal, a labor negotiation, a raise, or a job interview.

In this chapter we will learn the role language plays in the process of human communication. We will examine the origins of language, how we acquire it, its functions, and things that affect the way we use language in everyday life.

THE BEGINNINGS OF LANGUAGE

Early humans communicated primarily through touch. By about 100,000 B.C., evidence suggests that we were communicating through language. Yet to this day, researchers still debate whether our language developed through learning[1] or instinct.[2]

We do know that about 7,000 B.C., in addition to language, we began to communicate with *pictographs,* which were wall etchings on the insides of caves and temples. Even today, these pictographs remain vivid reminders of what life and religious beliefs were like for our ancestors. We know that between 3,000 and 2,000 B.C., pictographs became highly stylized. The first symbols came into existence, and primitive alphabets developed (Fig. 3–1). Our ancestors began to record sociocultural events, attitudes, values, and habits on the walls of caves, on animal skins, and on the bark of trees. From these records, we are also able to trace the development of their moral codes.

CONTEMPORARY LANGUAGE IN TRANSITION

Sixty years ago the words used to revise a large dictionary came from usage shaped and molded not only by scholars but also by newspapers. The way in which words appeared in the press was an important consideration in determin-

Figure 3-1
Stone tablets from the Middle East are
believed to contain the first elements of
written language. They are believed to
have been used to record units of land
and agricultural products. Experts have
offered the opinion that such tablets
represent the last stages of simple count-
ing that preceded the use of abstract
numbers. (Copyright, Royal Ontario
Museum, Toronto, Canada)

ing their common usage and sentence structure. Today, the press and its technology have given us access to instant communication with virtually any culture
or region of the world. We thus may be finding ourselves living in a period of
accelerated language change, one much more intense and compressed than in
past generations.

Understanding the changing characteristics of language and how we use
it is important for two reasons. First, by being able to understand how others use
language and by adapting our own use to others' use, we can decrease the
chances of misunderstandings. We thus increase our ability to understand the
true feelings and emotions behind the other person's words. Second, because we
first choose our words and sentences *intra*personally before we communicate
them *inter*personally, an understanding of language use will sharpen our "silent
language" skills. When we're aware intrapersonally of the fine distinctions of
words, sentences, and phrases that are possible, we can consciously or subconsciously use them to express our thoughts. In addition, the various ways these
distinctions are made determine our ability to use new words with even greater
clarity.

DEVELOPING LANGUAGE SKILLS

When we were about eight months old, we uttered those first familiar sounds of
"dada" or "mama." Soon thereafter, we were able to say such familiar words as
"hi" or "bye-bye." Around the age of 18 months, our ability to use language

snowballed. It was at that age that we combined words, and our vocabulary mushroomed.[3] In fact, within two weeks after we first joined together words with meaning, we uttered as many as 70 different combinations. Even more astounding is that one week later, we were entertaining anyone who would listen with as many as 700 different word combinations. By the time we reached the age of six, we had increased our vocabulary to as many as 8,000 words.

"Baby Talk"

The road from babbling to 8,000 words was not necessarily free of bumps. Along the way we encountered stern reprimands when our words and actions together headed us for an exposed electrical outlet or the path of a moving car. When we tried to communicate with others in a language they couldn't understand, we became frustrated. But we persevered.

We persevered not only with our embryonic verbal language but also with our budding nonverbal behavior. During the time we were learning language, we were also learning to react and interact by using eye contact and varying the tonal qualities of our voices. Many of the games we played with adults were eye-contact games, such as peek-a-boo. The next time you play peek-a-boo with a child, notice how the child's eyes will change expression in response to the change in your eyes. The child is learning to react to visual as well as audible stimuli. When you say "peek-a-boo," again notice how the tonal qualities of the child's voice try to match the tonal qualities of your voice.

Child psychologists have debated whether such "parent and child" language should be replaced by more "adult" talk and thus speed a child's learning of the language. More recently, however, research tends to suggest that less complex language is very appropriate, because the child is equipped to interact at the infant level and not at the adult level. Communicating with simple words is normal when interacting with children because they are capable of handling the language at that level, and they can interact this way with you and others around them.

Forming Sentences

Nonverbal cues also help children mold their words into sentences. Forming sentences is partly internal and partly external for children because they learn to use certain words in ways that adults do not. As the child is able to communicate with adults, he or she begins to assimilate certain rules of word arrangement. If a mother or father looks at a child and says, "Please bring me the toy," the child may go over to the other side of the room and pick up the toy. It may have taken this entire combination of cues, both verbal and nonverbal, to help the child respond correctly.

As children begin to use words, regardless of what meaning they may have for them, they begin to pick up the sentence structure used by adults around them.[4] At this time, the use of more advanced vocabulary by those adults can help children form correct and more complex sentences as they progress from "baby talk" to "adult talk." Gradually, children begin to use the "rules" of grammar common to adult language, acquiring the ability to generate the responses they desire from those around them.[5]

LANGUAGE AND CHILDREN

Understanding how children use language and the strategies they employ is central to a complete understanding of how we as adults acquire language and improve our language proficiency. One expert in the field of child language development has categorized the way in which children use language for different purposes.[6] These are pared down into four primary functions: (1) *directive,* (2) *interpretive,* (3) *projective,* and (4) *relational.*[7]

Functions and Uses

The *directive function* guides actions and operations. It may involve *self-directing,* where children talk to themselves. Or it may involve *other-directing,* where the child tells someone else what to do. *Interpretive functions* involve communicating information about events witnessed by the child. In interpretive functions, *reporting* permits the child to tell of his or her own experiences. Another use of the interpretive function is *reasoning,* which supports logical thought. The *projective function* permits children to project themselves into other situations. Uses of the projective function include *predicting, empathizing,* and *imagining.* The *relational function* serves the purpose of maintaining relationships between people. These include *self-maintaining,* where the self is maintained in relation to others, and *interactional,* where the views of others are taken into consideration.[8]

Interaction with Adults

The adults who took the time to talk with us when we were growing up are, more than anything else, responsible for the way in which we developed our language skills. Talking, both verbally and nonverbally, means interacting with children and responding to their communications. From this interaction, children can grasp the rudiments of the sender-receiver combination of human communication. Hugging a child is a form of communication from a parent that produces appropriate feedback. Children thus learn how to develop different kinds of cries, each expressing a different emotion or need. These first human contacts are the forms of dialogue that will later result in the "coupling" necessary to learn language.

In addition to picking up the ability to use words correctly, we also learned how to interact with others. We acquired certain "switching" skills that allowed us to judge when to speak and when to listen. Not only our language development but also our personalities were influenced by these early interactions. As we grew older and matured, we acquired complex language "storehouses" from which we arranged words in a myriad of ways.

LANGUAGE AND ADULT INTERACTION

Just as children use language to adapt to various environments, so do adults use language to encounter both themselves and others in their daily experiences.

Intrapersonal Communication and Self-Concept Maintenance

The most basic function of language is to communicate through intrapersonal communication. We need to form our thoughts intrapersonally before we can communicate them interpersonally. Yet we do not internally communicate with words as we know them. We do not know exactly how we communicate within ourselves or the role language plays in that communication. What we do know is that language helps us to organize our thoughts and helps maintain our self-concept.

To better understand both of these factors, stop and consider how you interact with someone in a sensitive situation. Perhaps you are asking your boss for a raise. Since it is a sensitive topic, you will want to predetermine the words to use by asking yourself, "What do I want to say?" Not only will you choose the exact words you want to say but you also weigh the amount of inflection you will give to those words.

Equally important to organizing our thoughts is the support that language gives to self-concept maintenance. Part of the reason you are choosing your words very carefully is to help maintain your self-concept, which will either be elevated or lowered after you speak. If you receive a "yes," then your self-concept will be boosted. But you know this before you ask, and thus take some care in thinking out what you are going to say. If you receive a "no" answer, then you are going to be disappointed. The saying "think before you speak" has enormous substance in addition to its obvious common sense.

Interpersonal Interaction and Attraction

It's a fact of life that the correct use of language is necessary in order for people to interact successfully with each other. First, we use language to *draw together our fields of experience.* By using language familiar to each of us, our interaction can improve and continue. Language becomes the yarn that knits together our conversation. As more and more yarn is added to our conversation, our fields of experience overlap and create a sweater of homophily.

Second, once we realize our fields of experience overlap, language becomes an exploratory device that enables us to look *deeper* into those fields of experience. The deeper we explore the other person's field of experience, the more opportunities we have to communicate with that person. In short, the more we discover what we have in common, the more things we can discuss. We can explore someone else's field of experience in many different ways. Asking questions is one of those. "Where are you from?" "Where do you live?" and "What's your major?" are typical exploratory questions.

Vocabulary and Self-Disclosure

Two key factors enhance our ability to explore another person's field of experience: (1) vocabulary and (2) the willingness of each person to participate in self-disclosure. The more extensive our vocabulary is, the more exact and refined our questions and disclosures can be. When we learn the fine distinctions between different words and can use those words with precision, we can communicate with greater clarity. Although we do not want to sound like an intellectual snob, neither do we want to sound ignorant.

The conversation may come to a quick halt if the people conversing are not willing to participate in even a limited degree of self-disclosure. Persuading the other person to engage in self-disclosure is accomplished by the effective use of language. Perhaps prefacing a question with a compliment will make the person feel more at ease. Or perhaps first disclosing something about ourselves will help.

Cultural Identity

Different regions have different dialects. The vocabulary, grammar, and pronunciation of one region may be completely foreign to another region. Understanding and accepting these dialects can be the first step in encouraging interaction among people of various regions. In order for us to gain credibility with the group we're with, we may have to adapt our language to that particular group. Without this credibility, without feeling we "belong," we deprive ourselves of one of the important human needs we discussed earlier—inclusion. To be included, we don't need to cast aside our cultural or regional identities, but being flexible in our use of language can help us communicate better. Learning the different meanings of words in different cultural settings enhances our vocabulary, strengthens our self-concept, and enables us to communicate with greater precision and understanding.

Society's Rules and Norms

Society, like communication, consists of various rules or norms to which we all try to adhere most of the time. The rules and norms have developed over the years as a way for society to operate smoothly and efficiently. Language is one instrument that helps us conform to these rules and norms. Specifically, it helps us to communicate effectively with others in a way that is acceptable and adhered to by society.

For example, when world leaders meet to discuss important international issues, they carefully choose their words to convey specific meanings to a specific audience. Many such meetings have a variety of "political norms" that are inappropriate to violate. Even during disagreement, some bodies require certain "niceties" of its members. One leader disagreeing with another, for example, may first refer to his or her opponent as a "colleague" or "distinguished leader." Let's expand the examples we have been discussing.

LANGUAGE AND COMMUNICATION SETTINGS

Different settings demand different kinds of language behavior. How you greet a judge in the courtroom differs from how you greet a friend on the golf course.

Adapting to Situations

Suppose you have lunch with a friend in the cafeteria. Your conversation is casual, the sentences are structured in a certain way, and the words exchanged are lighthearted and straightforward. Now consider what happens when you sit as a member of a company's board of directors and address that same friend, who happens to be the company's president. Your interaction, the words that are exchanged, and the way you address each other produce an entirely different language from what occurred over lunch. The board room language is more formal, more deliberate.

Getting Out of a Bind

Some situations are easier to adapt to than others. For instance, we may encounter a situation that leaves us with no way out. In a physical situation of this kind, we might respond by doing what is called "leaving the field."[9] Consider this example adapted from a research study examining how we use language to disqualify ourselves from situations, or verbally "leave the field."[10] Imagine someone you work with arriving at a staff meeting at which she is going to present a report. She is wearing a new dress and a new hair style. Both are awful.[11] She leans over and whispers in your ear, "How do I look?" Imagine now that you only have three answers to give her. You can say, "Your dress doesn't suit you." You can say, "Your hair doesn't look good that way." Or you can say, "Don't worry—you'll do fine."[12]

The first two responses might ruin her ability to present her report. The third answer, however, doesn't really answer her question. What would you do? Research suggests you would choose the third answer: "Don't worry—you'll do fine." That answer allows you verbally to "leave the field." It is language's answer to getting ourselves out of a bind.

Language and Lying

Just as our use of language changes when we rely on it to help us out of awkward and unpleasant situations, it also changes when we lie.[13] Research studies have examined the phenomenon of lying and have found that when we lie, we use fewer words than when we are telling the truth. Perhaps because we know we are lying and each word adds to the risk of being discovered, we minimize that risk by using fewer words. Another explanation is that lying is unpleasant, and we try to avoid the unpleasantness by minimizing the number of words we use. Research has also discovered that when we lie, we use fewer past-tense verbs.[14] An explanation is that it may be easier to verify past events than present or future events; our lies cannot hide as easily in the past. Thus, we try to use verbs that keep the conversation in the present and future but avoid the past.

Using Language to Control

To function in society, we need control of our environment. The ability to control does not mean that we need to become domineering or abrasive. It does mean that we need to acquire the skills necessary to control when we want or need to control. Language is one of those skills.

Routine uses of "controlling" language occur in everyday interactions with other people. "Please pass the sugar," "Set it over there," and "I need it tomorrow" are statements of control. We think little of being direct and stating precisely what we want when we interact with people who provide us with services, especially services for which we pay.

THE LANGUAGE OF COMMITMENT

Perhaps no person is more skilled at using language to gain a commitment than someone working in sales, especially direct-contact sales. Because of this ability, they're some of the highest paid people in business and industry. To hear and watch a talented salesperson work with language is to experience a master carpenter working with a tool, a symphony conductor using a baton, or a sculptor using a chisel.

At the heart of the sales presentation is what is called the "commitment," or "asking for the order." Asking for the order takes on many different forms. Sometimes it's direct, such as, "Can I sell you some today?" Although widely used, this request for commitment is risky because it opens the door for that dreaded one-word reply—"No!" Rather than risk using that approach, a skilled request for commitment involves a more subtle use of the language. Consider the person selling a stereo. Many a customer has left a store with a new stereo without ever having said, "I'll buy it" or "I'll take it." Instead, the salesperson has sold the stereo by effectively using language to ask a series of questions.

> "Do you like these models?"
> "Do you enjoy listening to music?"
> "What kind of a stereo were you thinking about?"
> "Have you heard this model's features [explains them]?"
> "Go ahead, turn it on [the customer does]."

At this point, the salesperson has engaged the potential customer in conversation, and the customer has made a partial commitment to the stereo just by turning it on. The customer may not buy the stereo, but the commitment of interest is much greater than when he or she first walked into the store. Moreover, the salesperson and the potential customer can now talk about something they have in common—the stereo and its features. Their fields of experience now overlap.

> "Here are the headphones. Sit down and enjoy it for a while."

After a short time the salesperson again engages in conversation. Most importantly, the salesperson determines what the customer's likes and dislikes about the stereo are and can then seek out and handle any previously unstated or hidden objections. Finally, the salesperson begins to ask for the order:

> "You would probably want FM and AM stereo capabilities, wouldn't you? (The question is fairly safe, since most people want to be able to listen to as many stations as possible. The purpose of the question is to generate an affirmative answer. Additional questions producing affirmative answers might follow.)
>
> "Does your current stereo have audio disc capabilities?" (Depending on the answer, the salesperson either affirms that cassette capabilities can be included with the new stereo or simply avoids the issue.)
>
> "Would you like it in silver or wood tones?"
>
> "Would you like us to deliver it, or do you want to take it home with you now?"

By now, the stereo has been "psychologically" purchased, and all that remains is completing the paperwork. Notice that at no time did the salesperson ask, "Can I sell you one?" Similarly, at no time did the customer say, "I'll buy it." The salesperson's skillful use of language helped to produce the sale. The final question, "Would you like us to deliver it . . . ?" took the place of, "Will you buy the stereo?" If the customer tells the salesperson, "I'll take it home," it is the same as saying, "I'll buy it." Skillful timing of the words is necessary along with using the right words. But without the words, without the use of language, the stereo would have never changed hands.

SEMANTICS: LANGUAGE AND MEANING

Semantics is the study of meaning, or, more appropriately, the science of meanings. Originating from the Greek words for *significant* and *sign,* semantics has evolved into a broad-based area of scholarly inquiry. The results of research in the field are providing valuable insights into the way we use language and apply meaning to language's various signs and symbols.

Differences in meaning, both of words and sentences, alter the way we use language and the way other people interpret what we say. This, again, is why having an adequate vocabulary is necessary to assure better understanding. At the same time, it remains important to understand where differences in meaning can occur. Being alert to the "stress points" of language where "breaks" or noise in the communication process can happen is an important step toward improving the way we use language in human communication.

Symbol and Referent

Written language, as we learned earlier in this text, evolved from simple drawings or pictographs on the inside of caves to the more complex symbols of words. Yet words are actually nothing more than modern-day pictographs (Fig. 3–2). In actuality, pictographs were more complex than words, at least small

Figure 3-2
The East-West Center in Hawaii invited visual communicators from the United States, Canada, Japan, India, and Iran to work at developing a means of visually communicating information about world population problems across cultures. The illustration is interpreted: "There are rising challenges in the changing world, caused by global situations of population, food, energy, and environmental pollution." (© East-West Center)

numbers of words, because they meant a great many detailed things to the people who read them. A squiggly stalk of corn, for example, was symbolic of the earth begetting life—fairly sophisticated for "a stalk of corn."

Today, we use words as the symbols that guide our thoughts and call forth images and meanings we have learned since birth. Consider the word *water*. If we wrote these five letters—w–a–t–e–r— or symbols, on the side of a cave, we would have a pictograph much like those of our early ancestors.

Now examine the different images that the word (symbol) *water* calls forth in our minds. Perhaps our vivid recollection dates back to the time we saw the pounding surf of the ocean for the first time. Or perhaps we remember the serene mountain lake where our family used to spend its vacations. Perhaps we recall the sprinkler hose we used to run through as a child to cool off on a hot summer's day. All of these images of water are *referents* to the symbol *water*. And while we were thinking of the water that had influenced our lives, others reading this passage had different thoughts of water that had influenced their lives.

Our discussion of the difference between the symbol *water* and the referent for the symbol leads us into examining how misunderstandings can develop when different people place different referents on the same symbol. Assume, for example, that you and your friend decide to send a gift to a third friend.

"Let's send candy."
"Great idea," your friend replies.
"I'll order it today. Will a five-pound box of chocolates be OK?"
"Chocolates? I thought fudge, perhaps fudge with nuts, would be better."
"Fudge with nuts? I don't think Jackie likes nuts. Perhaps just plain fudge would be more appropriate."
"OK, plain fudge. But it's going to melt."
"It won't melt. Godiva fudge is too thick and rich."

"Godiva fudge?! I can't afford that! What about Fanny Farmer fudge?"

"OK, Fanny Farmer fudge. But that white fudge reminds me of blue cheese."

"White fudge? I meant milk chocolate fudge. That's the best to send."

"Hold it right there. I suggest we send candy; you agree. I imagine us sending a five-pound box of chocolates and you're talking about milk chocolate fudge. Let's solve the dilemma and send flowers."

"Great idea! A bouquet or a live plant?"

We can quickly see the many misunderstandings these two people who encountered the word *candy* managed to picture in their own minds.

Language and Grammar

Language enables us to communicate and to prevent communication breakdowns. Language strives for this with its *rules of grammar,* which encourage certain arrangements of words in order to achieve a universal understanding. When the arrangement of words adheres to these accepted rules, we refer to the arrangement as good grammar. In a sense, grammar "glues" words into sentences and meanings. Yet even though the rules of grammar may be standardized and somewhat inflexible, many different words and organizations of words can be used to obey such rules. "Please go to the store and bring back some eggs" and "Please bring back some eggs from the store" are both grammatically correct, and either arrangement of words will produce the same results.

Connotation and Denotation

Another stress point in language occurs when we misunderstand the difference between *connotation* and *denotation.* From grade school on, we have heard that the denotative meaning of a word refers to its dictionary meaning. Although that statement is true, interpreting it literally has caused more than one communication breakdown. Dictionaries tend to look at multiple meanings of words. We saw this expressed in Chapter 1 when we defined "communication." By using other words to form those meanings, dictionaries immediately risk creating the same misunderstanding that took place in our example of the two friends buying candy. A much better way to refer to denotation is to say it is *a precise or explicit meaning of a word.*

Connotation, on the other hand, derives from the word *connote,* which means *to suggest or imply.* With connotation, we lack the accuracy we have with denotation. The judgments, prejudices, preferences, and experiences of people become tangled with connotation. Although a denotative meaning may exist, when we use words to communicate, the speaker may be using either his or her own connotative meaning of a particular word. Similarly, because of that person's own interpretation, the listener may receive a completely different meaning from what the speaker intended.

To achieve the greatest effectiveness when we communicate, we must keep in mind that because of backgrounds and life experiences, different people place different meanings on different words. In casual, everyday conversation with our friends, we may take the meanings of words for granted, knowing no serious consequences will happen if we make mistakes. But this attitude can cause us trouble when we engage in more important conversations or are in situations where the emotional content of our messages becomes more intense.

Meaning is only one variable of our language. Our language does contain other variables, though, and they are the "tools" that help us build good skills of human communication.[15] Among these tools are language complexity, language intensity, verbal immediacy, concrete or abstract language, vocabulary, language style, and language patterns. While we will discuss them separately, all are interrelated.

LANGUAGE COMPLEXITY

If we could sail through life uttering one-word expressions that had the exact same meaning for everyone, human communication would be a simple process. But it would not be effective. We would not have the ability to explain complex concepts, such as "compassion" and "peace." Yet along with the added capabilities of a more complex language comes new potential for misunderstandings. The more complex a concept, the more words are necessary to explain it.

Is language more complex today than in years past because of the increasing complexity of our world? Some say that the influx of new words entering our vocabulary every day just from science and technology is phenomenal. Add to this the fact that the mass media introduces these new words to us with ever-increasing speed, and we can begin to see that our language is changing at a much faster rate than it did in the past. New levels of complexity in society and new words and arrangements of words to meet that complexity place new importance on our knowledge of effective communication.

LANGUAGE INTENSITY

Imagine that you're conversing with a friend about someone you both know. Your feelings about that person are rather neutral. You remember meeting her at a company picnic, in an exercise class, and calling her about a budget problem. You describe her as "nice," "a good person," "competent." Nothing too exciting, but nothing negative, either. Your friend, on the other hand, has a different impression of the person. With gusto, your friend describes her as being "incredibly intelligent," having a "great sense of humor," and being "a person who really cares about people."[16] You are somewhat mystified about your friend's enthusiasm. Perhaps you missed something. Just then a third friend, who also knows the same person, enters the room. With words such as *selfish, egomaniac,* and *cunning,* the person gets a third evaluation that is totally negative.

The different degrees of language intensity in the above example are ever present when we describe our opinions about a person, an object, or an issue. Although this example used language that clearly reflected negative or positive opinions, much of what we say is more subtle. Descriptions are often not as clear-cut as "egomaniac" or "incredibly intelligent."

Research also suggests that the intensity of language plays a part in affirming or changing our opinions. When we face a stressful situation, for example, we may try to lessen that tension by using less intense language. One research study discovered that actual suicide notes exhibited lower language intensity than notes written by people who were role-playing suicides.[17] Other research indicates that language which is too intense can lower our opinion of the speaker, especially when that speaker delivers a message at odds with our own ideas.[18] Emotional involvement with an issue and strong opinions can cause us "internally" to become more intense and "outwardly" to express this intensity.[19]

VERBAL IMMEDIACY

The degree to which we associate ourselves with a concept can influence our use of language just as our feelings about something or someone can influence how intensely we use that language. We call this *verbal immediacy,* and it refers to *the amount we approach or avoid a topic.*[20]

The following statements will help to explain this concept. The first statement reflects strong verbal immediacy. The others follow in descending immediacy until we reach the last statement, which reflects weak verbal immediacy:

> We will gain a rich appreciation of human communication while taking this course.
> You and I will gain a rich appreciation of human communication while taking this course.
> Perhaps you and I will gain a rich appreciation of human communication while taking this course.
> Perhaps you will gain a rich appreciation of human communication when you take that course.

The first statement was assuring and all-inclusive. However, in the last statement, the speaker was removed not only from the feelings and expectations of the other person but also from the degree of involvement. In each statement, more and more disassociation took place.

Differences in verbal immediacy, much more than we are able to illustrate or discuss here, arise from variations in adjectives (*the* vs. *that*), verb tense (*past* vs. *future*), order of occurrence or reference in a sequence (*first* vs. *last*), implied volunteerism (*want* vs. *must*), mutuality (*Charles and I do something* vs. *I do something with Charles*), and probability (*Diane and I will* vs. *Diane and I may*).[21]

How are immediacy and language related? Research suggests that we use less immediate language when we are in a stressful situation. Using it is one of the ways we disassociate ourselves from the source of the stress. Journalism students under the impression that their program was being cut by the university administration used fewer first-person pronouns such as "I" when writing about that topic than they did in a less stressful situation.[22] Another researcher found anxiety can be related to verbal immediacy.[23] Still another study found that a former U.S. president "used language that was lower in immediacy when he was communicating in relatively uncomfortable (for him) situations."[24] When you listen to a speaker, converse with friends, or watch a televised debate, start to monitor immediacy as well as intensity. How do both variables influence the communication sent and received?[25]

CONCRETE VS. ABSTRACT LANGUAGE

Because language is changing more rapidly than in the past and the complexity of the concepts we encounter is increasing, our ability to communicate with clear and concise language to express our thoughts and ideas becomes even more critical. Both the words and the arrangement of those words that we use to communicate clearly and concisely can range between the concrete and the abstract.[26] *Concrete* words and sentences are *simple and direct*. "The boy put on his shoes" is straightforward and concise. Now consider this statement: "Children achieve satisfaction through small accomplishments." The first statement is concrete; the second statement is more abstract.

Which statement is more appropriate? The appropriateness depends on what is needed to communicate effectively and to meet a specific communication objective. If we only need to know what the boy has done, then our example of concrete language is acceptable and appropriate. If we need to describe a universal concept that is applicable across many situations, then our abstract statement is best. Although abstract language can help us to communicate complex thoughts, it is also susceptible to different interpretations and misunderstanding. Thus, it is best to use abstract language only to the degree that the communication situation requires it.

VOCABULARY

We talked earlier about the importance of vocabulary in making precise use of the language, achieving the ability to discuss and explain complex issues, and communicating with greater understanding. As a language variable, vocabulary helps us find those key points in others' fields of experience with which we can interact. The more extensive our vocabulary and the better use we make of it, the more adept we are at cementing thoughts and ideas with each other through human communication.

Again, the particular setting often determines how we use the range of or particular words in our vocabularies. Research results suggest that when we communicate in a highly stressful situation, we may use a much smaller vocabulary than we would under nonstressful situations.[27] Other studies suggest that people who use a wide vocabulary, and who are not doing so to show off, are perceived as being more competent, of a higher social and income status, and in control of themselves.

LANGUAGE STYLE

The way we use some or all of the language variables we have just discussed helps to determine our *language style*. Because there are so many different language variables, the way in which we combine them and, thus, the number of different language styles possible are infinite. Think of all the people you talk with and how your own style changes from one situation to another. Using humor and adopting a style to a particular situation are two examples.

The Use of Humor

All of us at times play the role of the humorist. We may offer a humorous anecdote, tell a joke, or relate a funny story as a communication "stretegy" to make another person laugh. Although some may call humorous people the life of the party, others may look upon their constant humor and laughing mannerisms as obnoxious or juvenile. Nevertheless, a humorist possesses a certain style in the way he or she uses language.[28]

Humor is a response "arising from the perception of incongruity or from wit and word play.[29] Jokes, for example, "depend upon language for a portion of their effect. Dialect jokes, jokes based on group stereotypes, . . . and shifts in meaning are all basic to humor. Puns and many forms of verbal word play are recognized and often highly appreciated forms of humor."[30]

Situational Style

We have all been in situations in which the language, such as cursing and swearing, is inappropriate. Such language can cause an unnatural strain on any encounter. Yet cursing and swearing are not necessarily or automatically inappropriate. Under certain circumstances,[31] even swearing or obscenity has its place.[32] Why would we use these language styles? The desire to draw together another person's field of experience with our own is one reason.

LANGUAGE PATTERNS

Words are joined together in a particular pattern to accomplish different communication goals. Consider the following different language patterns.[33]

Impulsive. An impulsive pattern is characterized by *short utterances*. There is little need for complex language structure. You are jogging and accidentally turn your ankle. "Ouch!" is your reaction. Or your friend invites you to an exciting rock concert. You immediately squeal, "Ooooooo." In most cases, we would characterize an impulsive pattern as "a speaker's vocal reaction to a situation."

Contactive. Slightly more complex than impulsive patterns are contactive patterns. We use contactive language patterns when *we try to initiate "contact" or gain the attention of another person.* "Hi there." "What's happening?" "How have you been?" are examples of contactive patterns. These patterns can be single-word statements such as "Hi," but they're more often composed of word phrases. It's the *intention* in making the statement, not the number of words, that distinguishes an impulsive pattern from a contactive one.

Conversative. In a conversative pattern, *our language style approaches human interaction.* Although a very limited vocabulary may be employed, this pattern goes beyond the impulsive reaction and the contactive phrase and approaches "conversation." Messages are sent and received, and feedback takes place or at least is expected. Examples are cocktail party chatter and elaborated greetings and farewells. A conversative pattern may take the following form: "Joan, you're looking terrific tonight. Have you changed your hairstyle or something? Did Sam come with you? You know, it's been too long since we've seen each other."

Descriptive or directive. In a descriptive or directive pattern, words are not only joined together in phrases but usually appear *in a definite sequence that tells a story or directs someone to do something.* Stop and consider how you would describe your favorite vacation spot to a classmate. The geographic location, the sights, sounds, smells, the people, and your feelings about the place all would be wrapped up into a specific package of words that would mentally take your classmate to that same location.

Elaborative. More complex than the patterns we have already discussed is the elaborative pattern. Here, language tackles the tasks of *moving from one concept to another, in much the same way paragraphs are used in a book.* A bank officer talking about the services of the bank would be using an elaborative pattern of language.

All through the day we constantly shift through these patterns. When we get up in the morning, the language patterns we employ may be very minimal. "Darn alarm clock!" may be the prelude to further grunts and groans as we struggle from bed to breakfast. Later we will nod a "Good morning" to a classmate or colleague. Still later we might find ourselves giving directions or explaining a complex idea to a co-worker or student.

Our ability to adapt and function successfully using different modes of speech is important to our ability to function in society. Although much debated and is some ways controversial, the research of British sociologist Basil Bernstein suggests that different social classes in Great Britain possess different patterns of speech, ranging from the more restrictive patterns for lower classes to the more complex and elaborative patterns for upper classes.[34] Bernstein's research has been interpreted to suggest that these different levels of language complexity cause lower-class children in Britain to fall behind their middle-class counterparts when they reach elementary school, where the more elaborative patterns of language are employed.[35]

AVOIDING SEXIST LANGUAGE

Avoiding sexist language is as much an attitude (Fig. 3–3) as it is attention to specific words. What follows are examples of biased and unbiased language.[36] But that is not enough. Avoiding sexist language demands a consciousness at all times and special attention to situations where sexist language may occur.

Occupations and Titles

Rooted in such basic words as "man," "mankind," "man-made," and "manpower" is a bias that has existed for centuries. Even the earliest descriptions of religious experiences refer to "wise men" and can leave the assumption that only men of the era were wise. Today, such familiar terms as "businessman," "foreman," "mailman," "policeman," "stewardess," "fireman," and others reflect sexist language. Consider instead the following terms replacing those just mentioned: "businessperson," "supervisor," "mail carrier," "police officer," "flight attendant," and "firefighter." Each is an unbiased alternative. Ask yourself what unbiased alternative titles could replace the following: actress, authoress, clean-

Figure 3-3
The changing role of women in all facets of society necessitates changes in our use of language. Avoiding sexist language is a sign of intelligence, sensitivity, and responsibility to the contributions of individuals without regard to sex and other characteristics. (Courtesy Exxon Company, U.S.A.)

ing lady, congressman, houseboy, housewife, salesman, woman doctor, and male nurse? Try the following alternatives: actor, author, household worker, member of Congress, servant, homemaker, salesperson, doctor, and nurse.

Omission

Another root of sexist language goes beyond titles to references that assume that either women were an afterthought, not represented in a particular setting, or treated as exceptional cases. Consider the following statements, comparing the biased with the unbiased alternatives:

Biased	Unbiased
The pioneers crossed the desert with their women and children.	Pioneer families crossed the desert.
Radium was discovered by a woman, Marie Curie.	Marie Curie discovered radium.
When setting up his experiment, a researcher must always check for error.	When setting up an experiment, a researcher must always check for error.
As knowledge of the physical world increased, men began to examine long-held beliefs.	As knowledge of the physical world increased, long-held beliefs were examined with a more critical eye.

Equal Treatment

A close examination of common language usage will turn up many examples of sexist comments that are patronizing or sexually oriented. Consider the following examples:

Biased	Unbiased
The poor women could no longer go on; the exhausted men. . . .	The exhausted pioneers could no longer go on.
Though a woman, she ran the business efficiently.	She ran the business efficiently.
Mrs. Acton, a statuesque blonde, is Joe Granger's assistant.	Jan Acton is Joe Granger's assistant.
All the strong young men of the village took part in the festival, as did the young girls.	All the young people of the village took part in the festival.
The line manager was angry; his secretary was upset.	The line manager and his secretary were both upset by the mistake.

Notice that in the last two biased examples, an unequal treatment is implied by statements that portray women as an afterthought. It is as important to include women in the main thought and expression of the statement as it is to avoid making a sexist comment in the first place.

Stereotyping Roles

Even though women have moved out of the typical stereotyped roles of past generations, we too frequently cling to perceptions and statements that reflect the past.

Biased	Unbiased
As a child, she was a tomboy; sports and not dolls were her main interest.	She was actively interested in sports as a child.
Most of the men in this plant are married heads of households.	In this plant, most of the married heads of household are men.
Current tax regulations allow a head of household to deduct for the support of a wife and children.	Current tax regulations allow a head of household to deduct for the support of a spouse and children.
The line manager is responsible for the productivity of his department; his foreman, for the day-to-day work of the girls on the line.	The line manager is responsible for the productivity of the department; the supervisors, for that of the workers on the line.
The secretary brought her boss his coffee.	The secretary brought the boss coffee.

Biased statements such as those listed above can leave the impression that only men fulfill certain roles. These statements also leave the impression that only men operate in positions of authority and that certain jobs, such as that of secretary, are held only by women. Children are seen as outdated role models, such as little girls being tomboys if they participate in sports. Do your statements contain sexist language that perpetuates these stereotypes?

The Generic 'His'

Many times the word "his" creeps into our language, but instead of referring to a man, it is used to describe an entire class of people. The personal pronouns "his," and "she" can be troublesome, and it is easy to slip into a sexist statement. The following examples illustrate this point:

Biased	Unbiased
A person's facial expression does not always reveal his true feelings.	Facial expression is not always an indicator of a person's true feelings.
Sometimes a doctor will see his patients only in a hospital.	Sometimes a doctor will see patients only in a hospital.
The clinician must take his measurements accurately and carefully.	The clinician must take accurate and careful measurements.
The typical child does his homework right after school.	Most children do their homework right after school.

Common Expressions Implying Bias

Through the years our language has acquired many familiar expressions that are sexist and biased. Being sensitive to these common sexist expressions is important when interacting with others.

Biased Expression	Alternative
The committee decided he was the right man for the job.	The committee decided he was the right person for the job.
The teacher must always remember that her role in the learning process is a vital one.	Teachers must always remember that their role in the learning process is a vital one.
Research has shown that the smart shopper knows what she wants before she enters the store.	Research has shown that smart shoppers know what they want before they enter the store.
Children need someone to mother them.	Children need a parent.

The examples cited here are a throwback to a time when women were not well represented in the work force. Today, in almost any job or profession—and backed up by laws guarding against sex discrimination—women hold positions of highest responsibility. Today, with two-career families and with fathers receiving custody in child-custody cases, a man may be the smart shopper and also the parent.

Balanced Treatment

Listen carefully the next time you are introduced to someone. For example, if you interview for a job and are introduced to the manager's assistant, is the assistant addressed by "Miss" or "Mrs." and an associate of the manager introduced by his or her first name? Such small slips, even unintentional, are examples of sexist language. Consider being introduced to Alice Smith and Jack Green. Alice is the manager's secretary and Jack is his associate. The manager says politely, "This is my secretary, Mrs. Smith, and my associate, Jack Green." The manager should have said, "This is my secretary, Alice Smith, and my associate, Jack Green." Even though Alice Smith is not at the same staff level as Jack, she should not be deprived of her first name in an introduction when that courtesy was afforded Jack.

Individuals with titles more familiar to us may be afforded preference in introductions. For example, if two corporation vice-presidents are introduced at a luncheon, it would be sexist to say, "Let's all welcome vice-president Smith and Mrs. Jones," especially when Mrs. Jones is also a vice-president and deserves the same courtesy as Smith.

Implied age differences can also creep into our everyday usage. Consider this statement: "The men in the office took the girls to lunch." A much better alternative would be, "The men in the office took the women to lunch."

The word "girls" not only implies a younger female but also less ability and maturity than "woman."

Avoiding Cliches

Before concluding our discussion of sexist language, we need to remind ourselves of some overused cliches that pop up frequently when we speak without thinking. Statements such as "the woman driver," "the nagging mother-in-law," "the little woman," "the henpecked husband," "gal Friday," "boys' night out," "dizzy blonde," "female gossip," and "man-sized job" are all statements that are outdated, demeaning, and that show a lack of sensitivity to the contemporary role of women in society.

It is hoped that by now we have become more sensitive to sexist language, but we should also understand that it still exists and that we may need patience with those who unintentionally and without any ill-will whatsoever still use sexist language in their everyday speech. Many people have not read this book or others that make them aware of the problems of sexist language. Moreover, from corporate training manuals of government documents, vestiges of sexist language still exist.

SUMMARY

Chapter 3 described our journey from the gurgles and goos of infancy to the acquisition of a sophisticated adult language. From approximately two to six years of age, our vocabularies mushroom from a few words to about 8,000. As we continue to increase our vocabularies and learn how to build sentences, we gain the ability to handle complex language tasks. Being around other people is very important in this stage of our language growth, for the opportunity to interact interpersonally helps us build our language skills.

One of the most basic functions of language is that it allows us to communicate within ourselves through intrapersonal communication. We are able internally to verbalize complex thoughts and processes in order to solve more complex communication problems that might confront us. Still another function of language is to assist us in meeting the expectations of certain societal norms through appropriate conversation, whether we converse with individuals or groups. Language helps us adapt to different situations. Whether we're asking someone out on a date or negotiating the price of a new car, language is the key to unlock understanding.

Two additional functions of language include achieving control and securing commitments. Control as a basic communication need can often be achieved by understanding the difference between assertive and nonassertive language. Directly related to control is our ability to secure commitments from people.

In discussing the important role of meaning in language, we encountered the term *semantics,* used to describe the science of meanings. Important to understanding meaning is to be able to distinguish between the symbol (a word) and the referent (what the word means). Grammar is the glue that holds meaning together, while denotation and connotation refer to the difference between the explicit, or "dictionary" meaning of a word, and how the word functions in a certain context. Language variables include how words are joined together, or language complexity; its intensity; verbal immediacy; concrete or abstract language; and vocabulary. How we combine these variables defines our language style. We form these styles with humor, the appropriate use of words, and language patterns which range from the impulsive to the elaborative.

Responsible use of the language means avoiding sexist language. Sexist language has its roots in centuries of tradition, much of it implying subservient roles for women. Occupations and titles are particularly troublesome when such words as "businessman," "policeman," and others have had such common usage. Faults of omission, unequal treatment, stereotyping roles, the generic use of "his," common expressions that imply bias, unbalanced treatment, and using cliches all contribute to sexist language.

QUESTIONS FOR REVIEW AND DISCUSSION

1. What are the four primary functions of language used by children?
2. Why is language in a constant state of transition?
3. How does language develop in children?
4. What is the study of semantics?
5. What is the difference between denotation and connotation?
6. What do the terms *language intensity, verbal immediacy, concrete vs. abstract language,* and *vocabulary* mean?
7. List and explain five different language patterns.
8. What is the difference between a symbol and a referent?
9. List the different categories of sexist language.

LEARNING EXERCISES

1. Select five buildings either on campus or nearby. Choose an architectural design from each building, such as an entrance, arch, trim around a window, or some other feature. Write a description of each one as though you were describing it to a friend. Compare your descriptions with others and notice carefully the choice of words each person uses. Without pictures, is it possible to "see" clearly the feature from each person's description?

2. Interview someone whose profession is sales. Discuss how the person "closes" a sale and the type of commitment language the person employs.

ADDITIONAL READINGS

BOLLES, E. B., *So Much To Say: How To Help Your Child Learn to Talk.* New York: St. Martins, 1982.

DEVILLIERS, J. G. *Language Acquisition.* Cambridge: Harvard University Press, 1978.

ELGIN, S. H. *Gentle Art of Verbal Self Defense.* Englewood Cliffs, NJ: Prentice-Hall–Spectrum Books, 1980.

HAYAKAWA, S. I. *Language in Thought and Action* (4th ed.). New York: Harcourt Brace Jovanovich, Inc., 1978.

MICHAELS, L. and C. RICKS *The State of the Language.* Berkeley: University of California Press, 1980.

MITCHELL, R. *Less Than Words Can Say.* Boston: Little, Brown, 1979.

PEI, M. *Weasel Words: The Art of Saying What You Don't Mean.* New York: Harper & Row Pub., 1978.

SAFIRE, W. *I Stand Corrected: More on Language.* New York: Times Books, 1984.

STEVENSON, V. ED., *Words: The Evolution of Western Languages.* New York: Von Nostrand, 1983.

4

NONVERBAL COMMUNICATION

OBJECTIVES

After completing this chapter, you should be able to

- Explain the concept of territorial space
- Describe personal space and the forces that can affect it
- Identify the nonverbal communication functions of complementing, repeating, substituting, regulating, and accenting
- Be aware of the nonverbal messages communicated by body types, shapes, and sizes
- Understand our bodies' natural clothes
- Realize basic body movements
- Compare and contrast emblems, illustrators, and adaptors
- Comprehend the language of posture
- Explain how we communicate with facial expressions
- Describe how we communicate with our eyes
- Discuss the qualities of the voice
- Identify the nonverbal messages of touch
- State how what we wear projects an image
- Talk about the influence of color on nonverbal communication
- Define the messages of time.

On Ocracoke Island off the coast of North Carolina is a safe harbor for Atlantic fishing fleets seeking refuge during storms. It is also a deep-water harbor for pleasure boats, U.S. Coast Guard vessels, and ferries that operate between the North Carolina coast and the island. Because of the vast number of boats that dock there, large pilings can be seen sticking up from the surface of the water. The tops of the pilings are fairly flat, a perfect place for seagulls to rest. At almost any hour you can find the gulls perched on their respective pilings, surveying the picturesque harbor. Perched, that is, until another seagull hovers in to claim a piling. What results is a rather comical spectacle of "piling jumping." The intruder usually approaches one of the perched seagulls from the rear and forces it off the piling. The displaced seagull, with much fluttering and squawking, in turn forces another seagull off its piling. What follows is a game of musical chairs until most of the seagulls change pilings.

TERRITORIAL SPACE

For the seagulls, the top of each piling represents *territorial space*. The intruding seagull is actually invading the territorial space of the other seagull when it challenges it for a perch.

Physical boundaries define territorial space (Fig. 4–1). They can be as concrete as the area behind a chain-link fence or as abstract as the perimeter of a beach towel. Also referred to as *territory* or *territoriality*, our territorial space affects the way we communicate with others. One research study identified the

Figure 4-1
Physical boundaries define territorial space. In this library, the desks are constructed with ledges defining the area each student occupies. If another student's books move into an occupied space, it would create awkwardness. Similarly, students occupying their own space are usually careful not to infringe on the territory available to other students. Where crowding is present or where survival is at stake, overt defensive behavior will result if territorial space is violated. (Laimute E. Druskis photo)

different territorial spaces that existed among prisoners at the Pennsylvania Correction Facility. It found, "When in the yard or other open space, someone crossing the eight-to-ten foot barrier is perceived as trespassing. In closed quarters, depending on the need for privacy, the distance is reduced to two or three feet. Conversational distance between two inmates is approximately two feet; between an inmate and a guard it increases to three feet."[1]

Most life forms defend their territorial space to some degree. Wild animals, for example, may lay claim to and jealously guard a water hole or hunting ground. When other animals venture too close to the claim, the animal who "owns" the territory may or may not permit the newcomers to drink or hunt, depending on the "owner's" thirst or hunger at the time. Protecting the claimed territory may be the key to the animal's survival. This protective behavior is particularly noticeable when natural resources are scarce, such as at a desert oasis.

The typical classroom usually has well-defined territorial space. At the front of the room is the source of authority, leadership, or knowledge. The teacher's desk or lectern is usually there. Although a student may be able to approach the desk and talk to the teacher, the student cannot take the liberty of occupying the chair behind the desk, unless asked by the teacher to deliver an assignment or some other task. Similarly, the student's territorial space is defined by the size of the classroom seat (Fig. 4–2). And although it may not be large, it is something the student returns to day after day. Even when assigned seating is

Figure 4-2   In classroom settings, the students' territorial space is carefully defined by classroom seating arrangements. The teacher is also assigned territorial space (a desk) at the front of the room which cannot be violated because of the differences in status and authority between student and teacher. Even when students are absent, a class will generally retain a seating arrangement similar to that at the beginning of the term. This occurs even when seating is not assigned. (Irene Springer)

absent, a class gradually adopts a fairly constant and defined seating arrangement.

PERSONAL SPACE

Psychological traits rather than physical structures are what distinguish personal space from territorial space. One way to understand personal space is to imagine that a bubble exists around each of us. If we are shy and introverted, our bubbles may be very large. Large bubbles prevent people from getting too close to us. The more extroverted or people-oriented we are, the smaller may be our bubbles. Yet these bubbles are also very flexible. They change from one moment to the next, depending on a host of factors, all of which influence the way we communicate with others.

The Relationship of Territory to Personal Space

Even though they deal with different concerns, personal space and territorial space are interrelated. In many cases, the amount of *available space* determines the amount of personal space we need. If we are in a crowded elevator, we do not normally feel awkward if someone else enters the elevator and stands with his or her shoulder touching ours. But if we are in an empty elevator, and someone else enters and stands with his or her shoulder touching ours, we not only feel very uncomfortable but will probably get off at the next floor. In these situations, available territory determines how much personal space is adequate for us to feel comfortable. Check-out lines, library tables, movie theaters, and park benches are all places where our personal space is flexible, determined by the available territory we share with other people.[2]

The Influence of Age and Status

Research has found that strangers who are similar in age will approach each other physically closer than strangers whose ages are apart.[3] Two elderly strangers in the same room will tend to stand closer together than will an elderly person and a younger person. Related to this concept is status. People of similar status will approach each other more closely than people whose statuses differ.[4]

Think about the people with whom you interact. If at work you go into your manager's office, do you stand as close to your manager as you would to one of your co-workers? Probably not. If you walk into the student union and your professor is there, you would be more likely to sit across from your professor rather than next to him or her.[5]

The Influence of Friendship

A significant factor influencing personal space is friendship. If we had the choice, we would rather be in closer proximity to our friends than we would with total strangers. Suppose that you decide to treat yourself to a pizza after your evening class. When you enter the pizzeria, you notice a close friend seated at a booth along with someone you do not know. You decide to join them. You are much more apt to position yourself closer to your friend than to the stranger.[6]

We also use personal space to communicate friendship. Sitting close to someone may be our nonverbal way of saying, "I want to be your friend"[7] or "I want to get to know you better." A risk is involved in such behavior, though, because violating another's personal space can hinder rather than enhance friendships.

Cultural Influence

Because we are more apt to encounter people of our own cultures, we can form the habit of assuming that everyone behaves with the same cultural and social norms that we do. Thus, often we are not sensitive to the personal space expectations of different cultures.[8] In some cultures, it is appropriate for men to kiss each other on the cheek as a greeting. Certain cultures deem it inappropriate to look a person in the eye while being reprimanded. Others consider this action a sign of disrespect.

Sexual Implications

When males talk with males, they tend to have different personal space expectations than females have when they're talking with other females. When men are talking to other men, they tend to stand farther apart than when women are talking to other women.[9] Some research studies have shown there to be as much as a one-foot difference in personal space expectations.

The Influence of Praise and Criticism

Seeking praise and avoiding criticism are human tendencies. They also infuence our personal space. When we are receiving praise, the personal space between us and the person praising us will be less than in situations in which we are receiving negative criticism.[10] If your manager calls you into the office to praise you, you will probably not feel uncomfortable about sitting in the chair next to your manager's desk. But if you are called in for a serious reprimand, you might feel much more comfortable sitting on the other side of the room.

Settings and Topics

Because every communication encounter is different, we must keep the setting in mind as a means of evaluating another person's personal space. One expert on nonverbal communication distinguished among different personal space distances based on the amount of intimacy or formality of an interaction. They are:

(1) intimate distance, for private interactions or physical contact, which is 0 to 18 inches; (2) personal distance, for situations involving less sensory

involvement, which is 18 inches to 4 feet; (3) social distance, for informal interactions with business associates and friends, which is 4 feet to 12 feet; and (4) formal distance, for public speeches and distances from public officials, which is 12 feet and beyond.[11]

These distances are not absolute, but they do show the variations in personal space that can arise in different situations.

Closely related to setting is the topic of conversation. If we are discussing a very intimate topic with a close friend, we do not hesitate to stand close to that person. If the topic is less personal, we may increase the distance between us (Fig. 4–3).

Psychological Effects on Personal Space

Although we can talk in general terms about territory, age, status, friendship, culture, sex, praise, criticism, situation, and topic, each of us is different. We cannot ignore the fact that our own psychological makeup will influence any communication encounter we may have. When we feel good about ourselves and have a good self-concept, we want to be with and communicate with other people. Because we have self-confidence in our ability to relate to others, and therefore perceive others as liking us, we are not offended when someone stands close to us, especially when we feel positive about the other person. This does not mean we go through the day hugging people, but a positive self-concept produces positive relationships with others. When positive relationships exist, it is more difficult to violate personal space, and communication is less likely to break down.[12]

Figure 4-3
The topic of conversation and the setting can affect the distance between the communicators. Topics of a highly personal nature or matters of secrecy can result in a reduction of physical distance.

THE FUNCTIONS OF NONVERBAL COMMUNICATION

Along with such factors as personal and territorial space, the way our body moves, our gestures, and the tone of our voice all affect the way we communicate. Because communication with our bodies is more subtle and less intentional at times than verbal communication, it may be more credible. We continually think about what we say, but we may pay less attention to our eye movements, whether or not we rub our hands, and a host of other nonverbal messages. Estimates of the different nonverbal symbols we send at any given moment run into the thousands. Skillful receivers of nonverbal communication are also skillful senders of human communication because they are able to "read" all of the messages others send them. To better understand how we use our body to communicate, we need to be able to recognize the functions of nonverbal communication.[13]

In addition to watching the seagulls on Ocracoke Island, I often stroll down to the docks and listen to the people who arrive in port after a long day of fishing. It is not the fish they caught that they talk about; they talk about the ones that got away. I remember listening to a father and son who returned to the harbor after a day of offshore fishing. While they had managed to bring back a large washtub full of fish, the father concentrated on telling me about the one that fell off the hook. As he described the fish, he placed his arms and hands outstretched before him and, spreading them about two feet apart, said the fish was "absolutely monstrous!" What amused me was the fact that if the flounder, not typically a large fish, had actually been as big as the man said it was, it would have been in contention for a world record.

The use of the man's outstretched arms to describe the fish was an example of the *complementing* function of nonverbal communication. Many of the things we do with our bodies *complement* what we say with our voices. In this case, the man was complementing the story of the big fish with a nonverbal gesture of outstretched arms.

Imagine the man had returned from his fishing trip and said, "I missed a fish that was two feet long," and then held his hands up next to a yardstick and placed his hands exactly two feet apart. He would have been *repeating* nonverbally what he had said verbally.

Nonverbal communication can also act as a *substitute* for words. An office with a large amount of territorial space may be a nonverbal substitute for the executive verbally saying, "I'm important." A hitchhiker doesn't stand by the road and yell, "I want a ride" to the cars whizzing by. Instead, the outstretched thumb becomes a nonverbal sign for the same message.

We can also regulate the flow of communication by using nonverbal communication. If we raise our hands when someone else is talking, it's a signal that we want to say something or that we want the other person to stop talking. A pause can have the same effect. Shaking our heads in a sideways motion can also prompt the other person to stop talking and ask us why we disagree.

Nonverbal messages accent interpersonal communication by accenting certain words or phrases we verbally express (Fig. 4–4). Imagine you've just

Figure 4-4
Nonverbal communication can accent words. Pointing while verbally giving directions, some gestures and other body movements are examples of this accenting function. Complementing, repeating, substituting, and regulating are also functions of nonverbal communication.

returned from a trip to Europe where you were particularly fascinated by the architecture of some of the European cathedrals. As you're describing the trip to your friends, you talk about the various people, the quaint countryside, and the delicious food. When you talk with excitement about the arched cathedrals, your hands gesture in front of you in an arch-shaped pattern. Forming the shape of the arch with your hands is an example of the accenting function of nonverbal communication.

Nonverbal communication goes beyond the simple body movements we have just discussed. It can reflect the activities of groups, even major events. A protest march and a sit-in are both forms of nonverbal communication. They are part of the way in which we express ourselves in a free society, and they are firmly entrenched in the law of free speech.[14]

BODY TYPES, SHAPES, AND SIZES

Aerobic dancers, weight lifters, joggers—taking care of our bodies is important to us. It's important for health reasons and for communication reasons. The size and shape of our bodies communicate nonverbal messages. Some of those messages are beyond our control, such as whether we are tall or short. But we may have more control over other messages, such as whether we are thin, chunky, or muscular. Some people may try to control the nonverbal messages communicated by their bodies so much that they become obsessed with that message. Cases of people starving themselves in order to communicate "thinness" may be the result.

There are three major classifications of body types: the *endomorph*, the *mesomorph*, and the *ectomorph*. The endomorph is characterized as being short and fat. The ectomorph, on the other hand, is characterized as being tall and skinny (Fig. 4–5). In between is the mesomorph, which is best described as being muscular and athletic. In some societies, although not all, the mesomorph is the ideal, the physically fit person who is admired, and the one we associate with good physical health.

A problem can arise when we let the messages communicated by different body types act as our only form of human communication. In other words, we let them become nonverbal stereotypes. Suppose that we are waiting to try

Figure 4-5
On the left is an endormorph; on the right, an ectomorph. We frequently have unjustified stereotypical opinions about a particular body type. (From an 1792 engraving published in *The Satirical Etchings of James Gillary*, D. Hill, ed., New York: Dover Books, 1976)

out for the basketball team. Into the gym comes a very tall, thin candidate. Immediately everyone looks up and greets the person with either a smile or a "hi." It is clear the tall, thin person is perceived as being a good basketball player, someone with whom others want to associate and communicate. But when practice starts, the tall, thin person cannot dribble the ball, cannot pass the ball, and cannot shoot the ball. Being tall does not mean a person will be a good basketball player any more than being short means a person will be a bad basketball player.

OUR BODIES' "NATURAL" CLOTHES

We know that the clothes we wear each day are nonverbal messages affecting how others perceive us and how we perceive ourselves. Yet what about our "natural" clothes? What nonverbal messages do our body smells, hair, and colors emit that can influence our total communicative impact?

Body Smell

Each of us has certain emotions that we associate with different smells. Many of these emotions are the result of prior experiences. When we communicate with other people, the smells each emits can play dominant or subtle roles in the interaction. Perhaps at some point in our lives we had an intense love affair with someone who wore a certain after-shave or perfume. The scent became the trademark of the individual just as much as the clothes he or she wore. Because we were close to the person, the scent also became etched in our minds.

A research study on the way in which we react to smell, specifically perfume, was conducted by a Purdue University psychologist (Fig. 4–6). Pairing up male and female college students, he asked the males to rate how attractive they found the females. Half of the women in the experiment wore a perfume called Jungle Gardenia, while the other half wore no perfume. Some women were more formally dressed in blouses, skirts, and stockings. Others wore more casual clothes, such as jeans and sweatshirts. The women in casual clothes who wore perfume were rated as being more sexy and warmer than those who did not wear perfume. In more formal clothes, perfume tended to make the woman seem less romantic and colder than their nonscented counterparts.[15]

How do you interpret these results? One suggested conclusion could be that in formal clothes the perfume was too overpowering. Perhaps Jungle Gardenia was too powerful a scent. Perhaps it was because the two people had just met each other and were not part of a relationship that had developed over time. Any other ideas?

Body Hair

A professor who moved to the Northwest noticed a large number of young men, especially college students, who wore beards. When he questioned a couple of colleagues about the apparent phenomenon, one of them pointed out

Figure 4-6

┌─ IN SCIENCE ─────────────────────┐

The allure of perfume

Does perfume make a woman as sexy as the ads promise? Robert A. Baron, a Purdue University psychologist, looked for the answer and came up with some unusual results—at least among college students.

Males, it seems, are attracted to perfumed females *only* if the women are wearing jeans, sweatshirts, or the like.

For the well-dressed female, perfume seems to have the opposite effect: It turns men off.

In the e..periment, Mr. Baron paired up males and females and then asked the males to rate how attractive they found the women. Half of the women in the experiment wore two drops of a perfume called Jungle Gardenia, the other half did not. Some women in each of the groups were neatly dressed (blouses, skirts, stockings), the others wore the most casual campus garb.

The women in casual clothes who wore perfume were seen as warmer and sexier than those who did not wear perfume. In nice clothes, the scented women were seen as colder and less romantic than the women who did not wear Jungle Gardenia.

Among the possible conclusions that can be drawn from his study, Mr. Baron says, is that perfume and dressy clothes "may be too much of a good thing."

Whatever the conclusion, Mr. Baron warns: "Unquestioning faith in the benefits of perfume, cologne, and similar products does not seem justified."

└──────────────────────────────────┘

that so much hiking, camping, and skiing took place there that the students found beards easier to care for then trying to shave in the wilds or having the icy wind hit their faces on a ski slope. Somewhat jokingly, the friend also noted that some of the students with beards liked to "leave the impression" that they hiked, camped, and skied.

We find that body hair communicates a symbol like any other type of message. Men with hairy chests may be seen as being virile. Long-haired women may be viewed as being feminine whereas short-haired women may be seen as being more professional. Although we may agree or disagree with each of these assertions, we nevertheless make judgments about people and communicate accordingly, rightly or wrongly, based on body hair.

Skin Color

We may feel that someone with the same skin color as ours may have a cultural heritage similar to our own and is therefore easier to communicate with and to get to know. The way in which language is used, the references, and the past experiences may in fact be similar. Or, they may not be. Stop and consider the people with whom you interact. What role does skin color play in the way you communicate with other people? Should it play that role? If communication is less than satisfactory, what can you do to improve your communication?

BASIC BODY MOVEMENTS

The importance of body movement in human communication is readily seen in a performance of a dance troupe (Fig. 4–7). Unlike the theater, where the voice plays a dominant role, dance relies almost totally on body movement to communicate. Carefully choreographed movements expressing love or hate can be exhibited by the same two dancers on stage. They can perform a caressing embrace or they can turn their backs to each other and fold their arms. No words

Figure 4-7
Body movement as a form of interpersonal communication can be witnessed in the performance of a dance troupe where movement is a substitute for words. (American Dance Ensemble)

are necessary to communicate their feelings. The positions and movements of the dancers' bodies "say" it all.

GESTURES

Some of the more obvious forms of nonverbal communication are gestures. Although we may think of them as primarily hand and arm movements, gestures can be communicated by other parts of the body as well. To help us understand them, we will break down gestures into types of movements: emblems and illustrators.

Emblems

Whereas *illustrators* are movements that accompany speech, *emblems* do not need speech to communicate meaning. They fulfill the "substituting" function we discussed earlier. Putting the tip of our index finger on the tip of our thumb up with a clenched fist (Fig. 4–8) is an example of an emblem. This recognized sign for "OK" or "success" does not need any accompanying words to identify it. What exactly are emblems?[16]

Emblems not only serve the substituting role in nonverbal communication we discussed but they also have *direct translations*. For example, a thumbs-up

Figure 4-8
Emblems do not need speech to communicate meaning. The clenched fist with the thumb upright is a sign of "OK" or "success." Emblems can come and go in popularity. The "V" for victory sign was popular in the 1940s, was used as an anti-war protest emblem in the 1960s, and today occasionally reappears as a victory sign at athletic contests. Different cultures also have different emblems. (Country singing star Kenny Rogers. Used through the courtesy of Kragen & Company, Los Angeles, California)

sign means "yes," or "go." A cupped hand behind the ear means, "I can't hear you." Each sign has an *exact meaning*. Emblems are also *directed at a specific receiver*. We don't walk around with our thumbs up or a hand cupped behind our ear unless we are sending a nonverbal message to someone. These messages are *consciously sent* and we must take responsibility for them. Nonverbal messages that have direct translations, that have exact meanings, that are directed at a specific receiver, and that are consciously sent are emblems.

Emblems also differ across cultures. In the United States, pointing your index finger at your temple with the thumb upright translates as "shooting yourself in the head." In Japan, an emblem depicting suicide is pushing a closed fist near your stomach to depict the plunge of a knife in your vital organs. In still other cultures, grasping one hand about the throat is an emblem for suicide.[17]

Illustrators

Illustrators complement rather than substitute for words. Used more frequently in conversations than emblems, illustrators are the typical expressive gestures we use in talking. Illustrators can still be identified, but they are *less precise* and pronounced than are emblems. We have all been in situations in which we cannot think of the words we want to say. We stop, hesitate, motion our hands outward in a circular motion, and say, "Oh, you know what I mean." We hope the other person will know what we mean, although there remains ample room for confusion and misunderstanding.

Illustrators *increase through involvement* what we are saying. I enjoy riding amusement park roller coasters. When the King's Island Amusement Park near Cincinnati unveiled "The Beast," heralded in advertisements as the "biggest," baddest, meanest roller coaster of them all," temptation was too great. After that ride, however, and shortly after a large picnic lunch, the illustrator consisted of holding our stomachs, uttering the words "I want to sit down," and looking for the nearest bench.

Research has also identified subcategories of illustrators, which we will describe in general terms. These subcategories are:

BATONS:	movements which account for or emphasize a particular word or phrase
KINETOGRAPHS:	movements which depict a bodily action or some non-human physical action
IDEOGRAPHS:	movements which sketch the path or direction of thought
PICTOGRAPHS:	movements which draw a picture in the air of the shape of the referent
DEICTIC MOVEMENTS:	pointing to an object, place, or event
RHYTHMIC MOVEMENTS:	movements which depict the rhythm or pacing of an event
SPATIAL MOVEMENTS:	movements which depict a spatial relationship[19]

How might you use these while carrying on a conversation? Under what topics or in what situations would each category find a use?

Adaptors

Adaptors are body movements that help us to orient ourselves or to adapt to our environment. Thus, they are more *intra*personal than *inter*personal. We tend to decrease our use of them when we are around others, because adaptors can become distractive and interfere with other communication. Consider the adaptor movement of scratching. Perhaps we are studying and are having trouble thinking of the answer to a question or the solution to a problem. We may breathe deeply, rub our chin, and scratch our head. But if we face the same problem in a meeting of corporate executives, we would be less visual in attempting to find the solution. We might only bite our lower lip or wrinkle our forehead, for instance.[20]

THE LANGUAGE OF POSTURE

When we were growing up, someone we knew invariably monitored our posture. "Stand up straight," "Don't slouch," or "Straighten your shoulders" used to echo in our ears because someone cared about how we presented ourselves to others. As we grew older and left home, the comments probably stopped. Unfortunately, bad posture didn't always stop. Posture communicates information just as much as hand and arm movements.

Messages Communicated by Posture

We would not want to slouch or sit with our arms folded during a job interview. It would communicate such messages as disinterest or defensiveness. A person who is tense and uncomfortable may stand artificially erect. On the other hand, when participating in a group discussion, a person's slight slouching posture may result from an air of confidence and relaxation. But do not plan on slouching at the next discussion just to project an image of being confident. You may discover that others do not perceive you that way; instead, you might be labeled as someone who does not pay attention. A good posture for most human interaction is to sit or stand upright enough to project an image of being alert and interested in the conversation.

Observing Posture in Others

One way to become sensitive to your own posture and how it affects communication is to observe the posture of others. Asking ourselves the following series of questions can form a good foundation for observing the positioning and posture of people engaged in human communication.

Do all of the people have the same posture? Why?
If one person is sitting and another person is standing, how does this relate to the perceived status one has in comparison to the other?

Are the people relaxed or tense?

Does posture change during the conversation? Why?

Are the people leaning toward or away from each other? Why?

Do their posture and the positions of their bodies tend to restrict others from entering the conversation?

How far apart are the people?

Do the positions of their arms or legs suggest personal warmth or coldness toward each other?

When one person changes posture, does another? What could this suggest?

How long is a given posture maintained?[21]

By observing others and monitoring our own postures, we can begin to use our postures to aid, not hinder, our human communication.

COMMUNICATING WITH FACIAL EXPRESSIONS

Facial expressions are some of the oldest, identifiable types of nonverbal communication by which we have reflected emotions and personality. Actors in the ancient Greek theater wore facial masks to portray different moods. Various African and South American tribes wear tribal masks in ceremonies or hold them on poles to illustrate pain and pleasure.

Physiognomy

Physiognomy, the study of the face and skull as indicators of various personality types, is an unscientific, inexact science that has managed to fascinate us since the time of Aristotle.[22] Some confusion has resulted in trying to use the term to apply to both the features of the face at rest, such as a high forehead or a snub nose, and the way our faces move as a medium of expression, such as puckering the mouth or wrinkling the forehead. The former has links to the speculations of soothsayers, whereas the latter belongs more to the contemporary study of nonverbal communication. Nevertheless, Socrates and A.T.&T. are among the individuals and corporations through history that have studied physiognomy to better understand human interaction.

We have no scientific evidence to suggest that a person with a long forehead is more intelligent than someone with a short forehead, or that someone with deeply recessed eyes has a better memory than someone whose eyes are less recessed. But we do still stereotype faces. What facial stereotypes come to mind for a librarian, a gangster, or a chef?

Functions of Facial Expressions

"Interaction management" is one way scholars of nonverbal communication view the functions of facial expressions. The face can "(1) open and close channels of communication, (2) complement or qualify verbal and/or nonverbal responses, and (3) replace speech."[23] These different functions can also occur simultaneously.

Try applying these functions to your own experiences. Imagine that you are taking part in a class discussion. If the class is large, you might raise your hand in an effort to secure your turn to speak. But if you are talking with just one other person, raising your hand would be inappropriate. In this instance, you might partially open your mouth to signal that you have something to say.

Facial Identities

What about the people behind different faces? Research has classified them into the categories of *withholders, revealers, substitute expressers*, and *ever-ready expressers*.[24] Many people fall across these categories depending on their personality traits or the situation in which the communication takes place (Fig. 4–9). For example, withholders hide their emotions and are difficult to read. Revealers, on the other hand, are just the opposite. Revealers wear their feelings openly. Substitute expressers display different facial expressions from what they are feeling. Ever-ready expressers react very quickly with facial expressions to any emotion they might feel.

Figure 4-9
Based on facial expressions, researchers have classified individuals as "withholders," "revealers," "substitute expressers," and "ever-ready expressers."

Components of Facial Expressions

We tend to use certain parts of our face to communicate certain emotions.[25] For example, research tends to support the notion that our eyes and eyelids are the most accurate indicators of fear. When we are afraid, our eyes are wide open and we may look straightforward with a "blank stare" until the threat passes or we learn to control our emotions. Happiness, on the other hand, is expressed primarily through our mouths and cheeks, but our eyes and eyelids also play important roles.

Communicating with Facial Expressions

Thousands of variations of facial expressions exist. By learning how these expressions affect our total communication efforts, we can improve our human communication skills.

The simple advice of "Try greeting people with a smile" is not trite when we consider that it begins communication with a positive feeling for both the sender and the receiver. Rather than adopting the facial expressions of a stern drill sergeant, a sales manager complimenting a salesperson can be much more effective by adding a smile.

Facial expressions can either reinforce or negate a verbal comment. Suppose a teacher calls upon a student to answer a question. The teacher, wanting to affirm the student's correct response, says, "That's a good answer, Susan." But the teacher's face shows a wrinkled forehead, eyebrows together, and rigid lips. Although the teacher thinks he or she has praised the student, the teacher's face has, instead, said exactly the opposite.[26]

COMMUNICATING WITH OUR EYES

Our eyes communicate through *eye contact* and *mutual gaze*.[27] In public speaking, eye contact refers to looking at the eyes of the people in the audience. Mutual gaze applies to a more intimate communication encounter, such as when two people are in an intense conversation, sitting only a few feet apart and looking at one another.

Eyes play different roles when we communicate with different people. For example, we can mentally regroup our thoughts when *receiving* communication from others by glancing away and pondering what has been said or how we want to respond. We can both *send* messages and we can *control* communication with our eyes. We are more apt to gaze at the other person when we have something important to say because we do not want to be interrupted and we want the other person to pay attention. Glancing away from the other person can also assist us in dealing with information overload—when too much information makes it difficult to comprehend the other person's message.[28]

QUALITIES OF THE VOICE

If you were asked to deliver a speech to the senior class, you would think very carefully about what you would say and how you would say it. You would consider how your voice would project to the audience, what role the public-address system would play, the difficult words you would need to pronounce, the tone of your voice, whether your voice would be authoritative or soft-spoken, and how you would articulate each word and syllable.

Understanding Paralanguage

The word *para* means "alongside." Paralanguage, therefore, is language alongside language. Specifically, *paralanguage* is the way we use the sounds of our voices to utter words. Stop and listen to a person who speaks with an accent. The way that person uses his or her voice may be different from the way you use your voice. You both could use the same words, but each of you would use different paralanguage. If we want to get scientific, we could analyze each person's voice using a voiceprint. A *voiceprint* provides a detailed "drawing" of a person's voice. In fact, some scientists claim that a voiceprint is much like a fingerprint in that no two voiceprints are exactly alike.

Paralanguage can be broken down into different categories. For instance, the *quality* of your voice is a form of paralanguage. Is your voice breathy? Does it become breathy in certain situations? The *resonance* of your voice is a form of paralanguage. Radio announcers are commonly known for their deep resonance. *Tempo* means the way in which you vary the rate of speech and your use of pauses. Being sensitive to paralanguage permits us to add another dimension to effective human communication.

Social Distance and the Qualities of the Voice

Earlier in this chapter we talked about personal space. A form of personal space is *social distance,* the comfortable physical distance between ourselves and the person with whom we are communicating. When the social distance becomes uncomfortable, because of violations of our personal space, our voice changes.[29] When someone stands uncomfortably close or uncomfortably far away from us, our speech becomes more wordy or verbose. It becomes this way because we are trying to compensate for the uncomfortable feeling that is present because of the awkward social distance.

Applying Good Voice Qualities

What we do with our voice, as much as what we say, plays a part in how we communicate with others.[30] In general, people who are perceived as being credible will have a greater fluency in their voice. They will have a self-confident command of the language and be able to speak without hesitation. Harshness will be absent, and they will possess a pleasant tone to their voice. They will speak slower than a less credible person and posses greater clarity and variety in their speaking.

The purpose of our speech also influences the way in which we use our speaking voice to achieve that purpose. For example, a manager who wants to resolve conflicts and express cooperative behavior among employees will engage in more actual speaking than those who want to avoid conflict by pretending it doesn't exist. People who employ criticizing and insulting communication tend to use a "hit-and-run" type of speaking with short bursts of speech.[31]

When interviewed by an employer, a prospective secretary was told, "You, more than anyone else in this company, will determine its success or failure." Looking a bit startled, the secretary asked why. The employer replied, "Because every bit of new business we receive comes from people who call us on the telephone. One hundred percent of their impression of this company depends on the quality of your voice. You have the job of every employee on your shoulder." The secretary suddenly realized the importance of being able to identify and use good vocal qualities. Sloppy English, a down-home lazy sound, or a brusque, impatient tone of voice would leave an instant negative impression on everyone who called the company. A truly excellent telephone voice is a valuable commodity and it will be recognized and visible when opportunity for promotion occurs. It is sad that so many people have never learned the importance of good voice quality, especially those who wonder why they have never improved their jobs or positions in life.

THE NONVERBAL MESSAGES OF TOUCH

Be it a kiss or a handshake, touch communicates the full range of emotions. From the minute we are born, touch becomes an important and, at times, the only means of communication we have with our world. Gradually as our eyes open and we take in the wonders of our environment, we begin to expand our communicative behaviors. Still later, social norms begin to influence touching behavior.

The Importance of Touch in Childhood

The bumper sticker that asks "Have You Hugged Your Kid Today?" carries more relevance than we may realize. Psychologists tell us that the amount of touching an infant receives can directly affect how well adjusted the child is later in life.[32] Yet historically, Americans have actually discouraged touching their children under the belief that touching transmitted infection and disease. What we may *not* have realized was that children who are *not* touched may be more susceptible to disease than children who are touched. Children hunger for touch and grow and respond to that touch.

As children enter elementary school, touch is a major form of reinforcement.[33] Because sexual connotations are not associated with touching at the preschool and early elementary levels, teachers are freer to touch and hug children to alleviate their fears of alienation, rejection, or insecurity.

As children develop a sexual awareness, touching behavior becomes limited between teacher and student and, in many cases, between parent and child. The latter can cause difficulties, because the transition into puberty can be an emotional trauma. The time when an individual's identity is being challenged may be the very time that touch and affectionate support from a parent is needed. Psychologists refer to this need for touching behavior in life as *anchoring*. When used to complement verbal, positive stroking, anchoring can play an important role in developing a positive self-concept and instilling confidence.

Where We Touch Each Other

Children may have a great latitude in their touching behavior. But social norms gradually define the appropriateness of that behavior as we grow older. Once again, the situation plays a large part in what kind of touching and when touching is appropriate. Consider touching by people of opposite sexes. In one study, researchers examined the relationship between unmarried, opposite-sex friends on the basis of four types of touching behavior—pat, stroke, squeeze, and brush. Monitoring the touching of more than 11 different parts of the body, the researchers found that strokes generally communicated sexual desire and warmth, whereas pats communicated playfulness and friendship. They were not able to say conclusively what messages squeezes and brushes conveyed.[34]

How we interpret messages communicated by touch depends on what parts of the body are being touched.[35] Touching hands is almost universally interpreted as being pleasant and communicating warmth. Touching the pelvic area is interpreted as being sexual. The setting, however, may alter the perceptions of touching behavior. For example, a coach who slaps the buttocks of a player being sent into a game is something different from buttock-touching that occurs while walking on a beach.

Where we touch each other also depends on our intentions. For example, one research study identified 12 different functions of touching behavior: "support, appreciation, inclusion, sexual interest or intent, affection, playful affection, playful aggression, compliance, attention-getting, announcing a response, departure, and greeting."[36] Ask yourself: What parts of the body and what type of touching would occur and also would be appropriate for these different functions?

Touching Behavior Across Cultures

Not only does touching behavior differ among different people but also among cultures. Studying couples in coffee shops, one researcher found that Americans touch each other an average of only two times per hour.[37] In France, that figure jumps to 110 times per hour. But in the Caribbean, the same researcher found that couples in Puerto Rico touch each other an average of 180 times per hour. Is there any place in American society outside of the home where a greater degree of touching appears to be socially acceptable? Yes; in airports. There, one research observed that 85 percent of the people touch each other during the period surrounding arrivals and departures.[38]

PROJECTING AN IMAGE: OUR DRESS

Fashion ads are constantly promising us a new love or the right job if we only purchase the correct wardrobe. Yet people do form impressions about the way we dress, especially during those critical moments when we first meet.

Dressing for Occasions

We all know how embarrassing it would be to show up at an informal picnic wearing evening clothes or at a formal dance wearing blue jeans. Yet we may unknowingly violate other occasions by equally improper, although more subtle, means. For years, one large corporation had an informal rule that executives should always wear dark blue suits, white, long-sleeved shirts, and black shoes. Although such standards of attire have been overdone, learning not to offend others is one of the best rules for dress. The adage of dressing not for the job you have but for the job you want is still good advice.

A consultant to the legal profession offered some advice for practicing trial attorneys.[39] She suggested that roles of authority and influence are played out in the courtroom and are determined partly by pinstripes and three-piece suits. Such attire may be best for prosecutors. For those attorneys representing defendants, the appearance of an underdog is necessary. Here a casual, more relaxed two-piece suit is appropriate. According to the consultant, women attorneys face special problems. Because authority uniforms are male-oriented, jurors may resent a woman who assumes a male role. She suggests women attorneys should dress for the cultural norm of their areas.

Dress and Self-Concept

A respected professor who directed the public-speaking courses at Purdue University required students to wear more dress-up attire when they delivered their speeches. He felt the use of suit jackets and ties for men and appropriate professional dress for women improved their self-concept and therefore their speeches. Students weren't always enthusiastic about Professor Bruce Kendall's requirements, but they did deliver some good speeches.

In retrospect, the idea has a great deal of merit. Research has shown that the way we dress affects our self-concept, and our self-concept plays a major role in how we perform in all walks of life. We know, for example, that the perceived effectiveness of psychological counselors has been linked to the formality of their attire.[40] Drawing from business examples, we know that job applicants feel more at ease during an interview if they are comfortable with their choice of attire. If applicants are worried about being dressed inappropriately, then it will affect the way they feel about themselves and the way they perform in the interview.

THE INFLUENCE OF COLOR

Magazing publishers know by looking at sales figures that certain color combinations on the cover of a magazine sell better on the newsstands than other color combinations. In some cases, this research has even suggested that certain audiences prefer certain colors. In our dress, colors not only say something about ourselves but also affect our self-concept. Do you sometimes want to wear something bright to make you stand out in the crowd? Do you sometimes want to wear something dark or neutral to blend in with what others are wearing and to belong? If you answered yes to any of these, then you are sensitive to colors.

Our preferences for color change at different times in our lives. For example, young children around five years of age have a definite preference for red, yellow, blue, or orange.[41] Putting red carpeting in an elementary school library increased the use of that library, and some school consultants have recommended bright colors to increase participation and expression.[42] Somewhere between 3 and 15 years of age, we begin to shift our color preferences from warm to cool colors.[43] Thus, in secondary school classrooms, consultants have recommended the use of green, blue, and gray. Our preference for color intensity shifts with age. Younger children seem to prefer bright colors while young adults shift their color preferences to pastel shades.[44]

THE MESSAGES OF TIME

Time has become a powerful communicative force in American culture. Our figures of speech reflect the importance of this elusive element: "Time is money." "Time is of the essence."

Consider the different ways that time helps or hinders our communication. If you begin your day without enough time to do everything necessary before leaving for school or work, the people around you may see an impersonal, harried individual.

When speaking, the timing of pauses can have a profound effect on meaning. Consider what happens when a person finishes a sentence and then simply ceases talking.[45] How long will you wait until you feel obligated to say something, regardless of whether or not you have planned to speak or had anything important to say? When a person who is criticizing another finishes with the criticism, what will the silence communicate? It can communicate various messages: "Well, what do you have to say for yourself?" "What do you think your punishment should be?"

Consider what happens in a classroom when the teacher asks a question. If no one knows the answer and the teacher just stands there not saying anything, you can literally feel the tension consuming the room. After such an experience takes place, the rest of the class period may also be filled with tension. The length of the silence was in itself a form of verbal punishment.

Our perceptions of time change with age.[46] The way children react to time is different from the way adults react. Between the first and third grade, a child's ability to judge the duration of time increases. The ability to judge the duration of stories and to reproduce accurately 60-second intervals increases between four and nine years of age. Young children perceive time as passing more slowly than do older children. This could be because the body temperature in young children is greater than it is in older children, and research has shown that people with higher body temperature perceive time as passing more slowly.

SUMMARY

We began our chapter on nonverbal communication by discussing territorial and personal space. Territorial space can be defined by physical boundaries. Personal space is more concerned with psychological space. It is influenced by such things as age, status, friendship, culture, sex, praise, criticism, settings, topics of conversation, and the psychological makeup of the communicators.

Nonverbal communication fulfills certain functions. It complements, repeats, substitutes for, regulates, and accents verbal communication. Football hand signals, for example, are a form of nonverbal communication that can substitute for a referee's verbal communication of the same information.

Many of the impressions other people have of us are formed by the nonverbal messages communicated by our bodies. Body shapes can be classified as endomorphic, mesomorphic, and ectomorphic. The first refers to a short and fat body, the second to a muscular body, and the third to a tall and skinny body. Although it is important to understand body types, it is equally important not to draw stereotypes from them. Our body odor, hair, and skin color also send nonverbal messages.

Body movements can be grouped into emblems, illustrators, and adaptors. Emblems replace words and have very specific meanings. Illustrators complement words and have less specific meanings. Adaptors, on the other hand, help us adjust to our environment. Our postures also send nonverbal messages as do our facial expressions.

Other components of nonverbal communication include our eyes, vocal paralanguage, touching behavior, dress, and color. Through eye contact and mutual gaze, we can control the channels of communication and adapt our eye behaviors to help us send and receive messages. Paralanguage is language that travels alongside of our words. The tempo, pitch, and resonance of our voices are examples of paralanguage. Touch plays a strong nonverbal communication role in early life and gradually adapts to social norms in less intimate relationships. What we wear can affect our self-concept, and color can influence emotion and establish credibility.

Because time is a valuable commodity in our culture, we use it as a means of nonverbal communication. Spending meaningful time with another person communicates a message to that person that he or she is important to us. Being late, disregarding appointments, and forgetting meetings send signals about others as well as about ourselves.

QUESTIONS FOR REVIEW AND DISCUSSION

1. The head of the household has a chair that no one else is supposed to use. What concept does this represent in nonverbal communication?

2. What distinguishes personal space from territorial space?

3. What are some factors that can affect (increase or decrease) our personal space?

4. Identify and describe the functions of nonverbal communication.

5. What are the three major body types?

6. Explain the difference between illustrators and emblems.

7. What does physiognomy refer to?

8. What are the differences between *eye contact* and *mutual gaze?*

9. How do dress, time, and color communicate information:

LEARNING EXERCISES

1. Visit the offices of some area businesses. Examine the design and location of offices within the building. How are these designs and locations reflective of territorial space?

2. Watch five different television interviews (news and sports programs are good sources). Identify and interpret the nonverbal behavior of the interviewer and interviewee.

ADDITIONAL READINGS

BAUM, A., and Y. M. EPSTEIN, EDS. *Human Response to Crowding.* New York: John Wiley, 1978.
COLTON, H. *The Gift of Touch.* New York: Seaview/Putnam, 1983.
HALL, E. T. *The Silent Language.* New York: Doubleday Anchor Books, 1973.
HOPSON, J. L. *Scent Signals.* New York: Morrow, 1979.
LEE, L. and J. CHARLTON *The Hand Book.* Englewood Cliffs, NJ: Prentice-Hall, 1980.
MEHRABIAN, A. *Public Places and Private Spaces.* New York: Basic Books, 1976.
MORRIS, D., P. COLETT, P. MARSH, and M. O'SHAUGHNESSY *Gestures: Their Origins and Distribution.* London: Jonathan Cape, Ltd., 1979.

5

LISTENING

OBJECTIVES

After completing this chapter, you should be able to

- List and describe the steps to good listening
- Explain the listening techniques of rephrasing, clarifying, and summarizing
- Separate content from emotion during the communication process
- Realize that listening is a developmental process
- Be sensitive to self-disclosure when listening
- Deal with loaded words
- Discuss the effect of dissonance
- Understand the fear of questioning
- Compare and contrast selective perception, exposure, and retention
- Be aware of the barriers of prejudice and stereotyping on good listening
- Talk about cultural obstacles to good listening
- Distinguish between the communication styles of the receiver and the sender.

Peggy Masterson, while serving as senior vice-president and creative group head of Benton & Bowles advertising agency, said, "I think the most important thing I've learned is to listen. So often a problem will start to be laid out and I immediately feel 'I have the answer for that! I have a solution. . . .' And the problem still hasn't really been laid out."[1] She pointed out how she had to keep reminding herself to listen and to reinforce that advice before every meeting. She was quick to admit it was a hard lesson to learn, and for someone who is quick-witted or very opinionated, there is a real desire to "jump in" and offer a solution.

Cynthia Swain, a senior news specialist for Sperry Corporation, documented that people spend an average of 80 percent of their working hours engaged in some type of communication. Of this time, 45 percent is spent listening.[2] Swain also noted that as one moves up through the corporate ranks, the amount of time spent listening increases dramatically. If that is not reason enough to concentrate on good listening skills, stop and consider this statistic—one person in a work force is easily capable of making a $10 listening error. In a work force of 100 million people, that represents a loss of $1 billion.

United Technologies Corporation, in a series of ads about business, told of a historic business mistake that was directly attributable to one person's unwillingness to listen. The ad described how an irate banker, instead of listening to how the telephone worked, told Alexander Graham Bell to get "that toy" out of the banker's office. The telephone and the companies it spawned, A.T.& T., were later worth billions of dollars.[3]

Of all the skills we are taught in high school and college, few receive *less* emphasis than listening skills.[4] Instead, we concentrate most of our time on speaking and becoming good senders of communication. But our success as senders is directly tied to our ability to understand the total communication process, and that involves listening. Listening is much more than just "hearing" what someone else is saying. In fact, being a good listener often requires greater skill than being a good speaker. When we are speaking, we can adapt and alter our messages at will. If we are able to tell that we are not being understood, we can change our messages. As listeners, we also become "senders" of communication in that we send back to the speaker information about the success of his or her message. Without being able to listen and respond to other people, we are unable to use the messages we receive effectively.

Some of the best men and women executives are successful because they have the ability to listen. They are able to reach goals they set for themselves because dealing with people is just as important as dealing with goods and services. Having delegated much of their work, as is the case with successful executives, these people spend much of their time acting as safety valves for the company by listening to the problems of employees. A corporation can seem almost overbearing to some employees. Hence, there is no substitute for gaining the ear of management. When truly able to understand and communicate with employees, these executives can do a great deal to alleviate the pressures for those employees before the pressures start affecting employees' ability to perform their jobs. Sadly, the reason employees feel they do not have the understanding of management in the first place is because management has not learned how to listen.

STEPS TOWARD BETTER LISTENING

We can witness a variety of "listening situations" when we stroll across the campus of any college or university. Students may be casually chatting, paying some attention to each other, and some attention to the sights and sounds of the moment. Rather than paying avid attention to what each is saying, they are content to just enjoy being with each other. At another place on campus, we might encounter two people in an intense conversation. Each can feel the emotions of the other person, and each is paying undivided attention to what the other is saying. Professors chatting with a group of students, a traffic officer arguing with a driver about an improperly parked car, research assistants discussing the results of a new experiment—all are involved in different steps of the listening process.

Our steps toward better *listening* begin with listening as a personal commitment, an *involvement* with the other person's fields of experience, *sensing, timing, empathy*. But the important rule is *never to close our minds to new ideas*.[5] It will be helpful to remember these steps because the first letter of each concept in the sequence above spells the word "l–i–s–t–e–n."

Listening as a Personal Commitment.

The first and most basic goal is to make a commitment to ourselves to become good listeners. Every time we meet someone and exchange information, even a smile, make a commitment to listen. Don't dismiss the presence of other people simply because they are not important to our daily lives. We may not be promoted for listening attentively to the office receptionist, but if we break this listening habit we run the risk of someday not listening to someone who can promote us. Remember, in order to be effective, listening must become a habit.

After we have made a commitment to become good listeners, we can then begin to turn each individual listening step and technique into a goal for us to master. Think of these steps and techniques as building blocks, much like the building blocks of self-concept we discussed earlier in the text. Each building block adds to our overall goal of becoming an effective communicator.

Involving Oneself in Fields of Experience

When we engage in conversation with another person, that person is reaching out by sending messages that we must integrate into our own thought processes. Think of that communication as a transmitter emitting pulsating signals, much like a rock hitting the surface of the water will send circles of water rippling out from its impact point. Those circles are really pulses of information and can be likened to the fields of experience discussed in Chapter 1 and diagrammed in the model of communication. When we are engaged in interaction with another person, we need to first lock into the other person's field of experience as it applies to that particular communication setting. For example, an employee might approach the manager about a personal problem. The manager must mentally separate other unrelated work concerns about the employee and devote full concentration to the specific problem the employee wants to discuss.

In this particular setting, the personal problem of the employee will identify where the fields of experience overlap. If the manager avoids the problem, talks about other issues, doesn't want to get to the heart of the issue, then the employee will leave dissatisfied because the manager has not engaged in active listening, has not "locked in" or become involved in the employee's field of experience.

Sensing

To appreciate fully the process of listening, to enjoy it and look forward to it, we must be able to use our senses to absorb everything we can about the person speaking. Many times we bypass sensing and jump ahead to hearing, and then wonder why we may not have "heard" what the person was saying. Using our senses to listen takes practice. If you were to take a walk in the park, your senses would pick up the sounds of birds chirping, children playing, and the slap of your shoes on the pavement or ground. You would feel the fresh air and see the flowers or bushes swaying in the sunshine. As in the park, when we encounter other people we need to listen to them with all of our senses and we need to pay attention to both their verbal and nonverbal messages. Listen to their eyes. Do they sparkle or squint? Are they saying, "I am sincere"? Are they saying, "I want to talk more"? Listen to their handshakes. Are they saying, "I am feeling positive about meeting you"?

Listen to more than mere words. For example, our ears can pick up the tone of a person's voice. Although most people are aware of vocal tones, they often do not "hear" those tones because they are listening to the other person's words. The next time you converse with someone, monitor all of the different changes in that person's voice and the relationship these changes have on the conversation. Do this for a series of conversations with various people. You'll find that each person's vocal qualities are unique. Scientists who specialize in reading voiceprints know that a person's voice is as identifiable as a fingerprint. By listening to a person's vocal qualities, you will begin to find that you can recognize that person's voice just as you recognize his or her face. By listening with your senses, you can pick up a great deal more information and be a more effective communicator.

A second important phase of sensing is *paying attention.* How many times have we been in a conversation with our classmates, our friends, our parents, or people with whom we work, and the person to whom we are listening says, "I'm boring you, aren't I?" Or perhaps the more direct statement, "You're not even listening to me!" jolts us to a new level of alertness. We probably then realize we had sent feedback to the person which made it obvious we were not paying attention. Perhaps we were shifting our feet while looking at the floor. Perhaps we were staring off into space. Perhaps we asked a question that had nothing to do with what the person was saying, or perhaps we asked about what that person just finished explaining. Perhaps we were just silent. The result was that the other person lost the commitment to continue because we had lost the commitment to listen. Not paying attention is another basic violation of good listening behavior. Moreover, it is a very noticeable violation.

A third phase of the sensing process is *understanding*. Some universities, for example, have what are called "instructional-response systems." At each seat is a series of buttons. The buttons are connected to a display monitor at the lectern. In large classes, the teacher can ask a question and give a series of possible answers, much like a multiple-choice test. Students then push the button corresponding to what they believe is the correct answer. The teacher is able to see instantly how many students understand the material. This electronic feedback system works particularly well in such subjects as mathematics where sequential learning takes place and where problems can develop quickly if the student doesn't understand the material.

The problem is that we have no human electronic-response system telling us if the person listening to us is truly understanding what we are saying. Moreover, people can look quite attentive while still not understanding what is being said. They thus give no verbal or nonverbal cues to the contrary, and we continue speaking. Only later do we discover that a serious communication breakdown took place. An order will not be filled, an examination will be failed, a group will not reach its goal, and we know someone may have been paying attention but was not understanding. Thus, we must develop our own listening skills so that we work not only at paying attention but also at providing feedback to the speaker when we don't understand something.

The fourth phase in the sensing process is *remembering*. We accumulate information during any conversation. Yet sometimes remembering the information we accumulate is difficult. Consider the politician who responded to a question that took three minutes for the reporter to phrase. By the time the reporter completed the question, the politician had forgotten the first half of it and couldn't give a complete answer. The reporter wrote the next morning that the politician had avoided the question. But the truth was that the reporter had compiled so much information into the question, that it was virtually impossible to remember, let alone answer. We cannot effectively understand what is being said unless we *remember* what is being said.

Timing

In Chapter 1 we learned about noise and how it interferes with communication. When speaking to another person, we would not think of throwing a glass of water in his or her face or stomping on that person's foot. If we did, we would interrupt the conversation by interjecting noise into the communication process. Yet many of us achieve the same result because we are not sensitive to proper *timing* in communication. We block both our ability to listen and the other person's ability to speak. In the physical sense, this is often called "interrupting" someone. But it also goes much deeper than that to *mentally interrupting our own listening behavior.* If someone is explaining something and we do not wait—both physically and mentally—until the person is finished, we (1) rob ourselves of the information necessary to make an intelligent and appropriate response to the person's statement; (2) inject a high risk of inaccuracy into the conversation by not fully understanding what the other person is saying; (3) run the risk of being perceived as rude because we interrupted; (4) may not obtain a complete picture of what is being said and therefore run the risk of using poor logic then or at a later point in the conversation; (5) waste time going back and restructuring missed information so that we can get the conversation or discussion back on track; (6) cause the other person to respond with inaccurate information because he or she is responding to our own misstatements; and (7) set an artificial pace to the conversation, which is filled with misperceptions and misstatements as one person tries to "contend" with the other's listening deficiencies.

Listening problems resulting from poor physical and mental timing become even more serious when tensions are high. Two people arguing, a superior issuing a reprimand, a counseling session on a sensitive subject, negotiating conflict resolution—these are all settings where things can go wrong because of poor listening behavior.

Empathy

Empathy is one of the least understood yet vitally important steps in the listening process. To *empathize* means to enter mentally into the feelings of another person. To a certain degree, empathy relates to the overlapping fields of experience or homophily we talked about earlier in the text. We cannot casually empathize. Rather, we literally transpose ourselves into the other person's position as a communicator and then develop an awareness of what that person is feeling.

The paraphrased American Indian saying, "Do not judge me until you have walked a mile in my moccasins," expresses the role of empathy. The therapist or psychiatrist should be able to understand and empathize with a patient in order to treat an illness. An attorney must be able to empathize with the problems of a client in order to represent that client effectively. Parents need to empathize with their child in order to provide help and guidance. In some situations, empathy gets pushed back in favor of more immediate steps in listening. In a corporate setting, the goals of the discussion and the desire of people to participate in specific kinds of behavior take precedence and often leave empathy far behind.

Adding empathy to our listening can improve any communication encounter. With empathy, we have the ability to gain a deeper insight into the person with whom we are talking. Not only can we monitor more types of messages the person may be sending but we can also become much more sensitive to those messages. If a person has been passed over for promotion and is participating aggressively in a business meeting, we may be less likely to react negatively if we can empathize and understand the reasons behind the behavior.

Another way to examine empathy is to look at it from two theoretical perspectives: (1) inference theory, and (2) role-taking theory.[6] Inference theory is our ability to interpret the experiences of another person. Our reference to "walking a mile in my moccasins" applies to inference theory. It is not possible to experience *exactly* what another person experiences. However, we can *infer* what the other person experiences and therefore empathize with that individual. As a result, our ability to make these inferences improves our listening skills since we, by inference, can relate to what the other person is saying.

Role-taking theory concentrates on self-concept. Empathy, from the approach of role-taking, is our ability to develop, through communication, a self-concept that can relate to the experiences of the other person. Imagination, not inference, permits us to experience what another person is experiencing. By relating our own self-concept to the other person and living in our imagination what the other person is experiencing, our empathy can enhance our ability to listen.

Never Block an Idea

At the beginning of this chapter we read about the irate banker who told Alexander Graham Bell to get the toy—which happened to be the telephone—out of the office. The banker blocked Bell's idea and the result was to miss out on one of the greatest technological innovations of our time.

Being open-minded is not always easy. The employee who constantly wisecracks may hold the spark that generates a new line of computers or a winning marketing strategy. Because the person is never serious around the office, we may fail to listen to an idea that could mean millions of dollars in profits. Perhaps we hold prejudices, perhaps a previous experience makes us too cautious to take a suggestion seriously, perhaps our culture or background interferes with our acceptance of the idea.

Blocking ideas can occur at any time. A company president abruptly rejected an employee's idea for a corporate training program that the president saw as too costly. The employee went to work for a competitor. There, the company president was more receptive. The employee not only started the training program but also sold it to other companies, thus opening up a whole new profit center for her new employer. The first employer missed out on the profits of the training program because he blocked the idea without seeing its full potential.

LISTENING TECHNIQUES

Closely related to the steps of good listening are techniques that can help us accurately consume what the other person is saying. These techniques are known as rephrasing, clarifying, and summarizing.

Rephrasing

Rephrasing means to mentally repeat in our own words what the other person is saying so that we might better understand the message. Suppose a friend tells us, "Driving to Lafayette is a long way, especially when the car isn't working and I have to buy groceries tonight. I also noticed that the bank is closed on Monday, and I forgot to cash a check." By actively listening and rephrasing this rather jumbled message, we could condense it into, "We are not going to Lafayette."

Clarifying

Yet we might want more information and therefore clarify our friend's statement with a question or a leading statement of our own: "If you're short of cash, I'll be glad to chip in for gas." Our friend might answer with, "Thanks for understanding and offering. I'll pay you back on Tuesday." We have now expanded the dialogue and received a more accurate message; namely, the person was short of money but was embarrassed to say so.

Summarizing

We might summarize our friend's second statement and say to ourselves: "This person is short of cash, and therefore he's going to borrow from me so we can go to Lafayette." We can also use all three techniques to listen carefully and develop a dialogue based on accurate and complete, rather than inaccurate and partial, information.

SEPARATING CONTENT FROM EMOTION

Two sets of emotions are present during the communication process—the emotions of the speaker and the emotions of the listener. When more listeners are involved, their sets of emotions also become intertwined in the process. Those emotions, when integrated as a part of the message exchange, help to build the communication relationship between individuals and complement the dialogue. Yet emotions can sometimes interrupt our ability to listen to the content of the communication message. A breakdown in the communication process can result.

Police negotiators deal with this problem every day. They often encounter a suspect who is extremely emotional, perhaps one threatening suicide or holding hostages. To communicate with that person, the negotiators must get beyond the emotions of the individual and concentrate on developing dialogue based on language content. They must concentrate on every word the suspect is saying. Those words are like baseballs flying by, and the police negotiator must reach out and catch each baseball, hoping to grasp the meaning of a key word that can lead to a game of verbal pitch and catch. As the game progresses, the police negotiator is able to catch more baseballs, and the suspect begins to throw the balls with greater accuracy. If successful, content, not emotion, becomes the prime component of the game.

LISTENING AS A DEVELOPMENTAL PROCESS

Communication, whether it is through a series of distinct interactions or a single conversation that moves from beginning to end, changes over time. To listen effectively, we need to keep this developmental perspective in mind. Language, for example, changes as we move through a conversation. Words may be spoken in one context at one moment and in a different context at another moment.

While we are listening, we must remember not to automatically take words at one point in a relationship at the same face value as would occur at another point in the relationship. Consider the words "I love you." If two people on their first date said to each other, "I love you," the words could hold the same meaning as the words, "I am infatuated by you," or "You sweep me off my feet." Five weeks later at a different time in the relationship, the words "I love you" could take on an entirely different meaning. On the tenth anniversary of the relationship the words would take on still another meaning. The words have changed in their context over time, and we need to listen to the differences. The words "I love you" on the tenth anniversary of a relationship may hold much deeper meaning than the words "I love you" on the first date.

BEING SENSITIVE TO SELF-DISCLOSURE

Earlier in the text we discussed the role of self-disclosure in the communication process. Central to the ability of both parties to participate in communication is the way in which listening contributes to self-disclosure. As self-disclosure progresses, the issues under discussion may become more personal or simply more opinionated and intense, and the speaker may become more ego-involved. Once this happens, more active listening is necessary. Reacting to self-disclosing messages demands a sensitivity to the fact that an individual is giving something personal and offering it into the conversation. As such, this gift must be treated with appreciation and care and acknowledged with appropriate sensitivity and listening skills.

DEALING WITH LOADED WORDS

Some years ago I attended a lecture given by a uniformed state police officer. The subject was drug abuse, and he graphically indicated what can happen when people suffer from a drug addiction and cannot control their actions. As he discussed what occurs in the body under the stress of drugs, he reached for his service revolver, pulled it out of the holster, pointed it at the class, and fired. What the class did not know was that the service revolver was loaded with blanks, and when it discharged, the students literally came out of their seats. From that moment on, every time the police officer's hand came within six inches of the service revolver, the class stopped listening to the lecture and instead focused on the service revolver. If the police officer had started the speech by saying that he would fire the gun, then the shot would not have been so surprising, and the class would have expected the blast. Since he did not, the students broke their concentration and stopped listening.

Similarly, our concentration can be broken and our listening stopped when another person unexpectedly uses words that do not fit the intensity or depth of the conversation. Someone once replied to my invitation to breakfast with the question, "What's your motivation?" The word "motivation" was out of place. The rest of the brief conversation became a blur as I wrestled with what the person meant by "motivation." It was a very defensive word. Since my only intention was to eat breakfast, I could only reply, "To get something to eat." The word "motivation" was a trigger that broke my concentration and caused me to stop listening, thus interrupting the flow of the conversation.

THE EFFECT OF DISSONANCE

Dissonance is defined as a disagreeable combination of sounds. In communication, we refer to dissonance as *a combination of messages that, together, are disagreeable.* The messages may be a combination of our perceptions of something plus our exposure to something else that conflicts with our original perceptions. For example, suppose that a speaker's message that we should eat cake to lose weight disagrees with our perception of cake as being fattening. We thus decide that the speaker's credibility is very low and we stop listening to the remainder of the message. By not listening, we miss the portion of the speech that describes how staying totally away from sweets at the early stage of a diet may cause us to consume too much of other foods and therefore gain weight. But we stopped listening in order to reduce the dissonance we felt for the conflicting messages we were receiving. Skilled speakers who are trying to change opinions know the value of leading gently into subjects that may contain opinions or facts at odds with those of the audience. They realize that dissonance can not only polarize opinion but also cause the audience to stop listening.

FEAR OF QUESTIONING

Asking questions is a way of clarifying information. Feeling uncomfortable about asking questions prevents understanding and interferes with communication. An acute fear of asking questions can cause us to block out that fear by not concentrating. We may stop listening to the other person. But why would we be hesitant to ask questions?

One reason we may hesitate to ask questions is because some people are so overpowering that they make asking questions almost impossible. They are insensitive to others and freely interrupt a conversation. Listening becomes a chore, for the chance to speak will be met with interruption. How can we actively communicate with such a person? Take the initiative. Courteously confront the individual with the fact that you find speaking with him or her difficult. It should get the person's attention and allow you to begin a responsible interaction. As that interaction develops, you can then take a meaningful part in the conversation, including active listening.

Fear of questioning can also develop when we lack sufficient information to ask intelligent questions. Imagine you are sitting in class and are unprepared. You are afraid to ask questions for fear of looking foolish. As a result, you separate yourself from your fears by not listening to the lecture. You thus place yourself in double jeopardy by not asking questions about what you don't understand and by not listening to new information. Keep this in mind the next time you aren't prepared for class.

SELECTIVE EXPOSURE, PERCEPTION, AND RETENTION

Among the most obvious obstacles to good listening is not applying the steps and techniques we discussed earlier or letting our feelings and fears block out the content of the other person's communication. Let's now look at the less obvious but broad-based obstacles to listening, including selective exposure, selective perception, and selective retention, and how they can affect the process of human communication.

Selective Exposure

We tend to think of listening as a skill employed when interacting with others. But we may be more selective than we realize in our interactions. Whom we choose to interact with is another way of determining to whom we want to listen. We can inadvertently narrow our own perspectives by limiting our communication to only certain people with whom we agree. Selective exposure means that we choose to come in contact with communication from others who we perceive to possess certain beliefs. This action can actually limit the number of people to whom we listen and can therefore reinforce and solidify our opinions and beliefs.

Selective Perception

Imagine that you and a friend attend a speech by a leading political candidate. Both you and your friend hold very strong but different views on a key issue that the candidate touches upon in the speech. When the speech is over, you discover that you and your friend have entirely different interpretations of what the candidate said. Yet you both heard the same speech. How could the two of you differ so greatly on what you heard?

Blame it on selective perception. This phenomenon explains that what we hear and, consequently, what we perceive often is determined by our preconceived notions about someone or something. Although the same message might be sent to two different people, each selectively interprets or perceives the communication differently. If you perceive yourself as being conservative, then you might react more favorably to something a conservative candidate says than to something a liberal candidate says, even though they say the same thing. We often hear what we want to hear; we are all guilty of selective perception.

Selective Retention

Remembering, as we have discovered, is one of the key steps in the listening process. Selective retention is the same as selective remembering. We selectively retain or remember communication that we perceive as having certain qualities. For example, we may hear a politician's speech and remember only those things with which we are in agreement. At home, parents ask their children to do chores around the house. Children have an uncanny ability to remember only the chores that are the easiest or the ones they want to do. In essence, they selectively remember.

When I was learning how to ski on the Three Sisters range in Oregon, my instructor gallantly tried to teach me the fine points of stopping and turning. On the advice of my instructor, we both headed up the chair lift to the top of the slope. Unfortunately, as I started down the run, the only thing I could remember was how to fall down at high speed without getting hurt or hitting a tree. With constant instruction at various intervals on the way down, I arrived at the bottom, remembering absolutely nothing about how to stop and turn. Later, on a more moderate run, I gradually began to develop my skill and become an avid fan of the sport.

This experience on the ski slope can be applied to listening. When we enter into a conversation, we may carry with us a certain priority of information and opinions. Regardless of what communication is sent to us, we remember only what we feel is important or that with which we agree. Even though I listened and paid attention to what my skiing instructor was saying about turning and stopping, it was not a priority, and I did not remember it.

THE BARRIERS OF PREJUDICE AND STEREOTYPING

In our society we tend to think of prejudice as something exercised negatively against another person. Clearly, negative prejudice can interfere with communication. When we prejudge people or when we permit our closed minds to block open communication and interfere with listening, then prejudice is working against us.

The Positive Role of Prejudice

Removing prejudice, however, is often difficult. If we can't remove it, we can at least work with it and turn it into a positive rather than a negative communication force. How? One way to do this is to recognize and identify prejudice, both in ourselves and others. Our listening can then take into consideration these prejudices and work toward developing a sensitive dialogue and understanding with the other person. With this dynamic, not static, use of prejudice, listening can achieve its greatest potential.

Dealing with Stereotypes

Closely related to selective perception is stereotyping, which, as used in this text, means prejudging a person. We frequently prejudge people before we have an opportunity to interact with them. Consequently, stereotyping sets up artificial barriers through which we selectively listen because we believe a person has certain qualities, stands for something, or represents something.

We can be guilty of stereotyping in any number of encounters. We often tend to stereotype and lump people together with others that we perceive to be similar. Perhaps we have known someone in our past who had certain qualities, and now we perceive everyone like that person to have the same qualities.[7]

How many times have we heard about stereotyping of the handicapped? Perhaps this unjust and "unskilled" approach to listening is felt deepest when a handicapped person applies for a job. The interviewer, seeing or hearing evidence of the handicap, often concentrates on that handicap and does not listen to what the person is saying. This may result in the interviewer stereotyping the applicant as being unable to do the job before ever considering what the person has to say on his or her behalf. In essence, stereotyping the handicapped and letting that block our ability to listen clearly to what a handicapped person is saying places a handicap on ourselves.

THE ROLE OF SOURCE CREDIBILITY

Source credibility is how much we accept, believe in, and respect the sender of communication. How intelligent we perceive the person to be about a given subject, even how dynamic the person is, is an additional dimension of the concept. People who possess these qualities influence us and form our opinions.[8]

Source credibility varies among people and even within a single conversation. If we are at a party and engage in conversation with someone, we may discuss a range of topics over the course of an evening. Suppose we are talking with a doctor. If the discussion deals with a medical topic, we probably would perceive the doctor as being a credible source on that subject. On the other hand, if we learn the doctor has never attended a ballet, we might place much less credibility on his or her opinions about ballet.

CULTURAL OBSTACLES

The verbal and nonverbal communication cues of foreign cultures may be entirely different from our own. Consequently, a person from a foreign country may think of the things we consider good qualities of communication as strange. Some cultures, for instance, do not encourage direct eye contact to the degree that other cultures do. Trying to read the nonverbal cues of another culture may result in our listening to conflicting information, misjudging behavior, or misunderstandings. When we have the opportunity to become more immersed in a culture, we can listen with a great deal more accuracy.

To better understand how cultural differences can affect communication, a sociologist at the University of Puget Sound in Washington conducted a study with Navajo Indian children and their mothers. He discovered that there was a considerable difference between the communication habits of Navajo Indian children and Caucasian children as perceived by their mothers.

A videotape of four Navajo Indian and four Caucasian children playing in a Los Angeles day-care center was shown to Navajo and Caucasian mothers. One child displayed by far the most verbal and physical activity of the eight children. The tape shows him running to the teacher and stating that he wants help in using a cartridge tape device that shows cartoons. He also tells the child already using the machine: "My turn." How did the mothers respond to this behavior? Eighty-five percent of the Caucasian mothers "stressed the positive. . . . They described him as being aggressive, excited, and interested. Only 35 percent of the Navajo mothers approved. . . . The other 65 percent thought he was mischievous. Not enough discipline."[9]

The sociologist concludes that:

> Navajo and Caucasian mothers attribute distinctly different meanings to active speech and physical behavior. The Navajo mothers tend to perceive extremely active speech and behavior to be discourteous, restless, self-centered, and undisciplined. The Caucasian mothers tend to see the same as self-disciplined, exciting to observe, and advantageous for the child.[10]

We can see that if the communication we receive from another person causes us to judge that person as "discourteous, restless, self-centered, and undisciplined," then that communication most likely will fail. When communicating with someone from a different culture, take the time to learn the meaning of various verbal and nonverbal symbols you do not understand. Instead of prematurely shutting out people, you may be able to adapt your own listening behavior to be more tolerant of their communicative styles.

COMMUNICATION STYLES: RECEIVER AND SENDER

A train coming to a crossing at which it changes tracks must slow down to pass over the switch. If it doesn't, it risks jumping off the track and missing its destination. The same thing can happen when we listen. The message must travel between the sender and the receiver, and how we receive the message and what we do with it is much like the train's switching to another track to follow a different route. We must throw our own mental switches. Throwing those switches takes time, literally measured as a fraction of a second. If the message does not slow down, it jumps the track. We either miss part of what is said or we may misunderstand what is said. These changes are actually the *switching of receiver styles*.

Switching Receiver Styles

We throw four basic cognitive or mental switches to receive and process communication: (1) agree, (2) disagree, (3) think, or (4) question.[11] Any time we switch this processing, we run the risk of jumping the listening track. Because we need to process information quickly, an information or switching overload can cause us to miss or misjudge information we receive. For example, some information remains in our memory for a few seconds, then is lost. Moreover, some kinds of information and information processing take more "storage space" in our brain than others. To understand these concepts, try listening to the radio while you're reading a book. The task is not too difficult and is even easier if the station is broadcasting background music rather than news. Now try watching television while reading a book. This becomes more difficult, and to some it's impossible. When watching television, we use more of the "storage and processing" systems in our brain than we do when listening to the radio. Consequently, we can't do as many other things or comprehend as much other information at the same time. The same principle applies to cognitive switching. It takes more intrapersonal effort to think and question than it does to agree with someone. Moreover, when the message switches from something we agree with to something we disagree with, it takes time to switch from one processing mode to another.

Reading Sender Styles

The noted Swiss psychiatrist Carl Jung established the theory that humans are of various psychological types. Paul Mok, a consulting psychologist, uses Jung's basic personality types to develop four predominant communicative styles:[12] (1) the thinker, the person who is deliberate in thought and action, is businesslike, and lives a highly structured life; (2) the feeler, an emotional, sensitive person who likes emotional involvement with people and may lead a more carefree life than the thinker; (3) the intuitor, a more imaginative individual but who can also be impatient with people who do not immediately see the value or lack of it in something or someone; (4) the sensor, who likes to absorb the things around him or her using all of the senses—for example, a person absorbing the sights, sounds, and smells of a mountain meadow.

What Mok and others suggest is that we can achieve much better communication by correctly "reading" the person with whom we are communicating. People in sales positions who must deal with many different personality types can immediately benefit from this suggestion. If they misread the communicative styles of clients, they may lose a sale.

LISTENING TO FEEDBACK

Human communication is a dynamic circular process. The sender communicates a message to a receiver, and the receiver, in turn, sends feedback to the sender. We continually alternate between being the sender and being the receiver of communication as we talk with other people. Feedback is extremely important for the success of these roles. Through feedback, we are able to influence and adjust the message being sent to us.[13] Without feedback, we have no way to alter the message, and the sender has no way to determine if what is meant to be communicated is being received with the desired effect.

Positive Feedback

Positive feedback can take a number of forms. *Clarification* asks for additional information in order to correctly process a message. We can request clarification through a variety of verbal and nonverbal cues. A frown accompanied by a smile may indicate we want to receive more information but of a different type from what we have been receiving. Or we can verbally request clarification by asking, "Would you please clarify that for me?" or "Could you be more specific?" or "I'm afraid I don't understand what you said."

Still another form of positive feedback is *evaluation,* which is feedback separated from the person with whom we are talking. It is normally objective and free from personal emotion or biased opinion. Evaluation is not to be confused with criticism, which in itself may be positive or negative. Suppose a student asks the professor, "What do you think of this latest best-seller?" When the professor replies, "I like it very much," this exchange is an evaluative statement about the best-selling book.

Empathy is another form of positive feedback. When we say, "I know how you feel" or "I understand what you are going through," we are empathizing with the other person. When sincerely expressed, empathy can enhance the self-concept of the sender and increase his or her desire for continued communication. As positive feedback, it is the kind of communication that can produce some of the most positive responses and solidify a relationship between people.

Start monitoring your own communication with other people. What types of positive feedback do you receive? How can you offer more positive feedback to others? To help your monitoring process, we now look at feedback you'll want to avoid—negative feedback.

Negative Feedback

You may have heard the statement, "Don't Rain on My Parade." Basically, the lyrics state that people don't appreciate negative reactions to their positive communication. The world is full of pessimists. They can lose friends, break up marriages, ruin companies, and perform a host of other ills. Do no become a person who rains on other people's parades.

Another form of negative feedback is to respond *partially* to what people are saying. This habit can signify to the sender that you only value part of what the person is saying. It also signals an inability to listen effectively because you have only heard part of the conversation.

Defensive communication is still another form of negative feedback. Accepting criticism gracefully is an art. No one likes to be criticized, and it is only natural that we react to it with some form of internal hostility, sometimes expressed verbally. It takes a strong self-concept to accept legitimate and valid criticism. In most cases we react defensively. A boss says, "I feel you could do better work." Outwardly you agree. Inside you are saying, "I disagree. I know my work is good; it is your supervision that is wrong." Unfortunately, your disgust may manifest itself in defensive, nonverbal feedback. Noticing that you are upset, you boss may withdraw further criticism, just when it may constructively improve your future efforts.[14]

SUMMARY

An ability to listen effectively is necessary for us to participate in any form of verbal communication. Listening takes practice and an acute awareness of the many subtle forms of communication that occur in any conversation.

A number of steps are necessary to travel down the road to better listening. These include: (1) listening as a personal commitment; (2) involving oneself in fields of experience; (3) sensing; (4) timing; (5) empathy; (6) never blocking an idea. Together, the first letter of each step spells l–i–s–t–e–n.

The techniques of rephrasing, clarifying, and summarizing are helpful. Rephrasing means restating to ourselves or to the other person what has been communicated. Clarifying includes gaining an understanding and new information. Summarizing involves a capsuled assessment of what has been said. In addition to the knowledge of the steps and techniques of good listening, we must be able to establish listening goals.

To avoid misreading the messages of others, we must be able to separate content from emotion. As an example, we discussed the police negotiator who must grasp language as a means of developing a dialogue with a suspect.

Listening is a developmental process; it is different at the beginning of a relationship than later when the relationship has matured. Moreover, as the relationship matures, self-disclosure increases. Personal opinions, attitudes, and feelings are offered into the conversation as gifts that must be sensitively acknowledged.

Good listening also demands understanding the barriers to good communication. Among these are the use of loaded words, the effect of dissonance, and the fear of questioning. Loaded words can distract our attention. Dissonance can make us stop listening while we try and resolve differences between our own perceptions and the messages we are receiving. Fear of questioning can cause us to stop listening to alleviate the fear.

Poor listening may be the fault of selective perception, selective exposure, or selective retention. It may also involve our ability to deal with prejudice and stereotypes. In addition, we must also understand the importance of source credibility, cultural obstacles to listening, and the disruptions of physical and semantic noise.

Different people have different styles of communication. Monitoring these communication styles may cause us to switch our listening styles in order to adapt to each communication encounter. By adapting to these different styles of communication, we will send accurate feedback to senders, thus giving listening its important place in the circular and dynamic process of communication.

QUESTIONS FOR REVIEW AND DISCUSSION

1. What are the steps to good listening?

2. How many of our senses do we use in effective listening? What are they?

3. Inference theory and role-taking theory are two perspectives from which we can approach empathy. Explain the differences between the two theories.

4. What role does listening play in self-disclosure?

5. What effect does stereotyping have on listening?

6. How can "source credibility" affect listening?

7. What are the four basic cognitive switches we throw to be able to receive and process communication?

8. How do selective exposure, selective perception, and selective retention affect listening?

LEARNING EXERCISES

1. Imagine you are the head of a new department titled the "Department of Listening." Design between 5 to 10 courses that would be included in the new department. For example, one course might be titled "Introduction to Empathy." Another might be "Elimination of Prejudice." Include a course description of exactly what would be included in the course and any classroom assignment that might help students learn about the subject.

2. The next time a speaker visits your campus, attend the speech with some friends. After the speech discuss with your friends exactly what the speaker said. See how many direct quotes you can remember. Discuss where you differed about what was said and why.

ADDITIONAL READINGS

BACHELLER, F. *Listening and Recall.* Englewood Cliffs, NJ: Prentice-Hall, 1986.

BROWNELL, J.L. *Building Active Listening Skills.* Englewood Cliffs, NJ: Prentice-Hall, 1986.

COLBURN, C. W., and S. B. WEINBERG *An Orientation to Listening and Audience Analysis.* Chicago: Science Research Associates, 1976.

GLATTHORN, A. A., and H. R. ADAMS *Listening Your Way to Management Success.* Glenview, IL: Scott Foresman, 1984.

HAYAKAWA, S. I. *Through the Communication Barrier.* New York: Harper & Row, Pub., 1979.

HIRSCH, R. O. *A Way to Process Information Aurally.* Dubuque, IA: Corsuch Scarisbrich, 1979.

WAKEFIELD, B. *Perception and Communication.* Arlington, VA: Speech Communication Association (ERIC), 1976.

6

INTERPERSONAL COMMUNICATION

OBJECTIVES

After completing this chapter, you should be able to

- Discuss the importance of good interpersonal communication
- Describe how the presence of homophily enables us to communicate on common ground
- Explain heterophily
- Talk about interpersonal communication from the situational approach
- Realize that interpersonal communication develops over time
- Understand that interpersonal communication both follows rules of behavior and obeys laws of behavior
- Discuss rhetoric and symbolic interaction
- List and describe the interpersonal needs of inclusion, control, and affection
- Think interpersonally.

Often in this text we have referred to examples in which two people were communicating face to face with each other. This is known as *dyadic communication*—the word dyadic meaning two of something, such as people or units. As we have learned, it is also called interpersonal communication.

THE IMPORTANCE OF GOOD INTERPERSONAL COMMUNICATION

Effective interpersonal communication is important in every encounter, every walk of life. From the most intimate interpersonal relationship to a casual discussion among corporate executives, it permeates our way of thinking about others and our effectiveness in dealing with people. To understand this importance, we'll draw from some examples.

Students spend a great deal of time in my office talking about a host of things, including their relationships with other students. One morning, a student mentioned she had had a terrific weekend because of a very enjoyable date. When I asked her what was so special about the date, she replied, "We went for a long walk, looked at the stars, then went back to the dorm and talked." Two weeks later she dropped by the office again. This time she told me the relationship with her new boyfriend was progressing and that she was very happy. I inquired what was so special about this person. She replied, "We have such good talks; I really enjoy our good talks."

While talking with her further, I found that they had often repeated the same kind of date as when they first met. They would go for a long walk, then go back to the dorm or a coffeehouse and talk. Whether or not the relationship had progressed past talking was not important. What was important was that she was putting such a premium on "the talk" that they had. Interpersonal communication had become the cornerstone of the relationship, the important part of the togetherness they were sharing. It was something she valued higher than anything else in the relationship, at least at that point in its development.

I thought about other students with whom I had chatted about their dates, campus weekends, or other personal relationships they wanted to share. I thought about the students who had said, somewhat jokingly, but with more seriousness than they would admit, that they really did not care for the people they were dating or that they just went out to have a good time. Many were disappointed with their relationships, disenchanted with their peers. One student exclaimed, "I even read the *Joy of Sex* and things still haven't improved."

I thought back to the student who had put such a value on the talks she had with her date. Perhaps the students who were disenchanted should have studied more about interpersonal communication instead of concentrating on the *Joy of Sex*. Many dating relationships break down before they have the chance to fully develop because one of the partners is not skilled in effective interpersonal communication. Perhaps neither one can listen effectively nor practice other communication skills necessary to communicate with each other.

The importance of interpersonal communication is reinforced again when we consider its role in world government. Diplomatic shuttle missions would be banished if nations did not think a special quality could exist when two people held face-to-face discussions. The rich rewards of interpersonal contact cannot be duplicated in a diplomatic memo, on a television screen, or through pomp and ceremony. Only interpersonal communication—people-to-people contact—can create a sensitivity to the myriad of emotions involved in making major political decisions. When we realize that the fate of millions of people can hinge on the effective interpersonal communication skills of two world leaders, we realize that interpersonal communication may be more crucial than military might for world survival. Leaders who cannot practice good interpersonal communication skills with other world leaders, or who cannot understand the delicate nature of face-to-face communication across cultures and through different languages, are a disservice to themselves and the countries they serve.

The world of business is filled with unfulfilled dreams, unobtained salary raises, unachieved promotions, and even terminations because some business people have never learned the importance of good interpersonal communication. They have been so caught up in competing with their peers that they never learned the importance of cooperation. They have been so concerned with graduating with a high-powered degree that they never stopped long enough to discover the importance of good interpersonal discussion. They have been so concerned with directing subordinates that they never developed the knack of interpersonal dialogue.

Those who possess good interpersonal skills are going to become increasingly valuable to their organizations. In addition, those who possess good interpersonal skills are going to be more effective friends, lovers, parents, associates, and, simply, human beings. Effective interpersonal communication creates encounters of substance with meaning, a foundation, something of lasting value rather than fleeting appeal. It helps to create true communication in which two people join ideas, thoughts, and feelings in an encounter of substance.

COMMUNICATING ON COMMON GROUND: HOMOPHILY

In Chapter 1 we talked about communication models, those pictorial representations of the communication process. Applying our model to interpersonal communication, we saw how the sender represented one person and the receiver another. Both were affected by such things as nonverbal communication, the self-concept of each person, their ability to listen, and homophily.[1] Although we dealt briefly with homophily earlier, we will now explore this topic in greater detail.

Homophily is concerned with where fields of experience overlap, that point at which two people communicating have things in common with each other and develop accurate shared perceptions upon which to base communication. Studies show that communication has a greater opportunity to succeed when considerable homophily exists between a sender and receiver. Suppose, for example, that after many tries, you cannot balance your checkbook so that it matches your current bank statement. You decide to talk to a bank officer or teller to work out the problem. What do you both have in common that will have a bearing on your conversation? First and foremost is the bank where you have your account and where the teller or bank officer works. Second is the bank statement, which does not reconcile with your checkbook. These, then, become the basis of your conversation. In essence, it is this commonality, this overlap of fields of experience, that causes you to communicate with the bank representative in the first place. Later, after conversing, you may discover you have more things in common.

Research has taken a close look at homophily, studying what attracts two people to one another. We are not necessarily speaking of romantic attraction, but rather of the acquaintances and friendships each of us makes in our normal life. This type of attraction centers around such things as similarities in attitudes, background, values, and appearance.[2]

Attitudes

When we meet someone and begin to interact with that person, a normal question we ask ourselves is, "Does this person think like me?"[3] If the answer to that question is positive, then our discussion may progress to topics that involve more self-disclosure, more intimacy, or greater depth and discussion. We want to know if the other person's attitudes, or their accumulations of opinions about a subject, merge with ours. If, as we continue to interact, the answer to the question remains "yes," then homophily is developing.

Background

Personal background is another area in which homophily can develop. Research suggests that social class is one link between people that can contribute to homophily. As you interact with another person, you make judgments on whether or not the person's social class is similar to yours, whether you are from similar economic backgrounds, whether the status of the person is similar to yours, or whether you grew up under similar conditions. This does not mean that we approach every communication situation investigating whether the other person appeared at the latest debutante ball or belongs to the country club. As we've said before, do not let biases hinder communication. It does mean, however, that such things as social class, economic status, and heritage *can* play a part in developing homophily. Our society is conditioned to these factors, and we should be alert to their presence.

Values

Earlier in the text we discussed how values play an important role in the development of our self-concept. We defined values as those qualities formed early in our lives and which are not easily changed. We can also use more general approaches to values in helping us to understand homophily. For example, when we form opinions about other people, we may ask ourselves such questions as, "Does this person have morals like mine?"[4] Or depending on the nature of the relationship, we might ask: "Are this person's sexual values like mine?"[5] Important to evaluating the individual would be a determination of whether the person shares our values or treats people the same way we do.

Appearance

Research indicates that nonverbal communication, especially in the form of appearance, influences homophily. People who accept positively the appearance of another person tend to generate more homophily toward each other than people who negatively interpret the appearance of the other person.

Our discussion of the building blocks of homophily has been in general terms. Relationships between people are based on many different qualities, affected by many different situations, and progress differently as the relationship matures. The dimensions of homophily that we have discussed *can* exist between individuals. They are not dimensions that necessarily *do* exist in every interpersonal encounter. Moreover, it is not enough to simply have something in common with another person. Homophily requires that this commonality is both known *and* perceived by each person as being an integral part of the relationship.

HETEROPHILY

Dissimilarities also play a part in communication patterns. Such *dissimilarities* are referred to as *heterophily*. Imagine that you are asked out on a date, and the initial homophily creates a very positive atmosphere to start the evening's conversation. You like the same food, the same restaurants, and the same music. But you have very different ideas about sex. You discover you come from different backgrounds, deal with people in much different ways, and have different values. On the other hand, you may try to focus upon the things you do have in common in order to develop some type of continuing relationship.

One sign of a good communicator is the ability to adapt to the different degrees of homophily and heterophily. Both operate in any communication situation. The world leader who negotiates an agreement is working across cultures, languages, backgrounds, attitudes, values, and a host of other differences. To be able to recognize that these differences exist while also realizing that communication must take place is a crucial quality of both people and governments.

With the role of homophily and heterophily as a foundation, we can begin broadening our understanding of interpersonal communication. In the sections that follow, we will consider different approaches to the study of interpersonal communication. As we examine these, keep in mind that all have important contributions to make, but some can be applied more readily to a particular interpersonal encounter than others. Interpersonal communication that takes place between you and a waitress, for example, is much different from that which takes place between you and a family member. Moreover, you probably will not have the *time to develop* much of a relationship with the waitress, whereas you make the time to develop that relationship with a family member.

INTERPERSONAL SITUATIONS

Let's begin by examining interpersonal communication from the perspective of different situations; this is aptly called the *situational* approach.[6] We should not analyze every interpersonal encounter based on a situation. Yet situations often influence the communication that takes place within them (Fig. 6–1).

Consider the chancellor of a university who has just commissioned a new meeting room to be built adjacent to his office. The chancellor wants the room to be large enough for comfort and to have two windows so that regardless of where people sit, they can see outside. The chancellor also wants the table to be round but only large enough to seat six people. The presence of more than six people, the chancellor believes, inhibits communication. Finally, the room is completed and the first meeting is held. The chancellor invites five deans to sit at the table for a discussion about the budget. Everyone has an equal chance to speak, and each dean spends an approximately equal amount of time supporting his or her own school's request for funding. Each feels equally important since no one can be considered at the "head" of the round table. If one dean notices something out the window, they can all look. When the meeting is over, the chancellor is delighted.

Figure 6-1
Interpersonal situations determine the content of the communication. The referee in this New York Rangers hockey game has little time to develop a relationship with the player. In other settings, the ability to develop relationships with individuals over time is an important skill dependent on understanding and using appropriate and effective interpersonal communication.

If we examine the interpersonal communication that took place in the new meeting room, we might consider it successful. The chancellor made all the necessary arrangements to see that a good interpersonal atmosphere existed: the round table, the two windows, the amount of equal interaction between the deans, and the successful conclusion of the task, which was the completion of the budget.

If we were to assume that successful interpersonal communication takes place every time people have the opportunity to interact equally, that the table is round, that there are two windows, and that the goal of the meeting is achieved, we would be sadly mistaken. What would have happened if the goal had been reached, but one of the deans had been rudely insulted by the other four? What would have happened if two of the deans had talked continually while the other three deans never got a word in edgewise? What would have happened if the chancellor had not permitted the deans to take part in the decision-making process? Moreover, what would have happened if one of the deans had received a job offer from another college and a new dean entered the picture? Situational perspectives are important, but they do have limitations in studying interpersonal communication.

For instance, the situational approach does not permit us to understand the *development* of communicative interaction over more than a short period of time. We do not know what effect on the organization the exiting dean will have when he or she talks to co-workers. Or suppose one dean's request is not funded. We do not know what pattern future communication will take when that dean vows at the next meeting to get his or her school funded "or else." In fact, the next meeting may turn into a fireworks display instead of a congenial gathering. And yet the fireworks were really fused in the first meeting, which we might have thought was relatively successful.

Keep in mind that interpersonal communication, like all human communication, is a dynamic process. Relationships change, perceptions of people change, and everything that happens in one encounter can affect subsequent encounters.

INTERPERSONAL COMMUNICATION DEVELOPING OVER TIME

Our example of the deans who were not able to say anything, of the dean who was rudely insulted, of the dean who accepted the new job even though the chancellor's "perfect" meeting room was used leads us to view interpersonal communication as more than situational. We realize that one communicative encounter can affect others. People who decide to marry, for example, usually have had reasonably good experiences communicating interpersonally. We could say that they have had a succession of good interpersonal "situations." Yet perhaps months or even years after the ceremony, these situations may become bad examples of interpersonal communication. What has happened is that the relationship between the two individuals has changed, and perhaps neither has the skill to replace bad interpersonal encounters with the good encounters of their courtship days. Sometimes it takes a marriage counselor to explain where the relationship broke down and how, if possible, it can be rebuilt. The reason for this is that the counselor can look at the entire history of the relationship, that is, its *development*, and not just a set of disconnected interpersonal situations.

Similarly, although group discussions within a corporation may enable the company to meet its goals, relationships between employees may actually be deteriorating. This condition develops to the point that one day, the goals are not met because the tension and animosity among employees makes it impossible for people to communicate with each other. Obviously an inept administrator felt everything was fine because he or she examined the organization in terms of short-range goals that were being met by a succession of interpersonal situations. What the administrator failed to do was monitor the interpersonal communication developing among the workers over the long term. Thus, we can see the importance of examining interpersonal communication from both the situational approach and the perspective of the developmental process.[7]

Keep in mind that a relationship may have different boundaries and time frames around it. What is important in looking at interpersonal communication from the developmental perspective is to be aware of how a relationship moves from the entry phase to the exit phase. Furthermore, relationships can progress through many more stages. Even the three discussed here can be broken down into many subphases. We'll learn more about communication as a developmental process in the chapter on developing relationships.

FOLLOWING RULES OF BEHAVIOR

During an entry phase of interpersonal communication, people exchange greetings and say polite and appropriate words to each other. These "appropriate words" are part of the rules-of-behavior approach to understanding interpersonal communication. Following social rules and norms can enhance interpersonal communication. Conversely, seriously violating those rules or norms may hinder it. Again, remember that rules change within different situations. Nothing is absolute.

Let's assume it's the first day of classes, and you have just arrived on campus to meet your roommate. Your initial greeting is tempered by certain appropriate rules of behavior common to society. Upon meeting your roommate for the first time, you do not exclaim, "I hope you will take as much care keeping this room clean as I will!" Chances are that if you greeted your roommate in such a fashion, you might find yourself sleeping in the hall. Even later in the semester when you ask your roommate to help keep the room clean, you will no doubt use a diplomatically phrased suggestion, "Could we work together to help keep the room clean?", which will promote a much better relationship. Certain rules of behavior and norms exist within our society, and adhering to them helps us in our communication relationships. Many relationships break down because people lose track of some of these basic rules and common courtesy.

RHETORIC AND SYMBOLIC INTERACTION

The term *rhetoric* calls forth images of politicians and demagogues using language to overpower opponents, camouflage issues, and retreat behind a barrage of verbal shots at the public. In the study of communication, however, rhetoric takes on a much more important and respectable meaning. Its roots are most firmly planted in the wisdom of the ancient Greeks who studied and reflected on the power of words to persuade. Long before the era of instant mass communication, million-dollar advertising campaigns, and sophisticated marketing strategies, the ability to speak on an interpersonal basis about the issues and events of the day was accorded the highest respect. Those who were skilled orators, who understood the importance and practice of public address, and who could persuade others to adopt their views through reasoned discourse were awarded the highest positions of government and power.

Today, rhetoric continues to be a critical and important tool of communication. Its modern definition can be stated as purposeful communication through symbols (language) providing alternatives of action. Examples of this definition are found in law, politics, education, and almost every other field of endeavor. An attorney, for example, must negotiate a settlement. To do this, the attorney must carefully choose language to achieve this goal. The communication between one attorney and another is purposeful, and each is involved in symbolic interaction. A senator addresses fellow senators and attempts to persuade them to vote for a bill. The strategies of persuasion and the words the senator uses are rhetorical strategies, rhetorical choices. A teacher wishes to impart a new concept to students. Thus, the communication the teacher uses is purposeful, as is the teacher's language. If we want to do a rhetorical analysis of the teacher's communication, we can examine the purpose of the teacher's remarks and the manner in which the lecture or teaching materials was devised. We can also examine the symbols used to communicate the lesson and the way in which the teacher and students interacted with each other.

To take a rhetorical and symbolic interaction approach to interpersonal communication, therefore, requires a sensitivity to the motives and purposes of our interaction. It also requires a sensitivity to the very powerful and important force that language plays in that interaction.

Studying interpersonal interaction from this perspective does not mean that we should look for an *ulterior* motive to the communication. Rather, it means we should look for whatever motive exists, regardless of how inconsequential it may be. Stated in other terms, we can say that interpersonal communication is a continual process of monitoring motives through the analysis of language. Language consists of symbols that represent objects, images, ideas, and other things. The key to the last sentence is *represent*. As we have already learned, symbols are not in themselves meaningful. What is meaningful is what they represent.

All of the approaches to understanding interpersonal communication can operate in symphony with each other. Assume that you are appearing for a job interview. You meet the interviewer and discuss your employment background. After the interview, the interviewer suggests that you meet the next day for lunch. You are pleased. You have made a good first impression. You appear for lunch the next day, the discussion goes well, and you are offered the job.

Applying our different approaches to your experience with the job interviewer, we can see that you had two distinct situations—the first interview and the later luncheon interview. Both situations were related to each other. If you had not performed well in the first interview, you might not have had an opportunity to have a second. One situation thus developed from the other. Moreover, you undoubtedly followed certain rules of interpersonal behavior in these interviews. The luncheon interview, for example, probably dealt with more personal issues, such as where you went to college, your hobbies and interests, and even your family, than did the first interview, where such personal discussions might have been inappropriate, depending on how the interview progressed. Moreover, there were undoubtedly certain "laws" also operating. If you dressed too warmly, you might have perspired and become uncomfortable, which in turn would have affected your ability to stay alert. And all of the interviewing interactions undoubtedly involved rhetoric and symbolic interaction.

INCLUSION

We began this chapter by talking about the student who placed a premium on her evenings out with a friend because they had such good conversations. She wisely saw these conversations as a prerequisite to a good relationship. We talked about the importance of interpersonal communication in a working situation and how goals could be accomplished in direct face-to-face interaction that could not be accomplished over long distances. All of these examples reflect certain needs that interpersonal communication helps to fulfill. William Schultz, a noted author and scholar, specifies three primary needs that interpersonal communication can help to fulfill: *inclusion, affection,* and *control.*[8]

Wanting to Be Included

Schultz states that inclusion

. . . has to do with interacting with people, with attention, acknowledgment, being known, prominence, recognition, prestige, status, and fame; with identity, individuality, understanding, interest, commitment, and participation. It is unlike affection in that it does not involve strong emotional attachments to individual persons. It is unlike control in that the preoccupation is with prominence, not dominance.[9]

Examining our own lives, we can find many examples of inclusion. Our desire to have friends is one example. Wanting to be popular is a natural desire, and when we first enter a new class or first arrive at our new job, we seek out new friends. Perhaps we go out of our way to invite another person to have lunch with us. Maybe we even join a club to acquire friends with interests similar to ours. When we associate with these club members, our fields of experience overlap, and homophily is present at the very beginning of our relationships because we have things in common. Thus, we probably find that conversation with other club members is much easier than it is with total strangers.

Levels of Inclusion

Different levels of inclusion can be found in different people. An *oversocial* individual is constantly overcompensating in an effort to belong. Joining every club on campus, wanting to be "in on everything," and trying to steal the show or attract attention all the time are characteristics of the oversocial person. The opposite extreme is the *undersocial* person. Undersocial people do not seek inclusion. They are said to be introverted and are sometimes called outcasts. This does not mean the need for inclusion does not exist, just that it is not fulfilled. Feelings of worthlessness and depression can result from extreme undersocial behavior. The person who is comfortable in any social situation, including being alone, is said to be *social*. This is the well-adjusted person who fits in well, has a positive self-concept, and can relate well to others in a relaxed atmosphere.

Effects of Non-Inclusion

Extreme failure to fulfill the inclusion need can result in serious psychological problems. School counselors deal with such problems regularly. The student who is rejected by a fraternity or sorority may lapse into a serious state of depression. When new "inclusive" relationships develop, the individual again adjusts to new people and begins to function properly in relating to others. If the person had likened acceptance into the organization as being the equivalent to either total inclusion or total exclusion, and if things do not turn out as planned, depression or even psychosomatic illnesses can occur. Some schools are sensitive enough to explain to students that it is not the end of the world if someone does not pledge or is not invited to join a fraternity or sorority.

A nine-year study of 7,000 people conducted by the University of California at Berkeley showed that those people who were lonely and without friends, without spouses, and without ties to the community had twice the death rate than those who experienced frequent interpersonal interaction.[10] A study conducted by the University of Michigan produced similar results.[11] Some psychiatrists suggest that the ability of a patient to recover from a serious illness is based on the patient's character. The key traits are a strong feeling of being needed and loved by someone. This is usually accompanied by the ability to share and communicate feelings with someone who is close to the patient.

Business and industry see the effects of strong social inclusion when employees are transferred to another city. An effort is made to make the employees feel part of the business and social community as quickly as possible. Since the previous network of social support has been lost by leaving friends and acquaintances behind, a new network must be rebuilt as quickly as possible or the lack of adjustment will affect worker productivity.

AFFECTION

Affection is a much more emotional relationship than that which exists in either inclusion or control. When affection is involved, such terms as love, infatuation, and intimacy are used to describe the relationship. All people need affection, although the degree to which they need it depends on the individual and his or her background.

We all know that different people seek affection in different ways. For example, people can be *underpersonal* and relate very superficially to others. This type of individual shies away from close relationships. Various reasons account for such behavior, such as a broken relationship that left unpleasant emotional scars or an unhappy childhood. Another level of affection can be the other extreme, the *overpersonal.* Overpersonal individuals are just that—overbearing in social relationships. We have all heard the phrase "he [she] tries too hard" at being liked. Such behavior is indicative of the overpersonal person who may even resort to deviousness in order to gain affection. Ideally, a person can be classified as *personal* when he or she has satisfactory relationships centering around affection. The personal individual is sensitive to other people's feelings, has the ability to "give people room to breathe," and does not crowd a relationship. Of course, matching one's own needs for affection to those of a partner is not always easy, and the needs themselves aren't constant.

CONTROL

Control is a range of behaviors that vary from strong or total control to being controlled by others.

Levels of Control

To better understand the range of behaviors, also expressed as different levels of control, let us imagine that we all went to work on a building construction project. At certain times under certain situations we may want strong control of others. For example, the construction supervisor is responsible for completing the job on time, making sure it comes in within budget, and for supervising the construction crews. When we supervise other workers we need their understanding of our responsibilities and we need to be in control of the project and personnel.

Now imagine we are members of the architectural firm that designed the project. We need less control over the construction crew than does the supervisor, but we still must have some control over the project or it will not be built to our specifications. Thus, as far as the construction crew is concerned, we fall into a mid-level of control. We are not directly supervising the crew but the crew must build the structure to the original design. If we engaged in an on-site discussion of a particular facet of construction we would defer to the supervisor when we interacted with a member of the construction crew. We would be much more directive, exercise a greater amount of control, and clearly express our expectations about how the job should be done.

A carpenter, on the other hand, would exercise more of a need to be controlled (directed by the supervisor) than to control others, for the carpenter has the responsibility for actually performing the work based on the architect's design.

At first we might assume that the architect or the supervisor has the most important job. Certainly there is some truth in that assumption but all three jobs are interdependent. No one person can work without the full cooperation of the other two. The owner or building inspector might even go so far as to say that the carpenter has the most important job.

Psychological Bases of Control

Another way to understand the control function is through the terms *abdicrat, autocrat,* and *democrat.* They are psychological bases for understanding the control need.

The *abdicrat* is a submissive individual. His or her control need is best fulfilled by being controlled, not by controlling others. In a company, this individual enjoys being supervised and might not normally seek positions that demand supervisory abilities and skills. In some cases, these people could be said to "know their limitations and accept them." In other cases in which deep-seated fears of failure might exist, we could say the individuals lack confidence in their ability.

At the other extreme is the *autocrat* who basically mistrusts those around him or her. This person's decisions may be dogmatic, based on his or her insecurity to maintain control. In organizations, such individuals may limit the amount of feedback they receive from subordinates, fearful that the information may be critical of their judgments.

The ideal level of control is to function as a *democrat.* To do so does not mean that we relinquish control, that someone else is in charge, or that decisions—even unpopular ones—are not made. What it does mean is that we have the ability to understand the feelings and desires of others and, whenever possible, to make decisions that take those feelings into consideration. A person must be capable and secure and have a positive self-concept to operate as a democrat. Organizations which possess such people are fortunate. More importantly, the manner in which such individuals are able to relate and talk with other people in the organization can make a great difference in the organization's success.

COMPLIANCE-GAINING BEHAVIOR

Compliance-gaining behavior is closely related to the control need we just discussed. Compliance-gaining behavior is really interpersonal persuasion. An expanded discussion of persuasion occurs in a separate chapter later in the text; for now, we will concentrate on how people use interpersonal communication to elicit specific behaviors in another person.

We use compliance-gaining strategies every day. We may persuade our roommate to help us clean up the room. We may persuade another person to go out on a date. We may persuade our boss to let us go home early.[12] One way to gain a deeper understanding of compliance-gaining behavior is to examine it from the perspective of compliance-gaining message strategies and compliance-gaining situations.

Compliance-Gaining Message Strategies

Compliance-gaining message strategies can be classified into four types: (1) activity messages; (2) power messages; (3) relationship messages; and (4) value messages.[13] For example, you may say to a classmate, "Let's go to the library and start our research for the term paper. If we start now, we may have a chance of getting an 'A' in the course." You have stressed the importance of the "activity" itself as a means of persuading your friend to get underway with the research. The positive outcome was a possible "A" in the course.

"Power messages" exert more control. For example, you might say, "Unless you agree to go to the library and start our research, I am not going to help you study for the final examination." Here the consequences of noncompliance were clear. Either go to the library or lose help with the final examination.

A "relationship" message might be, "We have a good friendship, and I don't want it ruined by your failure to do your share of the research." Here, the appeal was not on getting an "A" in the course, not on losing help on the final exam, but on ruining the relationship.

The fourth class of appeals stresses the values of the other person. For example, you might say, "You have always been a good student. Don't ruin your grades by not going to the library and starting the research." Here, the qualities of the individual, the "value" of being a good student, became the focus of the persuasion.

Compliance-Gaining Situations

Message strategies can be affected by different situations. Keep in mind that communication is a dynamic process that involves *both* the sender and receiver. This is especially true when we view compliance-gaining from the standpoint of situation, for how both the sender and the receiver perceive the situation will depend on the success of the message. Research has classified compliance-gaining situations into different categories. Some of these categories can be used to help us understand compliance-gaining behavior: (1) personal benefits of sender and/or receiver; (2) situation apprehension; (3) resistance to persuasion; (4) rights; (5) dominance; (6) relational consequences.[14]

For example, assume you are asking for a date of someone who does not know you very well. The simple question "Would you like to go out on a date?" may elicit different responses depending on how the other person perceives the situation. The other person may accept. A good dinner, an evening at the concert—there are "personal benefits" to saying yes. On the other hand, you may encounter "situational apprehension." The other person may feel that having dinner and going to a concert is too much involvement for a first date. You might have been more successful if you had asked the person to lunch instead. The other person may also decline because this individual perceives you as a person who would resist their own persuasion, should that become necessary. A commitment to go out to dinner and a concert is fine, but after that what happens if you will not take "no" for an answer? In the above three examples, we see how the presence of personal benefits, situational apprehension, and resistance to persuasion identifies three situations that influence compliance-gaining behavior.

Let us assume you were more sensitive to the situation. You know this is a first date, the other person has never met you, and therefore you do not feel you have adequate justification—you do not have the "right"—to ask the person to dinner and the concert. The reply to your request might be, "Gee, that sounds interesting, but I'd like to meet you first."

Perhaps you have a reputation for being an extremely "dominant" person. This makes the other person hesitant and concerned that accepting the invitation will mean an unpleasant evening. The dominance may be reflected in actions or the inability to participate in enjoyable interpersonal interaction.

Perhaps saying yes to the date will involve "relational consequences." On the positive side, the other person may like you and think that if the invitation is accepted it could result in a long-term relationship. The person may feel that accepting the invitation will make it more difficult to decline future invitations.

THINKING INTERPERSONALLY

Knowing about interpersonal communication is not enough to be an effective communicator. Being an effective communicator requires us to act interpersonally. By this we mean being constantly sensitive to the way we communicate with others. Too many people concentrate on good communication skills only when they feel it is necessary. Unfortunately, that is not good enough. Whereas it is possible to put on a good show once in a while, success demands constant attention to interpersonal skills. People who are experts in judging other people, such as corporate job recruiters, are not fooled by superficial communication skills. Too many people realize this too late and wonder why they did not land the job or the promotion.

Even though many students spend thousands of dollars getting an education, and take a wealth of courses ranging from political science to business, many fail to realize that the most important qualities they possess will be those they use in the first few minutes of a job interview. The knowledge and ability to practice good interpersonal skills *will*, not simply *can*, determine if the job is theirs or if it goes to someone who does a better job of communicating. Many qualified students who have superior grades, who participated in extra-curricular activities, and who worked hard at preparing for a career are cast aside in favor of someone who knows how to interact with another individual.

Being unskilled in interpersonal communication is the same as spending four years training for a marathon only to have your dream shattered on the day of the event. Each day you take great care with your training routine. You watch your diet. You read all of the running magazines and participate in a series of shorter races. On the day of the marathon you find yourself at the starting line. But instead of wearing a pair of running shoes, you have on a pair of wooden sandals. Terrified, you suddenly wake up to discover it has only been a bad dream. Unfortunately for many people unskilled in interpersonal communication, a job interview can be just as terrifying, and it isn't a dream. You may have prepared through four years of college with as much dedication as the marathon runner, but you may go to the starting line of your career, your job interview, with as much disadvantage as the marathon runner wearing wooden sandals. Moreover, poor interpersonal skills can also affect job performance.

Had you started thinking interpersonally long before the job interview and become a skilled communicator, you would have been prepared. Perhaps it meant taking additional courses in communication. Yet that, in itself, would not have been enough. It would have demanded putting that knowledge into practice. Take advantage now of the opportunity to improve your communication skills, and you will be at the starting line in running shoes, not sandals.

SUMMARY

Interpersonal communication, also referred to as dyadic communication, encompasses all of the components of communication we have discussed in the previous chapters. It becomes the means whereby nations negotiate treaties, reduce tensions, and carry on cultural exchanges. In the arts, direct contact with the public through everything from theater to symphonies results in a special bond between the participant and observer. In business, executives travel thousands of miles to be able to participate in direct interpersonal communication that can result in transactions of billions of dollars.

A review of the communication model we discussed earlier in the text highlighted the importance of overlapping fields of experience. In this chapter we expanded that concept to include homophily, a joining of these fields of experience to a level where two people develop a commonality of ideas, perceptions, and an awareness of each other. Heterophily represents the degree to which these commonalities are lacking.

The study of interpersonal communication involves many approaches, which, to some extent, are interrelated. We can view interpersonal communication as a series of interpersonal situations, each one self-contained with its own beginning and end. The changing nature of communication over time involves looking at communication as a developmental process. We can approach interpersonal communication as rules of behavior. More biologically oriented studies have begun to examine laws of interpersonal behavior. Approaching interpersonal communication as purposeful communication using symbols centers on the rhetorical-symbolic interactionist approach.

Interpersonal needs include inclusion, control, and affection. Inclusion is our desire to be wanted. Affection is our desire for positive emotional relationships. Control is our desire to be in control or to be controlled by others.

Related to the control need in interpersonal communication are compliance-gaining behaviors. Such behaviors can be addressed from the perspective of compliance-gaining message strategies and compliance-gaining situations. Messages can be classified as activity, power, relationship, and values. Situations can be classified as personal benefits, situation apprehension, resistance to persuasion, rights, intimacy, dominance, and relational consequence. Being an effective communicator means more than knowing about interpersonal communication; it also means thinking interpersonally.

QUESTIONS FOR REVIEW AND DISCUSSION

1. What can assist us in establishing homophily?

2. What is heterophily?

3. What is the drawback of the situational approach to analyzing interpersonal communication?

4. According to Schultz, what are the three primary needs interpersonal communication can help fulfill?

5. An oversocial individual differs in what way from an undersocial individual?

6. The most control during interpersonal communication would be exhibited by which of the following types of individuals—abdicrat, autocrat, democrat?

7. A person who is overbearing in social relationships would be considered underpersonal or overpersonal?

8. What is the quality that most determines the control need in interpersonal communication?

LEARNING EXERCISES

1. Interview a top executive of a large company. Ask what role interpersonal communication plays in his or her own exercise of responsibilities. Ask what role it plays in the jobs of people at different levels of responsibility. Ask what training programs the company has offered its employees and if these training programs included training on improving interpersonal skills. Find out if the executive received formal training in interpersonal communication either during college or after graduation. Find out what role interpersonal communication plays in the corporate philosophy or "culture" of the company.

2. Think of a close friend or family member with whom you have had a good interpersonal relationship. What things do you have in common with the person? Write these in a column labeled "homophily." In a column labeled "heterophily," list the things that are dissimilar. How do you maintain a proper balance with this person? Complete the same exercise but include someone you have worked with on a job.

ADDITIONAL READINGS

AMBRESTER, M. L., and G. H. STRAUSE   *Interpersonal Communication: A Rhetorical Perspective.* Prospect Heights, IL: Waveland Press, Inc., 1984.

BITTNER, J. R.   *Each Other: An Introduction to Interpersonal Communication.* Englewood Cliffs, NJ: Prentice-Hall, 1983.

BLOOM, L. ET. AL, EDS.   Facilitating Communication Change: *An Interpersonal Approach to Therapy and Counseling.* Rockville, MD: Aspen, 1986.

BRANDEN, N.   *If You Could Hear What I Cannot Say: Learning to Communicate With the Ones You Love.* New York: Bantam, 1983.

FOLGER, J.P. and M. S. POOLE   *Working Through Conflict.* Glenview, IL: Scott Foresman, 1984.

KENNEDY, A. K.   *Dramatic Dialogue: The Dialogue of Personal Encounter.* New York: Cambridge U. Press, 1983.

PHILLIPS, G. M., and J. T. WOOD   *Communication and Human Relationships: The Study of Interpersonal Communication.* New York: Macmillan Publishing Company, 1983.

SWETS, P.   *The Art of Talking So That People Will Listen: Getting Through to Family, Friends, & Associates.* Englewood Cliffs, NJ: Prentice-Hall, 1983.

7

DEVELOPING RELATIONSHIPS

OBJECTIVES

After completing this chapter, you should be able to

- Understand the importance of interpersonal relationships
- Distinguish between the depth and breadth of a relationship
- Deal with vulnerability
- Understand the importance of candor in a relationship
- Compare and contrast social, physical, and task attraction
- Describe the stages of coming-together and the stages of coming-apart
- Explain the communication strategies involved with ending a relationship
- List and describe the variables influencing relationship development
- Identify the orthodox, sharing, and cohabitant relationships.

Two stores are located down the street from each other. One is a small boutique that caters to high-income customers. The other is a larger department store that sells similar merchandise but prices it much lower than its smaller competitor. The boutique has a loyal following of customers who patronize the store on a regular basis. Despite its lower prices, the larger store does not enjoy customer loyalty. It can bring customers in for specials and sales, but it doesn't retain their loyalty.

INTERPERSONAL BONDING

How does the boutique survive even though it is adjacent to its price-conscious competitor? It survives because the owner and sales clerks of the boutique are trained to build relationships with customers; not just one-time, situational-based relationships, but long-term relationships bonded over time. Customers entering the boutique are treated as good friends. They are greeted by name. The owner and sales clerks also know the names of the customers' family members. Conversations center around personal matters, such as how a child is doing at college, how a spouse likes a new job, how a customer likes his or her new car. The owner and sales clerks make it a point to keep track of this information, making sure they understand much more about the customer than a simple, "may-I-help-you" inquiry. If the customer or a family member is sick or has some good fortune, the owner or sales clerk will call, write, even send flowers. They reach out and make contact with their customers the same way they would with a personal friend or family member. It pays off. The store can weather recessions, price wars by their competitors, and other business battles. Stated simply, the owner and sales clerks at the boutique know the art of building strong, bonded relationships over time.

MANAGING RELATIONSHIPS

The complex way in which business operates makes managing relationships more important now than at any other time in our history. In high-technology industry, for example, it is not enough for a computer salesperson to just place an order. The company becomes a long-term supplier of maintenance, software, and peripherals. Buyers are as concerned about the relationship with the company after the sale as they are about it before the sale.[1] The salesperson who doesn't understand this relationship and who is only concerned with the actual selling situation is at a significant, if not crippling, disadvantage. Those salespersons skilled in communication and developing lasting relationships can outdistance their competitors.

The salesperson begins a relationship with the prospective buyer as soon as the first contact is made. At that point, the salesperson must create an atmosphere that makes it possible to approach the prospective buyer again and again and again. It takes these multiple contacts—part consulting, part supplying product information, part developing a personal relationship—before the buyer feels confident to make a decision. If the salesperson is unskilled in interpersonal communication, the opportunity to go back again and again is lost. Another salesperson possessing good interpersonal skills will have the edge. In short, the other salesperson sets the standard for the relationship that will exist after the sale, when the true strength of the relationship is put to the test. What will this person be like if the equipment breaks down? Can I count on this person to be there when I need him or her? Will this person go the extra mile to service my business? Those questions must be answered in the buyer's mind *before* the sale. The relationship with the seller thus becomes as much a part of the total sale as the product itself.

Good communication is a process of relationship maintenance as much as it is a product of relationship formation. Bad communication, on the other hand, destroys business relationships just as it does romantic or personal relationships. When one party takes the other for granted, stops listening, or stops communicating, then the relationship deteriorates.

What we talk about is not necessarily new. We have already touched upon the basics of human needs and the different approaches to interpersonal communication. We now want to see how these concepts apply when we're developing relationships, from acquaintances to bonded relationships.

DEVELOPING COMMANALITY

We can examine relationships in many ways.[2] We can break them up into beginnings and endings and not worry too much about what happens in between. Our concentration in these instances would be on the communication at the "hello" and "goodbye" stages. Or we can examine relationships by relying on the developmental approach to interpersonal communication.[3] This approach follows the relationship from its beginning through its development to greater levels of intimacy. In some relationships, this development stops at friendship, an elusive quality in itself. In others, it gets much more intimate. We can, then, view relationships in terms of the different levels of involvement with each individual's rings of experience.

Relationship Depth

Imagine that the set of rings in Figure 7–1 represents one person, and that each ring represents different levels of information about that person.[4] At the center ring is our core of experience, our most private thoughts and feelings. Existing here are things we do not divulge to anyone, regardless of how intimate our relationships with them may be. Perhaps an inner ring of experience represents a favorite place where we can go to be alone and ponder the world. Although there would be nothing traumatic about telling our best friend or even our wife, husband, or lover about such a place, we cherish it as part of our individuality and simply have no desire to divulge it to anyone. Other inner rings may be even more intimate, such as sexual fantasies.

Figure 7-1 Relationships contain both breadth and depth. As the relationship develops, more intimate information may be disclosed. The most closely held thoughts are those which are the last to be disclosed. In certain situations, sharing with another person our inner thoughts can release pent-up emotion. We participate in selective disclosure, sharing information which we feel is appropriate at that stage of the relationship.

In the outside ring are pieces of information we don't mind revealing: the name of our dog, what we like to eat, or our feelings about the weather, for example. In between the outer and inner cores is a host of other information that may not be terribly confidential but which may be something we don't want to broadcast to the world. The amount of money in our checking account can be in this category. The process of divulging such information only to certain people is called *selective disclosure*.

Relationship Breadth

Not only do relationships have depth but also breadth. The two terms tend to be confusing, because they hinge on how people define breadth and depth. For our purposes, the word *depth* refers to the degree of intimacy in any given topic area. *Breadth* refers to the number of different subjects covered in a given topic area.

To best understand breadth and depth, let us consider the example of money. Suppose we reveal to a friend how much money we make a year. Because this disclosure is more important than our feelings about sports but not as important as our most private thoughts, on our concentric rings this information might appear halfway between the outer perimeter and the inner core. Sharing knowledge of our salary has a certain depth. Yet if, in addition to our salary, we also disclose how much income tax we pay, how much interest we earn on a certificate of deposit, what stocks we hold, and other similar information, then our revelation takes on considerable more breadth.

Flexibility in a Relationship

To conclude our discussion of breadth and depth, we should understand that the two dimensions: (1) can differ from one person to another, and (2) are flexible. We used the example of salary disclosure as being midway between the outer perimeter and the inner core of our rings. That may be fine for one person but not for another. Another person may consider this same information very important and would not dream of revealing it except to someone very close, and perhaps not even then. Similarly, within the same topic, some information may be more critical than other information. What types of stock you own may be less important to you than your salary.

DEALING WITH VULNERABILITY

Reflecting upon what we have discussed, we can see the potential for problems developing in any relationship. One problem comes from misreading just how far into another person's rings of experience a given topic lies.

Intrusion

Consider two people who are on their second date. Both are enjoying each other's company, but one person misjudges the level of the relationship. This individual asks: "How do you feel about having babies?" How the other person feels is not the point. What is the point is that the other person does not consider it an appropriate question to ask at this stage of the relationship. Rather, the question is an intrusion into the other person's more intimate rings

Figure 7-2
Intrusion occurs when one person misjudges the depth of the relationship and uses communication which is inappropriate. Advancing a relationship too quickly to the point where it makes the other person feel uncomfortable is an example of intrusion. The rules and norms of society, the stage of the relationship, and the psychological makeup of the other person will determine if intrusion takes place.

and, thus, an intrusion on the relationship (Fig. 7–2). As a result, that persons builds up a psychological defense, and the conversation regresses to superficial topics.

Tolerance of Vulnerability

To better understand intrusion, we can examine our *tolerance of vulnerability*.[5] Tolerance of vulnerability is defined as the amount of trust we place in another person to accept information without negatively affecting ourselves or the relationship. Researcher William Rawlins displayed this concept using four separate cells that show the relationship between needing to be open and having a high or low amount of trust in another person (Fig. 7–3).[6]

Suppose you are considering transferring to another college and need to talk this over with someone you trust. If you talk to the college admissions counselor, you feel the counselor will try to persuade you not to transfer. Moreover, the counselor might report the conversation to your faculty advisor who would take your desire to transfer personally. Finally, you decide to discuss the matter with a very close friend.

Let us look at what happened to your tolerance of vulnerability. If you plotted your concerns with the counselor in mind, you would find yourself in cell II. Discussing your desire to transfer with the counselor would require judgment, and you would be concerned about the counselor's ability to be discreet with the information. On the other hand, discussing this issue with your close friend, someone you trusted completely, would allow you to talk freely. Thus, your conversation would be plotted in cell I. What if you wanted to consider your tolerance of vulnerability in dealing with your faculty advisor? Here the situation would be similar to the counselor. You would retain the need to be open, but the decision would require judgment because of your lack of trust in the advisor's ability to be discreet.

Stop for a moment and consider where the following scenarios would be plotted on Rawlin's graph:

	High Need to be Open	Low Need to be Open
High amount of trust (in other's discretion)	I Very tolerant of Vulnerability (reveal)	III Judgment Required
Low amount of trust (in other's discretion)	II Judgment Required	IV Intolerant of Vulnerability (conceal)

Figure 7-3
Our tolerance for vulnerability and consequently the amount and content of communication that exists between two people is based on trust. (W. K. Rawlins, "Openness as Problematic in On-going Friendships: Two Conversational Dilemmas," *Communication Monographs*, 50 (March 1983), 8.)

You are guilty of stealing and are considering disclosing this information to a leader in your church.

You are guilty of stealing and are considering disclosing this information to an attorney.

You are guilty of stealing and are considering disclosing this information to a police officer.

You are guilty of stealing and are considering disclosing this information to a parent.

Vulnerability and Changing Relationships

Notice that in each of these situations the amount of trust placed in each individual and the need to disclose information varies. We should remember that our tolerance of vulnerability differs with the information and with the receiver of that information.

Yet even when we're dealing with the same individuals, our relationships with them change over time. Just as communication is a dynamic process, so are relationships. Some have more stability than others. All of them are influenced by such factors as society, peer pressure, self-concept of the individuals involved, and culture.

As an example of how changing relationships affect our tolerance of vulnerability, let's look at an example in which two people assume similar jobs at the same company at about the same time. The two individuals enter the company as equals and learn to develop a trusting friendship. They share opinions of peers and superiors. They share their insecurities. They become close associates. Gradually it becomes clear that their opportunities for promotion are limited, and only one of the individuals will be elevated to general manager of the division. The relationship now begins to change. They are still friends, but they are also beginning to perceive each other as competitors. While each retains the need to disclose information, there is an increased risk involved. Will information given to one individual create a competitive edge or show a weakness? The tolerance for vulnerability is changing in both individuals, and the trust factor begins to lower. Whereas earlier their interaction was comfortably plotted in cells I and II, it now begins to drift into cells III and IV.

CANDOR IN A RELATIONSHIP

Closely related to tolerance of vulnerability is one's *likelihood of candor,*[7] which is defined as the degree to which honesty can be displayed when disclosing information to another person. Rawlins provides us with graphic representation through which we can better understand the concept (Fig. 7–4).[8] It can be applied to communication between more intimate friends. For example, assume your best friend is consistently being turned down for jobs because of the way your friend dresses. You have a choice of telling or not telling your friend about this liability. You also have a choice, if you do decide to tell your friend, of how

	High Need to be Honest About Issue	Low Need to be Honest About Issue
High amount of restraint appropriate	I Judgment Required	III Candor Unlikely (avoid saying it)
Low amount of restraint appropriate	II Candor Likely (say it)	IV Judgment Required

Figure 7-4
Related to our tolerance for vulnerability is the likelihood of candor which is present. The need to be honest is closely tied to the amount of restraint a communicator perceives is appropriate. (W. K. Rawlins, "Openness as Problematic in Ongoing Friendships: Two Conversational Dilemmas," *Communication Monographs*, 50 (March 1983), 11.)

honest you will be. We'll assume your friend is easily hurt; thus, a high degree of restraint is appropriate. On the other hand, there is also a high need to be honest. You can't tell your friend he just needs to straighten his tie when, in fact, he looks like a total slob. Our example can be plotted in cell I.

INTERPERSONAL ATTRACTION

What brings people together to the point where vulnerability and candor are issues in a relationship? Why are some people attracted to one another? That last question has pulled at the minds of researchers for centuries. More recently, using sophisticated tools for research and analysis, we have been able to provide some answers to that question.[9] We find that we can break down interpersonal attraction into three broad categories: social attraction, physical attraction, and task attraction.

Social

Social attraction deals with the way in which another person is socially acceptable to us. Mentally, when we encounter another person, we tend to ask ourselves such questions as: Can this person be a friend of mine? Will it be difficult to meet and talk with this person? Will this person fit into my circle of friends? Can I establish a personal friendship with this person? Would I enjoy talking with this person? If the answers to those questions are mostly yes, then we may be socially attracted to the other person. Answering no to some of the questions does not mean we will automatically reject the other person. But it can be a gauge of how the relationship will develop and how intimate the friendship may become.

Physical

Physical attraction is another important force between individuals. We have already talked about how someone's appearance can cause us to make judgments about that person. Whether the person is physically attractive to us or dresses in a way that pleases us will influence the manner in which the relationship develops.

Task

Some years ago while working as a lifeguard, I had a disagreement with one of the other guards. What the disagreement was about was too insignificant to even remember. What I do remember, however, is how our supervisor made us friends again. The day after the disagreement, when there was still some tension between us, the supervisor assigned us the task of cleaning out the large swimming pool filtering system. Such a task cannot be accomplished easily by one person. Two people need to be present to monitor the flow of the water, add the chemicals, and remove the debris that invariably gets caught in the filter screens. At first, the idea that we work together was not popular with either one of us. Yet after a few minutes, we realized that if the job was going to get done, we had to cooperate with each other. Within an hour, we were laughing and joking together about all sorts of things. By the time we finished the job, we had become rather close friends. To this day, I recall the afternoon we spent cleaning the filtering system and look back upon both the task and my friend with nothing but positive memories. We had been brought together by a specific task, which today researchers would identify as *task attraction*.

INSIDE A RELATIONSHIP

Earlier we talked about examining relationships during their beginning and ending stages. We also discovered that we would miss a great deal about what happens in between if we just studied the point at which people say "hello" and "goodbye."[10] As a result, we will divide a relationship into more component parts for the following case study. Various scholars have used different terms and different divisions to explain developing and deteriorating relationships. In his book *Social Intercourse,* Mark Knapp chose to divide the "coming-together" of stages of interaction into: initiating, experimenting, intensifying, integrating, and bonding. Because all relationships do not stay together, we will also examine what Knapp calls the "coming-apart" process. These interaction stages are called: differentiating, circumscribing, stagnating, avoiding, and terminating.

We will follow the development of these communication patterns as two students named Gary and Linda meet in a college astronomy class. One day Gary arrives late for class and the only seat vacant is next to Linda. Gary moves across the row of seats, excusing himself as he maneuvers his way to the empty place. Sitting down, he looks at Linda and whispers,

> "Hi. Didn't know this class was so popular!"
> "It's a good class," Linda replies.
> "Has the prof said anything important?"
> "Not yet. She's just going over Monday's notes."
> "Good. Guess I didn't miss too much."

By now the professor is concentrating on new material, and the conversation between Gary and Linda stops as each begins to take notes.

Finally, class ends, and the two walk out of the room together. When they reach the hallway, Linda looks at Gary and says,

"Do you understand this material?"
"Some of it. I had to cut class last week when our soccer team traveled to the tournament, and I was afraid I would be lost forever."
"I know what you mean. I really don't think I was cut out to be an astronomy major."
"The exam next week has me uneasy. I need a B to make sure I get through the course."

Gary and Linda walk more slowly as they continue to talk, then introduce themselves to each other. Gradually the other students pass them. Gary, after a brief moment of silence, looks at Linda and says:

"I noticed your Boston sweatshirt. Is that your home?"
"No. I visited some friends there last month and picked it up then. Actually, I'm from St. Louis, but we haven't lived there since I was young. My family now lives in Washington, D.C. Where are you from?"
"Fort Lauderdale. I'm not sure how I ended up going to school in Maryland."

Both begin to sense the other's need to get to the next class. After walking partway across campus, they come to a point at which each goes in a different direction.

"I've enjoyed talking to you," Gary says a bit haltingly. "May I call you?"
"OK," Linda replies with a bit of hesitancy.

Over the next weekend, they date twice. At the end of the second evening together, Gary asks,

"If you aren't busy this weekend, would you like to get together and study for the exam? We could go to the mountains."
"I'd love to."

The weekend at the mountains turns out to be fun for both Gary and Linda, although not much studying is done. They spend a lot of time talking about each other's interests, friends, families, feelings, hobbies, and opinions about sex and personal commitments.

For the next few weeks, they are with each other almost constantly. When one is seen alone on campus, it isn't unusual for one of their close friends to ask where the other one is. Gary liked the Boston sweatshirt so much that Linda arranged for a friend to get one for him. Each seems to care for the other's needs. They review their astronomy notes together to make sure the other has not missed anything. Each is frequently the guest for meals at the other's apartment.

Spring comes, and both Gary and Linda manage to land jobs near Atlanta. By the end of the summer after their senior year, they are engaged.

At first, everything is fine, but then problems creep in. Each has spent enough time with the other to begin to know the other's feelings even when they aren't talking to one another. Gradually, when they do talk, their conversations deal more with things they do not share than with things they do. Finally, it becomes obvious that the relationship, which had developed in the atmosphere of a college campus, is not working in the real world. Each becomes involved in his or her own world and finds the other partner less and less interesting.

By November, the relationship has deteriorated to the point where both Linda and Gary realize it is better not to say anything to each other rather than bring up old memories that only cause hurt feelings. Any topic of discussion is on dangerous ground. Although they still see each other and remain engaged, their time together is spent avoiding conversation. Comments such as , "Let's not talk about that," "Do we have to discuss that again?", and "Let's change the subject," become more and more frequent.

During the month of November, the relationship seems to be in limbo. One topic of conversation that is definitely off limits is the relationship itself. Gary and Linda deliberately go out with other couples to avoid having to talk about their own relationship. When the evenings with the other couples end, Gary and Linda begin to feel awkward and engage more in unrelated small talk than in things of substance. Although each feels uncomfortable in the other's presence, neither wants to take the responsibility for dealing openly with the fact that nothing between them seems positive or even remotely related to what their lives had been like when they dated on campus.

Then one afternoon in mid-December, Linda tells Gary she wants to be with her parents over Christmas, and she feels he should then agree to the temporary separation. He wants them to be together up until the time Linda leaves for home, but she disagrees and tells him her work is too demanding. She simply cannot spend much time with him.

It isn't long after New Year's that Linda's phone rings. Gary wants to see her and talk. She agrees, and they make arrangements to meet for lunch at a local restaurant that had been their favorite place when they first arrived in Atlanta. When Linda shows up, Gary immediately notices she is not wearing her engagement ring.

"I really do not care to order," Linda states as she sits down, making no effort to unbutton her coat.

She then glances away from Gary and says, "It's over. You know it's over. I know it's over. There is no use torturing each other any longer with false hopes and illusions."

For the next few minutes, both utter a few putdowns, then realize they are being childish. It is over. Both understand that a relationship that had been created in the world of the college campus amid weekend parties, peer approvals, few worries, few obstacles, and few distractions has now taken on a different perspective.

CHANGES IN INTERPERSONAL INTERACTION

Linda and Gary's relationship can be analyzed in terms of Knapp's stages of interaction.[11] As we have already learned, these can be broken down into the stages that characterize the coming-together and the coming-apart processes.

The Process of Coming-Together

Initiating. *Initiating* is the beginning stage of any relationship, whether it lasts for a lifetime or for a few minutes. Initiating represents the first contact with another person. For Linda and Gary, that occurred as Gary sat down next to Linda in astronomy class and said, "Hi. Didn't know this class was so popular!" We could conclude that the initiating stage ended when the professor began to lecture. During the initiating stage, interaction is on a superficial level, with little breadth or depth.

Not all relationships begin quite as naturally as Gary's and Linda's. While aboard a friend's yacht, the late movie producer Nicholas Schenck noticed a "pert young woman" on the wharf. Unable to control an urge to push her in the water, and not even knowing if she could swim, he gave her a shove anyway. When she reacted by blinking the water out of her eyes and giving him a big smile, they hit it off, and were eventually married.

A friendly warning: Do not assume that this dramatic example is supported by research, which might suggest similar results on all occasions (or even a few).[12]

Experimenting. By the time Gary and Linda reached the hallway outside their astronomy class, their relationship had progressed to the experimenting stage. Here, the interaction took on more breadth. Their personal "rings of experience" began to merge as they exchanged the basic information about how well they were mastering the astronomy course. Although each may have been in some way attracted to the other, this wasn't the time for one of them to suggest spending the weekend in the mountains.

A required period of small talk must take place during this stage. The small talk is "safe," holding little risk for the other person. Mild disagreement has little consequences. Having a person tell you he or she doesn't like the traffic congestion in Boston is less shattering to the self-concept than turning down an invitation to spend a weekend in the mountains. Still, the small talk did perform a basic function. It lessened the risk for deeper interaction. ("We've agreed on some things; maybe Linda will agree to go to the mountains.") When the potential of a much more intimate encounter is on the mind of one of the people, the experimenting stage can be looked upon as a security blanket, something to cushion the fall if the conversation, upon approaching more personal depth, results in one person saying no.

Intensifying. For Gary and Linda, the intensifying stage occurred in the mountains. Although we were not privy to the conversations that took place there, we can assume that very personal information was exchanged. We read that they talked about each other's "interests, friends, families, feelings, hobbies, and opinions about sex and personal commitments." Their mountain talk was far more personal and informal than that which occurred in the hallway outside class. Nonverbal communication also played a larger role. For example, at times, touching may increase while verbal interaction decreases. Even though it may be perfectly natural to walk silently along a tree-lined trail holding hands, such behavior would have been awkward and unacceptable the day they first met and were walking across campus from astronomy class.

Integrating. The integrating stage appeared when Linda and Gary began to view themselves, and to be viewed by others, more as partners than as individuals. Their own commitment to interaction was seen in Linda giving Gary a Boston sweatshirt, in helping each other with astronomy, and in fixing meals for each other. Friends confirmed the integrating stage by asking where the other person was when seeing one of them alone. Gary's and Linda's interaction with each other and with people took on a dual quality. The word "I" was often replaced with "We."

Bonding. The bonding stage of Gary's and Linda's relationship occurred when they became engaged. In *Social Intercourse,* Knapp succinctly refers to the bonding stage as "a public ritual that announces to the world that commitments have been formally contracted."[13]

The Process of Coming-Apart

Differentiating. As Linda's and Gary's relationship began to come apart, they talked more about what they did *not* share rather than what they did. At this point, it was becoming obvious that something was going wrong with the relationship. Although they may not have openly engaged in heated arguments, they were in disagreement and did not see each other in the "we" stage that had preceded this stage of the relationship.

Circumscribing. The circumscribing stage evolved when Gary and Linda began to avoid interaction that referred to their relationship. When one said, "Let's not talk about that" or some other similar phrase, the circumscribing stage had arrived.

Stagnating. Gradually the couple began to feel uncomfortable with each other, and the relationship lapsed into stagnation. The month of November was undoubtedly painful for both Gary and Linda. Conversations were most likely unpleasant.

Avoiding. Avoiding the unpleasantness and pain characterized the avoiding stage. The decision to spend Christmas apart typified this. If the convenience of the holidays had not occurred, we might assume that the two would have gradually just stopped seeing each other.

Terminating.   The engagement ring no longer worn and the verbal confirmation of the ended relationship were rituals of the terminating stage of the relationship.

Not all relationships follow the exact same sequential pattern. Smaller or *micro* relationships may differ somewhat. For instance, during the time that Gary's and Linda's relationship was coming apart, there may have been short periods when things were going smoothly. During these periods, the relationship may have reverted back to the kinds of interaction that occurred when they first met.

In some relationships, interaction stages may be omitted. Bonding may never take place or termination may not exist until the death of one of the partners. Some relationships stay together and do not venture through the coming-apart stages. These "ideal" stages occur as the relationship parks or stops at a given stage at which the partners, for "better or for worse," try to meet each other's needs. Couples reach a point at which they accept each other's differences and do not feel they are sacrificing their own identities in accepting those differences as part of the relationship.

COMMUNICATION STRATEGIES IN ENDING A RELATIONSHIP

We can look even more closely at how two people remove or disengage themselves from a relationship by studying communication strategies. Researcher Michael Cody asked college freshmen, sophomores, and juniors at a New York State university to describe different strategies they employed in breaking off a relationship.[14] These were categorized and grouped together to determine why different people chose different strategies.[15] Cody grouped the strategies the students described into five subheadings: *behavioral de-escalation,* which involves actually removing oneself from the presence of the other person; *negative identity management,* which involves a lack of sensitivity to the other person's feelings; *justification,* which involves justifying the breakup to the other person; *de-escalation,* which involves gradually slowing down (cooling off the relationship over time); and *positive tone,* which involves an expressed concern for the feelings of the other person. Representative examples of each of these disengagement strategies described by the students include the following:

Behavioral De-Escalation

I didn't say anything to the partner; I avoided contact with him/her as much as possible.

Without explaining my intentions to break off the relationship, I just never called the person again and never returned any of his/her calls.

I never verbally said anything to the partner, but I discouraged our seeing each other again.

Negative Identity Management

> I told him/her that I was going to date other people and that I thought he/she should date others also.
>
> I told him/her life was too short and that we should date other people in order to enjoy life.
>
> I told him/her that I thought we should date around and left it at that.
>
> I told him/her that it was the best thing for both of us, that we need more time to date others, and that I wanted to be sure to find the right person.
>
> I told him/her that I wanted to be happy and that we should date other people.
>
> I said that I thought we might ruin our relationship all together if we didn't start dating around a little because I was not happy.

Justification

> I fully explained why I felt dissatisfied with the relationship, that it hasn't been growing, and that I believe we will both be happier if we didn't date anymore.
>
> I said that a good relationship meets the needs of both people and that ours wasn't meeting my needs. I said that I didn't want to change him/her and I would have to if he/she were going to meet my needs. So I don't think we should see each other anymore.
>
> I fully explained how I felt and that I wanted to break things off. I explained that a relationship was not good unless it makes both people happy, and that I wasn't happy and that I didn't want to date anymore.
>
> I said that I was really changing inside, and I didn't quite feel good about our relationship anymore. I said that we'd better stop seeing each other.
>
> I honestly conveyed my wishes not to date anymore.

De-Escalation

> I said that we are very close and that we shouldn't be anything but honest and open. If one is not happy, then the other wouldn't be happy either. I think the best thing for us is to let things cool off for awhile and see if we want to continue.
>
> I told him/her that I need to be honest with him/her and suggested that we break it off for awhile and see what happens.
>
> I told him/her that while I was happy most of the time, I sometimes felt that I can't do all the things I wanted to. I then said that we should call it quits for now, and if we still wanted to get back together, we will.

Positive Tone

> I told him/her that I was very, very sorry about breaking off the relationship.
>
> I told him/her that I regretted very much having to break off the relationship.
>
> I told him/her that I was very scared, too, and didn't want to hurt his/her feelings.[16]

Degree of Benefit

Why do some people choose one set of strategies over another? In examining how students felt about the relationship. Cody was able to draw some conclusions about this question.[17] The research suggested that for people who felt they had not benefited a great deal by the relationship (referred to as "under-benefited" individuals), the negative identity management and justification strategies were most suitable. For those individuals who felt highly benefited by the relationship or who felt they benefited more than the other party in the relationship (referred to as "overbenefited" individuals), the positive-tone strategy of disengagement was more appropriate. People who were angry as they disengaged from the relationship were more likely to employ a behavioral de-escalation strategy and less likely to employ a de-escalation strategy.

Placing Blame

Another way to examine the strategies chosen to disengage from a relationship is to examine why the relationship faltered. The students used as subjects in Cody's study cited a number of causes why their relationships failed. These were grouped into three broad categories: *faults,* which involved the other partner having certain faults that prevented the relationship from continuing; *no compromise,* where the other person was unwilling to compromise to prevent the relationship from ending; and *constrained,* where the party felt constrained by the other person.[18] Examples of each of these three categories are as follows:

Faults

> I realize that he/she had too many faults (personality and otherwise).
> The partner behaved in ways that embarrassed me.
> Generally, the partner's behaviors and/or personality were more to blame for the breakup than anything else.

No Compromise

> I realized she/he was unwilling to make enough contributions to the relationship.
> I felt that he/she no longer behaved toward me as romantically as she/he once did.
> I felt that he/she took me for granted.
> I felt that he/she wasn't willing to compromise for the good of the relationship.

Constrained

> I simply felt the relationship was beginning to constrain me, and I felt a lack of freedom.
> Although I still cared for the partner, I wanted to start dating other people.
> While this relationship was a good one, I started to get bored with it.
> The partner made too many contributions, and I started to feel suffocated.[19]

The cause perceived responsible for the breakup of the relationship would help determine which of the disengagement strategies would be chosen to deal with the partner.[20] For example, if one partner felt constrained by the relationship, this partner would be more likely to select positive-tone, justification, negative identity management, and de-escalation strategies. If one partner felt the other partner was unwilling to compromise, then that partner was more likely to avoid positive-tone strategies. If one partner thought the other partner's faults caused the breakup, then the partner was more likely to select such strategies as justification and behavioral de-escalation.

The research also suggested that the level of intimacy in a relationship will determine which strategies are used.[21] For example, relationships in which a high level of intimacy was present caused the person to select a justification strategy when disengaging from the relationship.

We still have a great deal to learn about why relationships break up, just as we have a great deal to learn about what makes a relationship grow positively and nurture into long-lasting bonds. Additional problems in researching interpersonal relationships are discussed later in this chapter.

VARIABLES INFLUENCING RELATIONSHIP DEVELOPMENT

A number of variables influence the way relationships develop. Nonverbal communication is one example.

Nonverbal Communication

Stop and consider the relationships in which you may have been involved. Regardless of whether or not such relationships reached sexual intimacy, think about the sequence of nonverbal contact you had with the other person. Now consider what could have happened or actually did happen if, based on societal or cultural norms, some of the sequences were violated. What effect did (or could) it have on your relationship with the other person? If such violations did occur, did they set back the relationship? In what ways did the relationship regain lost ground (or did it ever)?

Language Variables

If two people use language in different ways to convey their thoughts, the relationship stands a greater chance of ending. For example, if you like to speak in concrete terms whereas your date tends to speak in the abstract, you may become impatient and irritated with that person. Similarly, a discussion using intense language on the first date may not be comfortable for you to listen to or take part in.[22]

Topics of Conversation

Researchers Fern Johnson and Elizabeth Aries asked parents of students at the University of Massachusetts about their interactions with their friends. Results of the research suggested that close adult female friends conversed "more often than do close male friends about personal topics or personal problems"[23] Family problems, doubts and fears, and intimate relationships were some of the topics discussed. Moreover, women reported more in-depth conversations about such topics than did men. Male friends exceeded female friends in the frequency of interaction and in the depth of the interaction, but only for the topic of sports.

What causes the differences? The researchers suggested that females may find themselves talking alone with friends, whereas males spend more time in groups in which more personal topics of conversation may be less appropriate.

When you converse with friends, what do you talk about? Does the topic vary depending on how long you've known the other person? Compare your observations with someone of the opposite sex. See what he or she talks about to same-sex friends and if the topic varies depending on how long or how well they know each other. Do you feel there may be regional differences that could account for the topics of conversations among same-sex friends? Compare people you know from different parts of the country. Are there differences between Southerners and New Englanders? Westerners? Midwesterners?

Trust

Few factors can have more influence on a relationship than trust.[24] Trust is critical for two reasons. First, trust is a necessary ingredient for self-disclosure. If two people are going to create homophily and sharing—the type of deep sharing necessary for intimate communication—self-disclosure must take place. For self-disclosure to take place, positive reinforcement is necessary. If, in telling someone about yourself, you disclose personal qualities that you hold important to your self-concept, you do not expect those disclosures to be met with negative criticism and condemnation. You trust the other person not to critize or condemn.

Second, trust is important to keep the relationship intact and, in developing stages, to keep it progressing. A violation of trust, such as relating intimate information about someone to a third person, responding negatively to self-disclosure, or violating a "contract" of the relationship, may cause the relationship to falter. Let us look at the aspects of self-disclosure and relationship contracts in more detail.

Self-Disclosure

Self-disclosure is necessary to develop commonality and for effective communication to take place.[25] The particular type of self-disclosure plays a part in advancing or hindering a relationship. For example, research suggests that intimate information disclosed too early in a relationship will be perceived as inappropriate and will thus hinder the relationship. Deviant disclosure will be even less liked than normal but intimate information. Studies further suggest that as one person discloses more intimate information at the appropriate stage of a relationship, the other person will follow. Even the way we self-disclose information is important. You can shout something about yourself and get an entirely different reaction than if you whisper it. Although a few people feel that buying space on billboards and hiring skywriters is a great way to say "I love you," the best route may be to mention it quietly in intimate conversation.

Violating Contracts of a Relationship

Engagement and marrige—we tend to think of such things as forms of contracts. Unwritten contracts also exist between people. Communication plays a part in such contracts, because when they are violated, serious breakdowns in communication occur.[26] Let's return to our example of Gary and Linda. Although they dissolved their engagement, each agreed not to discuss their relationship with friends or, perhaps more importantly, with other lovers or mates. This contract is not in writing and may not even be expressed verbally. It is an unwritten contract both will abide by, so that despite their broken engagement, they remain friends.

Suppose that at a cocktail party, one of the two learns from a complete stranger the story of the broken engagement and ruined love affair. The contract has been violated and broken. The result is that whereas Gary and Linda managed to piece back their relationship to the point that they were no longer avoiding each other, they now cease to remain friends.

Cultural Differences

In our discussion of nonverbal communication we talked about touching behavior in different cultures. We learned of one research study that found that American couples observed in coffee shops touched each other an average of only two times per hour. The same researcher found that in Puerto Rico, the average was 180 times per hour.

Ask yourself what difficulties a relationship might encounter if two people from different cultures were attracted to each other, one from a high-touch culture and the other from a low-touch culture. Would the relationship progress faster or more slowly? By whose standards?

Differences in Japanese and American cultures offer additional perspectives on the way relationships are formed. In Japan, young adults do not form the close friendships between the opposite sex that they do in America. Such friendships occur only after an engagement.[27] This cultural factor thus has an effect on the type of conversations that occur over such topics as love and marriage. More intimate discussions that might seem appropriate to American couples in pre-engagement situations are not appropriate among some Japanese couples. Moreover, in Japan an individual's background, education, and other biographical factors play a more important role in relationships, especially among older Japanese, than they do in America. Whereas Americans might look upon such information as superficial, the Japanese give it a rather high priority and include questions of a biographical nature in early interaction.[28]

In Asia, for example, a large part of life is spent "honoring, overtly showing respect to another person."[29] Those not skilled or sensitive to this may come across as rude, overbearing, and boisterous. Americans sometimes make the mistake of trying to be "one of the gang," even though an Asian host has deliberately deferred to the American associate as a higher-ranking individual. American business executives shunning such honoring can find themselves looked upon unfavorably for rejecting the respectful overture. Americans also differ from Asian people in the way they express their emotions. Americans tend to show emotion and anger in an outward fashion, whereas people from Asian cultures tend to stress being polite. Canadians, South Africans, and Australians also come across as being too overpowering to many Asians. Loud voices, unreserved behavior in public places, and offhanded remarks are not looked upon favorably by most Asians. Yet in certain casual social settings in Western cultures, such behavior would be considered acceptable.

As business and industry become more international in scope, the ability to understand cultural differences in the way relationships are built and nurtured will become increasingly important. If the management of two companies operating across national boundaries cannot build long-lasting relationships, then the succession of sales through which a solid financial base is formed will not succeed.

Sex

Research suggests that females approach relationships somewhat differently from males. In general, females tend to be more personal in their interactions and engage in more talk for the sake of talk.[30] As women enter business and the professions in greater numbers, these differences may be reduced. We could speculate that as more women become associated with men as equal partners in the work place, men will begin to see the importance of placing value on interpersonal relationships. We have already seen at the beginning of this chapter how changes in the way business and industry operate demand the ability to create relationship bonds. Women have traditionally been more skilled at this bonding process than men. Many men have operated in the macho-based approach to management, and the strong competitive nature of business can create an adversary-oriented individual instead of a cooperatively oriented one.

TYPES OF RELATIONSHIPS

Thus far we have discussed the importance of building relationships, how people develop commonality, how they deal with vulnerability and candor, interpersonal attraction, how relationships come together and come apart, and what can influence the development of relationships. Merging all of those elements together, we will now turn our attention to three general types of relationships.[31] As you read about them try to classify those relationships with which you may be familiar into these categories.

Orthodox Relationships

An orthodox relationship is a traditional relationship. Each partner functions in the "we" state and has little individuality outside of the relationship. If we were monitoring the interaction between partners in an orthodox relationship, we might find their identities to be tightly linked to the relationship itself, as opposed to being linked to their own uniqueness as individuals. We might also assume that as an orthodox relationship developed, interpersonal communication was quite successful at the integrating stage when the two people merged into one. To others, such a couple might be known as "the Johnsons" rather than as Sam Johnson and Lisa Johnson. Least satisfactory to this type of relationship would be the avoiding stage, because in the face of conflict, orthodox couples would rather meet together to talk things out rather than avoid each other.

In an orthodox relationship, each individual is dependent on the other, and each does not hesitate to express feelings and wishes to the other person. Self-disclosure is the norm for this relationship. Few things are kept hidden from the other partner, and each person builds upon the strength of the other. Both partners in an orthodox relationship do not hesitate to express affection for the other person, and orthodox couples are more likely to express satisfaction with the relationship itself. Because of this high degree of emotional psychological linkage, both partners find it easy to agree on issues that directly affect their relationship. More traditional sex roles are common in such a relationship, such as the woman taking care of the children while the man works.

Sharing Relationships

In a sharing relationship, each partner retains a great deal of autonomy in his or her own life. The autonomy itself can be one of the things the couple has "in common." Couples whose partners pursue their own careers fall into this category. Other qualities of the sharing relationship include a couple's outspokenness, which is directly related to the individuals' autonomy. In many ways, this outspokenness will carry over into social situations as well, and the partners may openly disagree with each other. On the other hand, orthodox couples may be more reserved in social situations, reflecting their "public" commitment to their relationship and support for each other. Sharing couples have more difficulty expressing affection than do orthodox couples. Furthermore, because they do not hesitate to disagree on matters in which each is ego-involved, each tends to be less satisfied with the other person's ability to communicate interpersonally.

In traditional bonding terms, such as engagements or marriage, it may seem that sharing relationships are off to a rough start. This may not be the case. Because of each partner's strong self-concept, which is strong enough to allow autonomy to exist in the relationship, enough individual self-worth is present to sustain each other's independence. Each might contribute substantially to the family income and might share equal housework chores. They also can be tolerant of a role reversal in which the man stays at home to take care of the house while the woman works.

Cohabitant Relationships

Couples who exist in what we commonly call a "separate world" characterize a cohabitant relationship. Both in verbal and nonverbal communication, interaction plays a small role in their relationship. Although they may sleep in the same room, much of their time is spent in different parts of the living quarters, outside of each other's presence. Although they may have little in common, they avoid conflict by staying out of each other's way. Although they stay together, there is little commitment by both partners to the relationship itself. Because of the separateness, they are mostly undemonstrative to the other partner. Affection, empathy, and understanding may be perceived as absent in the relationship.

Think about what can happen and what kinds of communication patterns can result when someone who is basically a sharing person is involved in a relationship with someone who is a cohabitant or an orthodox. How can a knowledge of interpersonal communication help each individual adapt to the other person?

SOCIETAL VALUES AND RELATIONSHIP TYPES

For purposes of the study, we have separated relationships into three different types. Our changing society, however, makes it difficult to classify any relationship as exclusively adhering to any one given type. What effect do such things as no-fault divorce, living together without marriage, and less traditional relationships have on life styles and the different stages of interaction in relationships?

If we viewed a cohabiting relationship, for example, some might feel it is foolish to keep the marriage together. Others, who deeply believe in traditional values built upon family or religious experiences, may feel differently.[32] The point is that in some segments of our society, both choices are being made more freely than in the past. Economic conditions may cause a cohabiting relationship to exist and even be practical. The bonding stage never occurs, but two people, for economic necessity, decide to become roommates and share the cost of rent and food.

A couple considered as cohabitants on one issue may be considered as orthodox on another. For example, both partners may be autonomous in their relationships, pursue different careers, and need little support from the other person. On the other hand, they may be intimately involved sexually, not share that intimacy with anyone else, and, in their verbal and physical interaction with each other, be very supportive and able to participate in a great deal of shared affection.

Anyone who has been romantically and intimately involved with another person realizes just how close to one's inner core the relationship penetrates. Yet the very fact that the relationship does penetrate close to the inner core may make it difficult to relate the "total" experience to someone else, such as a researcher.

Adapting what we know about communication patterns between individuals is a difficult, somewhat elusive, process. But it is not insurmountable, and you can participate in the experience. By taking a serious approach to learning about the good qualities of human communication and by adapting those qualities to your own relationships, you will be in a much better position to have meaningful, satisfying experiences, whether they be intimate or casual. You may not avoid the experience of breaking up or feeling the pain of a deteriorating relationship, but you will be able to understand it. Understanding in itself is a very valuable commodity.

SUMMARY

The ability to build relationships with other people is critical for both our personal and professional success. Communication skills are the keys to this success. To learn more about building successful relationships, we studied how people develop commonality. Each person has different rings of experience that merge during a relationship. Depth refers to the penetration into our personal lives that we disclose and share with others. How wide the range of topics is that we disclose or share refers to the breadth of our relationships. Knowing how wide a variety of topics can be and knowing the depth of our conversations and interactions with others permits us to be sensitive to the many communication breakdowns that can occur the deeper and more involved a relationship becomes.

Understanding that we are vulnerable when we disclose information about ourselves also increases our sensitivity to good communication. How honest we can be with another person and how much trust we place in that individual will be reflected in the candor of our conversation. As relationships change, as topics of conversation and communication change, so does our tolerance of vulnerability and the likelihood we will express candor in communicating with the other partner.

We applied Knapp's stages of interaction—initiating, experimenting, intensifying, integrating, bonding, differentiating, circumscribing, stagnating, avoiding, and terminating—to a hypothetical relationship between Gary and Linda. We then took a more detailed look at the coming-apart process of a relationship by studying disengagement strategies. Those included behavioral de-escalation, negative identity management, justification, de-escalation, and positive tone. To some degree, we can predict which disengagement strategies a person will choose by examining whether the relationship began to deteriorate from the faults of one of the partners, their refusal to compromise, or the feeling of one partner of being constrained in the relationship.

We examined such communication variables in relationships as the role of nonverbal communication, language, topics of conversation, trust, self-disclosure, and violating the contracts of a relationship. We also studied three different types of relationships. We learned about orthodox relationships, in which both people are closely tied to the relationship itself; sharing relationships, in which both individuals have an autonomy and are less attached to the relationship than in orthodox couples; and cohabitant relationships, in which people exist together but have little in common, have little interaction, and express little affection for one another. Because of changes in our society, it is more difficult to categorize any given relationship. Contributing to this difficulty are such factors as the relative ease with which some people make and dissolve bonds, economic necessity, and the different levels and varieties of involvement.

QUESTIONS FOR REVIEW AND DISCUSSION

1. What is the difference between a relationship in breadth and depth?

2. A relationship in which both partners' identities are closely linked to the relationship, with little individuality, is what type of relationship?

3. How does candor affect a relationship?

4. What role does trust play in developing relationships?

5. How is trust related to self-disclosure?

6. Where might the following topics fall within your circles of experience? (1) the classes you are taking, (2) the grades you received last semester, (3) how much money your parents give you a month, (4) your career ambitions

7. What are the differences in "sharing" and "cohabitant" relationships?

8. What are communication strategies for ending a relationship?

LEARNING EXERCISES

1. Re-create a log of the stages encountered in a relationship with another person. What identified each stage? How did transitions between stages take place?

2. Think of places where you have done business. Did you patronize the business because of the relationship you had with someone who worked there or was it because of the product or service?

ADDITIONAL READINGS

ALBERONI, F. *Falling in Love.* New York: Random House, 1983.

ALTMAN, I., and D. TAYLOR *Social Penetration: The Development of Interpersonal Relationships.* New York: Holt, Rinehart & Winston, 1973.

AMODEO, J. and C. AMODEO *Being Intimate: A Guide to Successful Relationships.* New York: Metheun, 1986.

COOPER, C. L. *Improving Interpersonal Relationships.* Englewood Cliffs, NJ: Prentice Hall, Inc., 1982.

EDWARDS, M., and E. HOOVER *The Challenge of Being Single.* Los Angeles: J. P. Tarcher, Inc., 1974.

EPSTEIN, J. *Divorced in America.* New York: Dutton, 1974.

GATHORNE-HARDY, J. *Marriage, Love, Sex, Divorce.* New York: Summit Books, 1981.

JEWETT, C. L. *Helping Children Cope with Separation and Loss.* Harvard, MA: The Harvard Common Press, 1982.

KRANTZLER, M. *Creative Marriage.* New York: McGraw-Hill Book Company, 1981.

LIEBOWITZ, M. R. *The Chemistry of Love.* Boston: Little, Brown and Company, 1983.

VILLARD, K. L., and L. J. WHIPPLE *Beginnings in Relational Communication.* New York: John Wiley, 1976.

8

SMALL-GROUP COMMUNICATION

OBJECTIVES

After completing this chapter, you should be able to

- Distinguish the qualities of small groups
- Explain how factors such as size, bonding, interaction, member roles, member rewards, and time affect interaction
- Distinguish among policy groups, problem-solving groups, task-oriented groups, brainstorming groups, social groups, and therapeutic groups
- Understand how to become a responsible participant in group discussions
- Understand the role of power and status in small groups
- Know how member roles play a part in small-group interaction
- Be sensitive to the way trust, personalities, and group size affect interaction
- Learn the skills necessary to lead a group discussion
- Distinguish among different leadership styles
- Understand the role of an agenda.

At the edge of the swirling river that ate its way through the jagged mountains, we started our river raft trip. All of us were strangers. No one really thought about how we were communicating with each other. No one thought about such things as the roles of the different members of our party, the role of the guide, or the role of the outfitters. But by the time we had roared through our first rapids, all of us had become participants in the process of small-group communication. We possessed many of the same qualities as the groups that solve problems in business and industry, tackle tasks of planning strategy for the next big game of the sports season, or diagnose a disease and discuss the cure. We possessed a leader in Dave, our guide. We also possessed other leaders, depending on the nature of the discussion. Sometimes the group members interacted in a calm and relaxed manner. Other times the foam and the surging rapids would add excitement and even a touch of fear.

As you discovered at the beginning of this text, those of us on the river trip became good communicators by the time the day ended. Through the natural evolutionary give-and-take of personalities, problems, tasks, and other forces that controlled our communication, we learned to adapt to each other the same way members of other groups must adapt to each other. In our own case, the stakes of adapting were not too high. There were no corporate mergers to discuss, no diseases to cure. In other settings, however, the risks could have been much greater. Our ability to engage in purposeful and productive small-group communication could have determined whether we would be accepted as part of a new research team, be asked to join a group of high-level executives, or be selected to lead a group of astronauts on a space mission. This chapter on small-group communication is designed to sensitize us to some of the forces that make groups successful components of the decision-making process.

QUALITIES OF SMALL GROUPS

Small groups have qualities that distinguish their communication patterns from dyadic, one-to-one communication. Let's look at some of those qualities.

Size

One-to-one communication involves two people. Group communication requires at least three or more people. These additional people translate into more relationships and "channels" for human communication.[1] As the number of group members increase, the factors affecting communication increase. For example, a group with 10 people has 45 possible relationships; a group of 20 people has 190. Breaking down the relationships still further into nonverbal and verbal communication, the number of possible relationships among members of the group quickly reaches into the thousands.

Imagine you are responsible for leading a group discussion and solving an important problem at your school or workplace. If the group consists of yourself and two other people, the interaction and relationships are probably manageable. But if five people participate your job becomes more difficult.

Much more skill is necessary to lead the group through the problem-solving process. Many more variables come into play.

Bonding

The word *bonding* takes on many different meanings in communication. In long-term relationships between lovers, it involves a merging of personal feelings and an agreement to be sensitive to the "us" qualities of the relationships in addition to the "I" qualities.

In small-group communication, bonding refers to the commonalities that can cause a small group to evolve into a cohesive body of people interacting with one another.

Leadership bonding.   Leadership bonding occurs when the leader of the group is looked upon as an individual with integrity and respect. Effective leaders are quickly recognized. This does not mean that a leader cannot develop these traits of loyalty as the group develops.

Procedural bonding.   Procedural bonding happens when the rules of the organization dictate how the group will be formed. The procedures of Congress and its subcommittees, for example, are clearly established as matters of law. The bonds that hold these subcommittees together are created out of procedural necessity. Sometimes these official groups are so loyal to tradition that no one questions why or how they are bonded.

Task bonding.   Task bonds are created by the specific task the group is designed to accomplish. The astronauts on a space shuttle are part of a group that has the specific task of flying the shuttle and conducting experiments in space. A group of engineering supervisors overseeing the construction of a new bridge is bonded together by the need to see the bridge completed on schedule. A group of doctors meeting together to discuss a major operation is bonded by the need to see that the patient receives the best care possible.

Social bonding.   Social bonding occurs when people desire to be with other people in the group. These social groups may meet formally at specific times, but the seriousness of purpose is much less than in formal task-oriented groups. Social groups are present in every area of life. Business executives who are part of a corporate planning department may also have a social bond that operates outside of the office. These social bonds are not automatically set aside when a formal task arises.

Interaction

Small groups participate in frequent face-to-face interaction. Clubs, trade organizations, academic and government committees, or groups charged to meet until a job is accomplished or a goal is met exemplify this characteristic. We will thus distinguish small groups by the frequency of those interactions.

These many interactions permit us to view small groups as a *developing* process of communication. For instance, as the members become better acquainted and realize what to expect, the group begins to change to meet the demands of these more developed relationships.

Member Roles

Every person participating in small-group communication has a particular function. Members of the group, for example, are responsible for providing information to the group. A leader is responsible for guiding the group's progress and assuring that every participant's view is heard. A group of building inspectors might be called together to discuss licensing procedures. One inspector may work in the western part of the state, another may work in the mountains, and still another may work in the city. Each provides information about the opinions and practices of inspectors in his or her particular area.

Member Rewards

Each member of the group can receive some form of reward for participating. We can divide this reward structure into two categories: direct and indirect. For example, a group of friends meet at work to help plan a company picnic. Meetings are held in which the location, date, time, food selection, and activities are planned. The result is a well-attended picnic, and many new friendships are formed among the members of the group who planned the event. The direct reward is the successful picnic, for the group accomplished what it set out to accomplish. Indirect rewards are the friendships that were formed. To some, the indirect rewards are more important and satisfying than the successful picnic. A number of concepts we have already discussed in this text come into play in the reward system. Because the group members were working on a common project we can assume that task attraction was present. Inclusion played a part because the group activity contributed to a feeling of belonging. The successful picnic and newly formed friendships contributed to the group members' self-concept.

Meeting Over Time

Small groups usually meet over a specified time period especially in more formal situations. This time factor affects how group members interact with each other. A crisis with little time to plan a solution to a serious problem will result in a tense, hurried, even combative style. Ample time for planning will result in interaction that is more thoughtful, more deliberative. In group discussion, interactions with others become the building blocks upon which future meetings and future interactions are constructed. In essence, when we interact with someone in a group discussion, what we say will affect our relationship with that person and the group the next time the discussion group meets.

Small groups can be classified into policy groups, problem-solving groups, task-oriented groups, brainstorming groups, social groups, therapy groups, and T-groups. To some extent, they overlap one another. As we discuss each type, think of what you have already learned about human communication and consider what freedoms or restrictions would be inherent in each group.

POLICY GROUPS

Implementing Policy

A student committee that sets up new visitation policies for a living unit is actually implementing policy. Implementing policy is a frequent function of small groups, especially in organizations or government agencies. Such agencies as the Federal Trade Commission, Small Business Administration, and the Federal Communications Commission regularly meet as policy-implementing bodies. School administrators and teachers meet to establish policies for student athletic-eligibility requirements.

Recommending Policy

Groups also recommend policy. A corporation's personnel committee may meet to discuss who should be promoted and then recommend the names of those people to the managers responsible for the promotions. A committee of nurses might meet to discuss training requirements and recommend that those requirements be implemented by the state nursing board. The committees of legislative bodies, as opposed to legislative agencies, meet to discuss and recommend policy to larger groups.

PROBLEM-SOLVING GROUPS

Problem-solving groups seek solutions to problems. They may either implement those solutions or recommend that other bodies implement them. Because something may be wrong or need changing when the group meets, problem-solving groups often exist in somewhat restrictive atmospheres. Thus, they often do not know beforehand what direction they will take. The purpose of the group is to find a solution, and the collective efforts of the group are designed around that goal. All of these characteristics determine the group's interaction.

TASK-ORIENTED GROUPS

A task-oriented group sets out to accomplish a specific goal. In many ways the task-oriented group is related to the problem-solving group because both have a task to accomplish. Yet the task group can exist without being a problem-solving group. An example of a task-oriented group might be a city council considering bids on a construction of a new library. Another example would be a group of students meeting to set the theme and plan the entertainment for a school dance. No specific problem needs to be solved, but the group does have a goal.[2]

BRAINSTORMING GROUPS

Brainstorming is a particular type of communication, and when it is used as a strategy in group interaction, the group is referred to as a *brainstorming group.* Brainstorming allows one of the freest atmospheres of discussion to take place. The primary objective is to get as many ideas into the discussion as possible so that the "right" idea or the "best" solution will not inadvertently be missed because of interactive restrictions.

As a process, brainstorming can be employed in many different ways. In a problem-solving discussion, a certain amount of time can be set aside to give everyone a chance to offer solutions. With the emphasis on quantity rather than quality, the discussion leader can encourage even the more hesitant members of the group to offer solutions. Brainstorming can also be effective in a task-oriented agenda when the discussion centers around different ways of achieving a goal.

The key to effective brainstorming is for every member of the group to understand that criticism of any other person's ideas or comments is inappropriate during a brainstorming session. Such criticism can stifle discussion. Remember, the goal of a brainstorming session is to stimulate, not inhibit, interaction. Regardless of how unusual or out of place some suggestions may be, they are perfectly legitimate in an open, unrestrictive, brainstorming atmosphere. Because ideas may be presented in rapid succession, it is sometimes best to have someone record or write down each person's comments.[3]

SOCIAL GROUPS

Although much of our discussion has been of small groups in corporate and other organizational settings, small groups function in other situations for a variety of purposes. Many social groups meet by chance—students dropping by after dinner, bridge players spontaneously arranging a game of bridge. Cocktail parties, receptions, luncheons, and similar settings are where social groups congregate. Such groups do not have fixed agendas, and the makeup of the groups may change from one minute to the next.

THERAPEUTIC GROUPS

Still other groups operate outside the traditional organizational or formal setting. In counseling and psychiatric sessions, therapeutic groups bring people together to enhance their abilities to deal with others and with life in general. Participants in such groups range from highly psychotic individuals involved in therapy to those people who simply want to enhance their awareness of others by participating in "encounter groups." Such encounter groups have also been called T-groups or training groups, confrontation groups, and sensitivity groups.[4]

T-groups and therapy groups are primarily intensive communicative experiences. Both groups concentrate on emotional arousal.[5] "Members are encouraged and expected to drop their facades and inhibitions and reveal as honestly as possible their feelings about one another. Such openness typically leads to emotionally arousing confrontation and even interpersonal conflict."[6]

Still another similarity involves what can be called the "here-and-now" orientation of such groups. Each participant taking responsibility for what is being said and what is happening at that moment can become the main task of the T-group.[7] Feedback is also in reference to what is being said at the moment, without any need for an external referent, such as a particular problem to be solved by the group as a whole. The agenda, to a certain extent, is set as the group moves through its discussion.

A basic difference between T-groups and therapy groups is in the characteristics of the participants in each group. T-group members generally consist of well-functioning individuals who are seeking greater competence on their abilities to experience life. Therapy groups, on the other hand, are often made up of individuals who want relief from problems with which they cannot cope. Even everyday stress may be too much to handle, and they seek relief through group counseling.[8]

Another difference lies in the task each group faces. Whereas T-groups try to resolve conflict within the individual, therapy groups permit that conflict to become a tool by which the individual can search out and resolve interpersonal dilemmas and stress.[9] Acceptable discussion content for therapy groups includes personal thoughts of which members may be deeply ashamed, such as hostility toward loved ones, lust, and a lack of self-confidence.[10]

BECOMING A SKILLED PARTICIPANT IN GROUP DISCUSSION

We have been discussing the characteristics and types of small groups in order to distinguish small-group communication from interpersonal communication. We now shift our emphasis to understanding the process of small-group interaction and the skills necessary to be a responsible participant in small-group discussions. Although we spend more time talking to other people on a one-to-one basis, the important decision-making aspects of life, from a family discussing personal matters to a congressional committee deliberating tax appropriations, group discussion impacts on all our lives.

Becoming Alert to Others' Interactions

Good group discussion is dependent on a succession of comments from different people. Each comment builds upon other comments as the discussion moves forward. The first step in becoming a skilled participant is to learn to recognize and categorize different *statements* within the group.[11] By doing so we will become both better listeners and better participants. The statements can be grouped into: (1) procedural statements, (2) solution statements, (3) unity statements, (4) personal-involvement statements, and (5) superficial statements.

Procedural statements are easy to recognize and deal with the rules by which the discussion will operate. For example, a group of nurses meets to discuss a staffing problem caused by budget cuts. Nurses from different floors of the hospital attend. The nursing supervisor is chairing the meeting and begins by saying:

> "I'd like Sandra Smith from the budget office to speak first and then the floor representatives can comment. After that we'll open up the discussion to anyone who wants to offer additional insights and comments."

Here the supervisor is establishing the procedural rules for discussion. Procedural rules are important but not as important as the actual decision making. Careful attention must be given to procedural statements, for not following the rules can result in embarrassing mistakes that lessen a participant's credibility. If one nurse were to respond to another nurse's statement before all had the opportunity to react to Sandra Smith, then the person who interrupted is seen as being a poor listener. That person's credibility can be affected later when he or she has something more important to say.

Solution statements either offer a solution or refute a solution. For example, one nurse might say:

> "I think we should ask the volunteer corps to help with some of the duties in the less-critical-care areas."

This statement offers a solution to the budget-staffing problem. Someone must now respond to the statement. Another nurse disagrees with the solution:

> "That's an interesting idea, but the latest figures on the volunteer corps show a decline in interest. Until we institute some new recruiting, perhaps we should consider a different solution."

The solution was disrupted and a reason backed up by evidence (a decline in interest in the volunteer corps) was offered why the solution was unworkable. Notice that the statement softened the rejection by using the phrase "That's an interesting idea. . . ." Had the nurse responded to the solution by saying, "That idea is ridiculous," or responded with a harsh tone of voice, or interrupted the other person, the result would have been negative, not positive.

Remember, when a person offers a solution to a problem, he or she is setting out one's own judgments and reasoning for evaluation by the rest of the group. That person's ideas are important to the group's success. If the person is made to feel ill at ease, if the person's solution is openly ridiculed, or if the reply is too quick and becomes an interruption, then the person who presented the idea may withdraw and not offer additional ideas or perspectives. That is dangerous; it cuts down on the total brain power of the group to solve its problem. It may also offend other members of the group who feel one member was treated too harshly. The person making the unpleasant response may be isolated by the other members of the group and find their own input becoming limited. It is not necessary to preface every remark, but a responsible group avoids offending another member of the group.

Unity statements support a solution or an idea advanced by another member of the group. Unity statements are accepted positively by the group but only when they are made with sincerity. Agreeing with a bad idea is counterproductive.

One nurse who thinks using the volunteer corps is a good idea responds by saying:

> "The idea of a volunteer corps is excellent. I spent two years as a volunteer before going to nursing school. Volunteers are dedicated and caring, and patients respond to them as well or better than they respond to nurses."

The nurse expressed a unity statement. A personal-involvement statement was also contained in the response.

Personal-involvement statements can be powerful forms of evidence. Because no one else can have exactly the same personal experience as another person, such statements cannot be refuted without inferring that the other person is lying or inept. Personal-involvement statements are very ego-involved, and a person using a personal statement is participating in self-disclosure. As we learned earlier in the text, when people self-disclose, they offer something of themselves. That "gift" must be treated with respect.

Superficial statements have the least importance, especially in problem-solving or policy groups. Such statements can, however, help to alleviate tension and create a comfortable atmosphere in which the group operates. For instance, some business executives are preparing to discuss a sensitive, tension-filled personnel matter. While they wait for one of the group members to arrive, someone jokingly says, "For these more serious matters we should all take a week's vacation in Bermuda. After all, we need a relaxed perspective to make the right decision." The comment is not taken seriously, but everyone laughs and the tension is eased.

Many things are said that are variations and combinations of the statements we have just read. What is important is to begin to be sensitive to the different characteristics and the motivations behind what people say so that responses contribute to, not detract from, the dynamics of the group and the group's ultimate goal.

Pacing and Flow of the Discussion

We have isolated different statements to categorize and understand them. Equally important is understanding how a discussion flows from one phase to another.[12] For example, when participants meet for the first time, more emphasis will be spent on procedural statements. Also, we can expect more statements of unity as people test out each other and learn more about the issues. Later, when the topic is well understood and relationships and ideas can stand more criticism, solution statements—both supportive and nonsupportive—emerge.

Based on the ideas being discussed and the relationships that form between group members, statements from one participant will influence statements from other participants. Gradually these interactions will develop into a pattern. Assume we have a group that meets to solve the problem of drinking on campus. During the initial state of the interaction, the comments are mostly congenial and "expressions of unity." We could predict that if one person utters an expression of unity, it will be followed by another expression of unity. Later in the discussion, the sequence of comments—also called the structure of the discussion—may change. During that period, when problem solving begins, we are analyzing the interaction between two people whose ideas do not mesh, and we might predict that a "solution" statement from person A will be followed by disagreement from person B. We might also predict that such an exchange will go on for only so long, until other members of the group draw the discussion back on course through a sequence of "procedural communications" or "expressions of unity."

UNDERSTANDING POWER AND STATUS

People who generate numerous ideas in a brainstorming group perceive other people in the group as being more equal in status to them.[13] They also perceive themselves as high-status group members. Perhaps it would be ideal if all groups could function productively in a leaderless atmosphere in which the quantity of information, not the quality, determines the success of the group. Power and status do, however, directly affect the interaction of the group.

Distinguishing Between Power and Status

In group interaction, the discussion leader may have the power, by using procedural statements, to control interaction. This does not necessarily mean the leader has status. Status is more closely related to the desirability, satisfaction, and prestige inherent in a given position.[14] For example, the head of a store's retail division sits in on a meeting of department managers to discuss a new marketing proposal where each department will share the cost of a new advertising campaign. Although the retail division head may have a great deal of status (and at times power over the department heads), in this setting the real power is with the department heads.[15] They must unanimously approve the plan or it will not be instituted. Every department head has veto power over the proposal. Even though the division head may like the advertising campaign she knows it cannot work unless everyone supports it. Thus, the real power lies with the department heads, not the division head. At other times and with other issues, the power status roles may be reversed.

Effects of Power and Status

With the distinction between power and status in mind, we can examine the role each plays in group interaction by coming to grips with the term *ego-defense mechanism*. Having an ego-defense mechanism means protecting our egos. In other words, it means keeping our self-concept and guarding our self-confidence. It also can mean exercising that interpersonal need we learned about earlier in the text—control. In group interaction, power and status center around protecting our egos and retaining some degree of control over ourselves and our relationships with others.

To better understand these concepts, let us create an example of a discussion among a group of business executives. Carlos is of low power, whereas his boss, Manuel, is of high power. Manuel has control over Carlos and can determine whether the relationship will be good or bad, productive or unproductive. Let us also assume that Manuel determines whether Carlos advances in the company. What does research suggest about the relationship between Manuel and Carlos when they take part in the group discussion with other executives?

First of all, among members of the group, Manuel will have more communication directed at him than will Carlos. Not only will Manuel receive more messages but the messages will also be longer.[16] If Carlos perceives that Manuel has the ability to influence his upward mobility in the company, then when Carlos communicates with Manuel, Carlos will make statements of unity.[17] In other words, Carlos wants to make a favorable impression on Manuel. Because of this the accuracy of his communication to Manuel may suffer in the attempt to filter out negative comments. Carlos may have access to facts that Manuel does not have, but Carlos may not divulge those facts if doing so would endanger the relationship with Manuel. Because of the "psychological link" between Carlos and his boss, Carlos will make more statements of unity toward persons who are like Manuel or who also agree with Manuel.[18]

We can see from the preceding examples and research that unless a leader is skillful, unless a leader has the power to permit open and free discussion and uninhibited responses, the discussion can get bogged down in "niceties" and false flattery at the expense of accurate information and group productivity.

THE RELATIONSHIP OF ROLES

In discussion groups in which the roles of group members are easily identified and adhered to, everyone has a fairly good understanding of what each person's relationship is to other group members. In some situations, this understanding will determine how interaction will take place.

Clearly Defined Roles

Consider a professor leading a class discussion (Fig. 8–1). The professor is the person in authority. Although the professor may try to make sure that everyone's ideas are expressed, the professor still holds final control over the

Figure 8-1
In many group discussions, clearly defined roles exist. A leader of the group can direct discussion and serve as a rather strong authority figure over other members of the group. This individual is also in control of the content and direction of the discussion as well as determining who speaks when. (Laimute E. Druskis Photo)

group. If the professor interrupts, then whoever is talking stops. If the professor changes the subject, the group shifts gears. The roles of the professor and student are easily defined. Authority figures—whether they be professors, a gang leader, high-ranking individuals on a board of directors, or police officers—play a large role in determining group interaction. Depending on how much authority people have and how they use it, regardless of whether or not they are "officially" designated group leaders, they will influence group interaction.

Role Conflict

Role conflict can be experienced at any time by any member of the group, and it can affect the behavior of both a single individual and the interaction of the entire group. For example, assume that you are a member of a committee deciding personnel cuts for a large company. You have two close friends working in one of the company's divisions that is steadily losing money. You know of no other place in the company where these people can be transferred. The company president asks your opinion of the losing division. Speaking in front of the other corporate officers, you find yourself hesitating; your verbal statements are contradicted by your nonverbal cues. You know you will sound ridiculous if you suggest anything other than eliminating the division. Yet you are sensitive to the people who work there, especially your two friends. Other members of the group who have no personal relationships in the division are puzzled by your hesitation. You begin to feel self-conscious and wonder if you will be perceived as being weak and ineffective as a future administrator. The process is painful. You have experienced role conflict; not only has it affected your own behavior but also that of the group as a whole.[19]

HOW TRUST AFFECTS INTERACTION

We traditionally think of trust as something we want from others, sometimes more in their absence than in their presence: "I am dating a very wonderful person, and we have a meaningful relationship based on trust. Therefore, if I am away or must spend the weekend studying, the other person will not go out with someone else behind my back." "My partner and I are a team; my partner would not cut me down behind my back." These statements imply the trust we place in someone else. We have certain expectations about what the other person will do, especially in relation to our own feelings and behavior. Similarly, it is our responsibility to earn the trust others may place in us.

Developing Trust

Trust is implied in the communication process from the time we begin to talk. A child trusts that a parent will react positively to his or her beginning words. Think of how difficult it would be for a child to learn to talk if every time the child uttered a new word, an adult or parent said, "Be quiet!" The child would gradually become reserved, withdrawn, lack self-confidence, and be hindered in his or her ability to interact with others. Now consider how important trust is when we meet another person for the first time and begin to engage in self-disclosure. But how much self-disclosure would take place if trust were not present? On a date, one person may say, "I like to play the piano." The other person replies, "I do not see how anyone can sensibly sit still for hours on end and press down keys on a keyboard, getting sore fingers in the process." In essence, the second person has just said, "Anyone who likes to play the piano is stupid; therefore, you are stupid!" A much more tactful way to have expressed those feelings would have been to say, "I'm glad you enjoy playing the piano. I enjoy listening to records."

Trust and Group Interaction

Trust not only helps us to develop our communication skills and build relationships with other people but also assures good group interaction.[20] If certain members of a group feel that when they present an idea, they will be humiliated or chastised, they will not participate in the discussion. The result may be the loss of the very idea that solves the problem. At the same time, the morale of the entire group may be affected. Research has taught us that trust-destroying communication between two people can hinder the interaction among all members of the group. Even though the trust-destroying exchange may only be between participants *A* and *B*, participants *C, D, E, F,* and however many others in the group can become defensive, protecting their own ideas against attack.

HOW PERSONALITIES AFFECT INTERACTION

Being sensitive to the personalities of different group members is important not only for the group leader but equally important for other members of the group who may be affected by particular personality types. Especially recognizable is the *dominant* personality who may try to control a discussion or interrupt other group members. Some people possess a more dominant personality than others, and sometimes individuals who are part of a group cannot recognize when their dominance is hindering group interaction. Left unchecked, a dominant personality can monopolize conversation, stifle the comments of other group members, and cause the group to flounder out of control of the leader. If you see yourself as having a particularly dominant personality, guard against interrupting others and spending more than you share of the group's time talking.[21]

HOW GROUP SIZE AFFECTS INTERACTION

The difference between your discussing an issue with a friend and discussing it at a city council meeting is clear: The first situation gives you much more opportunity to be heard than does the city council meeting. Your friend may be more responsive to your feelings or more courteous and less impersonal than the city council members. Part of the difference in your interaction between you and your friend and you and the council members is the number of people involved in the conversation.

Amount of Interaction

With larger groups, each member has less time for interaction. Sheer numbers dictate this constraint, especially when the group has a limited time to interact. An hour set aside for a meeting of three people will produce a completely different atmosphere from an hour set aside for a meeting of 12 people. Your chances of being heard will be diminished, and the time you have to interact may be much more limited.

The more people present for a group discussion, the more varied the input placed into the discussion. Two, three, four, or more heads are sometimes better than one. If you have a particular problem to solve and are responsible for bringing together a group of people to solve the problem, there may be advantages to inviting every person who might be able to contribute information and possible solutions.

Reaching a Consensus

Even though involving more people may improve input into the discussion, such involvement can also hinder the discussion. The more people, the more chance for disagreement. Group members or leaders accustomed to reaching a "consensus" rather than taking a vote for majority rule sometimes find larger groups difficult to deal with. Everyone may not agree, and the time necessary for a person to persuade others to a certain way of thinking, or even for every member to be heard, may prohibit true consensus decision making in larger groups. At some point, the leader may simply need to say, "It is time to vote on the issue."

LEARNING TO LEAD A GROUP DISCUSSION

Learning to lead a group discussion is much like running a railroad. The leader can be compared to the engineer in the locomotive. For example, the train has a predetermined route along the tracks. A schedule must be followed with key stops along the way. If the train is moving too slowly, the engineer must increase the speed. If the train is on the wrong track, the engineer must make sure switches are thrown so the train can return to its route. The train could not operate without a conductor and others who cooperate with the engineer and with each other.

In many group discussions, such as problem-solving discussions, the leader also has a "route" to follow that is reflected in the agenda. If the discussion gets bogged down on irrelevant topics then it must be brought back on the right track. The discussion could not function without participants who cooperate with the leader and with each other.

To understand the qualities that distinguish leaders from other group participants, let us begin with a definition of *leadership*. In essence, leadership is a behavioral quality that influences group members toward meeting their goal, maintains cohesiveness, and generates unthreatened interaction among all group members. From our definition, we can begin to extract and identify qualities of a leader.

Exerting Influence

Our definition used the term *influence*. To be effective, a leader must be able to exert influence over the group. This does not mean that an all-powerful or authoritarian individual makes a good leader, but it does mean that a leader lacking control or lacking influence over a group will not produce results. Exerting influence and maintaining good relations with other members of the group takes talent. Skill in human communication is an important quality in maintaining those good relations.

Maintaining Credibility

The credibility of a leader is another quality that can spell the difference between success and failure of a group. More importantly, the group must *perceive* the leader as being credible. A leader may have the title of "leader" but unless the group respects the leader and is willing to adhere to his or her influence, the group's progress toward its goal will be limited. Sometimes the inherent authority of a leader provides the needed credibility to function in a group. A sergeant meeting with a group of privates may lack certain qualities of leadership, but the rank itself can provide the credibility needed to reach the group's goal. This does not mean that the group will "like" the leader or even be satisfied with the group's achievements, but the power inherent in the rank will eventually get the job done.

Goal Commitment

Despite all of the personal qualities a leader may possess, the leader's success will be limited unless the group perceives him or her as being committed to the group's goals. Consider the student who is appointed to head a group planning a class field trip. The student lets it be known that instead of going on the field trip, she would be much happier spending the day studying for exams. From the outset, the group proceeds but with little enthusiasm. When the leader attempts to influence the group's progress, she is perceived as suspect. Suggestions from the leader are met with suspicion. A good leader is perceived by the group as being committed to accomplishing a task. Without that commitment, credibility suffers, the ability to exert influence is lessened, and the productivity of the group and satisfaction of the members with the group's progress are reduced.

Group Maintenance

Simply being committed to a group's goals and following an agenda is not enough to be a sensitive and responsive leader. Maintaining the relationships that exist among group members is also important. At any moment, members of the group can become involved in dialogue which, unless skillfully handled, can endanger the cohesiveness of the group. When ideas are being bantered about, members of the group often become highly involved with their own opinions to the point that they take comments personally that are in disagreement with their own. At that point, communication relationships can break down. Carried to the extreme, communication among members of the group can become so strained that the group ceases to function. Here is when good leadership qualities come into play. Being sensitive to these "breaking points" in group communication means a leader can help steer clear of crisis situations that may develop, and can keep the group cohesive and progressing uninterrupted toward its goal.

When communication crises do occur or when relationships among group members become strained, then the leader may need to adapt to the situation and place emphasis on group maintenance as opposed to reaching the group's goals.[22] From a personality standpoint, this means that a leader may have to shift from being a director to being a negotiator.

Being Sensitive to Comment Flow

Consider the following dialogue from a problem-solving group:

PARTICIPANT A: "I feel we should route all of our trucks through Oklahoma City. Then we would have full loads before reaching our service depots in Amarillo and Albuquerque. After we fill up in Albuquerque, we can make additional stops in Flagstaff, Las Vegas, and on into Los Angeles."

PARTICIPANT B: "That's a good idea, but why couldn't we go through Oklahoma City and then route south through Dallas and Fort Worth, and let the next truck service Amarillo?"

The interaction of participant *A* and participant *B* was in sequence, and both statements were interrelated. Good group discussion follows such a sequential structure, with one comment related to and following another.

Larger groups, however, risk a lack of sequential structure. Let's look at another interaction, this time between participants *C* and *D:*

PARTICIPANT C: "Let me make another suggestion. Bring one of the trucks out of Denver and let it service such places as Colorado Springs, Greeley, and Cheyenne. Have a different truck leave Little Rock and work west toward Oklahoma City."

PARTICIPANT D: "Have we had our trucks inspected this year? I was noticing the other day that the state police are cracking down on inspection violations."

Participant *D*'s comment is not related to participant *C*'s. "As the size of a group increases, it becomes easier for members to ignore messages and pursue other topics of conversation, since the intended receiver of any message may not be clearly understood, and the responsibility for providing a suitable response falls on no one participant."[23]

Member Dominance

The larger the group, the greater the chance that dominant personalities will be present. Those of less-dominant or even submissive personalities may consequently feel isolated, and eventually may withdraw from the group altogether. Not only are there fewer opportunities to be heard in a large group but also when one does speak, many more people are watching and listening. A leader must guard against any one member dominating the group and limiting interaction.

LEADERSHIP STYLE

Leadership styles vary depending on the setting, the goal of the discussion, and the personality of the leader. Some leaders take a hands-off or laissez-faire approach. They let the participants proceed and offer little guidance. This works when everyone is comfortable with the subject and has a basic understanding of good participant skills. Strategic advantages exist for the laissez-faire approach as well. For example, if the leader wants to separate himself or herself from the ultimate decision, the leader may deliberately remain distant from the issues. An assembly line supervisor calls together key employees to discuss a slowdown in production. Solutions to the problem must be implemented by the employees themselves. Thus, the supervisor remains aloof from the discussion because it will take a self-motivated cooperative effort by the employees, not the supervisor, if the solution is to work.

Opposite from the laissez-faire leader is the authoritarian leader, one who exercises a great deal of control over the discussion. A police captain is unhappy with a newspaper story about officers taking excessively long lunch hours. He calls together the sergeants who have daily supervisory responsibilities over much of the force. As each one speaks, the captain responds to their comments and determines who will speak next. The captain is directly involved in the matter because he is ultimately responsible for stopping the practice and making sure the sergeants understand the seriousness of the problem.

A leader may also be a strong participant in the discussion process. For example, a school principal has spent many years in the school she heads. She greets the teachers on a first-name basis, has good relations with the school board and PTA, and is respected by students and staff. When some parents complain about the school's academic scores on a national achievement test, the principal calls together the department heads to discuss the matter. The principal takes an active part in the discussion. She speaks from experience, having been a department head herself and before that a teacher. No one is threatened by her presence, and her open approach to administration permits her to speak with candor and receive candid comments in return. While still leading the discussion, she is also a strong and active participant.

Combinations of the above three leadership styles exist, sometimes in the same discussion. Whereas a laissez-faire approach may be appropriate in the early stages of a discussion, the need for leader participation may emerge, or even an occasional authoritarian emphasis.

THE AGENDA

The route the discussion takes is reflected in the *agenda*. Agendas differ depending on such things as the purpose and goals of the discussion, the number of participants, and the organization within which the discussion operates.

As an example of how purposes and goals affect a discussion, assume an insurance company brings its regional sales representatives together for a meeting every six months. The agenda will be long for many of the business matters that have occurred over the past six months will need to be discussed. The agenda might include such things as reports on the past six months' billings, projections for future business, a new insurance policy being offered for the first time, advertising and marketing strategies being planned, competing companies—all of which will take time and can result in a lengthy agenda.

The number of participants can also affect the agenda. For example, if all the regional sales representatives must report to the group, then the time necessary for this task may limit the other items that will appear on the agenda. In some settings, the number of participants may necessitate breaking up into subcommittees.

In the above examples, the agenda dictates certain responsibilities for the leader. For instance, the leader must understand the pacing of the discussion. Experience will dictate that the reports of the previous six months' sales will not take much time. Explaining a new policy will, however, take time, and until everyone understands the new policy, it will not be possible to continue to other matters. The leader will need to be sure the six months' sales reports are completed in the time allotted. If the discussion of new policies leaves little time for other matters, then what comes after the discussion of new policies may need to be handled at a faster pace.

Many agendas are determined by the organization within which the discussion operates. A government agency may meet every month as required by law. The agency is made up of different bureaus, and each bureau must report at the monthly meetings. The agenda consists of a listing of each bureau's report, followed by time for new business. On occasion, there are additional items such as personnel matters or special topics that have been made part of the agenda by Congress, the courts, or the public. The leader, who also frequently serves as the agency chair, is responsible for seeing that each bureau is able to make its report and that new business is at least introduced. Rarely do the monthly meetings run overtime, for new business is continued to the next meeting and becomes part of the individual bureau reports.

Agendas may appear in written format or simply occur as the discussion develops and are reflected later in the minutes of the meeting. Many discussions operate without any official agenda. A goal is stated by the leader and the discussion proceeds toward the goal. The leader's responsibility, then, is to see that the discussion stays on course and that comments are pertinent to the topic and the goal.

SUMMARY

In learning about small-group communication we began by discussing the qualities of a small group. Group size determines the number of possible interactions, which can range into the thousands when relationships between group members and the intervening factors of verbal and nonverbal communication are considered. For our purposes, we characterized small groups in the general range of three to five members. In addition to group size, other characteristics of a small group include bonding, the degree of interaction among group members, member roles, direct and indirect member rewards, and the time over which the group meets.

We next looked at the various types of small groups. There are groups that implement and recommend policy. Other groups are task-oriented and strive for specific goals. Problem-solving groups are designed to tackle specific problems. A brainstorming group encourages unrestrained interaction to take place. Social groups traditionally operate without fixed agendas, and the consistency of the groups frequently changes. Therapeutic and T-groups function in clinical and introspective settings.

To better understand the content of small-group interaction we examined procedural communications, expressions of unity, solutions, expressions of personal involvement, and superficial statements.

When groups interact, power and status among group members contribute to the interaction. In addition, roles of group members and the conflict of those roles influence group interaction. Trust, which is implied in all communication, functions in the small-group setting as well. Personalities, group size, and the time a group meets affect the interaction.

At the helm of a group is the leader, who is sometimes appointed, but who sometimes evolves from the group without being appointed. A good leader exerts influence on the group, possesses credibility, is committed to the group's goals, and can maintain the group, sometimes in the face of crises.

Different leadership styles exist in a discussion and can include a laissez-faire, authoritarian, or participant approach. In some discussions an agenda helps guide the progress of the group.

QUESTIONS FOR REVIEW AND DISCUSSION

1. What happens to the number of "channels" for communication when you move from dyadic to small-group communication?

2. What different types of bonding can take place in a small group?

3. How do policy groups function?

4. What are the differences between problem-solving groups and task-oriented groups?

5. Why is criticism, even constructive criticism, out of place in the brainstorming group?

6. How does a therapeutic or T-group differ from a task group? How does conflict affect each of these groups?

7. What are the differences between power and status?

8. What are the qualities of a successful leader?

LEARNING EXERCISES

1. Solve the following problem by beginning with a brainstorming group of three to five other people. Problem: Only 1,000 parking spaces are located on campus, but there are 3,000 requests on file for parking permits. (The number of cars and spaces can vary depending on the size of your campus.) You have a 10-minute time limit.

2. Select a different problem and arrive at a solution through a problem-solving group of three to five people.

ADDITIONAL READINGS

BRAMSON, R. M. *Coping with Difficult People.* Garden City, New York: Anchor Press/Doubleday, 1981.
CARNES, W. T. *Effective Meetings for Busy People.* New York: McGraw-Hill, 1980.
DYER, W. G. *Insight to Impact: Strategies for Interpersonal and Organizational Change* (Rev. ed.). Provo, Utah: Brigham Young University Press, 1976.
GILMORE, J. V. *The Productive Personality.* San Francisco: Albion Pub. Co., 1974.
LOYE, D.   *The Leadership Passion.* San Francisco: Jossey-Bass Publishers, 1977.
MACCOBY, M.   *The Leader.* New York: Simon and Schuster, 1981.
MURRAY, S. L.   *How to Organize and Manage a Seminar.* Englewood Cliffs, NJ: Prentice-Hall, 1983.
SUDHALTER, D. L.   *The Management Option: Nine Strategies for Leadership.* New York: Human Science Press, 1980.

9

ANALYZING THE AUDIENCE

OBJECTIVES

After completing this chapter, you should be able to

- Understand the importance of analyzing the audience
- Describe the importance that audience demographics play in audience analysis
- Explain the use of psychographics in audience analysis
- Discuss the significance of audience motives in both preparing and adapting speeches
- Become aware of the obstacles to audience attention
- Identify nonverbal aspects of audience analysis.

A business executive who was an acquaintance of mine decided one day to change careers. He became a professional public speaker. For some of us, the thought of making a living giving speeches might seem terrifying. After all, public speaking has been rated as one of the tasks people fear the most. But this individual found public speaking exciting and enjoyable. Having been a successful sales manager, he was accustomed to giving talks to local business groups and motivating his own staff to reaching sales goals. For him, it seemed only natural to combine these roles into a full-time job as a public speaker. Today, his annual income is substantial. Although he travels a great deal, he has found high job satisfaction by making a living doing something many of us want to avoid.

Few of us will make a living giving speeches. We will, however, find that as we go through life, public speaking will be a requisite in almost any profession. Few business executives, both men and women, can achieve advancement within an organization without possessing good public speaking ability. Corporate executives spend a great deal of their time representing their company before stockholders' groups, student assemblies, government agencies, employee gatherings, and other similar functions. Whether it is a monthly meeting of a parent-teacher's association or testifying before a Congressional committee, knowing how to deliver a speech and doing it well are attributes that can pay big dividends. Whether it is a student government election, a class assignment in an introductory communication course, or just speaking out on an issue at a residence hall meeting, leadership and effective communicating begins with the ability to think and talk on our feet.

The chapters that follow are designed to give the beginning public speaker an introductory awareness of the basic talents necessary to succeed. In a college classroom, that success may determine a grade. Yet not every speech we deliver will be in front of a classroom. That is why this text is designed to take us beyond the immediate assignment and sensitize us to things we will need to know long after we graduate. Thus, the ideas and concepts that follow should be taken in the broader context of different speaking situations, not just a given assignment. Public speaking involves many of the factors of human communication we have been discussing throughout this book. It also involves analyzing every speaking situation individually to identify the factors that are present and unique to a specific speech. Part of that analysis begins with the audience.

AUDIENCE ANALYSIS

An attorney approached the appellate court representing a client who had a good chance of winning an appeal.[1] The attorney had spent considerable time preparing his oral arguments for the appellate judges. He began by discussing the merits of the case, and then concluded by explaining why the judge in the lower court had erred and how the decision should be reversed. The judges listened politely, something they are not always willing to do, asked few questions, and without much deliberation affirmed the decision of the lower court. The attorney was stunned and wondered what had gone wrong.

With a better audience analysis, the attorney would have successfully placed himself in the position of the judges and not made the simple mistakes that cost him the case. What were those audience-related mistakes?

First and foremost, the attorney should have understood that the audience consisted of judges, not jurors. Most judges have experienced the difficulties of sitting on lower courts and can empathize with lower-court judges. They understand that many procedural decisions made by lower-court judges do not influence the outcome of a case. In this instance, a decision had been made by another judge, which, on the surface, may have seemed at odds with standard judicial procedure. The decision did not, however, infringe on the rights of the accused. Thus, while the attorney was quick to point out where the lower court erred, he did not show how those decisions did harm to his client.

Instead of structuring his argument as if he were one of the judges, he acted as an adversary to the judges. Instead of talking *with* the judges, he talked *to* the judges. They, in turn, talked back with a decision contrary to what the attorney had expected. A skillful attorney who had analyzed his audience would have taken a position that said, "I understand your role and the decision you must make. It must be based on a procedural error that infringed on the rights of my client. This is where I feel your decision must concentrate." By using this strategy, the attorney would have rhetorically placed himself on the bench alongside the judges. He would have created homophily. Instead, he presented the case much in the same way it was presented to the jury. The only problem was that the jury wasn't making the decision.

AUDIENCE EXPECTATIONS

The attorney made another audience-related mistake. Instead of concentrating on just the important parts of the case and advancing the strongest arguments, the attorney briefed the judges on the entire case. The judges, expecting a brief summation of the major procedural errors, instead were confronted with too much information. The valuable time of the appellate court had been wasted. While the facts of the case may have been important to the jury that heard the case in the lower court, a much more succinct presentation was necessary at the appellate level. Thus, the attorney had not met the judges' expectations.

The mistakes made by the attorney were the same that many other speakers make. The result is a speech that fails to capture or hold the attention of the audience, fails to impart information, and results in a negative evaluation of the speaker. Remember, a speech begins with the audience, not with the speaker. It is the audience that must endure the presence of the speaker, not the speaker who must endure the presence of the audience. If the latter is the case, then the speaker has failed to take the time to analyze the audience and prepare a presentation that will make the audience want to listen. Forcing an audience to listen is next to impossible. Audiences will smile. They will sit politely while you finish your speech. They may even ask questions and applaud. But they cannot be forced to listen. If the speaker does not meet the audience's expectations, members of the audience will permit their minds to wander everywhere but on what the speaker is saying. Even if they manage to pay attention, they will not actively listen. They will become passive observers, and what they do learn or remember will soon be forgotten.

PITFALLS TO AUDIENCE ANALYSIS

Some speakers have been confident that they knew their audience and were prepared to deliver an effective, information-packed speech. To their dismay, they were badly disappointed. I can remember one afternoon when I received a telephone call and was invited to address a group of dentists from a prestigious dental school. The dentists were meeting at a nearby convention center as part of a "teaching retreat." I was invited to speak to the group in the afternoon and explain my philosophy of teaching.

For two weeks before the speech I thought about what to say. I arrived prepared to offer a step-by-step guide to better teaching. As the time to deliver my speech came nearer, I reviewed my notes and walked one more time into the empty auditorium where I was to speak. Fifteen minutes later, I was in front of the 100-plus dentists who, I thought, were eagerly awaiting my remarks. Thirty minutes later, my speech concluded. I received a polite round of applause, but I knew inside that everyone in the room would have rather been somewhere else. What had happened?

My strategy for analyzing the audience took into consideration everything, or at least I thought it did. I had considered their ages, their profession, the "teaching" theme of their conference, and had followed explicitly the directions of the program chair. But I had not considered what the audience *wanted* to hear. As such, I had completely bypassed the audience's reason for being present at the speech. They weren't present because they wanted to hear me. They were present because they were required by the dean of the dental school to be there. Had I taken the time to contact a couple of the faculty and solicit their opinions of the conference, I would have been in a much better position to deliver a speech that held their attention. A strategy offering some light-hearted comments about teaching would have been more successful. Making the entire speech a series of humorous stories about my own experiences with students might have helped. But a speech heavy in content and adding to the drudgery of being required to be present was not successful. In short, I had not sufficiently analyzed my audience.

While it is possible to know something about the characteristics of an audience, a good speaker looks deeper into the minds and background of an audience to try to determine the motive for being present at a speech. Although it will never be possible to know exactly how an audience approaches a speech, it is a much better strategy than merely considering how the speaker should approach the speech.

AUDIENCE DEMOGRAPHICS

When we think of audience analysis, the *demographic characteristics* of an audience come to mind. Demographic characteristics are *vital statistics about an audience*. In analyzing an audience for a speech, for example, some of the most familiar statistics to study are age, education, sex, race, income, religion, national origin, and group membership. While these factors alone are not sufficient to analyze an audience, they do provide a gauge for analyzing more complex psychological characteristics. Examining some typical speaking situations will help to show how demographic characteristics make a difference.

Applying Demographic Analysis

Assume you are assigned to deliver a speech to a group of students. We'll assume the speech is set for a local community college where students are studying advertising. Your assignment is to talk about the ways in which a successful advertising executive can make a presentation and land an account. You know that the students are in their second year of an associate degree program. How do demographic characteristics contribute to the planning of your speech?

Consider the demographic of age. When you question the instructor, you are told that the students are of various ages. Some students are just out of high school and are taking the course as an elective portion of other degree programs. You know, therefore, that although these students may end up working in advertising, they will probably not be owners or senior partners and therefore will not be making presentations to clients. However, other students in the class are older and already work in some type of advertising, either for an agency or for a company involved in in-house advertising work. These students probably have some desire to move on to more senior-level positions and will want to know how to make a successful presentation. In addition, they most likely will be making a higher income than their younger counterparts. Income is a demographic that can correlate with age, although not always. Thus, while you do not know very much about each individual student, you do know something about their ages and to some degree their income. This information will be helpful in determining how you will approach your subject.

Assume you are going to deliver a speech about parking problems to a group of college students. What demographic information is important? First, it would be helpful to know how many students own cars. Unless you have some idea of that statistic, you'll have a hard time relating to your audience. You stop and think for a moment. You realize that the entire group of students you'll be talking to is made up of freshmen and sophomores. You also realize that at your school, freshmen and sophomores rarely have cars because seniors and juniors get first choice of your school's limited vehicle permits. With this knowledge, you can begin to develop your speech. Your strategy will be to suggest to the group that if the parking problem is solved, freshmen and sophomores will have a much better chance of obtaining vehicle permits. Knowing something about the demographic characteristics of your audience—in this case, what year they were in school—helped you plan your speech.

Settings for Demographic Analysis

Other settings show the importance of demographic information. A gathering of religious leaders representing a specific denomination will guarantee that the group has a specific church membership in common. A group of senior citizens not only has age demographic in common but also attitudes and beliefs that may be indicative of that age group. A speech to a local civic club about crime prevention would at first seem to be a general topic designed for a general audience. Further analysis of the group, however, determines that many of the people in the group are senior citizens who live alone. Crime prevention takes on special importance to them. We might discover that many members of an audience come from an ethnic neighborhood where strong family ties are important. All of these facts about the audience will help make our speech more effective.

AUDIENCE PSYCHOGRAPHICS

The *psychographic characteristics* of an audience refer to the psychological characteristics of the audience or those derived from the mind or emotions. Values, attitudes, opinions, beliefs, feelings, perceptions, mental images, and prejudices are all part of these psychological characteristics (Fig. 9–1).

In teaching, I have found a certain classroom exercise to be a good way of sensitizing students to the psychographic characteristics of an audience. To

Figure 9-1
The diverse makeup of a large audience necessitates analysis which may take into consideration both the demographic and psychographic characteristics of the audience. To be effective, the speaker must research and understand the composition of an audience. (Jim Kalett, Photo Researchers)

start the class, I ask everyone to stop and think what image comes to mind when I say the word "flower." After a few moments, I ask them what that image is. Some see a field of daisies. Others visualize a rose. Some describe red roses. Some describe yellow roses. Others describe pink roses. Still others, not presented with the spelling of the term, tell of imagining hot, fluffy biscuits made from "flour." The exercise underscores how much more complex the psychological characteristics of an audience are than the demographic characteristics. It also shows that when preparing a speech, we need to consider more than the demographic characteristics.

Applying Psychographic Analysis

Assume you are making a speech to persuade a group of community leaders to vote for a new zoning ordinance. In order to be effective, it is vital to know where these leaders stand on the issue before you begin. If their attitudes are against major development and change, then you will need to work toward changing their minds about new development before you can persuade them to consider the zoning ordinance.

Similarly, suppose you are a politician delivering a speech on gun control. If your audience is against gun control and you are for gun control, you have a twofold task before you. You must first convince them of your own credibility. You next must change their minds about gun control.

Value Analysis and Appeals

Analyzing the basic values of an audience can often help a speaker identify the goals and aspirations of that audience. Think back to the basic values we discussed in Chapter 2 when we learned about self-concept: aesthetic, humanitarian, intellectual, material, power, and religious values. Now imagine you are scheduled to speak before the city council about the allocation of downtown space for city parks. You might decide to base your speech around the aesthetic improvements that would occur in the downtown area because of the parks. The opposition could argue that the land would be put to better use as an office building, but could not effectively argue that improving the aesthetic value of the downtown area was inherently bad.

A humanitarian value might also be employed. Assume the opposition's plan for the office building will involve tearing down a nearby apartment house. The families living in the apartment will need to find alternative housing if the office building is built. Because many of the families are on fixed incomes, the move is frightening to them. You argue persuasively that not only will the office building cause the downtown area to lose its aesthetic appeal but also the office project is insensitive to the humanitarian needs of the residents of the apartment complex. The opposition will have a tough time arguing against your humanitarian concerns for the residents.

You are aware that in attendance at the council meeting are a number of parents and teachers concerned about a nearby school and library that will fall victim to the office building. You next discuss the importance of the intellectual life of young children. You argue that disrupting their education will harm their educational opportunities and further disrupt the community.

Using materialism and power values as part of your argument will be much more difficult. Our society tends to place a premium on material things, but it is not something universal to all individuals. Moreover, there are times when public opinion swings heavily against materialism. More than one trial jury has ruled against a business because a company is perceived as being overly concerned with profits and not enough about people. To argue at the city council meeting that the opposition is only interested in materialism, profits, and power might seem to be an ideal strategy. None of the residents will gain financially from the office complex, only the developers. You plan your remarks around that theme and eloquently present your speech to the city council.

Now it is time for the council to hear from the opposition. Their representative is a skillful speaker who has argued in front of city councils before. You are surprised to hear your opponent agreeing with you on virtually everything you have said. Your opponent champions the cause of the aesthetic values of the downtown area and points out that the new office building has been designed to fit into the theme of other buildings in the downtown area. It will also have a fast-food restaurant with an inside playground which small children can use for neighborhood parties.

Your opponent agrees with the need for housing, but challenges the city council to seek out developers who will construct more apartment buildings. Perhaps the new office building will be just the thing to spur this development. Your opponent also agrees that some disruption may occur if the school is moved, but suggests the new school should be constructed with better facilities than the old one and that it should incorporate a library. On the subject of profits, your opponent says little but indicates that profits and progress go hand in hand and that the council members should realize this since many of them own their own businesses.

As you listen to the vote of the council members, you realize you have lost. You have also learned a lesson. Your appeal to basic values was sound and well presented. That becomes evident as many council members point this out before casting their vote. Even those who vote for the office complex state they are sensitive to the need for a pleasing downtown appearance and the need to take into consideration the lives of the people living in the apartment complex.

The next morning when you read the newspaper account of the council meeting, you gain a better perspective of what happened. The newspaper states that general agreement existed between yourself and the business representative who appeared at the council meeting. You ask yourself, "How could that be? The opposition wanted the office complex and I wanted the park." You realize now how skillful a communicator your opponent was, so skillful that the reporter saw little difference in your two arguments. You also analyze the vote tally. Your research shows that the members of the council who voted for the office complex are independent business people who own their own businesses. They were not persuaded by your criticism of profits and power. They sided with your opponent who said "profits and progress go hand in hand." Much like the attorney who failed to place himself in the shoes of the appellate judges, you failed to realize that many members of city government are business people. Your negative appeal based on materialism and power spawned the opposite effect you desired.

Attitudes and Opinions

Attitudes and opinions are also part of our psychographic profile, yet not as deeply held as personal values. If you are preparing a speech about banning phosphates in detergents, you will want to know how strongly your audience feels about the subject. Although phosphates in detergents are not part of the audience's basic values, the audience may harbor some attitudes and opinions about the subject.

Regardless of what values, attitudes, and opinions we hold, an effective speaker must make a match between the topic and the psychographic characteristics of the audience. Yet simply knowing about the attitudes and opinions of an audience is not enough. We must dovetail our topic and the content of the speech with those same attitudes and opinions.

AUDIENCE MOTIVES

At the beginning of this chapter it was noted that it is important for a speaker to know the motives of an audience. That may seem strange, since as prospective public speakers we naturally concentrate on ourselves. Yet even though we may analyze the audience, we need to go one step further and ask, "Why are these people here?"

Audience-Centered Preparation

Answered skillfully and correctly, that last question can make the difference between delivering a good speech and delivering a great speech. Too many speakers fail to take an audience's motives into consideration in preparing for a speech. Let's be honest. Some people are in attendance because they want to hear the speech; they want to learn something new, be motivated, be inspired. But for other people, the speech is secondary. They may be attending because of the fellowship of the group. Others may be there for social reasons or to "be seen." Still others may be there for political reasons, or that attending is the correct thing to do to advance one's career. Still others may be looking for a diversion, something to do to escape boredom. We need to prepare our speech with all of these potential listeners in mind.

Audience Adaptation

Because there may be people in our audience who are there for reasons other than to hear our speech, we must adapt our thoughts to get these people involved. Actually, the effort will improve our speech. For example, the extension agent who talks to a local civic club about agricultural production or the state fair will more than likely receive a polite reception. But if the extension agent adds something extra to the speech, then the reception will be more enthusiastic. Weaving comments about specific members of the civic club into the presentation will keep the audience alert, interested, and listening. For instance, a civic club member may own a farm in the area. The extension agent could make reference to that person's farm and how it applies to the topic of the speech. By doing this, not only can the rest of the audience relate to the speech better but this action also shows that the speaker has taken the time to learn something about the club and its members. The speaker, therefore, takes on the role of being part of the group, not of being an outsider asked in to speak.

A personal speaking engagement brings to mind a similar situation in which I was asked to address a local service club about a research project I had completed on human values. The club president was nice enough to provide me with a list of the members, and I was able to identify three people I recognized as well-known members of the community. I planned a personal reference around all three individuals, knowing that not every member attends every meeting. One member happened to be a funeral director, and it was around that individual that I wove part of my speech.

I explained that if we were to test this individual to determine his personal values, he would test high in humanitarian values because he liked to work with people so much. The club members broke into laughter. I then made reference to a local banker and said he would also test high because he likes people, but for different reasons. This comment brought a second roll of laughter, and the rest of the speech was a success. After lunch, I was approached by more than one member of the group and invited to join their club, something I discovered that was not extended to every speaker. Understanding why the members were in the audience—which was for the fellowship with their club members—made it possible for me to better adapt my speech to the occasion.

OBSTACLES TO AUDIENCE ATTENTION

In the chapter on listening, we learned of three obstacles that can interfere with good listening: selective exposure, selective perception, and selective retention. Each can be reviewed and applied to audience analysis. They especially pertain when we examine the psychographic characteristics of an audience. Let's examine this further.

We selectively expose ourselves to information because of preconceived ideas and opinions about the content of that communication. This determines whether or not we will be in the audience and if our motive is a personal one. However, if the speech is required, or we feel it is advantageous for us to attend, we can still selectively expose ourselves to the speaker's message by simply not listening.

We may also perceive a speaker as being unimaginative and uninteresting and thus pay little attention to what is being said. Similarly, we may retain only that information that was relevant to our lives, forgetting the rest.

Being sensitive to selective exposure, perception, and retention means knowing that the audience can bring to a speech certain preconceived ideas about what we are going to say. For example, if we belong to a campus fraternity, then when we deliver a speech about belonging to a fraternity, the audience will perceive that we will take a profraternity stance. If we want to change the minds of people in the audience who are opposed to fraternities, we must convince them that we understand their position as well. In other words, we must change their selective perceptions before they will truly listen to us and remember what we say.

NONVERBAL ASPECTS OF AUDIENCE ANALYSIS

A professional public speaker, one who frequently addresses groups of people in settings ranging from business meetings to civic gatherings, always takes the time before the speech to visit the room where he will deliver the speech. This individual long ago learned not to take anything for granted. He makes a livelihood by not being surprised and leaves nothing to chance. A receptacle too far away to plug in an overhead projector, a speaker's table arranged so that a chart cannot be displayed, and a seating arrangement that prohibits a slide projector from being located the right distance from the screen are things that must be discovered ahead of time, not a few minutes before a speech begins. All of these nonverbal forces can greatly affect the outcome of a speech. What other nonverbal factors should we take into consideration?

Size and Seating Arrangements

The size of the audience and the seating arrangements are a good place to start. If the number in attendance is small, no one will have difficulty seeing or hearing the speaker. If the group is large but seated in an auditorium where each row is elevated, then the speaker is assured of being seen. If the group is large and the seats are on a level surface, then special care may be necessary to communicate with people seated in the back rows.

Larger audiences and certain seating arrangements can be particularly difficult when visual aids are employed. Some overhead projectors and slide projectors do not have high-intensity lamps. When a large auditorium is used, special equipment may be necessary in order to correctly display the visual aids. It may also be necessary to control the lighting. Yet instead of planning ahead, some speakers will wait until they show their slide or overhead transparency, then ask for someone to "dim the lights." The only problem is that no one knows who is supposed to dim the lights. No one even knows where the light switch is! A well-prepared speaker would have made prior arrangements.

Interruptions

In addition to the above nonverbal interruptions, physical noise can also interrupt a speech. How many times have we been in an audience listening to a speech when the rear doors to the room are opened as someone walks in late? Everyone in the room turns and looks, and the speaker loses the attention of the audience. Finding out what entrances and exits exist in the room prior to a speech can keep interruption surprises to a minimum for the speaker. If it looks as though a number of people will be arriving late, making sure the doors to the room remain open can cut down on the distraction. If it is critical to the success of a speech that no interruption takes place, then prior arrangements must be made for someone to be stationed at the door to halt late arrivals, or at least be responsible for quietly opening and shutting the door.

Dinner speeches can be particularly difficult. The noise of clanging glasses, banging silverware, and the stacking of food trays can be disconcerting. If the speech begins before the meal is finished, the speaker may end up watching the audience eat instead of listening to the speech. Equally distracting to a speaker is trying to talk while waiters and waitresses walk around the room serving dessert. If you will be speaking at a dinner setting, try to coordinate closely with the food service personnel what you would prefer. They are usually quite cooperative; after all, they want your repeat business.

SUMMARY

Public speaking involves many of the factors of human communication which we have been discussing throughout this text. It also involves analyzing every speaking situation individually and identifying those factors unique to a specific speech. That analysis begins with the audience.

Audience analysis is accomplished by placing ourselves in the role of the audience, not the speaker. The audience brings to every speech certain expectations which the speaker must understand and meet. Yet this analysis is not without its pitfalls, and the speaker may misjudge an audience's expectations or other factors.

When we analyze an audience, we need to consider the members' demographics, which include such things as sex, age, income, race, national origin, group membership, year in school, and similar data.

We should also consider the audience's psychographic characteristics, or those derived from their thoughts and emotions. Values, attitudes, opinions, beliefs, feelings, perceptions, and mental images are all part of an audience's psychographic profile. Analyzing the basic values of an audience can help a speaker identify the needs and goals of that audience. Knowing an audience's opinions and attitudes toward a topic is necessary for effective speech preparation. We must dovetail the topic of our speech with these attitudes and opinions in order to elicit effective audience reaction.

Knowing why people are attending the speech and what their motives are can help us adapt our speech for a better reception.

Selective exposure, selective perception, and selective retention—those obstacles to good listening also can become obstacles to audience attention. Many audiences hold captive members who would not be present unless it was required. Realizing that people may daydream and tune us out because they may have preconceived notions about us can help us prepare our speech and remove these obstacles to audience attention.

A good speaker will prepare for every eventuality, including an analysis of nonverbal factors in speaking situations. The size of the audience, the seating arrangement, and the potential for distractions are three important things to check before delivering a speech.

QUESTIONS FOR REVIEW AND DISCUSSION

1. Assume you are delivering a speech to the following audiences. How would you analyze and adapt to each one: (1) college students enrolled in a basic communication class? (2) professors meeting at a retreat? (3) business people with both men and women in the audience? (4) a group of professional women?

2. How can a speaker become "part of the audience"?

3. What is the difference between talking "with" an audience and talking "to" an audience?

4. What are audience expectations?

5. What are the pitfalls to audience analysis?

6. What are the differences between audience demographics and audience psychographics?

7. How do basic values contribute to audience analysis?

8. Why are attitudes and opinions important to audience analysis?

9. What is meant by audience motives and how do they affect a speaking situation?

10. What are some nonverbal aspects of audience analysis?

LEARNING EXERCISES

1. Consider the following audiences: nursing-home residents, nurses, local service club, the basketball team, a group of managers where you work, the meeting of managers of area fast-food restaurants, owners of dry-cleaning establishments in your state, car salespersons, fraternity or sorority presidents from your school. For those audiences with which you would be most familiar (you may add others) select different topics for an after-dinner speaking engagement.

2. Visit different lecture rooms or auditoriums on campus or at a local conference center or hotel. Analyze the room and seating arrangements and determine how these would affect the presentation of a lecture or speech.

ADDITIONAL READINGS

DONNELLY, J. H., JR., and J. M. IVANCEVICH   *Analysis for Marketing Decisions.* Homewood, IL: R. D. Irwin, 1970.

GIBSON, J. W., and M. S. HANNA   *Audience Analysis: A Programmed Approach to Receiver Behavior.* Englewood Cliffs, NJ: Prentice-Hall, 1976.

SHEA, G. F.   *Managing a Difficult or Hostile Audience.* Englewood Cliffs, NJ: Prentice-Hall, 1984.

10

SPEECH ORGANIZATION AND SUPPORT

OBJECTIVES

After completing this chapter, you should be able to

- Choose not only a topic but also a manageable topic
- Realize the importance of organization in speech preparation
- Compare and contrast the spatial, chronological, problem-solution, cause-effect, and related-topics plans to organizing speeches
- Develop an introduction to a speech that gains audience attention and a summary that ties into the introduction
- Understand the importance of supporting your speech through a number of ways
- Explain the role of source credibility
- Describe perceived homophily and its relation to a speech
- Distinguish between ethos, pathos, and logos
- Talk about the use of both deductive and inductive reasoning
- Define and discuss the *post hoc, ergo propter hoc* fallacy
- Be aware of attributing information in a speech
- Distinguish between primary and secondary sources of information
- Explain analogies
- Speak from personal experiences
- Know how to use statistics in a speech.

Audience analysis is an important first step in planning a speech. But it is only the first step. A good speech is well organized and, where appropriate for the occasion, supported with facts, sound reasoning, and solid proof. Part of the support a speech receives comes from the credibility of the speaker—credibility already present in the minds of the audience or which is placed there by the speaker as the speech develops. Other support is the product of hard work and research, which involves using the library efficiently and effectively. In this chapter, we will examine topic selection, speech organization, support for what is said, and key skills in using the library to research a speech topic.

CHOOSING THE TOPIC

At the beginning of this text we visited with Dave, the river guide. When Dave spoke to the people waiting to take the plunge down the rapids he didn't have to worry about choosing a topic. Dave knew everyone would pay attention. The topic of Dave's speech was manageable and dealt with the few important points of riding the raft down the river and not capsizing. It wasn't an overly broad topic such as the history of river rafting. Nor was it confusing or poorly organized. Dave talked about the basics, and by the time he finished you were able to understand exactly what he wanted you to do.

Not all speeches enjoy the clarity of Dave's talk. Some are so broad that the audience can't figure out what the speaker really wanted to say. The speech has been a rambling assemblage of disjointed topics. This chapter is designed to help you prevent that from happening.

Adapting the Topic to the Audience

Many beginning speakers make the mistake of not adapting the topic to the audience. For example, assume you are on the college golf team. You know something about golf but simply delivering a speech about golf is not sufficient. You need to adapt what you know about golf to your audience. Thus, a speech about *why* the class should learn to play golf is more interesting than a speech about *how* to play golf. Similarly, if you are involved in an unusual club or hobby, talk about why the class might like to learn about the subject. Simply assuming that because you are interested in something your audience—even your classmates—will be interested in the same thing is a fallacy of audience analysis. *You* have the responsibility of interesting the audience in your topic. It is not the responsibility of the audience to be interested. As we learned when studying listening, the audience may appear to listen attentively, may be polite and courteous, may show emotion and express positive feedback, but the audience still may not be really interested in what you have to say unless you make audience members interested.

Try to envision what some of the other speeches will be like. Realize that in any school there are students who have already taken the course and that ideas get passed along from one class to another. Thus, in a typical class there are predictable topics. To avoid falling into this trap, don't pass up the opportunity to be original and talk about something of which you personally have knowledge or experience. Realize also that your instructor has probably heard enough speeches to know when you have not taken the necessary time to intelligently select a topic and plan your speech.

Choosing a Manageable Topic

Narrow the topic and make it manageable. This accomplishes two things. It helps guard against your speech being superficial. After all, you can't give the definitive speech on the topic of "love" or "war" in a few minutes. Narrowing your topic also makes it more comprehensible. Your audience will have a difficult time remembering and understanding all about love and war, but if you deliver a speech about "The art of saying hello and goodbye," or a speech about "The effect on society of the military draft," your audience will be more apt to pay attention and comprehend the speech. Even with these more manageable topics it is still the responsibility of the speaker to adapt the topic to the audience.

Read the topic in the left column and then examine the more narrow, manageable topic in the right column.

Too Broad	More Manageable
Defense Spending	The effect of defense spending on appropriations to higher education.
Career Preparation	The importance of internships in locating a job after college.
Athletics	How athletic gate receipts are used in the university.
Safe Driving	Traffic patterns and their effect on pedestrians on campus.
Success in College	How study habits in the first weeks of school affect the outcome of a semester.
Sports	How good physical conditioning can improve academic achievement.
Cycling	The need for the community and the college to cooperate in developing bike paths.
Crime	How college students can protect personal belongings.

Writing the Specific Purpose

The specific purpose is a statement that clearly identifies the purpose and content of the speech. It helps the speaker keep in mind what he or she wants to accomplish. The logical follow-up step to topic selection is to write a clear, concise, specific purpose. For example, we can use our examples of speech topics which we just discussed. For the topic "defense spending" a specific purpose could read: "To explain to the class how defense spending limits appropriations to higher education."

Developing a clear specific purpose is helpful because it prevents many of the pitfalls of selecting a topic that is too broad, unclear, or inappropriate. By reading the specific purpose you can ask yourself such questions as: "Is this speech going to cover too much ground?" "Is this speech going to apply to the audience?" "If I were required to listen to a speech on this subject, would I consider it interesting?" "If I do not consider it interesting, how can I possibly do a good job?" "What kind of proof must I gather or will my own credibility on the subject carry me through?" After answering the questions yourself, ask someone else to look at the specific purpose. Ask them if it is clear what you are trying to accomplish and how they will feel about the speech. It is this kind of deliberate care and attention to your speech that will make it not just a good speech, but an excellent speech.

THE IMPORTANCE OF ORGANIZATION

A simple exercise shows the necessity for organizing our thoughts.

Organizing Our Thoughts

Read the following list of numbers and then immediately shut the book. On a separate piece of paper, jot down as many numbers as you can, in any order. Remember, shut the book as soon as you read the list:

36   64   24   72   52   60   44   68   48   28   40   32

How did you do? If you are like most people, you had a difficult time remembering the numbers. Try this same exercise on a friend. Read the list of numbers to a friend and then ask your friend to jot down as many numbers as he or she can remember.

Now let's add some organization to the numbers. Look for the lowest number in the list. It's 24. Now count how many numbers there are. You will find 12 numbers. Starting with the number 24, the remainder of the list consists of 28, 32, 36, 40, 44, 48, 52, 60, 64, 68, 72. If you read this list to friends and ask them to jot down as many of the numbers as they can remember, they will fare much better than they did with the list that was disorganized.

Applying Organization to Speech Preparation

Our exercise shows the importance of organization. In making speeches, this same attention to organization can improve the impact of the speech. For example, assume you are delivering a speech about pollution of our major rivers. You might choose a random selection of rivers to illustrate your point. The Snake River, the Mississippi River, the Columbia River, the Missouri River, the Allegheny River, or the Monongahela River might be some of the rivers you could discuss. Unless the audience is familiar with geography, simply listing the rivers will not permit the audience to remember or identify them with any more success than our first list of numbers. If, however, we add some organization to the list of rivers, our ability to comprehend and remember them is made much easier. We could begin our speech by informing the audience that we are going to talk about pollution and discuss six rivers. We could also tell the audience that we will start by selecting two rivers from the West, two from the Midwest, and two from the East. Already we have added some structure and organization to our speech. The audience knows the speech will move from West to East. In the mind of the audience we have created a receptacle into which we can plug the information.

We now move to the body of our speech by choosing two rivers from the West, the Snake River and the Columbia River. Both waterways are located in the upper Northwest and are famous for fishing and outdoor sports such as rafting. We now move to the Midwest and deal with the Missouri and Mississippi Rivers. The Mississippi is the most famous. The Missouri runs through many of the Great Plains states and feeds into the Mississippi. In the East, namely near Pennsylvania and West Virginia, we encounter the Allegheny and the Mononga-hela Rivers. These rivers run through part of the industrial region of the United States that is filled with coal mining and steel production.

By creating an organizational plan to our speech, we have made it much easier to identify with and remember the content of the speech. The six rivers may not have meant a great deal to us when we first heard their names. However, by arranging them in a spatial plan that ran from West to East, we were able to keep track of where the rivers were located. When we were learning about the Snake and Columbia Rivers we already were aware that the next two rivers would be in the Midwest and the two after that in the East. We had laid down a figurative road map which we could follow and walk across from one region of the country to another.

PLANS AND SAMPLE OUTLINES FOR ORGANIZING SPEECHES

The organizational plan used in our example is called a "spatial" or "geographical" plan. Other commonly used organizational plans in addition to the spatial plan include the chronological, problem-solution, cause-effect, related topics, and combinations of these different plans.

The Structure of a Good Outline

Regardless of which plan you choose, standard rules apply to outlining. First, each point in the outline should contain only one complete thought. If more than one thought is included then it should be subdivided or another main point should be added. Second, if subdivided, a main point or subheading should have at least two subdivisions. If not, then another main point or subheading should be used. Consider the following example, which is correct:

I. Radio is a specialized advertising medium.
   A. It reaches audiences with preference for a particular programming format.
   B. Cost-efficient commercials can reach a narrow segment of the mass audience.

1. Commercials airing on stations with hard-rock formats reach the 18–34-year-old age group.
2. Commercials airing on stations with classical music formats frequently reach audiences with higher than average incomes.

Notice that a main point (I) was subdivided into two subheadings (A and B), which were further subdivided into two more subheadings (1 and 2). Whenever a subdivison occurred it always resulted in at least two subdivisons.

Now consider an incorrect structure:

I. Radio is a specialized advertising medium.
  A. It reaches audiences with a preference for a particular programming format. (Subheadings 1 and 2 would follow)

In this structure we failed to subdivide I into at least two subheadings. If the only information we wanted to communicate was that information contained in I and A it could have been presented in one of two ways. The first would have been to combine I and A into a single main point.

I. Radio is a specialized advertising medium reaching audiences with a preference for a particular format.

Or we could have added a second main point.

 I. Radio is a specialized advertising medium.
II. Radio reaches audiences with a preference for a particular programming format.

Third, keep all of the main points of equal importance. Points of lesser importance should be reduced to subheadings.

Fourth, make each subheading a complete thought. Avoid one-word statements or statements so brief they don't communicate complete thoughts. These rules will become clearer as we begin to develop examples of our different organizational plans.

Spatial Plan

We will develop our example of a spatial plan by outlining a speech about pollution. In addition to a specific purpose, each of our outlines will contain an "Introduction" and "Conclusion." We will deal in more detail with these parts of a speech after we learn about outlining.

SPECIFIC PURPOSE: To point out the threat of pollution to some of America's major rivers.
INTRODUCTION
 I. In the West, recreational use contributes to the pollution of two major rivers.
  A. The Snake River frequently carries the debris left by campers and other recreational users.
  B. The Columbia River is affected by increased recreational use in the vicinity of Portland, Oregon.

II. In the Midwest, the Missouri and Mississippi Rivers are threatened.
   A. The Missouri River is collecting sediment from blown-off soil in the Dakotas.
   B. The Mississippi River is being affected by residential and industrial use.
      1. New housing developments are springing up and some sewage run-off problems have occurred.
      2. Increased river traffic by industrial and recreational users have contributed to pollution
III. Two rivers in the East, the Allegheny and the Monongahela, face the daily threat of pollution from the coal mining and steel industries of Pennsylvania and West Virginia.
   CONCLUSION

By referring back to our rules of outlining we can see each rule has been applied to our spatial organization plan. Each main point (I, II, III) contains a single thought. Each thought is of equal importance.

When a point is subdivided, it is subdivided into at least two subheadings.

Chronological Plan

The chronological plan is organized around time. We can start now and go back in time or we can start in the past and work toward the present. The latter is more common. Consider the following outline, which uses a chronological plan:

SPECIFIC PURPOSE: To explain the contributions of great inventors to the development of radio.
INTRODUCTION
I. Guglielmo Marconi began his experiments in Italy and later successfully received the first transatlantic wireless signals.
   A. Under a prodding father and with home-built equipment, Marconi first transmitted a wireless signal over a short distance near his home in Italy in the 1890s.
   B. On December 12, 1901, from the receiving station at Signal Hill, Newfoundland, Marconi successfully received the letter S sent from the transmitting station in Poldhu, England.
   C. Marconi's American Marconi Wireless Telegraph Company developed after worldwide attention to his transatlantic broadcasts.
II. Lee de Forest announced the development of the audion vacuum tube to a gathering of the American Institute of Electrical Engineers meeting in New York in 1906.
   A. The tube contained a third element consisting of an iron grid, which amplified the electrical current.
   B. The audion significantly improved the sensitivity of early radio receivers.
III. Dr. Ernst Alexanderson, a General Electric engineer, had developed the Alexanderson alternator by 1920.
   A. The alternator made it possible for improved long-distance voice communication via wireless.
   B. The alternator improved America's position in international broadcasting after World War I.
   CONCLUSION

Notice in the chronological plan we started in the 1890s with Marconi and concluded in the 1920s with Alexanderson. None of the subheadings broke this chronological path. It would have been confusing to have used an early date for main point I, an even earlier date for II, then a much later date for III. All three points, I, II, and III, followed in order from 1890 to 1906, to 1920. It was not necessary to deal with specific dates in the subheadings since these were an expansion of the main point and the time frame had already been established. While this outline moved from the past to the present, a chronological plan can also move from the future or present into the past.

Problem-Solution Plan

Problem-solution plans are divided into two parts: the statement of the problem and the solution(s). Some complex presentations may deal with multiple problems and solutions. Below is an outline for a speech examining a water shortage problem and a solution to that problem.

> SPECIFIC PURPOSE: To propose a solution to the water shortage problem in Elmville.
> INTRODUCTION
> I. Because of the increased population growth in the valley, more demands are being placed on our water supply.
>   A. Three new housing developments started last year will increase water demand by thousands of gallons per month.
>   B. Additional enrollments at area colleges further increase the demand for water.
>   C. A new manufacturing company has decided to locate in the area and will be transferring employees to Elmville.
> II. The lake's capacity can be improved by increasing the height of the spillway.
> III. A pipeline from the northern watershed will be completed by 1990.
> IV. Water-saving devices can be distributed to all residences.
> CONCLUSION

In the problem-solution plan the problem is stated in main point I and further discussed in subheadings A, B, and C. The solution to the problem is outlined in subheadings II, III, and IV. The subpoint arrangement was chosen arbitrarily by the author and can be restructured into many different combinations. For example, when outlining a problem-solution plan, the problem can consist of any reasonable number of main points followed by the solution(s), which can also include any reasonable number of main points. Each main point can be expanded in subheadings. The key is to begin with the problem and then follow with the solution. In some speeches, more than one problem and solution are offered. To make it easier for the audience to understand the speech, each problem should be stated, then followed by the appropriate solution(s). It becomes confusing when all the problems are stated and then a variety of solutions offered, some fitting one problem and some fitting others. That much complexity may need more than one speech or be accompanied by a written report. One final caution when dealing with a problem-solution plan: Be careful not to state a problem as a main point and then a solution as a subheading. For example, an *incorrect* arrangement would be as follows:

I. In some Midwestern states the lack of rainfall has resulted in dust bowl conditions.
  A. Irrigation is improving soil conditions and crop yields.

The correct way to state the solution would be to elevate subheading A to main point II.

Cause-Effect Plan

Much like the problem-solution plan, the cause-effect plan is organized around one or more causes followed by the effect(s). A cause-effect organizational plan dealing with the subject of poor study habits could look like this:

> SPECIFIC PURPOSE: To show the effect of poor study habits on academic achievement.
> INTRODUCTION
> I. Many students enter their freshman year of college more concerned about social acceptance than academic achievement.
>   A. New surroundings and few friends contribute to this concern.
>   B. Some schools stress fraternity or sorority membership early in the school year.
> II. New freedom associated with fewer in-class hours results in less time devoted to studying.
> III. The student gets behind in his or her studies in the first few weeks of the semester and is not able to catch up.
> IV. Fewer examinations result in less opportunity to bring up low grades.
> V. By the fourth week of class, too much information must be comprehended for the student to pass the course successfully.
> CONCLUSION

The speech, while being divided into different subpoints, is still basically organized into two parts, the cause (I, II, III) and the effect (IV, V). Care must be taken in organizing the cause-effect plan. It is too easy to fall into the pattern of using subheadings as an effect and main points as the cause. Remember that subheadings are used to expand on a main point. In a cause-effect plan, we have done this with main point I and subpoint A and B. This is a correct representation of "cause." which is stated in the main point and expanded upon in the subheading. It would have been incorrect to state the cause in the main point and then state an effect in the subheading.

Related-Topics Plan

A related-topics plan is one of the more frequently used organizational plans because a wide variety of information can be included in the speech without that information being compartmentalized into one of the previous plans we have discussed. Consider the organization of a speech centered around a related-topics plan:

> SPECIFIC PURPOSE: To explain the role of advertising in society.
> INTRODUCTION
> I. Advertising agencies provide talent, research, and distribution.
>   A. Media buyers, art directors, and graphic artists are some of the individuals found in an advertising agency.
>   B. Agencies are involved in researching both the product and the market before the advertising campaign is launched.

    C. Critical to the success of the campaign is the ability to choose the most effective medium of distribution.
      1. Radio reaches specialized audiences who have a preference for a particular format.
      2. Television provides a visual dimension to an ad but is expensive and cannot be targeted as easily as radio.
      3. Magazines are effective when high-quality color reproduction is employed.
 II. The majority of our attitudes about advertising are centered on the credibility of a message and its entertainment value.
    A. A popular advertising campaign for a fast-food hamburger chain developed around a slogan.
    B. Financial institutions, brokerage houses, and banks are considered by some to have credible advertising.
III. As the nation moves toward service industries and as new media such as cable television develop, the outlook for job opportunities in advertising is bright.
CONCLUSION

Speeches that deal with contemporary issues are often organized around a related-topics plan. This plan will frequently contain other plans incorporated into subheadings, as we'll now discuss.

Combinations of Different Plans

Not all speeches fit into a single organizational plan. Some speeches include combinations and variations of the plans that we have just examined. For example, a speech dealing with crime prevention could include a related-topics plan and then be subdivided into other organizational plans.

SPECIFIC PURPOSE: To persuade people to take part in the Community Watch crime-prevention program.
INTRODUCTION
  I. Many new residents to the area are unfamiliar with the Community Watch crime-prevention program.
 II. The program is designed to enlist the help of citizens in identifying and marking valuable property.
    A. Many stolen items cannot be claimed by their owners because the items cannot be identified.
    B. Special electronic marking pencils label each item with the owner's identification number.
III. Local police departments work with citizens groups to develop Community Watch programs for each street or neighborhood.
    A. Years ago officers spent more time on foot patrol and knew everyone in the neighborhood.
    B. Today, increased use of vehicle patrols has lessened the personal contact between citizens and police officers.
IV. The Community Watch program has been especially effective in suburban areas.
    A. In the inter-city and downtown areas residential and business housing is close together and surveillance by tenants and police is much easier.
    B. Outlying suburban neighborhoods result in detached housing on large lots, making police protection more difficult.
CONCLUSION

In our speech about the Community Watch crime-prevention program, four different plans have been incorporated into the outline. A related-topics plan has been employed for the main points of the speech (I, II, III, IV). Within the main points are subheadings representing a problem-solution plan (II, A and B), a chronological plan (III, A and B), and a spatial plan (IV, A and B).

HANDLING INTRODUCTIONS AND CONCLUSIONS

You may wonder why we are discussing the introduction and conclusion of a speech after discussing outlining. You might ask, Why not talk about the introduction first? Too many people begin a speech thinking about the introduction. Consequently, they determine the topic, not on its appeal to the audience, not on its ability to be managed, but on whether the speaker can come up with a good introduction. Planning a speech should not begin with what you are going to say in the introduction. That comes after you have selected a topic, written a specific purpose, and outlined the speech. This does not lessen the importance of the introduction. An introduction serves some key purposes that are critical to the development of the speech.

An Introduction That Gains Attention

Without the attention of the audience, a speaker has little hope of communicating information. Many ways exist to gain attention. One of the simplest is to make a statement that elevates the emotion of the audience. A speech dealing with the importance of early career preparation in college and delivered to a group of college freshmen began with the following introduction:

> Let me begin by asking each of you a question. How many of you in this class are freshmen? [Virtually the entire class raised their hand.] Then pay close attention to my next statement. [The speaker paused and looked slowly around the room.] You only have three more summer vacations left in your life.

The class groaned. What the speaker wanted to emphasize was that, a lot sooner than the class realized, student would be searching for a job and marketing themselves to employers. If they didn't begin now to think about what their résumé would look like when they graduated, it would be too late when they were seniors. The speaker went on to stress the importance of internships, taking advantage of opportunities in college, and collecting letters of recommendation.

Another example of gaining attention can be found in the introduction of a speech about drug abuse. The speaker was addressing a group of parents. This is the introduction that gained their attention:

> One of the biggest problems I face when addressing parents is making them understand how easy it is to become a drug addict. What you may not know is that at one time or another more than 95 percent of you were drug addicts, and

at least 75 percent of you are drug addicts right now. [After a short pause to let what had been said sink in, the speaker continued.] You probably think I am wrong, but every one of you who gets up in the morning and must start the day with a cup of coffee is a drug addict. You are addicted to the drug caffeine. You may not think you are, but tomorrow just try and go through the entire day without a cup of coffee. Go ahead, try it. And how many of you smoke? [Knowing what was coming next, only a few people sheepishly raised their hands.] You are also drug addicts. You are addicted to nicotine.

In each of the two examples, the speaker went on to develop the main points of the speech and supported the points with facts and personal experiences.

Using Humor

Humor can be a good way to gain audience attention, instill a positive feeling toward the speaker, and begin the speech on an upbeat note. It can also fail miserably. Too many people use humor without realizing that if a joke or humorous anecdote fails at the beginning of a speech, the speaker will need to use the rest of the speech to regain both composure and credibility. Some speakers have used tasteless jokes or, worse yet, tasteless jokes based on stereotypes related to sex or race. The stupidity of such statements is matched only by their lack of effect. Others use humor but make no connection between the humorous statement and the speech. A funny story about what you did on your vacation will not tie into a speech on foreign policy. You may have managed a few laughs but you will leave the audience asking, "So what does that have to do with the speech?" Others will feel you are wasting their valuable time, and still others will feel you lack the intelligence, professionalism, and courtesy to adapt your humor to the audience and the speech.

This does not mean that you should avoid using humor. It can be effective if done correctly. First, do not try for the big laugh. An anecdote that is not meant to be particularly funny but has some humor is better than a joke that simply falls flat on its face if no one laughs. You can easily recover from the former. The audience did not detect in your delivery an expectation that they should be rolling in the aisles with laughter.

Concluding a Speech

Two common ways of concluding a speech are a summary statement or a tie-in with the introduction. For example, in the speech on career planning the speaker used the following conclusion:

Even though you only have three summer vacations left in your life, take the time now to investigate internships and other opportunities that will give you professional experience before you graduate. Develop a resume now, not later. It will help you understand where your weaknesses are so you can begin to fill in the gaps. Develop relationships with individuals who can write letters of recommendation. Do not wait until you are ready to graduate. Good letters of recommendation occur when you are fresh in the mind of the person writing the letter. Do these things and you will be in a position to compete in the job market. The three summer vacations are ones that can be enjoyable but also productive.

In this conclusion, the speaker not only tied in the introduction but also tied together and summarized the main points of the speech.

THE IMPORTANCE OF SUPPORTING THE SPEECH

The sample introduction used by the speaker to address an audience of parents on the subject of drug abuse captured their attention. The speaker also helped to hold the audience's attention because of his own credibility. He was a state police officer who had investigated a number of drug-related cases. He possessed the credibility necessary to support much of what he said. Although he also used statistics and other forms of support, his own experiences supported the speech.

A good speech is well supported by any number of things. The credibility of the speaker, the speaker's ability to develop homophily with the audience, and the speaker's use of reasoning are just some of the ways in which a speech and the speaker are believable.

THE ROLE OF SOURCE CREDIBILITY

A speaker's credibility centers around how dynamic and authoritative the speaker is as well as the speaker's character.[1] The former, often called *dynamism*, is controlled by the way in which the speech is delivered. For example, a speaker who is more aggressive than meek, more bold than timid, more energetic than tired, and more extroverted than introverted, will be perceived by the audience as having certain dynamic qualities that will contribute to the speaker's credibility. Similarly, if the audience perceives the speaker as informed, reliable, qualified, intelligent, and an expert on the subject, then this will contribute to the speaker being perceived as authoritative. If the audience perceives the speaker as honest, friendly, pleasant, unselfish, and virtuous, then the speaker will be perceived as having good character. The adjectives just used to illustrate the "dynamic," "authoritative," and "character" dimensions of a speaker are adjectives that research has frequently identified as labels for a speaker's credibility.

Source credibility is related to the topic of the speech and the audience which hears the speech. For example, a lumberjack, while appearing dynamic and of good character, might have little authority speaking about the history of French cooking unless the lumberjack was a recognized expert on the subject. Similarly, the dynamic qualities of a speaker can help to reinforce the speaker's authority. An expert may not be perceived as an expert if the individual is so timid and introverted he or she cannot effectively communicate thoughts and ideas to the audience.

Many readers of this text will be delivering speeches to classmates. Stop and ask yourself what topics you could select to address an audience of your peers and how will they perceive you on the dimensions of source credibility we have just discussed. How good a public speaker are you? Do you know enough about your subject and can you support it with facts or other data that will make your presentation authoritative? Are there personal qualities about you which will be communicated to the audience? Will these personal qualities reflect on the content of the speech or how you are perceived by the audience?

PERCEIVED HOMOPHILY

Earlier in this text we learned that homophily consists of perceived shared experiences, attitudes, opinions, and other qualities of senders and receivers of communication. As it applies to this chapter, homophily relates to the speaker and the audience. The amount of homophily that exists will be reflected in the way the audience perceives the speaker as understanding the audience and sharing in the audience's feelings and emotions. In some cases, a speaker will have achieved homophily before starting the speech. For example, a political figure may have achieved such a following that those who are attending the speech will already perceive the person as having the same opinions, attitudes, and experiences. They may, therefore, as we learned in the chapter on audience analysis, take the time to expose themselves to the speech, perceive what the speaker says as being similar to their own opinions of the issue, and remember more than if they were not positively predisposed to the speech.

When preparing a speech, ask yourself to what degree homophily can help support your presentation. For example, if you are a student speaking to a group of students, then already you enjoy the advantage of having something in common with your audience.

ETHOS, PATHOS, LOGOS

The ancient Greeks were serious scholars of the process of communication. Although sophisticated research methodologies and contemporary results of research have cautioned us against overgeneralizing about what the Greeks told us, we still find that much of their wisdom is of value. To the Greeks, the qualities of ethos, pathos, and logos were important to supporting a speech, especially persuasive speeches.

Ethos: Character and the Central Governing Principle

To some degree we have already studied ethos. Ethos refers to the character of the speaker and we discussed character as part of source credibility. Ethos also goes beyond character. Character itself, when approached from ethos, is a central governing principle that is possessed by the individual and which separates the individual from other individuals. Thus, a world leader held in high esteem by contemporaries enjoys that status because of more than just character. The ethos is created by a foundation of support for control issues which others also support. Mere knowledge of a subject is not enough. Neither is personal character by itself. Commitments, beliefs, attitudes, willingness to defend one's beliefs—all are central to ethos.

Pathos: Call to Emotion

Whereas ethos refers to the central character of an individual, pathos is based on emotion. A speaker who supports a speech with pathos arouses the audience in support of the speaker's cause. Feelings of pity, tenderness, and sympathy are examples of pathos. Pathos is also the subjective evaluation of a message. For example, a speaker who tells us that undernourished children are suffering and dying in major cities may arouse our sympathy. That arousal is a subjective quality which may or may not be the same as the arousal experienced by another person hearing the same speech. The statement may be further supported by a statistic that shows that last year more than 1,000 children died every month from diseases caused by malnutrition. The latter statement, while also arousing emotion, is more objectively evaluated by the audience. The statistic is communicated as fact, not emotion (even though it may elicit emotion).

Pathos, used by a skillful speaker, is a powerful form of support. Consider the following pathos-based excerpt from a speech on neglected children.

> We walked down the row of houses which had been beaten by the weather and neglected by the city. On the front steps of a sagging unpainted porch a young child about two years of age was sitting with her head between the porch railings. She was giggling at two rats gnawing on the carcass of a dead, dismembered dog stretched on the ground about three feet below. Flies were covering the carcass and buzzing about the child's face. Now and then a fly would land on the child's lips and tongue and she would wince.

It would make little difference what statistic accompanied the above paragraph. The emotion generated by the words of the speaker are enough to arouse our feelings.

Logos: Call to Reasoning

Logos refers to support based on logic and reasoning. Readers who have taken a course in logic know both the power and fallacy of logical support. Central to understanding logic is the *syllogism*. A syllogism contains a major premise, a minor premise, and a conclusion. For example, consider the following syllogism: All members of the college debate team are good speakers (major premise). Cindy is a member of the debate team (minor premise). Therefore, Cindy is a good speaker (conclusion). The syllogism resulting in the conclusion that Cindy is a good speaker employed what we call *deductive reasoning,* reasoning from the general (members of the debate team are good speakers) to the specific (Cindy is a good speaker).

THE USE OF REASONING

Reasoning, as discussed in the example of Cindy, is of two basic types: deductive and inductive. Deductive reasoning, as we have just stated, moves from the general to the specific. Inductive reasoning moves from the specific to the general. For example, we could go back to Cindy and determine that because Cindy is a good speaker, and because she is on the debate team, that all members of the debate team are therefore good speakers. Or we might determine that if a certain movie director is responsible for an Academy Award–winning film, then other films by the same director will win Academy Awards. That, of course, is not the case, and we can immediately see the fallacy of trying to reason inductively without a great deal of additional proof beyond the syllogism. We can see that it is much more difficult to support an argument through inductive reasoning than it is through deductive reasoning, although in many speeches we tend to use more inductive than deductive reasoning, simply because we have access to more limited amounts of information.

For example, much of research, by its very nature, uses small samples of information to make inferences about larger samples. Consider the public opinion poll. A random sample of people is selected (each person in the sample population having an equal chance of being chosen), the sample is then polled, and inferences made about the larger population. Translated into information for public consumption, the television news commentator at station WAAA reads the results of the poll: "Candidate Jones is leading candidate Smith by 5 percentage points. A poll of 250 registered voters shows candidate Jones with 54 percent of the vote and candidate Smith with 46 percent of the vote. Thus, on this sample we can predict candidate Jones will be the winner in tomorrow's election."

The next day, candidate Smith, not Jones, wins the election. WAAA's news polls suffered from some of the fallacies of inductive reasoning. First, the data upon which the initial premise was based was in error. The sample chosen for the WAAA poll was too small to make sound predictions, especially when the margin of error for a sample of 250 is more than 6 percent. Thus, while the sample chosen by WAAA showed Jones ahead of Smith, the voter preference of the total population might have been as much as 6 percent in the opposite direction. The premise upon which WAAA based its prediction was faulty. Similarly, other factors were omitted, such as the number of people who intended to vote as opposed to those who registered to vote.

Faulty inductive reasoning is common. Using the example of Cindy, we can immediately see that although she may be a good speaker, it is risky to infer that because she is on the debate team that everyone on the debate team is a good speaker. We might also challenge the premise, used in deductive reasoning, that everyone on the debate team is a good speaker. We might ask, By what standards has it been determined that everyone on the debate team is a good speaker? Who has applied those standards and are they qualified to apply those standards?

A FALLACY

The *post hoc, ergo propter hoc* fallacy (after this, therefore because of this) is the assumption that because something precedes something it is the cause of something.[2] The fallacy is particularly important when using the cause-effect plan of organization. A newspaper article originating from an Associated Press wire service story illustrates this fallacy. It seems a California assemblyman pointed out to the press that a controversial sex education textbook that was to be used in the California public schools was discovered in the home of a man linked to 27 murders of young men in Texas. The assemblyman charged that the textbook and similar material contributed to warped minds and a warped sense of values and therefore were responsible for the murders. A further investigation turned up the fact that along with the textbook there was also found a copy of the Bible, and a number of issues of *Reader's Digest.* The assemblyman was guilty of the *post hoc, ergo propter hoc* fallacy and tried to convince the public that the controversial textbook was the real reason behind the murders.

The fallacy appears frequently in arguments to ban what some consider to be pornographic material. Such material, when found in the possession of sex offenders, is linked to the crime. There are those who then argue that if pornographic material were banned, sex crimes would decrease. The truth is that the sex crimes may be the result of psychological instability and a host of other causes.

Television violence has also faced the *post hoc, ergo propter hoc* fallacy. Critics claim that violence on television results in more aggravated assaults and those convicted of such assaults are heavy viewers of violent programming. What critics fail to point out is that aggravated assaults can be caused by factors other than television and that those same factors can be responsible for people watching more violent television. Similarly, the influence of parents, interaction and influence of peers, even diet can result in children becoming aggressive toward other children. Such children also tend to watch cartoons because they are frequently left alone by their parents. Assuming that the cartoons cause the aggressive behavior would be committing the same fallacy.

ATTRIBUTION

When facts, statistics, quotations, and other more "objective" information are used to support a speech, the question arises: Where did the information come from? When attributing information to a source, including another person, the speaker not only needs to be sure the information is accurate but also that the source is reliable. For example, scholars studying mass media, including newspapers, books, and magazines, know that some media are more credible than others. If you are delivering a speech on national economic policy, a writer for the *Wall Street Journal* will generally be more credible than a local storekeeper who is quoted in a small-town weekly. The storekeeper could be used for feature material in your speech and add some interesting local applications of more complex national economic policy.

PRIMARY VS. SECONDARY SOURCES

A primary source is an original or first-reported source of information, whereas a secondary source contains a second report of the original source. For example, if we want to quote statistics on business and industry we can consult a primary source such as the *Statistical Abstracts of the United States*. Or we might quote a newspaper article that quotes the *Abstracts*. Whereas the newspaper article might be a satisfactory source of information, it is not a primary source. Similarly, when quoting another person, unless you have personally talked to that individual, the source of the quote will more than likely be a secondary source such as a newspaper or a newsmagazine. Colleges and universities are good places for primary source material. Professors from many different diciplines offer an opportunity for first-hand interviews on a wealth of subjects. Professors can be a primary source of information which a college audience can easily relate to and identify with.

ANALOGIES

Analogies are a form of inference between two different things perceived as being alike. An analogy can help to support a speech by becoming an example, sometimes more vivid than the point being made. For example, in a speech about career preparation a speaker emphasized that letters of recommendation should be written by people who know the applicant well and who have dealt with the person recently. The speaker advised students participating in internships to have their supervisor place a letter of recommendation in their placement file as soon as the internship is completed. The letter will reflect more detailed positive information than if the student goes back six months or a year later and asks for the letter. In emphasizing this point the speaker used an analogy.

> Near the end of the internship, or as soon as possible after the internship ends, ask your supervisor if he or she would be willing to write you a letter of recommendation. If you have a final exit interview or lunch with your supervisor, this is a good time to request the letter.
>
> Waiting until later to ask for the letter places you at a disadvantage. It's like spending an evening enjoying a good meal with good service at a fine restaurant. At the end of the meal the waiter or waitress brings you your bill and you leave a nice large tip.
>
> Now ask yourself, how much of a tip would you leave if the waiter had not asked for the tip the night of the dinner but instead waited six months or a year and then asked for the tip? Not very much if anything. Now you can understand the importance of asking for the letter of recommendation when you are fresh in your supervisor's mind.

PERSONAL EXPERIENCES

Many beginning speakers eschew personal experiences to support a speech because they feel those experiences aren't important enough to share with others. They feel more comfortable with facts, statistics, quotations, and information developed from sources other than themselves. Still others are self-conscious about relating their own experiences to others.

If we think back over what we have read, personal experiences can be an effective way to support a speech. Personal experiences provide you with a primary source of information. Who could be more of an authority on your experiences than you? Your experiences can add a personal dimension to a speech that can generate not only warmth and understanding but also factual information. People, including audiences, are interested in the lives of other people. You move beyond the abstract world of supportive information when you interject a human dimension into your speech through a retelling of personal experiences.

USING STATISTICS

Statistics consist of numerical data, usually grouped in summary forms. We have learned from our example of inductive reasoning that statistics can represent smaller portions of a whole and can be used, sometimes incorrectly, to predict the characteristics of a larger population. The slogan "statistics lie" may not be entirely accurate, but then again, statistics do not always tell the complete truth. Take for example, the research study that listed the best and worst states in which to live.[3] Containing some 40 categories, including the number of television sets in use, the number of Lincolns and Cadillacs, crime reports, and other statistical information, the final list ranked states in order of life style. The top 10 states were: Connecticut, Minnesota, New York, Illinois, Massachusetts, Hawaii, New Hampshire, Rhode Island, California, Utah. Is a statistic which reports the number of Cadillacs and Lincolns a valid statistic upon which to base assumptions about overall lifestyle? Does a major metropolitan area in a smaller state lose its position on the list because of high crime in that particular city? Would industrialization be the cause of more television sets and not necessarily reflect on the overall life style of the state? These are questions that an intelligent audience will ask and which a speaker may need to defend.

Another study developed a list of the best football teams based on their won-lost record. A statistician at Harvard argued the list was faulty because it did not take into consideration the difficulty of the opponents and the overall playing schedule.[4]

Ratios can also cause faulty reasoning. Ratios consist of one unit of analysis divided by another. Averages are actually ratios of larger numbers divided by smaller numbers, such as the average age of the class, which is determined by adding all of the ages together and dividing that number by the number of people in the class. You cannot, however, average two ratios, which would be the same as averaging averages. For example, if the average age of freshmen is 18.5 years of age and the average age of seniors is 20.5, then the average age of freshmen and seniors together is *not* the sum of 18.5 + 20.5 divided by 2. Because there are many more freshmen than seniors, the correct average of the age of the two classes would be found by going back and computing the original data, which would necessitate adding together the ages of all seniors and all freshmen and dividing the summation by the number of students in both classes.

When statistics are part of your speech or used as a basis for other information, be prepared to look behind the statistics to achieve the real meaning and importance of the information.

SUMMARY

The first step in developing a speech is choosing a topic that takes into consideration what your audience wants to hear and what you as a speaker are qualified to talk about. Manageable topics take into consideration both the content and time limits of your speech. After the topic is selected, a clear, concise, specific purpose is written. This helps prevent some of the pitfalls of speech preparation, such as selecting a topic that is too broad, unclear, or inappropriate.

For an audience to be able to comprehend a speech, the speech must be well organized. Typical plans of organization include: the spatial plan—arranged around geographic areas such as West to East or from the inner city to the suburbs; the chronological plan—which moves from a point in history to the present or future or from the future or present into the past; the problem-solution plan—which states a problem(s) followed by a solution(s); the cause-effect plan—which is similar to the problem-solution plan except that a cause(s) is preceded by an effect(s); the related-topics plan—where similar topics are presented and where no other plan fits the organization scheme of the speech. A speech can also be arranged around combinations of each plan just discussed.

An effective speech contains an introduction that captures and holds the attention of the audience. If used effectively, humor can complement both the introduction and other parts of the speech. Conclusions to a speech frequently refer back to the introduction or review the main points of the speech.

Effective speeches rely on support mechanisms. Source credibility, which consists of the dimensions of dynamism, character, and authoritativeness, is one form of support. Ethos, pathos, and logos are others. Ethos is related to source credibility. Pathos is the use of emotional appeals in a speech, whereas logos appears to logic and reason. Both deductive and inductive reasoning help support a speech, although fallacies can be present in both. Another fallacy is the *post hoc, ergo propter hoc* fallacy, which infers that "after this, therefore this."

Many beginning speakers overlook the use of personal experiences. Credibility and a primary source of information are two of the benefits of including a personal reference in a speech. An analogy can also support a speech by providing an example and emphasizing a main point. Facts and statistics can support a speech, but care must be used because statistics can both mislead and inform.

QUESTIONS FOR REVIEW AND DISCUSSION

1. What important things must a speaker take into consideration when choosing a topic?

2. Why is it important to organize our thoughts before presenting them to an audience?

3. Why is caution advised when using humor in a speech?

4. How is source credibility a form of support?

5. How are ethos, pathos, and logos used as support for a speech?

6. What causes deductive reasoning to be unsound?

7. What is the *post hoc, ergo propter hoc* fallacy?

8. What are the differences between primary and secondary sources?

9. Why must a speaker be careful when using statistics to support a speech?

LEARNING EXERCISES

1. Using the five plans of organization outlined in the chapter, develop a sample speech outline for (1) an informative speech on cold remedies, and (2) a demonstration on ceramic/pottery making.

2. Attend a speech or watch a speech on television. Take notes and outline the speech. Determine if any other plan of organization would have been appropriate for the topic the speaker chose.

ADDITIONAL READINGS

Bower, S. A. *Painless Public Speaking: Develop and Deliver Your Train of Thought Anytime, Anywhere.* Englewood Cliffs, NJ: Prentice-Hall–Spectrum Books, 1981.

Capps, R., C. H. Dodd, and H. J. Winn *Communication for the Business and Professional Speaker.* New York: Macmillan, 1981.

Dellinger, S., and B. Deane *Communicating Effectively: A Complete Guide for Better Management.* Radnor, PA: Chilton, 1982.

Jefferies, J. R. and J. D. Bates *An Executive Guide to Meetings, Conferences, and Audiovisual Presentations.* New York: McGraw-Hill, 1983.

Koehler, J. W., and J. I. Sisco *Public Communication in Business and the Professions.* St. Paul: West Publishing Company, 1981.

Leech, T. *How to Prepare, Stage, and Deliver Winning Presentations.* New York: AMACOM, 1982.

Lieberman, G. F. *3500 Good Quotes for Speakers.* New York: Doubleday, 1983.

Vardaman, G. T. *Making Successful Presentations.* New York: AMACOM, 1981.

Wydro, K. *Think on Your Feet: The Art of Thinking and Speaking Under Pressure.* Englewood Cliffs, NJ: Prentice-Hall–Spectrum Books, 1981.

11

RESEARCHING THE SPEECH

OBJECTIVES

After completing this chapter, you should be able to

- Be familiar with basic library procedures
- Develop a research strategy
- Use the card catalogue
- Be aware of reference sources
- Be able to use indexes
- Know how to use abstracting services
- List some key statistical indexes and abstracts
- Cite legal sources
- Realize journals and trade publications are excellent sources of information.

The two previous chapters conditioned us to the importance of audience analysis, organization, and support in speech preparation. These important concepts are necessary before starting to research a speech. When we begin our research we need to be able to recognize information as valuable or of little use, and we need to know how it falls into place in our organizational plan.

MAKING FRIENDS WITH THE LIBRARY

For many of us, the word *research* brings to mind long lonely hours in the library. Libraries suffer from this image because for many students their first serious visit to the library is under the pressure of a deadline to finish a paper or report. A library can be an enjoyable, even exciting place when we understand how to use it and how much benefit it can give us. Preparation for a speech can begin by just browsing in a periodical room to get ideas. Once the idea has emerged and the topic refined, the research strategy begins. The strategy involves knowing something about the location of books in the library, which is best accomplished by visiting the library and taking the necessary time to study the floor guide. Most people only to go the library for the purpose of checking out a book. They then go to the card catalogue, find a call number, and start their search by trying to locate the floor area in the vicinity of where they believe the publication can be found. To their dismay, they find the book isn't there. They become discouraged and complain that something is wrong with the library. In many cases the researcher has not taken the time to become comfortable in the library, not taken the time to let the library become a friend, not taken the time to find out how the library is organized, and not developed a strategy before beginning a search.

A good way to begin this chapter is to spend an afternoon or evening in a friendly visit to the library. Browse through the lobby, wander through the periodical room, look through periodicals from different disciplines, different universities, different countries. Walk casually among the stacks and read the titles of books. Pull some from the shelf and scan their contents. Take the time to expand your mind to other horizons; begin to break down some of the subconscious barriers to research many of us possess.

A STRATEGY

The first step in our strategy is to search for more general information. Unless we are experts on a subject and know a great deal about the topic, our research strategy will move from the general to the specific. Reference materials, such as encyclopedias, are valuable first steps. With information located in background sources we can narrow our search to more specific information found in journals and books. Many times the more general information will give us key terms that will make looking for more detailed information that much easier. For example, while browsing through a book about popular music we might encounter the term *videodisc*. We learn that recorded music has become both a visual and a sound medium. As a result, we want to learn more about videodiscs and we go to the card catalogue or indexes to locate information.

Looking for more general information to support a speech makes a search strategy much easier. Beginning researchers frequently do the opposite. This makes the research strategy more difficult for three reasons. First, the more specialized information can be difficult to find until after one has become familiar with the library. Second, it is easier to comprehend more detailed information about a subject after one has grasped its more general principles. Third, these more general sources may contain bibliographical information or references that can direct the research to additional sources.

Abstracts, annual bibliographies, literary reviews, and government documents can be helpful in locating more detailed information.

Different speech topics will mean different levels of research. However, it is not possible to know too much about a subject, and the more a speaker knows, the more opportunities to advance a credible, authoritative presentation. Where a class assignment may require an outline, being able to show that you have gone beyond beginning sources could be a plus.

USING THE CARD CATALOGUE

Not all catalogue cards are alike, even for the same book.

Subject-Heading, Author, and Title Cards

When we have some idea of what our topic will be, the subject-heading card is a good place to start. It groups the catalogue cards by heading. For example, if we wanted to research a speech on radio we can look under "Radio" in the card catalogue. If we're not sure what heading to look under, the *Library of Congress Subject Headings* will give us a good start. This guide refers us to specific subject headings dealing with the general topic of our speech. Let's say we want to deliver a speech about radio; the Library of Congress subject guide would refer us to some of the following headings:

> Radio
> Radio—U.S. Laws and Regulations
> Radio Advertising
> Radio Announcing
> Radio as a Profession
> Radio Audiences
> Radio Authorship
> Radio Broadcasting
> Radio in Education
> Radio Journalism
> Radio Plays

Two other cards that can be useful are the *author card* (Fig. 11–1) and the *title card*. The author card lists the name of the author first and can be used when the author's name is known. Similarly, the title card lists the title first and can be used when we know the title of the book and thus can go directly to the title card.

```
PN207
.B6
 1983          Bostrom, Robert N.
                   Persuasion/Robert N. Bostrom. --
               Englewood Cliffs, N.J.:  Prentice-Hall,
               c 1983.
                   xiv, 296 p. ; 24 cm.
                   Bibliography:  p. 255-281.
                   Includes index.
                   ISBN 0-13-661157-5

                   1.  Persuasion (Rhetoric)
                   2.  Persuasion (Psychology)        I.  Title

 NcU      8554226            LIZE              NOCCde     82-12190
```

Figure 11-1   The author card lists the author's name, followed by the title of the book. In the upper left corner is the call number, which can help locate the book on the library shelf. Other information includes the publisher and year of publication, the number of pages, whether there is a bibliography and index, and the ISBN number. At the bottom of the author card are tracings which provide additional topics where similar works can be found. Two other types of cards are subject-heading cards, which list the subject of the book, and a title card, which begins with the book's title. Both subject-heading and title cards contain basically the same information but in different order.

Call Numbers

In the upper left-hand corner of the card you will find the *call number*. The call number refers us to the location of the book in the library and is assigned so that books on similar subjects are shelved together.

The call number may be used to peruse the shelves or find a specific book on a specific topic. Usually a subject-heading card is not assigned to a book unless a significant portion of the book is on that topic.

REFERENCE SOURCES

Reference books can provide such things as general overviews of a topic, definitions of terms, bibliographic information, bibliographies, and introductory essays. Reference books can also help to search for information in more extensive library sources.

Bibliographical Sources

Most school libraries have numerous sources of bibliographical information. Three of the major ones are:

Contemporary Authors: A multivolume work containing bibliographical information on living authors from every nation, giving personal data, avocations, writings, and works in progress.

Current Biography (1940 to date): A multivolume set of biographies of people in the news, both in the United States and abroad, often with photographs and obituaries.

Who's Who in America. The standard source of current biographies of noted men and women in the United States.

Dictionaries and Encyclopedias

General dictionaries and encyclopedias such as the *Encyclopedia Americana* and others are common to most libraries, but more specialized ones include the *Encyclopedia of Psychology,* the *International Encyclopedia for the Social Sciences,* and the *Encyclopedia of Educational Research.* Two examples of even more specialized encyclopedias include the *Great Soviet Encyclopedia* and the *Encyclopedia of Library and Information Sciences.*

USING INDEXES

Once we have narrowed our speech topic and want to go to more specialized sources, indexes can be used to locate relevant articles in magazines, journals, books, and newspapers. Some good ones to start with are:

Applied Science and Technology Index: Science and technology journals are indexed, and the AST Index is a good source of information on high-technology and computers.

Business Periodicals Index (1958 to date): An index to over 100 journals on various aspects of business.

California News Index: Indexes the *Los Angeles Times, Sacramento Bee, San Diego Union, San Francisco Chronicle and Examiner,* and *San Jose Mercury* and Sunday *Mercury-News.*

Current Index to Journals in Education: One of the larger indexes, covering more than 700 journals including publications directly and peripherally related to education.

Education Index: An index to over 200 periodicals relating to education.

Humanities Index: Formerly part of the *Social Sciences and Humanities Index,* an index to over 260 journals in the humanities.

Index to Legal Periodicals: Indexes in major law publications.

Index to Periodicals Relating to Law: Articles indexed are not usually found in main legal periodicals.

International Index to Multimedia Information: An index of material found in audio-video services.

National Newspaper Index: Indexes the *Christian Science Monitor*, *The New York Times* and the *Wall Street Journal.*

National Observer Index: Indexes the *National Observer* from 1962 through 1977.

The New York Times Index: Indexes *The New York Times.*

Newspaper Index: Topic index of articles appearing in the *Chicago Tribune, Los Angeles Times, New Orleans Times-Picayune* and the *Washington Post.*

Public Affairs Information Services (P.A.I.S.): A subject index to "current books, pamphlets, periodical articles, government documents, and other materials in the field of economics and public affairs."

Reader's Guide to Periodical Literature: A subject and author index to over 100 periodicals of popular interest.

Social Sciences Index: Formerly part of the *Social Sciences and Humanities Index,* and index to over 260 journals in the social sciences.

Social Sciences and Humanities Index 1965–1972 (formerly *International Index 1920–1965*): An index of over 200 journals, which in 1973 was divided into two indexing services: *Humanities Index* and *Social Sciences Index.*

Wall Street Journal Index: Index of the *Wall Street Journal.*

You will notice some of the indexes are newspaper indexes. In addition to these, other newspaper indexes are available including indexes for the *Chicago Sun Times, Denver Post, Detroit News, Houston Post, San Francisco Chronicle, Arkansas Gazette, Baltimore Evening Sun, Barrons's, Charleston* (West Virginia) *Gazette and Mail, Cleveland Press, Des Moines Register, Flint* (Michigan) *Journal, Honolulu Star Bulletin, Minneapolis Tribune, Raleigh* (North Carolina) *News and Observer, Durham* (North Carolina) *Sun, Washington Star, Atlanta Constitution, Bergen* (New Jersey) *Record,* and others. Some are indexed by the newspapers themselves and housed on-location or in nearby libraries. Others are available from companies involved in commercially producing indexes such as the Microfilming Corporation of America and Bell & Howell.

Also consult the indexes in most scholarly journals and magazines. Each is designed for quick reference to that particular publication.

USING ABSTRACTING SERVICES

An abstract not only contains information about how to find a particular journal article, just as an indexing service does, but it also summarizes the article. Usually the abstract is short—50 to 150 words. An abstracting service often indexes and abstracts many different sources.

Dissertation Abstracts International: A monthly compilation of abstracts of doctoral dissertations submitted to University Microfilms International by more than 375 cooperating institutions in the United States and Canada.

Education Abstracts: Summary of articles related to education.

Historical Abstracts, International Political Science Abstracts: Source for policy-related subjects.

Journalism Abstracts: Covers theses and dissertations in journalism and mass communications.

Psychological Abstracts: An abstracting service for the world's literature in psychology and related fields.

Resources in Education: Published by the Government Printing Office, this source indexes and abstracts material from clearing houses in the Educational Resources Information Center (ERIC). Included are reports, documents, and conference proceedings.

Sociological Abstracts (1953 to date): An abstracting service for articles on sociology from many journals.

LOCALIZING SOURCES

Not all libraries have access to all of the indexes listed here. When one becomes familiar with a specific library, it is possible to develop a research strategy based on that library's holdings. At first it may seem remote that we would use one of the more specialized indexes. But consider the audience. A speech delivered to an audience in Pennsylvania can be more informative and authoritative if it deals with information about Pennsylvania. A speech to an audience in California can be more interesting if it deals with a subject related to California; thus, the *California Newspaper Index* may be more valuable than an index for a national newspaper or publication. We need to think carefully about a topic. While making the topic manageable, we also have the opportunity to localize it.

STATISTICAL INDEXES AND ABSTRACTS

When statistics are appropriate for supporting a speech, various statistical indexes and abstracts can be used. Some of the major ones found in many libraries include the following:

Statistical Abstracts of the United States (annual): U.S. Bureau of the Census. General data for major industry groups with notes on statistical sources.

Standard & Poor's Statistical Service (monthly): Basic figures for generally used statistical data of trade, industry, agriculture, banking, price, and financial trends.

Predicasts Basebook (annual): Provides annual statistical data from the last 16 years for products and industries, including annual growth rate.

Predicasts Forecast (quarterly): Short- and long-range forecasts and statistics on specific U.S. industries and products. Includes citation to current journal article, which is the source of the statistic.

Survey of Current Business (monthly): U.S. Department of Commerce. A statistical summary of current business, industry income, and employment; usually covers past four years.

American Statistics Index (monthly; annual cumulations): Descriptive guide and index to statistical publications of all U.S. government agencies. Indexes by detailed subject, by commodity or industry category, by titles and report numbers; provides abstracts.

Statistical Reference Index: A guide with index and abstracts to American statistical publications from sources other than the U.S. government, including trade associations, business organizations, commercial publications, and so forth.

Almanac of Business and Industrial Financial Ratios (1983, ed. L. Troy): Reports the operating and financial information for 182 industry groups; uses current information from the Internal Revenue Service.

Industry Norms and Key Business Ratios: Dun and Bradstreet. Includes financial data and ratios for retail, wholesale, manufacturing, construction, transportation, communication businesses, utilities, agriculture, and mining.

LEGAL SOURCES

Legal sources, especially court cases, can provide authoritative support for a speech. A number of legal periodicals and law journals are available, and some of the more interesting reading can come from actual cases. Researching legal publications is a bit different from researching more traditional sources, and legal citations are somewhat different from standard bibliographic citations. For example, a legal publication might look like this:

ANGEL, D. "Legal Protection for Titles in the Entertainment Industry," 52 *Southern California Law Review 279* (1979).

The name of the author appears first, followed by the title of the article, the volume of the publication (in our example, volume 52), the title of the publication (*Southern California Law Review*), and the first page number of the article. The year is the date of publication. Articles about law are listed and cross-referenced in a number of indexes, including the *Index to Legal Periodicals* and the *Index to Periodicals Relating to Law*.

Locating court decisions, the "primary" materials of law, is an easy process once we understand how to start. Consider the following citation:

New York Times v. United States, 403 U.S. 713, 91 S.Ct. 2140, 29 L.Ed.2d 822 (1971).

This citation refers to the case of *New York Times v. United States.*

Actually, three citations are included, referred to as parallel citations, which are three different sources where the case can be found. These include the *U.S. Reports* (abbreviated as: U.S.), *Supreme Court Reporter* (abbreviated as: S.Ct.), and *U.S. Supreme Court Reports, Lawyer's Edition, 2d series* (abbreviated as: L.Ed.2d). The date in parentheses (1971 in our example) refers to the year of the decision. The numbers represent volume and page citations.

Some exceptions do exist to the citations we have just discussed. Some sources, such as the *U.S. Code* and other statute volumes, use section numbers.

JOURNALS AND TRADE PUBLICATIONS

Journals and trade publications offer excellent information about virtually any subject. These publications are designed and read by people who work, do research, and are many times authorities in specific fields. The periodical section of the library is the place to find journals and trade publications. In larger academic institutions, individual departments sometimes house the books and periodicals related to their discipline.

COMPILING INFORMATION

As we develop our strategy and begin to locate sources important in supporting our speech, the information can be recorded on index cards. If our instructor requires it or we want to compile a bibliography, then we can record each source in the format for a bibliography. We would then number the index card. Other index cards need only contain the number; it will not be necessary to recopy the complete citation. If the instructor requires a bibliography, then the index cards can later be alphabetized and the bibliography typed. If footnotes are required, these can be typed from the bibliography. A good style manual is the best source of information to check the correct style for both footnotes and a bibliography.

Part of speaking with confidence is being prepared. Being prepared means knowing that you are comfortable with the subject and have ample material to prepare for a sound presentation, which will be perceived by the audience as authoritative and well researched.

SUMMARY

Too many people associate the library with deadlines, and too few have taken the time to get to know the library and approach it from a positive perspective.

The library can be the source of a wealth of information and the place where we begin a strategy to support our speech. A good research strategy moves from the general to the specific, going from such sources as encyclopedias to more detailed information found in journals and books.

The card catalogue can help us locate books. Three types of catalogue cards are found in the library: subject-heading cards, author cards, and title cards. Subject-heading cards are more general than author or title cards and can tell us where groups of books on the same subject are located. Author and title cards are used when we know the author or exact title of a publication. If we are unaware of what heading to look under, the *Library of Congress Subject Headings* will be helpful. Call numbers refer us to the location where a specific title and related titles can be found.

Before using the card catalogue, however, it is a good idea to consult more general reference works. Bibliographical sources, encyclopedias, and dictionaries are helpful.

Indexes are important for locating specific information found in journals and trade publications. Some more familiar ones are the *Reader's Guide to Periodical Literature*, the *Humanities Index*, and *The New York Times Index*. Newspaper indexes can help us to localize our research to a specific geographic region.

Statistics can be found in statistical indexes and abstracts. *Statistical Abstracts of the United States, American Statistics Index,* and *Statistical Reference Index* are three examples.

Legal sources, especially court cases, can provide authoritative support for a speech. Researching legal periodicals and cases is a bit different from other research strategies.

Journals and trade publications offer important content. Much of the information in these publications is written by people who work in or are experts in a particular field.

Being prepared is an important part of speaking with confidence, and that means a well-researched presentation.

QUESTIONS FOR REVIEW AND DISCUSSION

1. Why is it important to become familiar with the library before planning a search strategy?

2. How are books grouped by call number? What function do call numbers serve other than helping you to locate a book on the shelf?

3. List three bibliographical sources mentioned in the text. Where would you find famous writers? The biography of a foreign leader?

4. What are some examples of specialized encyclopedias?

5. Why would a specialized state index be of value to a speaker?

6. Which index would we use to locate publications dealing with the law?

7. What is meant by the term *localizing a source?*

LEARNING EXERCISES

1. Visit a local library. Acquaint yourself with the card catalogue, the available indexes, the reference section, the periodical section, the government documents section, and any statistical and abstracting services.

2. Interview a knowledgeable librarian about the available electronic data bases and services with which that person is familiar.

ADDITIONAL READINGS

Downs, R. B., and C. D. Keller   *How To Do Library Research* (2nd ed.). Urbana, IL: University of Illinois Press, 1975.

Dutta, Dwijendraneth   *Libraries and Their Uses: A Guide for the Users.* Calcutta: World Press, 1975.

Fenner, P. and M. C. Armstrong   *Research: A Practical Guide to Finding Information.* Los Altos, CA: W. Kaufman, 1981.

Gates, J. K.   *Guide to the Use of Books and Libraries* (4th ed.). New York: McGraw-Hill, 1979.

McIlvaine, B.   *A Consumers' Researchers' and Students' Guide to Government Publications.* New York: The H. W. Wilson Company, 1983.

Ryans, C. ed.   *The Card Catalog: Current Issues.* Metuchen, NJ: Scarecrow Press, 1981.

Todd, Alden   *Finding Facts Fast: How to Find Out What You Want to Know Immediately.* New York: Morrow, 1972.

12

SPEECH DELIVERY

OBJECTIVES

After completing this chapter, you should be able to

- Overcome communication apprehension
- Describe how we produce speech sounds, including our pitch and rate of speaking
- Distinguish between pronunciation and articulation
- Explain how a speaker uses posture, gestures, and eye contact in his or her physical presence
- Compare and contrast impromptu, extemporaneous, manuscript, and memorized speaking
- Discuss the benefits and liabilities of using visual aids.

Anyone who has witnessed an accomplished actor perform Mark Twain can imagine the presence and impact that Mark Twain himself must have had on his audiences. Twain was a master speaker who brought charisma and presence to a speech. In his later years he was actually forced to become a speaker to pay his bills; reportedly, he was a huge success:

> He starts his audiences laughing with the very first sentence he utters, and for two hours keeps them in a continual roar. The only serious moments occur when, with the unutterable pathos of which the true humorist alone is capable, he interpolates a few pathetic touches which almost make the tears mingle with the smiles. . . . His characteristic attitude is to stand quite still, with the right arm across the abdomen and the left resting on it and supporting his chin. In this manner he talks on for nearly two hours; and, while the audience is laughing uproariously, he never by any chance relapses into a smile.[1]

Thinking of getting an assignment to speak for two hours, and be humorous the entire time! There's also the story of newspaper reporter Tim Woodward. Tim works for the *Idaho Statesman*. His column is well written and filled with a number of humorous anecdotes, many of which are drawn from his personal life. One column talked about public speaking. It seems Tim managed to enroll in a college public speaking class and . . . well, he tells it best.

> The assignment was a three-minute speech entitled "What I Like Best About Boise." It had to be exactly three minutes, give or take a tenth of a second. I wrote and rehearsed it in my bedroom, thinking of as much fluff as possible and surrounding it with the most pompous and long-winded of verbiage. The thing came to a maximum of 45 seconds. Frank Church couldn't have stretched it to more than 50.
> The class convened right after "lunch," a formality for a man unable even to face breakfast. As usual, the goat whose name began with "W" was last to the chopping block. Only a few minutes of the hour remained. My palms were sweating; my mouth was a grave for my tongue.
> "Mr. Woodward," Professor Flapjaw called out.
> I rose and walked to the podium, attempting to affect an air of breezy nonchalance while stifling an urge to vomit.
> "The thing I like best about Boise is skiing," I began. "The mountains around Bogus Basin rise to more than 7,000 feet."
> At this point my mind became an empty vault. The speech rehearsed so many times in the safety of the bedroom, the simple speech that was virtually memorized, might as well have been a dissertation on nuclear fission. My notes, printed ever so carefully on index cards, had turned to Sanskrit. Nothing written thereon was legible, let alone sensible.
> A long time passed, perhaps 15 seconds. My temperature rose to 110; my cheeks began to sizzle. Realizing the next step was madness, I took it anyway. It was the only way out.
> "Thank you," I said, and returned my desk.
> The stunned audience maintained a polite and frozen silence in the remaining seconds before the bell rang. When it did, I got up and slunk out for the last time. History shall record that I flunked. To the best of my knowledge, my speech remains the shortest in the school's history.
> Now, when some misguided soul asks me to address his bowling cronies, I give

the official explanation in a firm, businesslike way. It's the truth, and it makes sense, and people seem to believe it. I sincerely thank the caller for asking, gently hang up the phone, and heave a long sigh. My mind is far away, in the mountains around Bogus Basin.[2]

If you have been concerned about delivering your next speech, now you can relax. Chances are you will not be asked to deliver a speech that lasts two hours with the humor of Mark Twain. And you have already learned too much about communication to end up like Tim Woodward, who only managed a few words about a nearby ski slope. To make your job even easier, we'll spend a few paragraphs talking about how to lessen even the few apprehensions that are perfectly normal for everyone who is asked to deliver a speech. After all, if some apprehension is not present, then you are not challenged and are not going to grow from the experience. The experience can, however, result in a tremendous number of positive benefits including the ability to gain more and more self-confidence until you discover that on some subjects in front of some audiences you would find it possible to speak for hours. Mark Twain did, and the things he talked about were his own experiences and those of his friends.

OVERCOMING COMMUNICATION APPREHENSION

A speaker's job is actually much easier than it seems, because if a speaker stops long enough to realize that everyone in the audience has some apprehension about public speaking, the speaker will discover that he or she is actually among friends. Apprehension of any kind is a function of our body tensing and reacting to stimuli. Interestingly, we fail to realize that the real cause of this stimuli is not the audience but ourselves.[3] When we find ourselves apprehensive about something it is the internal reaction to our mental and physical processes. Therefore we have a great deal of control over those processes. Where many beginning speakers make the mistake is to place the cause of that apprehension outside themselves.

Another way to approach a speech is to realize you begin a speech at an *advantage*, not a disadvantage. You retain that advantage because the more you speak the more the audience can identify with you personally, what you are saying, and what you are feeling. Even when controversial issues are involved, those who disagree with you still must respect your willingness, desire, and ability to state those views. It is also important to realize that even where audiences may seem to differ with a speaker, that does not preclude "agreement within differences."

Communication Apprehension vs. Other Types of Apprehension

Do not make the mistake of confusing communication apprehension with other types of apprehension. If we went on a short vacation trip and lugged along all of the clothes in our closet, we probably wouldn't enjoy the trip. We sometimes lug with us other types of apprehension, of which communication apprehension is just part of the load. For example, just because you receive an average grade in school doesn't mean you will be an average speaker. It does not mean the last grade you received on an examination or term paper—the one you're not too proud of—is going to appear on your chest in neon lights. It doesn't mean the fact you were rejected on your last date or didn't get asked to the weekend party that your speech will not be up to par, or for that matter, that you will be rejected the next time you ask someone on a date. Nor does it mean that because you did not set the world on fire with your last speech your performance should determine how well you will do this time.

Remember, we all carry around psychological baggage, and much of it is excessive and unnecessary. The average day brings too many good things to dwell on the bad, too many positive friends to dwell on our enemies, too many accomplishments to dwell on our failures. Communication apprehension is just one type of apprehension. Try not to let other types of apprehension contribute to communication apprehension.

Strategies for Relaxation

When Tim Woodward started to think about a ski area outside Boise, Idaho, he may not have realized he had seized one of the keys to lowering his apprehension—using pleasant thoughts as a means of relaxation. When we become nervous, our blood vessels contract. We are apprehensive and "uptight." Sometimes a physical experience will cause this to happen, such as being in an accident or simply working too hard for too long. Other times our mental processes will cause us to become tense when we think of unpleasant or tension-producing experiences.

We can control many of our physical and mental processes. These processes control our body functions. Therefore we have the ability to lower some of the tension within ourselves. One of the ways this can be accomplished is through physical relaxation. The other is through mental relaxation. Physical relaxation usually means getting enough rest and eating the right foods before delivering a speech. It stands to reason that if we are tired and edgy then it is natural that we would be tense and apprehensive, both during the preparation and delivery of our speech.

Mental relaxation is equally important. For example, if we think of pleasant thoughts our body will relax. However, trying to think of pleasant thoughts when our mental or physical processes are overridden by something negative will not work. We must actually "work" at becoming relaxed. Remember, some apprehension is a natural occurrence, and it affects each of us.

Preparation and Practice

A good speech, especially for beginning students, is much like a fine statue that has been carefully and laboriously carved from stone by a skilled artisan. It was not created by a few moments spent molding some poor-quality clay. It was certainly not created the night before it was to be displayed at an art exhibit. The artist, who will also be at the exhibit, would display apprehension if the statue was rough around the edges. Much like the artist, there is no substitute for preparation and practice for the speaker.

THE SPEAKER'S VOICE

People who do a lot of business on the telephone will tell you they can recognize hundreds of voices. Voices are the same as fingerprints and faces; no two are exactly alike. A machine called a *voice stress analyzer* analyzes the "tremor" in a person's voice and charts the words much like a lie detector. A speaker uses the voice to express feelings, emotions, convey meaning, and generate a response from an audience.

Producing Speech Sounds

The vocal mechanism permitting us to make sounds and form words consists of a series of physical components through which air is controlled and moved over the tongue.[4] The human voice is produced in the *larynx* (Fig. 12–1). Above the larynx is the *pharynx,* which is followed by the *soft palate* called the *velum,* which operates much like a valve. To produce sound, such as a "t" or a "d," the tongue moves upward and forward making contact with the upper gum ridge. To make sounds such as "k" or "g," the rear portion of the tongue is lifted to touch the soft palate. This creates an effect much like a dam, but instead of

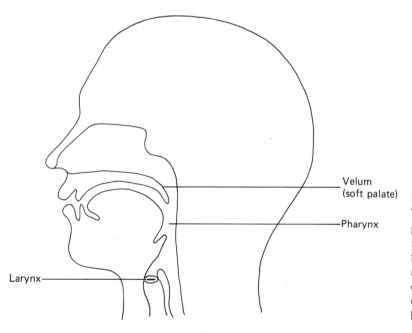

Velum
(soft palate)

Pharynx

Larynx

Figure 12-1
Voice sounds are produced by changing the position of the parts of the mouth and throat and fluctuating the air flow from the lungs.

holding back water, the tongue and soft palate create a dam of air that is released when the tongue moves back down. Different vowels produce different contours of the tongue. The lips then add to the control of air flow. The mouth itself helps because there are some sounds that can only be made by having our mouth in motion. Called *glide sounds,* they consist of the "w" as it is pronounced in "wind," and the letter "y."

Although sounds are not made with the ear, speaking without the ability to aurally audit what we say seriously restricts us. This is especially true in young children who are learning to develop their speech patterns.

Pitch

Imagine a 200-pound football player who appears at a speech pathologist's office and says:

> Yes, I was one of those sopranos and my music teacher loved me. I soloed in all the cantatas and programs and sang in the choir and glee clubs, and they never let my voice change. I socked a guy the other day who wisecracked about it, but I'm afraid to open my mouth. Strangers start looking for a Charlie McCarthy somewhere. I got to get over it, and quick. Why I can't even swear but some guy who's been saying the same words looks shocked.[5]

The 200-pound football player is suffering from a problem with the pitch of his voice, a problem that the speech pathologist will be able to help. But why should he worry about the pitch? Because we make judgments about people based on the pitch of their voice. As a speaker, you can be aware of the pitch of your voice but not be overly concerned. It is also possible to change the pitch of your voice. Over enough time, it can be altered to the point where the change is more normal than abnormal.

Some years ago I wanted to get a job as a radio announcer. I went to a local radio station, was given permission to cut an audition tape, but didn't get the job. The man who owned the radio station in Latrobe, Pennsylvania, was nice enough to permit me to stay around and learn all I could about the station. It was enough incentive to work on my voice, which was too high pitched. After practice, and also years later when I was older, the pitch lowered.

When pitch does become an issue, it is helpful to know the different ways in which pitch can be affected. These include a too-high pitch, a pitch that is too low, and monopitch.

Too high and too low a pitch is relative, and to some degree it is based on the perceptions of the audience. Every day we hear people with different pitched voices and we think nothing unusual of these varieties of sounds. When a pitch sounds unnaturally high or low, then it attracts our attention. Unless someone tells you your voice projects a pitch that is too high or too low, then there is little with which to concern yourself. Monopitch, a pitch that doesn't change, can also be distracting, and this is far more frequent than a pitch that is too high or too low. A speech instructor or someone critiquing your speech may suggest you vary the pitch to avoid a noticeable monopitch.

Rate of Speaking

When Dave was lecturing to the group of weekend river rafters, he didn't have to worry about changing the rate of his speaking. His audience paid attention to every word. Other speakers are not as fortunate. To emphasize a point, to gain and hold attention, we vary our rate of speaking. Many beginning speakers talk too fast. The faster they talk the more uncomfortable they become, and the more uncomfortable they become, the faster they talk. In short, they want to end the speech so they can sit down.

When practicing a speech, ask one of your friends to listen. Several listeners are even better. As part of their critique, ask them to evaluate your rate of speaking. When you deliver your speech, be conscious of your rate. If you feel yourself speeding up, pause slightly longer between thoughts as a way of getting your rate back under control. Deliberately place a sentence or phrase in your speech that can help slow you down. For example, one speaker talking about the ability of Congress to pass legislation said, "The slow, cumbersome wheels of Congress trudged along, delaying, sometimes debating, but mostly falling farther and farther behind until the technology had gone out of control." The words were not spoken at the same pace as other words in the speech. They were deliberately spoken at a slow pace to create attention. The pauses were deliberate and effective. As delivered in the speech the sentence would look more like this: "The slow . . . cumbersome wheels of Congress trudged along . . . delaying . . . sometimes debating . . . but mostly falling farther . . . and farther . . . behind . . . until the technology had gone out of control." Statements such as this one will help slow a pace that has become too rapid *if* the speaker remembers they are there as a reminder that says, like a speedometer, "check your speed."

Another plight of beginning speakers is to use rate simply as a means of highlighting a speech when a more natural flow would be more appropriate. The speaker, without taking the care and attention that is necessary, says to himself or herself, "This looks like a good place to speed up." Or, "This looks like a good place to slow down." In fact, neither is the case. The words stood alone and the deliberate slowing down or speeding up for emphasis came across as unnatural. The best rule to follow is to develop a good, even flow to your speaking and emphasize rate only when it is appropriate for the content of your speech.

Articulation

Articulation is our ability to give each syllable, each sound of the word, the emphasis it deserves. Poor articulation is not so much concerned with whether we pronounce the "ing" in "coming" but it is concerned with whether we fail to say the "com" and "ing" completely or whether we mumble the word so that it is not comprehended by the audience. Four types of articulation problems exist.[6] For instance, the *distortion* of a standard sound, such as not clearly saying the "ing" in coming, is an articulation failure.

A second category of articulation failure is the *omission* of a sound normally heard when the word is spoken correctly. Omitting the letter "s" from the word "sky" is an example. Young children sometimes omit the letter "s" from the word "sky" and the word is pronounced as "kye."

Still another category is the *substitution* of one sound for another. For example, the actual word "substitute" is sometimes said by substituting "th" in place of the "s" sound, and the word "thubstitute" occurs.

A fourth articulation problem *adds* a sound that would not normally be present. For example, young children reciting the rhyme "twinkle twinkle little star" sometimes pronounce the words "tinko tinko itto tah." In the word "little" they add sounds that would not normally be present; thus, changing the way "little" and "star" are pronounced. This last example also points out that the four categories are not necessarily represented individually. Many times combinations of articulation problems exist, such as in our last example, where both substitution and addition take place.

THE PHYSICAL PRESENCE OF THE SPEAKER

Lucian Lupinski is the artist in residence at the *Saturday Evening Post*. When time permits, Lucian manages to accept a few of his numerous invitations to speak to college art classes. What many people do not know about Lucian, especially if they have never seen him in person, is that he was once a collegiate wrestler at Ohio State. Lucian has what we call *physical presence*. People listen, not only because they are somewhat enamored of his artistic genius but also because this kind gentleman is housed in the frame of a Big-Ten wrestler.

Few public speakers bring to a speech the credibility of Lucian Lupinski. Most of us must work much harder at getting our audience to listen and to remember what we said. Along with everything we have learned up to this point, we need to be conscious of the physical qualities that will affect our speech. That starts from the time we get up from our seat and approach the podium.

The First Few Steps

The audience begins paying attention to a speaker the moment he or she is introduced. Sometimes that includes a rather long introduction. Other times it simply means having the instructor call a name; instantly, "you're on!"

For students, the instructor calling a name is where everything starts. At that moment we begin to have an impression on everyone around us. When you leave your seat and walk toward the front of the room, the first opinions are formed. Think of posture then, not later when you are behind the podium. If you slouch, correct the slouch and stand upright. When you get to the podium, stop behind the podium and stand still. Look at the audience for a few moments and begin to create a bond. Shifting from side to side or shuffling papers or notes detracts from your presence behind the podium. Place your hands relaxed on top, not at the sides, of the podium. Be careful about clutching the podium. While delivering a testimonial speech one evening I mistakenly thought the podium was part of a larger structure anchored to the floor. As I began to speak, and added some enthusiasm to my remarks, I realized that I had clutched the side of the podium and had actually lifted it about three inches off the table. I gently lowered it and stepped back. My gestures gave me the physical emphasis I needed, and I was able to continue my speech.

Posture

Posture behind the podium is even more important than one's posture approaching the podium. In the late 1800s, public speaking was taught by methods that paid a great deal of attention to where the person stood in relation to the podium and audience. Today, we realize that a speaker should be natural while not appearing sloppy. The posture we exhibit when speaking communicates a nonverbal message. It tells the audience whether we are confident or apprehensive. It tells the audience if we really believe in our topic or are just getting through the assignment. Although a speaker is not expected to stand rigid, a good, strong shoulders-up posture is appropriate for both men and women.

It may also be natural for a speaker to move from behind the podium to the side or front. If a speaker is uncomfortable or the speaking situation or physical characteristics of the room make it uncomfortable, then remaining behind the podium may be more appropriate. Do not try to add emphasis to a speech by deliberately moving away from the podium to the point where it appears awkward. If a more relaxed atmosphere exists, such as a question-and-answer session, then moving away from the podium may be natural. A different communicative atmosphere, one less formal, sometimes develops during these sessions, and speakers may want to reduce the distance between themselves and the audience.

Too much rigidity can cause a speaker to appear as a tin soldier. Thus, being relaxed but not slumped, being casual but not sloppy, is the best rule of thumb. Some beginning speakers, until they become comfortable with public presentations, shift from one foot to another and engage in an excessive amount of eye contact with the podium. Becoming more relaxed and reducing apprehension are two ways to help avoid this tendency.

Gestures

Throughout history many famous people have developed a sort of trade-mark by their gestures. Some gestures have stood alone and been substitutes for words. The two-fingered "V" for victory sign is one example. President John Kennedy was famous for his "chopping hand" gesture, which has also been used by other politicians.

Gestures not only emphasize our words but they also provide us with a type of linguistic-physical balance. Try describing to a friend how a spiral staircase is constructed. It is difficult unless we use a spiraling hand gesture showing the way the staircase goes upward. Not to use the gesture seems awkward, unnatural, and uncomfortable.

When speaking, permit gestures to flow naturally. We do not talk with our friends by keeping our hands on our laps or at our sides. We use gestures subconsciously. The audience receives the "message" of gestures as a very natural, almost unnoticeable part of the communication process. Think of the last person you heard deliver a speech. You can probably remember some of the things he or she said but would have a difficult time remembering the speaker's gestures. The exception would be if the gestures were so accentuated that they distracted from the speech. That's not what we are looking for. What we do want to achieve is a natural balance, employing gestures that emphasize key thoughts and statements.

The Function and Obligation of Eye Contact

In public speaking, keeping eye contact with your audience, even when the audience is large, can develop a bond and hold attention, giving words a greater impact. We sometimes forget that public speaking is still face-to-face communication, and the same principles apply to the speaker-audience relationship that apply to communication between two people. When we converse with another person a great deal of eye contact is present. Moreover, the verbal interaction is more balanced.

A speaker is awarded a privilege when given the opportunity to address an audience. The speaker, not the audience, has a monopoly on verbal communication. The audience must listen to the speaker, usually finding it awkward to get up and leave. We can use these two premises as a basis to argue that the speaker, if through nothing else than common courtesy, is somewhat obligated to engage in eye contact with the audience.

Eye Contact Problem Areas

Speakers fail in their eye contact in a number of ways: Either because the speaker is tied to the manuscript or because of apprehensiveness, he or she fails to look at the audience. Instead of linking eyes with the audience, the speaker finds it psychologically safe to look at the podium or the space immediately in front of the podium.

Some speakers will concentrate their eye contact on only part of the audience. Sometimes the arrangement of a room contributes to this problem. Rooms where a large aisle separates the audience in half can result in the speaker concentrating eye contact on one side of the aisle or the other. Similarly, a speaker may avoid eye contact with people sitting in either the extreme right or left sections of a room or auditorium. People in the balcony can also be slighted.

If the speaker begins to receive positive feedback from a particular area, then the eye contact may stay with that section of the room.

Sometimes the speaker will identify with one individual in the audience and concentrate eye contact on that one person.

Rapid eye contact occurs by either quick glances up from the podium— too quick to be meaningful—or by glancing at the audience and then rapidly sweeping one's gaze across the audience. The speaker sees the audience but does not take the time to really communicate with the audience.

Improving Eye Contact

Problems with eye contact are easily corrected with practice. A common remedy for poor contact is to begin by picking out one or two people you know or feel comfortable with and concentrate your eye contact on them. Then, as the speech continues, gradually increase your eye contact with others in the audience.

Another way to aid eye contact is mentally to divide the room into parts and then move eye contact from one part to another. By stopping long enough on each section to create a feeling of awareness and contact between yourself and the audience, a bond develops that can contribute to an effective presentation. The more comfortable one becomes with the speaking process, the more natural eye contact becomes. We do not hesitate to look people in the eye when we feel confident and assured about our own worth and abilities as a speaker.

THE PRESENTATION: IMPROMPTU, EXTEMPORANEOUS, MEMORIZATION, AND MANUSCRIPT

My friend Lucian Lupinski begins some of his speeches about art by reading a statement of the philosophy of art and aesthetics. This portion of his speech is in what we call manuscript form; other portions are delivered extemporaneously while still others are memorized. Speeches are rarely 100 percent devoted to one specific type of presentation: impromptu, extemporaneous, memorization, or manuscript. Even professional speakers who seem to be delivering a professional extemporaneous presentation have memorized much of what they say.

Impromptu Speaking

The class begins and on the first day the instructor looks up and says, "Let's get to know each other better. I'd like each of you to stand and tell us something about yourself." One by one each member of the class stands and tells something of his or her background. The exercise permits every student to participate in impromptu speaking.

Speech contests and classroom exercises sometimes use a secret list of topics. Each student draws one of the topics by chance and then delivers a speech on that subject. More than one business executive has been asked to explain something to a business meeting, which involves giving an impromptu speech. Sometimes the executive's career skyrockets through just such unexpected visibility *if* the executive knows how to deliver the speech.

If you are asked to deliver an impromptu speech, make a quick mental organization plan about how you want to organize your thoughts. Concentrate only on two or three main points and then expand on them. Some of the best people capable of delivering impromptu speeches are radio reporters who cover fast-breaking news events. They are accustomed to arriving at the scene of a news story, making some mental notes on what is happening, consuming as much visual information as possible, and then going on the air live from a mobile news vehicle. To the listener it sounds as if the report is rehearsed and delivered from a script. In reality, the reporter is an excellent impromptu speaker.

The reporter knows how to construct a "mental" organizational plan. It might include a geographic survey that permits the reporter mentally to scan a city block destroyed by a tornado then deliver a live report—an impromptu speech to an audience of thousands—or it may be a report from a courtroom where an important decision has just been rendered. The mental plan is chronological and the reporter tells the history of the case. Some important lessons can be learned from these experts in impromptu speaking. Some use what we call the S O S method. *See* what you are going to talk about—create the visual image. *Organize* your thoughts. *Speak* on the subject. S O S.

Extemporaneous Speaking

Extemporaneous speaking is a popular and effective method of presentation since it involves both preparation and more natural delivery than the formal manuscript speech. Extemporaneous speeches begin with careful audience analysis, research, and delivery. While we may still use notes, the notes carry a synopsis of the information the speaker wants to convey to the audience. That information may involve quotations or statistics to support the speech; it may involve the main points of the speech; it may involve an abridged outline that the speaker can follow. Each speaking situation is different and each speaker is different. One topic may demand detailed information, another a few notes.

Extemporaneous speaking is sometimes confused with impromptu speaking, and it is assumed to have little preparation. While that is sometimes the case, a good extemporaneous speech is still well researched and developed. While we may not write down the speech word-for-word, we still have a good idea of what we want to say. We have practiced the speech, and we are comfortable with its contents.

An advantage of the extemporaneous speech is that it provides a natural open delivery style with good eye contact while still permitting us to use notes. If we want to change our emphasis or expand on a point, the freedom is there; with a manuscript speech we are more tied to a script.

Manuscript Speaking

The manuscript speech provides a word-for-word guide. The complete speech is written and then delivered from the manuscript. Where every word counts, and where accuracy is critical, the manuscript speech is unequaled. Politicians find is helpful where an important policy statement may determine legislation or their career. Manuscript speeches can be duplicated and distributed to voters, can become government policy, can be published, such as in the *Congressional Record,* can be excerpted and released to the press.

Both advantages and disadvantages exist in a manuscript speech. Advantages include control over exactly what is said. We can be assured of precise language. For the less accomplished speaker, the manuscript provides an anchor whereby the speaker can read and then accentuate the speech with the voice and gestures.

Disadvantages include much less eye contact since the speaker must concentrate on the manuscript rather than the audience. If the speaker loses his or her place in the manuscript, the attempt to recover and find one's place again is quite awkward.

The manuscript can prove beneficial for the accomplished speaker who must reduce the chance of error or a poor presentation to an absolute minimum. The speech is researched and then written in manuscript form. The manuscript is edited, rehearsed, then edited again. A final version, which emerges from both the written and oral drafts, is typed and becomes the manuscript used in the final presentation. This may be rehearsed again until the speaker is completely comfortable with both the contents and the delivery.

When the speech is delivered to its intended audience, the speaker is so familiar with its contents that eye contact and delivery do not suffer. A quick glance at the manuscript permits the speaker to grasp longer portions of the speech (two to five sentences), which are delivered with direct eye contact, gestures, and a natural, effective style.

Memorizing a Speech

A memorized speech means the speaker will deliver the speech without the aid of notes or a manuscript. While some extemporaneous speeches are delivered this way, a truly memorized speech has the exactness of a manuscript speech but without the manuscript. While a good memorized speech can be effective, the biggest problem occurs when the speaker forgets a line. The only way to recover is to ad-lib, for you are speaking without notes or manuscript.

USING AUDIO AND VISUAL AIDS

One day while I was instructing a public-speaking class, a student completed his assignment speech in which he chose to explain the correct way to raise turkeys. The class learned about feeding, breeding, even the sale and shipment of turkeys at Thanksgiving time. Near the end of the speech the student reached under the desk in front of the room where he had earlier placed a large burlap bag. What the class did not know was that the bag contained a very large, live turkey. Reaching into the bag the student pulled out the turkey and placed it on top of the desk. Everything was fine for a few moments until the turkey became excited and beat its wings, flapping the student in the face. He lost control of the bird, which went sailing off the desk about half-way across the room and landed on another student. That student screamed, which further frightened the bird as well as some of the other students. Finally, another student, who had some experience with animals, managed to tackle the bird. Eventually the turkey was returned to the bag and the class returned to normal . . . well, almost normal.

Complementing vs. Distracting

While the visual aid chosen by the student certainly illustrated how healthy a turkey can become, it was not entirely appropriate for the speech. A visual aid should complement a speech, not distract from it. A speaker lecturing on the motion picture industry stopped using a film about special effects since it was the only thing the audience really wanted to see. The film dominated the speech.

When using a visual aid, we need to stop and ask ourselves if the visual aid is appropriate for the speech and complements the presentation. After all, the purpose of a speech is to place the audience in human contact with the speaker. If that human contact is diminished, then there may be another method of presentation more appropriate to the occasion. In other words, it might be more appropriate to visit a turkey farm if live turkeys are necessary to effectively tell about raising turkeys.

Selecting a Medium

Whereas many of us choose charts and graphs to emphasize a speech (and we'll talk about those in more detail), many other media are available. Videotape, film, slides, overhead transparencies, and audio recordings are just some of the choices. To be effective the medium must match the purpose of the speech. For example, some topics lend themselves to charts and graphs. The rise of tuition in colleges can be plotted chronologically on a graph. A speech about appreciating classical music is best complemented with an audio or videotape of a symphony. Some charts and graphs can be transferred to overhead transparencies and made much larger for larger audiences.

Whatever medium is chosen, the speaker must know beforehand how to operate the technology. It is a sinking feeling to arrive for a speech with a well-prepared slide presentation and not know how to operate the projector.

Assets and Liabilities

Audio and visual aids can be both an asset and a liability. As an asset, audiovisual aids add information. As a liability, they can be cumbersome objects, that need to be set up, moved, lifted, folded, and turned on and off. A camera might make a good visual aid for a speech on photography, but if the speaker keeps clicking the shutter and doesn't know when to set the camera down, the presentation will suffer. Be sure you are comfortable with the audio or visual aid. Before your speech visit the room where you will make your presentation. Look at the setting, the positioning of the podium, the seating arrangement. Then determine how you will set up and use the aid. Stopping midway through a speech to rearrange a poster or change a recording tape breaks the audience's attention span and destroys communication.

Charts and Graphs

Many speakers not familiar with using visual aids try to include too much information in the aid. They either end up not using much of the information or the visual aid is so jammed the audience can't see clearly. Neither is satisfactory and both are distracting. Take the time to have your visual aid critiqued by someone other than yourself. Place it in the room where it will be used and then walk to the rear of the room to see if you can read all of the information on the chart or graph. If you cannot, then the visual aid must be changed.

Related to the problem of including too much information is not making the visual aid large enough. Some speakers go to the trouble of developing a clear, uncluttered visual aid and then making it too small. Special problems exist with numbers and letters. What may look large to someone at a drawing table may be entirely inadequate when placed in front of the audience.

Permitting visual aids to dominate a speech lessens their effectiveness. Moreover, an audience can only remember so much information. The visual aid should be employed to highlight only the most important parts of your speech, not everything you say.

Integrating Aids Into a Speech

If you are delivering a speech about the benefit of athletics to the learning process you could decide to include a poster of a basketball player. Although the poster might attract attention, it would be of minimal benefit in supporting your speech. Stop and ask: Does this audio or visual aid support the speech or is it just window dressing?

With these few guidelines, audio and visual aids will add a professional element to your presentation, increase its effectiveness, and enlarge your own self-assurance.

SUMMARY

Some apprehension is a normal part of speechmaking. Without apprehension we cannot grow, learn, and succeed. Excessive apprehension can result in dysfunction. Speakers can lessen apprehension through some basic steps. Because our body is a function of our physical and emotional states, learning how to relax is a good first step in lessening apprehension. Also important is recognizing the differences between communication apprehension and other types of apprehension. Past experiences resulting in apprehension should, as much as possible, be left behind when approaching a communication situation. In addition to relaxation, preparation and practice are necessary for an effective apprehension-free presentation.

A speaker's voice is generated by the larynx, which is located in the throat cavity. Just above the larynx is the pharynx, which is followed by the soft palate, called the velum. The velum, in conjunction with the tongue and lips, works much like a valve controlling air pressure and producing sounds. Pitch and rate are important components of an effective delivery. Three categories of pitch exist: a pitch that is too high, one that is too low, and monopitch.

Effective communication demands good pronunciation and articulation. Pronunciation is concerned with saying each syllable correctly. Articulation is more concerned with the entire word and ensuring that all sounds are included. For example, the word *coming* consists of the syllables "com" and "ing." In pronunciation, we want to be sure that the "ing" does not become "in." In articulation we want to be sure the entire word is communicated in a clear, distortion-free manner and that both syllables are included.

The audience's perception of a speaker begins as soon as the speaker leaves his or her seat and approaches the podium. Good posture reflects positively on the presentation. Effective delivery is complemented by gestures and eye contact.

The types of presentation are impromptu, extemporaneous, memorization, and manuscript. Each has its advantages and disadvantages.

Speeches can be complemented with visual aids, charts, and graphs. When using visual aids, care should be given to their construction and their incorporation into the speech. Not engaging in information overload, making visual aids large enough, and not using more visual aids than necessary are additional safeguards for an effective presentation.

QUESTIONS FOR REVIEW AND DISCUSSION

1. How does our body function when we are apprehensive?

2. Why is it important to distinguish between communication apprehension and other types of apprehension?

3. What are the physical components of the throat cavity and mouth that are employed in the production of speech sounds?

4. What are the differences between pronunciation and articulation? How are they related?

5. In what way do posture and gestures complement a speech?

6. What are the eye contact problem areas and how can they be avoided?

7. What are the differences that distinguish impromptu, extemporaneous, memorized, and manuscript speeches?

8. In what way can audiovisual aids distract from a speech?

9. What are the rules to follow when using charts and graphs?

LEARNING EXERCISES

1. Deliver a three- to five-minute speech in which you incorporate at least one visual aid. Be sure the visual aid is easily understood, does not contain too much information, is well integrated into the topic and outline you choose, and is large enough to be seen by everyone in the audience.

2. Review the text of a speech in the publication *Vital Speeches,* which is available in most libraries. Outline the speech.

ADDITIONAL READINGS

BENNETT, C. W. ET AL. EDS.   *Contemporary Readings in Articulation Disorders.* Dubuque, IA: Kendall-Hunt, 1982.
DIEDRICH, W. M. and J. BANGERT   *Articulation Learning.* San Diego, CA: College-Hill, 1980.
MAYER, L. V   *Fundamentals of Voice and Diction* (7th ed.). Dubuque, IA: Wm. C. Brown Company Publishers, 1985.
SOMMERS, R. K.   *Articulation Disorders.* Englewood Cliffs, NJ: Prentice-Hall, 1983.

13
PERSUASION

OBJECTIVES

After completing this chapter, you should be able to

- Be aware of our persuasion-filled environment
- Realize how persuasion fits into the communication process
- Explain rhetoric and rhetorical criticism
- Describe the learning theory approach to studying persuasion
- Discuss balance and consistence theory as it relates to persuasion
- Define and discuss cognitive dissonance
- Explain the social-judgment theory approach to studying persuasion
- Talk about our resistance to persuasion.

We cannot escape persuasion. It starts from the time we wake up with the first commercial on the local radio station. If our clock radio turns on to the local news then we might hear a politician or a local community-action group calling our attention to some issue that demands public awareness. As for the commercials, we not only hear them on the radio station but also see them on the television game show. When we open the kitchen cabinet, we see an example of persuasive advertising in the cereal box that held our attention long enough in the grocery store so that we picked the box off the shelf and placed it in our shopping cart. We may even dip inside the box to find a coupon that we can redeem at the same grocery store where more fancy labels, more colorful boxes await us. Even the simple generic labels may have been devised by an advertising campaign bent on convincing us to try these "inexpensive" brands.

By the time we leave the house and head for school we are bombarded with billboards telling us what radio station to listen to, what car to buy, what record is on sale, what airline to fly. On campus, posters on bulletin boards invite us to attend meetings, to appear at the next intramural athletic contest, to listen to a controversial speaker. Other, more fancy posters try to persuade us to take a vacation in January by showing us the warm beaches of the South or the lush green meadows of an English countryside where we can study next summer.

Persuasion exists in our everyday encounters with others (Fig. 13–1). While we tend to think more in terms of a specific persuasive message, such as a speech or television commercial, we may be persuaded by a friend to go to a movie, by a date to go out to dinner, by a subordinate to award a raise, by our boss to get a job done, by our teacher to have an assignment completed on time.

Persuasion follows us into the classroom where the label on a classmate's shirt, or blouse, or jeans calls our attention to the latest brand in clothing. After all, if you see someone wearing something you like, chances are you will want one for yourself. The manufacturer doesn't want to take the chance of your finding another brand, so the label is in plain view. If the manufacturer is lucky and the horse with the polo rider, the strange-sounding French name, or the unusual monogram catches on, millions of dollars will be made in a commercial fad directed at those who don't dare to be different. What better way to persuade you to buy name-brand apparel than to have the brand name staring at you on the sleeve or hip of the person next to you.

We consume much more persuasion than we realize. Persuasive messages, both those that are highly visible and detectable and those that are more subtle, hit us at every waking hour. We can sit back and passively permit ourselves to be swayed by these messages, or we can become much more responsible consumers of persuasion. We can take the time to learn to tell the difference between persuasion directed at our well-being and persuasion with less honorable intentions. We can take the time to recognize the difference between well-disguised propaganda and messages that truly inform us of all sides of an issue.

To be a participant of the communication process we must also be aware of persuasive messages and the way we react to those messages. It is here that we defer to the process of rhetorical criticism or psychological-based theories of

Figure 13-1   Knowing about the theory and practice of persuasion is important in many situations other than public speaking. An attorney must draw information from witnesses to persuade judge and jury of the merits of a case. Similarly, members of a jury should be responsible consumers of persuasive messages to be able to sort out fact from opinion, truths from untruths.

persuasion, where we look to the research of years of laboratory and field studies to help draw conclusions about how messages are developed and received. Questions arise such as, Why is this particular message being presented to me at this time? Am I the intended receiver or is someone with different attitudes and different opinions from mine the real audience for this commercial? The answers to these questions, and knowing the strategy as well as the content of persuasion, make one a responsible consumer of both interpersonal and more media-oriented communication.

PERSUASION AND THE COMMUNICATION PROCESS

Persuasion is communication and, as such, it is capable of moving in a circular process between sender and receiver. But the sender-to-receiver dimension is only one part of the process. In a group discussion on a controversial issue, for example, people are both persuading and being persuaded simultaneously. When one individual changes his or her view because of what others in the group have said, persuasion has occurred. A compromise or negotiated settlement involves persuasion among specific individuals in a give-and-take process. In politics we know that politicians can change their stands based on the views of the electorate. Similarly, the editor of a newspaper trying to persuade readers to adopt a particular viewpoint may be the one who ends up being persuaded by "letters to the editor."

An advertising campaign is a circular persuasive process, although at first it may seem the purpose is one-way communication designed to sell soap or the latest-model automobile. The advertising agency that designs the campaign plans the message and then distributes the message any number of ways, from free samples to television commercials to demonstrations of the product. But the public to which the campaign is directed takes an active part in the communication process the instant the first message appears. If the product does not sell, the advertiser must open up more dialogue—not one-way communication but *dialogue*—with the public to learn more about either what is wrong with the product or what is wrong with the advertising campaign. Gradually, the public persuades the advertiser or manufacturer to make adjustments in the campaign or product. While the message from the public may not be direct, such as a speaker persuading an audience, it still has a decisive impact.

RHETORIC AND RHETORICAL CRITICISM

The study of persuasion is not new. Although a great deal of attention has been paid to modern media and their persuasive impact on our lives, especially in political campaigns, we have learned elsewhere in this text that the ancient Greeks recognized the importance and wisdom of persuasion. The term *rhetoric* in this classical sense is an analysis of the persuasive appeals within messages and their effect on the audience. To examine persuasion from a rhetorical perspective is an excellent way to grasp in broad general terms how persuasive messages function and how we can evaluate and analyze them. Central to this analysis and understanding is the awareness that persuasive messages do not just happen. They are planned and executed by individuals who have specific purposes in mind, specific messages to communicate, specific audiences to reach.

Message-Based Criticism

We can analyze some persuasive messages firsthand. We can read a speech, for example, and conduct our own analysis of the appeals employed and what strategies the speaker had in mind when he or she delivered the speech. Language may be our only clue to what was meant, what was said, and the effect of the speech on the audience. We may examine the components of the language to see how forceful were the speaker's convictions. For example, the speaker may choose to use metaphors, words used to describe other things.[1] How important are these metaphors to the development of the persuasive message? Are the metaphors designed specifically to appeal to a certain type of audience? "The twilight of her years" means one thing to a group of old people and something else to a group of business people. Why was it chosen by the speaker? Why was it important to the speech? If the lack of any consistency among metaphors is present then this may tell us something else. We can also examine the power and forcefulness of the language. Such information will help to tell us how committed the speaker might have been.

Sender-Based Criticism

With additional information we can expand our analysis to include more speaker-based criticism. For instance, if the speaker is a contemporary, we may be able to examine other speeches delivered by the same individual. We can conduct research about the person to determine from what background, from what ideology, from what political, economic, or social orientation the thoughts and persuasive strategies evolved. We may go beyond the speeches to study other analyses of the speaker made by scholars or journalists. If the person is famous, these analyses will be plentiful.

We may make judgments about whether the persuasive strategy was the product of some other individual. For example, the Rev. Jesse Jackson was likened to the Rev. Martin Luther King, Jr., during much of the early 1984 race for the Democratic nomination for President. Certainly Jackson knew Dr. King and was closely associated with King's early civil rights efforts. Jackson's persuasive strategies could therefore have been influenced by the King era.

Audience-Based Criticism

Still another way to examine a speech would be to stress audience analysis. If we were part of the audience we might have been able to view audience reaction firsthand. Perhaps we discussed the speech with others who were present. Knowing something about the makeup of the audience could aid our analysis.

More detailed criticism of a persuasive message could be conducted by employing a research methodology known as *content analysis*. To illustrate, we might place in one category all of the metaphors used in the speech. In another category we might place all of the specific references to the audience. After completing our analysis of these and other categories we would then count the number of times metaphors were used, count the number of specific references, develop summaries and examples from the categories, and arrive at conclusions about the persuasive strategies employed. While we might look at this method of analysis as more systematic than a more general rhetorical criticism, we would to some degree be confined by our categories, and would need to be aware of this shortfall. The fact that one speech contains more references to an audience does not mean that it is more effective.

Important contributions have been made by scientific approaches to communication, and a full appreciation of persuasion includes an awareness of these theories. While we tend to separate them to facilitate study, many are related to each other and function together in any communicative act. The more traditional is *learning theory* in which classical conditioning and instrumental or operant theory are found.

Classical Conditioning

Classical conditioning is based on a stimulus-response model of persuasion. A message is disseminated from sender to receiver, and the receiver changes his or her attitude based on the message; thus, the stimulus (message)-response (change of attitude).

Classical conditioning has its roots in the work of psychologist Ivan Pavlov.[2] Four elements are contained in classical conditioning. The first two are the *unconditioned stimulus* and the *unconditioned response.* Pavlov used the experiment of a salivating dog to demonstrate classical conditioning. The unconditioned stimulus was food; the unconditioned response was a dog salivating. The third component of classical conditioning is a *conditioned stimulus,* which Pavlov demonstrated with a bell. The bell would ring before food was presented to the dog until only the ringing of the bell made the animal salivate. Salivation resulting from the bell but not the food was the *conditioned response,* the fourth element in classical conditioning.

Many persuasive campaigns have employed the classical conditioning approach as a means of getting consumers to buy products. When it works, especially in advertising, a bonus is afforded the advertising campaign. Slogans incorporated into advertising campaigns are one example. For instance, the slogan "Where's the beef?" was used in a fast-food restaurant chain's television commercial. "Where's the beef?" became a conditioned stimulus.

Instrumental or Operant Learning Theory

Whereas classical conditioning is concerned with prior stimuli, instrumental or operant learning theory concentrates on postreinforcement.[3] Applying instrumental learning to our fast-food commercial, the favorable visit to the restaurant outlet becomes a reinforcing mechanism that increases even more the effectiveness of the commercial. Instrumental learning is therefore dependent not only on postreinforcement but also on *positive* postreinforcement.

The store that advertises a special sale and then doesn't have the merchandise on hand when the customers arrive may have designed an effective persuasive campaign based on classical conditioning but neglected to take into consideration instrumental learning—to assure a positive postreinforcement to the ads. If the store does take instrumental learning into consideration and the postreinforcement experience is positive then the customer will pay attention and have faith in other messages from the same source.

Intervening Variables

Other variables can enter into a persuasive campaign and affect both classical conditioning and instrumental learning. For example, the time lapse between the conditioned stimulus and the unconditioned stimulus will affect learning. A ringing bell that immediately precedes the food will create an environment in which learning will take place. On the other hand, if the bell is heard and food doesn't appear for ten minutes, learning will be inhibited. Similarly, an advertisement for a department store sale will have less effect if the advertisement appears too far in advance of the sale.

BALANCE AND CONSISTENCY THEORY

Balance theory suggests that we seek balance in our lives as a means of reducing stress.[4] This does not mean that imbalance is bad. Being madly in love may result in a temporary imbalance in our emotional and physical systems but the sensation is what makes it so wonderful. Unfortunately, a state of suspended infatuation can cause dysfunction in other parts of our lives such as the inability to concentrate in school, the constant need to be with the other person at the expense of friends, irrational behavior, and a host of other irregularities. Sooner or later we must descend from the clouds and come to terms with the relationship, balancing it with the other forces in our life. For example, if we flunk out of school, our attractiveness to the other party will immediately lessen. Thus, we must choose a balance between being with the other person and remaining academically eligible to continue in school.

In persuasion, the message attempts either to create or to return attitude balance. For example, the former is designed to create resistance to forthcoming or simultaneous persuasion such as candidate A delivering a series of speeches that raise doubts about candidate B's honesty. The speeches create attitude imbalance in the minds of B's supporters who do not like dishonest politicians. Therefore, the supporters have three choices: (1) to disagree with candidate A to the point where imbalance does not occur, (2) find other communication that confirms the honesty of candidate B, or (3) vote for candidate A.

Meanwhile, candidate B has the job of refuting the charges of dishonesty and therefore returning attitude balance among candidate B's supporters. Candidate B might deliver a series of speeches calling for honesty in government. The voters would therefore be able to return to a balance between their own perceptions of the candidate and the communication they are receiving. In other words, they could sleep nights knowing candidate *B* was honest after all.

Three components will help us to better understand balance theory: the perceiver (A), which in our example of the politician would be the voters; a second person (B), which would be represented by candidate *B*; and the object (X), which was the issue of honesty in government. A triangle with *A*, *B* and *X* presents a pictorial representation of these components. What candidate *A* tried to do was disrupt the balance between *A*'s perception of *B* and also *A*'s perception of *X*. In a balanced state, *A* would be favorably predisposed to both *B* and *X*. But when candidate *A* placed doubts in the minds of the voters, it was an attempt to create imbalance in the way *A* perceived *B* and the way *A* perceived *B*'s feelings about *X*. *Before* candidate *A* arrived on the scene, the triangle looked like this:

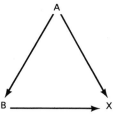

A is positive toward both *B* and *X* and perceives *B* as also being positive toward *X*. The system is balanced. When doubts arise, the triangle looks like this:

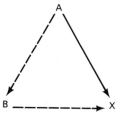

A begins to feel negatively (illustrated by the dotted line) toward *B* precisely because of the way *A* perceives *B*'s feelings about *X*. In other words, the voter will not vote for *B* because *B* is not disposed to honesty in government. Candidate *B*'s speech about honesty in government returned balance to the system.

COGNITIVE DISSONANCE

Directly related to balance and consistency theory is the theory of cognitive dissonance. Dissonance theory initially emerged from the work of social psychologist Leon Festinger.[5] Since the publication in 1957 of Festinger's book *A Theory of Cognitive Dissonance*, the concept has been tested and retested. It has a direct application to persuasion for many of the same theoretical reasons we discussed in balance and consistency.

Basic Premise

In its simplest form, cognitive dissonance theory suggests that dissonance—a psychologically disagreeable combination of elements—is a cause of stress and that, presented with a dissonance-reducing alternative, we will work toward reducing the dissonance or avoiding it altogether.

Reducing Dissonance

The more serious the dissonance the more forceful our desire to remove or avoid it. For example, let's return to our example of being madly in love. To return a semblance of balance to the system, to reduce dissonance between being with the lover or studying, alternatives are available. First, you could avoid the dissonance-producing situation. You might throw up your hands in despair and say, "I just can't handle this relationship. I am not ready for this type of commitment. It's too disrupting to my life and I have to get through college first!" You have chosen to reduce the dissonance by avoiding the situation.

You could have also avoided your studies and taken the attitude, "If I lose this individual my studies won't make any difference to me." Or, "Right now I just want to be in love and be with this person. It is the most important all-consuming thing in my life and my studies will just have to wait." The alternatives resulted in physical action to reduce dissonance.

Psychological avoidance is another alternative. For example, you might be an honor student and suddenly decide that good grades aren't as important as being with someone you love. After all, being successful but lonely isn't fun. Or you could reevaluate the other person and decide that he or she isn't so attractive after all, and you really do not need to spend as much time with that person. You have equally important things to attend to, namely, your studies. Had dissonance not been present you might have been perfectly content to make a total commitment.

Another person comes into your lover's life. Suddenly the prospect of losing your lover to someone else tips the scales. If that happens you will be so depressed your studies will surely suffer. Not spending as much time with someone is one thing but losing that person to someone else is another matter. You would suffer humiliation and embarrassment. Now the dissonance is reduced by your rationalizing that you must hold on to your lover. All kinds of persuasive messages emanate from your friends and acquaintances. Your love affair is a hot item on campus and advice is around every corner. Finally, you leap at the first suggestion that will reduce all the dissonance—you become engaged and move in with your lover. Now you can, at least for the time being, stop worrying about losing the one you love to another person and begin concentrating on your studies.

A large payoff, for example, money, can also reduce dissonance and make a choice between alternatives somewhat easier. For instance, let's say your lover's father showed up and offered you a huge sum of money to stop the love affair; you might decide to accept the cash. Although that alternative might seem reprehensible to most of us, others will say, "It depends on how much money is involved." Exactly. If the payoff is large enough you may not have any difficulty accepting the money and feeling perfectly OK about leaving your lover. You would readjust your psychological orientation to reduce dissonance, convincing yourself the money was worth it. Others may argue that no amount of money would make them leave the person they love.

SOCIAL JUDGMENT THEORY

The study of persuasion is also based on social-judgment theory. Developed by social psychologist Muzafer Sherif, social judgment theory consists of four elements that are primary to attitude change.[6] These four elements include three that make up an attitude scale: (1) *latitude of acceptance,* (2) *latitude of noncommitment,* and (3) *latitude of rejection.* The fourth is *ego-involvement.* Think of the first three as being on a horizontal line with latitude of acceptance on the left and latitude of rejection on the right (which side is not important). In the middle is the latitude of noncommitment.

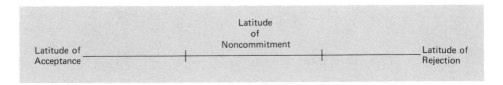

Positioning Attitudes

For purposes of example we have divided the line into three equal parts, although when applied to a person's attitude, one section may be larger or smaller than the others. We can plot our attitude on the line. For example, assume a public official delivers a speech in which she complains about the telephone service. A person hearing the speech would react to it based on his or her own *prior orientation* to the issue. For instance, if a long-time resident of the area felt the telephone service was poor, that person's orientation (or attitude) might be anchored within the latitude of acceptance. After having trouble making phone calls, the person developed an attitude that accepted the public official's view. If we positioned that person's opinion, as it relates to the speech, on a horizontal line, it would appear within the latitude of acceptance.

Perhaps another person in a rural area had just had a telephone installed and was so glad to be hooked up to the world that this person thought the telephone service was excellent. Thus, in the attitude of this individual would be in the latitude of rejection and they would disagree with the official.

A third person may have just moved to the area and was away from home a great deal. This individual rarely used the telephone and did not have strong feelings about local service. We could position that person's opinion in the latitude of noncommitment.

Ego-Involvement

We have been discussing attitudes in terms of agreement and disagreement. The remaining dimension to consider is how ego-involved someone is with the topic. For example, the person who doesn't own a telephone is not very ego-involved with the topic of telephone service. On the other hand, someone who owns a business involved in long-distance telephone solicitation will be very ego-involved. That person will respond to a speech about telephone service in a much different way from the person who doesn't own a telephone.

Research has provided us with some insights into how our attitudes and ego-involvement affect the way we react to persuasive messages. For example, we judge communication based on how close or far away from our own attitudes we perceive the message. If we are disappointed with local telephone service and hear a speech calling for improved service, then we will accept the message and perceive it to be close to our own opinion, even closer than it actually is. If, on the other hand, we are extremely satisfied with telephone service and hear a speech complaining about the service, we will reject the message and perceive it to be farther away from our own opinions than it actually is. Remember, theoretically our attitudes are positioned on the scale before communication takes place. We are "anchored" into our world, and that anchor determines how we react to persuasive messages.

Persuasive Strategies

How would we use what we know about social judgment theory to plan persuasive messages? To begin with, we would plan our messages to fall within the receiver's latitude of noncommitment or latitude of acceptance. It is in these areas that we would have the most success.

When an attitude is positioned in the latitude of noncommitment but close to the latitude of rejection, special care is necessary. Too much discrepancy between our persuasive message and the attitude of the receiver could push the receiver's attitude across the line; then our problems would be compounded. In a media campaign, such a mistake might be very costly. The impersonal nature of the mass media might make it difficult to pull back the attitude and the cost of reeducating (re-persuading) the receiver could be economically prohibitive.

A person highly ego-involved and strongly anchored to an issue will be more difficult to change. For example, if candidate A walks into candidate B's headquarters and begins a negative speech about candidate B, chances are everyone in the audience will be squarely in the latitude of rejection. People at headquarters are working for candidate B and are ego-involved with candidate B's campaign. The chance of changing attitudes is slim. On the other hand, citizens with little interest in politics aren't ego-involved with either candidate and their opinions are more easily changed. In politics the goal of many persuasive strategies is to find people ego-involved enough to vote but not anchored to a particular candidate.

RESISTANCE TO PERSUASION

Sophisticated persuasion involves setting up barriers to counter communication. Some theorists suggest that resistance to persuasion works best on topics that are rarely challenged, where debate has not taken place, and where issues are not open to attack. When we are made to believe an attack is imminent, then we are more likely to build a psychological fort to protect the idea.[7] For example, a basic belief is that the First Amendment to the U.S. Constitution provides a free press and therefore safeguards democracy. Few people actually debate the "value" of a free press. But assume we wanted to build stronger opinions about the value of a free press and therefore ward off challenges to those who would disagree with its premise. Assume that in a nearby country, which does not subscribe to our own political philosophy, we discover that a powerful radio station is being built and the broadcasts, directed toward our country, will be to attack basic principles of the U.S. Constitution.

How do we develop resistance to the persuasion and propaganda we know are about to be directed toward us? One method is to provide messages about the importance of a free press in a democracy. While that would be helpful it may not be as effective as informing the public of some of the arguments against a free press, which people will more than likely hear, and then refuting those same arguments. We would have presented *both sides* of the issue, then refuted the anti–free-press side. We also would have wanted to inform our own listeners that the broadcasts were about to begin. After all, one sees little reason to build a fort unless there is something worth defending. We know we have an opportunity to make the defense successful, and the approach of the enemy is imminent. It works much the same way with persuasion.

As we conclude this chapter we should remember that any attempt to analyze persuasion must take into consideration not only the sender, the message, and the receiver but also a host of other intervening variables that can affect the message and its outcome. Moreover, the design of message strategies and their distribution are much more sophisticated than ever before. We must take it upon ourselves to consume critically the messages that surround us and to use responsibly the understanding of persuasion that we have acquired.

SUMMARY

We are surrounded by messages. From the sound of the first morning radio commercial to the exposure of our work and educational environment, we are bombarded by persuasion. Like communication, persuasion is a circular process. The sender of communication is constantly being affected by the receiver.

Although there are many ways to study and analyze persuasion, rhetorical criticism is a good way to grasp the overall structure of a persuasive campaign. Depending on the amount of information that is available to us, that criticism can take a message-based, speaker-based, audience-based approach or a combination of these approaches.

From a behavioral perspective, persuasion can be studied through many psychologically based theories. Classical conditioning, which developed through the work of psychologist Ivan Pavlov, employs conditioned stimulus to gain a conditioned response. Instrumental or operant learning theory concentrates on postreinforcement communication. A number of intervening variables can affect both, including the strength of the message, motivation, and the time lapse between the conditioned and unconditioned stimulus.

Balance and consistency suggest we seek balance in our lives as a means of reducing stress. To illustrate this approach we employed a pictorial representation containing the three components of balance theory: the perceiver, the second person, and the issue. The manner in which the perceiver views the second person, the issue, and the second person's orientation to the issue will affect the balance of one's psychological system.

Perhaps the most famous theory and the object of major research is cognitive dissonance, which is also concerned with balance and suggests that when we are faced with dissonance we will seek to reduce or avoid the dissonance. Where a clear alternative is available or a payoff exists for a specific choice, this will make dissonance reduction easier. It is when choices are equal and no clear justifiable alternative exists that dissonance is the most difficult to reduce.

Social judgment theory is one of the most easily applied theories to persuasion. Social judgment theory involves four components: three latitudes— acceptance, noncommitment, and rejection—and a fourth component, ego-involvement. Persuasive messages that fall in our latitude of acceptance and latitude of noncommitment have the best chance of succeeding. Not effective are persuasive messages that fall in our latitude of rejection. Such messages can actually polarize our opinion, making it more difficult to accept future persuasion.

Less research is available on resistance to persuasion. However, where seldomly debated issues are concerned, presenting both sides of an issue and then refuting one side can build up defenses against future messages that might support the refuted position.

Regardless of whether we employ rhetorical criticism or more behavioral approaches to the study of persuasion, the knowledge about how we react to persuasive messages carries with it the obligation to use that knowledge responsibly.

QUESTIONS FOR REVIEW AND DISCUSSION

1. What is meant by the phrase "persuasion is a two-way process?"

2. In what way did the ancient Greeks define the term *persuasion?*

3. What conditions might exist that would result in a message-based approach to rhetorical analysis?

4. How does classical learning theory differ from instrumental or operant learning theory? Do you believe one is more effective than the other?

5. What intervening variables enter into classical or instrumental learning theories?

6. What are the three components of balance theory?

7. What are the two actions we customarily take when confronted with dissonance?

8. Is persuasion more effective when it reaches a latitude of acceptance or a latitude of rejection? Explain.

9. What strategy can be employed to create resistance to persuasion?

LEARNING EXERCISES

1. Role-play with another student a scenario whereby you must borrow $100 to lend to a friend who is in desperate trouble. Reverse the roles and have the student persuade you to lend him your car for a week.

2. Collect 10 advertisements from newspapers and magazines. Analyze each advertisement and explain the persuasive appeal of the ad.

ADDITIONAL READINGS

BOSTROM, R. N. *Persuasion.* Englewood Cliffs, NJ: Prentice-Hall, 1983.
CIALDINI, R. *Influence: The New Psychology of Modern Persuasion.* New York: Wm. Morrow, 1985.
FUNKHOUSER, R. *The Artful Persuader: Giving Up Control or the Way to Power.* New York: Times Books, 1986.
JOWETT, G. and V. O'DONNELL *Propaganda and Persuasion.* Beverly Hills, Sage, 1986.
KARLINS, M., and H. I. ABELSON *Persuasion: How Opinions and Attitudes Are Changed.* New York: Springer Pub. Co., 1982.
NEWELL, H. H., and H. S. SCHWERIN *Persuasion in Marketing: The Dynamics of Marketing's Great Untapped Resource.* New York: Wiley, 1981.
QUICK, T. L. *The Persuasive Manager: How to Sell Yourself and Your Ideas.* Radnor, PA: Chilton Book Co., 1982.
REARDON, K. K. *Persuasion, Theory and Context.* Beverly Hills: Sage Publications, 1981.
SANDERS R. *Cognitive Foundations of Calculated Speech: Controlling Understanding in Conversation and Persuasion.* Albany, NY: Sony Press, 1986.
SMART, J. J. *Ethics, Persuasion, and Truth.* New York: Metheun Inc., 1984.

14

ORGANIZATIONAL COMMUNICATION

OBJECTIVES

After completing this chapter, you should be able to

- Compare and contrast the classical, human-relations, human-resources, and systems approaches to management and communication
- Describe the four communication networks in organizations
- Distinguish the types of communication flow in organizations
- Describe both controlled external communication and uncontrolled external communication, or whistle blowing
- Discuss rumors and grapevines
- Recognize communication roles in organizations
- Explain the five factors on which power is based in organizations
- Talk about power sharing
- Outline the power structures in an organization and how they affect communication
- Realize that an organization and its communication are a cultural phenomenon
- Describe nonverbal communication in organizations
- Discuss the importance of negotiation in organizational communication
- Understand communication skills in organizations.

For college students, registration can be a difficult and formidable task. I was reminded of just how frustrating it can be when a certain student, whom we'll call Julie, needed a course to graduate. Unfortunately, the course was already filled by the time she registered. Frustrated, she came into my office to talk, and the conversation went as follows:

"Which course do you need?"

"Speech 142."

"Why can't you take Speech 150 instead?"

"Because if I take 150, I can't take English 98, which I also need for graduation."

"Is there anything besides English 98?"

"Only English 77, which meets at the same time as Speech 142."

"Your best bet would be to go to the head of the speech department and see if she could do anything for you."

"I did that, and she said that if nothing else worked, she would design an independent study for me, which would fill my requirement."

"Are you going to take the independent study?"

"Only as a last resort."

"What about your advisor? What did he say?"

"My advisor is 'Mr. Diplomat.' That's what we call him because all he wants to do is to keep everyone happy. He's nice and everyone likes him, but he doesn't want to make waves by calling the instructor of the Speech 150 course and asking her if she can open up another place and let me enroll."

"Have you talked to the dean?"

"Oh yes. He said to check with my advisor, and if that didn't work, he would order the Speech 150 professor to let me in."

"So what have you decided?"

"I guess I'll head back to talk with the chair of the speech department and see about the independent study."

"I think that's a great idea."

A few weeks later, I ran into the student again. She had enrolled in the independent study, was planning to graduate on schedule, was enjoying the course, and had developed a sincere friendship with the department chair, who was encouraging her to attend graduate school.

APPROACHES TO MANAGEMENT AND COMMUNICATION

In solving her scheduling problem, Julie encountered four common approaches to organizational structure that directly affect the way communication travels and is used in organizations: the classical, human relations, human resources, and systems approaches.

Classical Approach

The dean who was ready to solve Julie's problem by ordering the professor to enroll her in the course represented the *classical approach*. The *authoritarian approach to management* is one of the most common in business. It evolves from an organization-chart approach where the person at the top has the most power. Power that is left over is then distributed downward to subordinates.

One small company has a chief executive who tries very hard to leave the impression that he is a modern-thinking company president who knows a great deal about modern management techniques. His meetings include clearly defined objectives. But he is the only one who sets the objectives because he resists advice from his subordinates. His meetings begin and end at a specific time, regardless of whether or not the agenda is completed. He has a beeper phone and a small compact dictating machine attached to his belt. Although he is constantly sending memos, he pays little attention to the ones he receives. When employees want to talk to him, he complains that talking to employees takes up too much of his time. In the rear of the building that houses the company is an area where materials are packaged and shipped. Here he has established complex quota systems recorded on large tally boards. Workers plot their weekly progress in packaging and shipping.

Aside from his being looked upon as a complete nitwit, his approach would be looked upon as antiquated by anyone knowledgeable in organizational behavior or organizational communication. He is a living example of the classical approach to organizational theory in which the organization chart is the only chart to live by, and the workers' output is divorced from their own feelings or relationships with others in the company. He is threatened, insecure, and only manages to keep the employees in line by letting them know that if a union is ever voted in, the company will go under. Because the employees are paid little and jobs in the small community are scarce, his tactics keep the company in operation despite his tenuous relationships with the employees.

Our examples, both of the dean and the company manager, are somewhat extreme. Not all managers or organizations that subscribe to the classical approach (and to some degree all do) should be viewed from a negative perspective. Some charismatic leaders operate in a classical structure without having to give direct "orders" or make decisions that are perceived as being "bossy" or "heavy-handed." Rather, they manage through respect, not fear, from their subordinates.

Human-Relations Approach

Julie's advisor, who was liked by the students but who did not want to make waves, can be described as employing a *human-relations approach*. In the same town where our classical manager works is a manager who practices a human-relations approach in his organization. A casual, likable person, he believes in a very personal democratic approach to running his business. He frequently invites employees to his home for meals. He makes sure everyone is satisfied with the working conditions. The employees speak of him as a "nice, pleasant person" for whom to work.

When the competition in town began to cut into his company's profits, the nice, pleasant manager held a series of staff meetings, about pricing and other market factors. Gradually, however, the talented people in his firm became restless. The leading salesperson left to join the competing company. Morale was affected, other employees became concerned and restless, and the company ran into financial difficulty.

Even though morale may be high (although sometimes temporarily), productivity can suffer under a "pure" human-relations approach to management.

Human-Resources Approach

A corporation that the author has worked for as a consultant employs about 800 people. The company has developed a training and development program that gives employees the skills necessary to move up within the organization. A performance review and appraisal program has also been instituted.

This company is sensitive to a *human-resources approach* to management, recognizing the importance of nurturing the relationships between each employee-level of the company. The company's management also understands that communication within the company should not always flow in one direction—down from management. Realizing that the talents of one employee might be used in another division of the company, management established new divisional lines of communication to increase awareness of company-wide employment opportunities. This has made managers more aware of the talent that exists within the company, talent that can possibly be used to fill an opening they may have.

What about Julie? Did she encounter a human-resources approach to her problem? The chair of the speech department, who was willing to develop the independent study, was sensitive to a human-resources approach that would make it possible for Julie to graduate.

Systems Approach

Julie encountered the *systems approach* when she discovered that some courses were offered at times that conflicted with other courses. One part of the system, the English schedule, was affected by another part of the system, the Speech schedule.

The systems approach becomes especially evident in rapidly growing companies. The marketing people plan campaigns; the salespeople increase sales. These, in turn, translate into a heavier production schedule for manufacturing. The entire "system" is now operating at a higher level of output. The expansion of this output is maintained by hiring more people. Horizontal communication is stressed between different "parts of the whole" in order to get the job done. Each division, therefore, and the corresponding people who make up the divisions are functionally dependent and interrelated to each other.

Yet with the increased output and more personnel, transfers and promotions occur at a rapid pace. Although all divisions are dependent upon each other, the relationships between division heads have little time to develop. Because the company is expanding so rapidly, division heads rarely remain at their jobs more than a few months before they are promoted, transferred, or replaced by more "aggressive" high-growth-oriented managers.

Combinations of Approaches

We can see from the four approaches to management that organizations operate in different ways. However, a corporate commitment to a given management approach does not mean that that approach exclusively is practiced by everyone in the company. In fact, all four approaches frequently can be found within the same organization. Thus, these approaches sometimes work best when they are viewed as "management philosophies," indicating that perfection is impossible.

Moreover, roles and approaches shift depending on the specific tasks to be accomplished and the personalities of the individuals involved. In the company practicing human resources, for example, there may be times when a manager must instruct a supervisor in very businesslike language or reprimand an employee for being late for work. This "classical" approach to a single situation may be necessary to solve a problem or clearly state objectives.

In each approach, communication varies. We can see this more clearly by examining communication networks in organizations.

COMMUNICATION NETWORKS IN ORGANIZATIONS

In order to understand how communication varies in organizations, we will examine communication networks: formal, informal, internal, and external. Although we have deliberately separated these networks for purposes of study, they can be closely interrelated.

Formal Networks

Structured, sanctioned, identifiable, official—these words best describe formal communication networks. They are decreed every day by such things as organization charts, appointed committees, and other identifiable characteristics known by management and employees. Whether people are getting the job done, meeting goals, accomplishing objectives, or performing other "task functions," formal networks carry communication between people who are in a position to make decisions and carry on the work of an organization.

How these formal networks are structured will have an impact on the leadership within the network, the satisfaction of the network participants, and the team effectiveness of the network in solving the task. Often, it becomes a matter of who is talking to whom.

The more central a communication role that a person has in a formal network, the more likely that person is going to emerge as the leader. For example, the leader of a committee usually coordinates, among other tasks, the communication flow among committee members. This person assigns certain members to work with other members, or is the sole person to read the final reports of the other members. By controlling these message flows, either consciously or unconsciously, the chairperson leads the committee. Someone other than the chairperson may become elevated in stature by obtaining a vital piece of communication or being able to provide an important communication link in solving the task at hand.

Usually, the more structured the task, the more centralized is the communication network. If a committee is set up specifically to hire a new secretary, committee members know their responsibilities and can communicate accordingly. On the other hand, had the committee been set up to generate ideas about new products the company might manufacture, the committee would want to have the ability for more diverse, open communication.

Informal Networks

Organizations do not operate exclusively by organization charts and appointed committees. Just because three people are brought together at a corporate board meeting does not mean that they will always interact with machine efficiency or that their meetings will produce predictable results. Human nature, with all of its variables, spawns relationships and communication that may have very little to do with formal communication networks.

We talked earlier about the manager who subscribed to the classical approach of directing his organization. His greatest weakness was his inability to listen. Upward communication, even simple questions from subordinates, was difficult to handle because he perceived communication as only being appropriate when it flowed downward. When a problem did arise, he rarely waited to hear more than one side of the story, and he immediately made a decision to solve the problem based on the chain of command. He was most fearful when an employee communicated outside the division. Horizontal communication, or communication to one's superiors, was life threatening and was met by serious reprimand.

Because communication to the manager was, for all practical purposes, blocked for the employees, they began to communicate with another staff member who had equal professional seniority to the manager. This "phantom" manager, in an attempt to keep morale high and under pressure from other employees, began to make management decisions using the secretaries (who also found it difficult to talk to the manager) as a source of information and a channel of communication around the manager. Small subgroups began to form. When committees were assigned by the manager, committee members made decisions based on the wishes of the informal subgroups to which they belonged. Finally, enough informal networks had been developed that the organization moved along in spite of the manager. When the periodic evaluation of the manager took place, the corporate officers replaced him with the "phantom" manager.

Internal Networks

Internal networks are those that function inside an organization. Our discussion of formal and informal networks dealt with communication that was internal. Most of our examples in this chapter deal with internal communication, and for three reasons. *First,* the great majority of communication directly concerns the people within the organizations. *Second,* many organizations are themselves "private" entities. Corporations, for example, do not typically make all their records available to outsiders. Competitive business strategies, such as protecting patents, new products, and marketing plans, demand a certain amount of secrecy. *Third,* employees are "private" persons, unless they are politicians or public figures. Their private lives both at work and elsewhere are protected by law. Organizations are thus not at liberty to divulge this information to outsiders or the press. The private nature of organizations was expressed by reporter John Lewis of the *Wichita* (Kansas) *Journal,* who noted in a symposium on corporate communications that, "The corporation is, in fact, only a legal fiction that serves as a vehicle for a complex set of relationships between individuals."[1]

External Networks

External networks link the organization with people outside the organization. These people could be either the general public or the news media, which help carry the information to the general public. The power of the electronic media and the speed with which the media disseminate information have made business leaders keenly aware of the importance of these external networks of information. A television newscast can send the price of a company's stock soaring or crashing, depending on how favorable the news is to the company.

External networks are made up of both formal and informal networks. For example, a public-relations director is part of a network of people that not only includes corporate management but also members of the news media. The public-relations director may be asked by management to talk to a reporter—an example of a *formal* external network. At the same time, the reporter's secretary, who happens to know when a good story is needed, can be a valuable *informal* contact for a skilled public-relations person.

COMMUNICATION FLOW IN ORGANIZATIONS

So far our discussion has dealt with the channels used to convey communication. We can also become better organizational communicators by studying the *direction* in which messages flow.

Downward Communication

The manager who was replaced by the phantom manager was someone filled with a belief in the importance of downward communication. Yet even though downward communication placed a serious handicap on the manager's

Figure 14-1   One of the functions of downward communication in organizations is an analysis of the employee's job effectiveness. Many organizations incorporate performance review and appraisal as a regular part of supervisor-subordinate relationships. Such programs demand skill in interpersonal communication. When done properly, they permit employees to better know where they stand in the organization and what skills or improvements may be necessary.

effectiveness in that example, it does serve important purposes in organizations (Fig. 14–1). Traditionally, downward communication has been tied to a classical approach to management. Yet even in the most forward-thinking organizations, downward communication is still very necessary. The following are some of the functions of downward communication.[2]

Job instruction. Directives from management on what is to be done, how it is to be achieved, and what results are to be expected are all a part of job instruction.

General information. General information to assist in getting the job done also finds its way into downward communication. For example, management will share with subordinates information about how another company is approaching a problem.

Rules and regulations. Rules and regulations—every organization is faced with a host of them. In many companies, management has the responsibility, sometimes a legal obligation, to disseminate information about government rules and regulations to employees. Job discrimination, working conditions, safety factors, and equal pay are just some of the issues that flow from top to bottom. Other information may flow from top to the first or second level under top management, such as legal decisions affecting the company and competitive pricing policies.

Performance appraisal. Informing employees how well they do their jobs, how they can improve, and how the company can help them improve are three types of appraisal information that can flow downward from management. At the same time we should remember that truly effective performance appraisal necessitates two-way, and thus upward, communication as well.

Management philosophy. Organizations, especially larger corporations, utilize such diverse methods as internal public relations and motivation seminars to develop employees' awareness of the philosophy and goals to which the company subscribes.

Too much downward communication can overload the system to the point that much of the communication goes unheeded. A lack of sensitivity to timing can also destroy the effectiveness of the communication. Reprimanding an employee the morning after his wife had a miscarriage may not be the wisest management decision. Inadequate communication can have the same effect, such as firing a popular employee without fully explaining to key staff members why the decision was made.

Upward Communication

Organizations sensitive to employee feelings and opinions encourage every opportunity for upward communication.[3] Some of the more common examples are:

Self-appraisal. When employees communicate to supervisors how they feel about their success on the job, they're expressing self-appraisal. Self-appraisal is often required by organizations that have a well-developed performance appraisal program.

Appraisal of others. Communicating to supervisors about the performance of subordinates is standard upward communication. However, when employees communicate to supervisors about the performance of other employees, appraisal of others may take on the characteristics of "tattletale" communication.

Organizational policy. Opinions of how things should or do operate and of normal and abnormal policies and procedures are forms of upward communication (Fig. 14–2). This type of communication can be very valuable if received with an open mind by management.

When a person communicates upwardly in an organization, research suggests that to get the best results, communication should (1) be positive, (2) be timely, (3) support current policy, (4) go directly to the person who can act on it (although not necessarily an "end run"), and (5) conform to the perceptions of the receiver.[4]

Figure 14-2
Upward communication is important for management to receive a clear understanding of employee concerns. Opinions about organizational policy and suggestions for change are just some of the subjects contained in communication which flows upward.

Horizontal Communication

Horizontal communication occurs between people at similar levels of responsibility within an organization. It can be used to form some of the strongest relationships between people, because this communication often occurs in an atmosphere of mutual trust. Such communication can be voluntary and nonappraising. Suppose a police officer on patrol has a question about procedures. As the officer's sergeant may evaluate the officer negatively because he or she does not know what procedure is appropriate, the officer is much more likely to turn to a fellow officer for advice.

Horizontal communication is sometimes difficult to monitor. This is one of the reasons management should be receptive to upward communication. If management places a lid on upward communication, that communication can be diffused horizontally within the organization. This can cause serious problems if the horizontal communication is negative and creates tension and a loss of morale within the organization.

Controlled External Communication

A great deal of an organization's external communication is under management's control. In addition, management is becoming increasingly aware of its effects. In the Kansas symposium on corporate communications, James Boyd, of the Vulcan Materials Company, said: "Business must recognize the growing need of the community to be informed and to respond to that need when an interest is shown. Business, for its part, wants assurance that the information it imparts is treated in a manner which is fair."[5] Frank Hedrick of Beech Aircraft Corporation suggested that through external communication, a broader understanding and appreciation of the system of free enterprise is necessary to avoid government encroachment.[6]

In another forum, James D. Robinson, III, chairman of the American Express Company, suggested that the business community must have a change of attitudes toward the function, power, and role of communications, and that business leaders must be committed to philosophically "speaking up" and "speaking out" on issues. He quoted *Wall Street Journal* columnist Vermont Royster as saying: "Only when the business community recognizes that its chief executives must be less narrow of thought, less inarticulate . . . and less fearful of the fray, will the voice of business be heard in the land."[7]

UNCONTROLLED EXTERNAL COMMUNICATION: WHISTLE BLOWING

Another type of external communication, one management does not control, is called *whistle blowing* or *leaking*. Both terms describe unauthorized communication where an employee complains outside the organization to the public or press,[8] or sometimes to a government agency. Little is known about whistle blowing because the person who blows the whistle often ends up being fired.

In a whistle-blowing incident, the employee becomes aware of something he or she feels is unethical, immoral, or illegal. When little or no action is taken after complaints have been made to immediate and higher-up supervisors, the employee takes the complaint outside the organization. Because of this action, the employee often is forced out of or becomes isolated within the organization. In other cases, the employee may voluntarily resign over the issue that precipitated the complaint.

Although every organization is different, certain conditions can create an atmosphere that encourages whistle blowing. Organizations lacking a planning and policy division or some other mechanism for quality control may produce products that are unsafe.[9] If workers discover defects in the product but their concerns go unheeded, they may feel their only alternative is to inform the public or the press.

Another atmosphere for whistle blowing exists in organizations in which the lower-echelon staff has little respect for the next level of management. Sometimes this occurs when employees feel their immediate superiors are managers only because of bureaucracy, not because of their qualifications or expertise.[10] Under such conditions, employees may believe the only way they can communicate with top management is to do an end-run around their supervisor, something that may get them fired.[11]

In an effort to control whistle blowing, some organizations hire *ombuds-*

men, people whose job is to listen to complaints and try to find solutions.[12] Ombudsmen are safety valves that can help alleviate tension among employees and sometimes eliminate the need for whistle blowing.[13]

What little we do know about whistle blowing offers some lessons for organizational communicators. Management may not perceive that an issue is serious enough to result in whistle blowing especially when management does not listen to all levels of the organization. Those managers may not have experienced the resounding frustration of the whistle blower. They may also smugly feel that an employee will not risk his or her job to engage in whistle blowing. Similar naive notions are held by whistle-blowers, who may not realize the serious ramifications of communicating outside of the organization.

RUMORS AND GRAPEVINES

If you have been part of any organization for any length of time, you are aware that information cannot always be trusted as being accurate and that informal networks often operate unpredictably. Both of these phenomena can involve rumor and the use of the grapevine.[14]

Rumors

History has been filled with examples of information run amok. In ancient Rome, Mark Antony lost a major military battle because he thought Cleopatra's barge was sailing away and pulled back to follow. More recently, two major automobile companies, Volkswagen and Chrysler, fought unfounded rumors that the two were going to merge. A fast-food chain combatted rumors that it had worms in its hamburgers. Political conventions are notorious for rumors about candidates for office, running mates, and cloakroom deals. False shortages of everything from gasoline to aluminum foil to toilet paper have plagued merchants for years. Rumors are unavoidable. Simply defined, they consist of sometimes difficult-to-confirm information passed through informal channels of communication. Sometimes rumors prove uncannily accurate. Other times they have little basis in fact.

Rumors are passed from one person to another for a number of reasons, such as the desire to verify information. One person asks another: "Have you heard anything about Juan's resignation?" The other replies, "No, but I bet Felipe does!"

The desire to be included in a group that possesses the information is another motivation for rumor transfer. "Don't leave me hanging. Tell me what's going on." Wanting to give something to someone else can aid rumor transmission. "You're my roommate, so I'll tell you what's happening."

Psychologists have classified rumors into four types.[15]

> ***Wedge drivers.*** Some of the most serious rumors divide or simply relay untrue and damaging information (Fig. 14–3). "I heard he is drunk on the job more than he's sober."

Pipe dreams. Pipe dreams can best be described as wishful thinking. "I hear we're getting a raise." Sadly, paychecks stay the same.

Bogeys. Bogeys are untrue rumors that create fear or lower morale in an organization. "I heard our division will close."

Homestretchers. Homestretchers anticipate something. "It's almost certain. Consolidated Oil will sign the contract next week."

Although realizing rumors are inevitable, many organizations do try to control them. Some operate special phone lines and rumor clearance centers where a staff member can call to try to verify information. When these centers are operated in an atmosphere of trust and commitment to the free flow of information, they can be helpful. Although they will not stop the spread of information through informal channels, they can help keep it accurate.

Grapevines

Grapevines are informal communication networks that carry rumors. Research suggests that grapevines are not the same as the informal networks used on a regular basis for job-assistance information, such as asking a co-worker how to complete a task. Grapevines are irregular, can change rapidly, and carry information that is about 75 to 95 percent accurate, although not complete. Because information carried on the grapevine is not totally complete, management considers that information to be 0 percent accurate.[16] Research has also found that only about 10 percent of the people involved with a grapevine actually transmit information. The rest of the people aware of the event or the issue receive the information from those 10 percent.

COMMUNICATION ROLES IN ORGANIZATIONS

Regardless of whether we ask for help with our job, participate in rumor transmission, or deal with top management through established channels, we serve given communication roles in an organization.

Role Behavior

The communication roles we perform in an organization may vary, depending on the situation, the topic under discussion, the task to be performed, or the goal to be reached. Different role relationships can exist in an organization.[17]

Within an organization are groups with *group members.* You may be appointed to serve on a committee, become a member of the board, or work as part of a construction crew. In each case, you are a member of a group. The people responsible for bridging the gap between different groups form *bridges.* Examples of bridges can be found in large committees that break up into smaller subcommittees in order to solve parts of a problem. In solving the total problem, it becomes necessary for one subcommittee to communicate with another subcommittee. A bridge (person) is appointed. *Liaisons* are the "linkers" of information, serving a vital role in transmitting and receiving information. Usually such people have high status in the organization, at least among the staff if they are not on a formal organization chart. He or she may be someone to whom everyone turns to talk something out or to ask questions. Liaisons can act as the links between multiple groups of people. They can also be members of a group. *Nonliaisons* are group members who do not have contact with other groups. *Isolates* are the most removed from the decision process.

Role Fulfillment

From our knowledge of the various roles people play in an organization, we can see that to be an effective part of any organization, it is necessary both to have and to use properly many of the skills of human communication we have been talking about throughout this book. In decision making, the ability to work effectively within a group is critical to achieving even the simplest goals. Even more responsibility rests upon a group member acting as a bridge between groups. The ability to communicate information accurately, to understand the give-and-take process of listening and reacting, and to be sensitive to the communication dynamics of organizations determine the difference between success and failure. It may also determine how the individuals involved serve most of their roles, from liaison to isolate.

POWER IN ORGANIZATIONS

A company supervisor tells a group of steelworkers, "The president of the company says we have to increase production by 20 percent by the end of the month. If you do not raise your own productivity by 20 percent by the end of the month, I will fire you, and you will not receive a recommendation from the company." At the end of the month, overall production has increased by 31 percent.

Does this sound like a show of power? You bet it does. Even though interpersonal communication, self-concept, group processes, and nonverbal communication all helped the supervisor communicate the message to the steelworkers, the very *power* of the supervisor to control the jobs of the workers may have been the only incentive for meeting the goals.

Power plays a major role in all organizations.[18] Sometimes it is subtle, such as a co-worker's knowing more than a colleague about the operation of the grapevine. At other times it is overt, such as the company president's unquestioned authority to hire and fire.

In studying communication in organizations, we should remember that power can play an important part in interaction. Because power usually evolves from above, we tend to pay more attention to messages reaching us through downward communication. If we are closely associated with power—for example, by being an executive assistant to the company president—we will pay attention and react differently to communication from the president than, say, from a division head. Because of the power relationship to communication, it is important to know the basis of power.[19]

One basis of power is *knowledge*. Knowing how to do something can mean knowing how to succeed. Whether it is investing money or assembling an automobile, those who have knowledge are in a position of power to give or withhold that knowledge from someone else. Showing a new student the ropes, training a salesperson, and helping a recruit learn the basics are examples of using knowledge as a basis for power.

People who can *reward* us have power over us. They can determine how much we are paid, what hours we work, whether we are promoted, and other "rewards," both tangible and intangible. The power may not always be evident or even stated, but whenever someone else has something of value to us, we find ourselves operating in a power relationship. For some people, any kind of power imbalance is unsatisfactory. Many times such individuals find their greatest satisfaction in being the owners and operators of their own companies in which they sign paychecks, make the decisions, and reap the profits. They also take all the risks.

People who exercise power through *identification* find they can manage an organization even when they're absent. Employees identify with the manager and carry out that manager's wishes whether or not the manager is present. Let's look at an example. A manager the author knows left for a vacation. Not long after he had gone, the organization began to have problems. Even the substitute manager was unsuccessful in keeping things under control. The problem was that no one in the organization identified with the manager, no one wanted to be like him, and many people actually disliked him. Because no one *identified* with him, when he left, they stopped behaving like a group of coerced subordinates and more like individuals. The substitute manager did not have the time to develop his own management style before the organization began to flounder.

The power to *coerce* is often interrelated to the power to reward. If a person has the power to reward, he or she also has the power to punish. Perceived power to coerce can be just as powerful as actual power, and the person holding that power does not need to set examples by firing people to gain results.

When someone enlists in the military, he or she *agrees* to the rules of power that are part of the military structure. Admirals have power over ensigns, majors have power over captains, sergeants have power over privates, and so on. In organizations, similar power by agreement operates within these constraints. Companies' social clubs and professional societies consist of people who are part of the organization because they recognize and agree to abide by the power structure that is part of the organization.

What kind of power we best respond to or what kind of power we can best administer depends on our individual psychological makeup. Remember that communication is an important part of an organization, and power plays a major role in determining the results of that communication.

POWER SHARING

We have talked a great deal in this book about communication as a process of sharing. Power can also be viewed as a sharing process. One cannot have power without having someone over whom to have power. The success of using power is determined only by how another individual responds to that power. If a police officer walks up to an individual and tells that person to be quiet, the police officer has used power. If, on the other hand, the person's response to the officer's request is to yell even louder, the police officer has had little original success in using power.

We hear the phrase *balance of power* used to describe the relationships between two countries. A balance of power can also exist between people, both in and out of organizations. The president of a company hires a talented executive assistant. Because the president needs more time to consider the growth and expansion of the company and wants relief from daily personnel problems, the president entrusts increasingly more authority to the executive assistant. It is not long before the executive assistant is handling all personnel problems effectively.

One day when touring the assembly line, the president invites a supervisor to have lunch. To his surprise, the supervisor tells him that she appreciates the offer but that the executive assistant wanted to have lunch sometime this week, and before the supervisor can have lunch with the president, she needs to check with the executive assistant. The president discovers that by placing responsibility with the executive assistant, he has also shared his power with the executive assistant.

This example demonstrates that power relationships are an exchange, much like that of goods and services. Because the president wanted to spend more time helping the company expand, he had to give up much of his direct power to the executive assistant. Of course, the president still has at his disposal all sorts of other bases for power and can overrule, even fire, the executive assistant. But then the president would be back spending even more time on personnel problems. While understanding the basis for power, do not forget the costs implied in the use of power.

POWER STRUCTURES

One way to view the relationship of power and organizational communication is to interpret power from (1) a surface structure, (2) a deep structure, and (3) communication that helps identify the presence of power in each structure.[20] Although these may seem complex, some examples will make them readily understandable.

The Surface Structure

On the surface structure of an organization, dialogue is being exchanged about solving the practical problems of the organization. A small-group discussion would be one place to witness power on the surface structure at work.

Three vice-presidents meet to discuss a new product. One is a vice-president for production, another is a vice-president for corporate relations, and the third is a vice-president for marketing. Each has a vested interest in the product and its success. As the discussion continues, each sets forth ideas on the qualities of the new product, consumer acceptance, and how the new product should be marketed. Some participants feel more strongly about some issues than others, and these feelings are reflected in the comments they make. Their discussion is an example of the surface structure at work.

The Deep Structure

Now consider how power in the deep structure of the organization affects the discussion. The three vice-presidents actually have varying amounts of power in the organization. Knowing their roles in the company and the relationships from which they function adds to our understanding of the deep structure. For example, one vice-president may be a "liaison," whereas another may be more of an "isolate." This information is part of the deep structure of the organization. For purposes of example, let's say that the vice-president for production is the isolate without key contacts in the organization. Let's assume the vice-president for marketing, on the other hand, has an open line of communication to the chairman of the board. In a situation requiring a power play, the vice-president for marketing could squelch a product by not offering effective marketing support. Thus, while the vice-president for production will offer opinions, those opinions are tempered by the knowledge that opposing the vice-president for marketing or raising issues with which that person might strongly disagree is ineffective and even dangerous. The deep structure has outlined the battlefield, the soldiers, the battles to be fought, and which battles will be won or lost.

Communication Among Structures

The communication through which the vice-presidents deal with issues and solve problems in our example is affected by both of the structures just described. In turn, communication can, itself, affect both of these structures. While communication is most visibly present on the surface of an organization, communication can influence greatly the deep structure of the organization. For instance, a stockholders' meeting may generate criticism of the company's policies and even its executives, but too much criticism may produce a change in the deep structure. Similarly, too many negative comments from customers may result in a change in personnel and thus a change in the deep structure of an organization.

The Politics of Power Structures

Knowing about the deep structure of an organization is necessary to function successfully within the organization. The "politics" of the deep structure guides an employee in knowing how and with whom to communicate. You don't criticize the boss if the boss doesn't like to be criticized. Furthermore, not knowing whether or not someone has the power to impose penalties on you means you are communicating in a vacuum, a vacuum that can whisk you into a position of little authority.

CORPORATE CULTURE AS ORGANIZATIONAL COMMUNICATION

An organization is in many ways like a small society. It is held together by many of the same things that hold a society together—values, beliefs, customs, rituals, lifestyle patterns, and symbols. All of these qualities are what anthropologists call *culture.* They are what distinguish one society from another. Organizations reflect their own culture much in the same way that a society reflects its culture. For instance, we will experience a different culture working inside the laboratory of a high-technology company than we will working on a cruise ship.

In some cases culture is experienced verbally, such as the Monday morning sales meeting where the motivational messages send the sales force roaring into the marketplace. In others, the culture may be expressed nonverbally, such as the blue-gray wall color and carpeting of a corporate boardroom, which mimics the same color scheme used in the corporate logo. Culture is transmitted among members of a society through communication. It is transmitted to large groups of people through mass media and sometimes to smaller groups through direct face-to-face interaction.

Expression of Culture

Within any organization, we can identify different expressions of culture by examining some of the dimensions of communication that take place. Rituals, for example, are an expression of organizational culture. The company that hosts a Friday afternoon party in the cafeteria is reflecting corporate culture. The executive roast that pokes fun at the chief operating officers after the annual stockholders' meeting is an example of corporate culture.

Rituals can be divided into different subrituals: personal, task, social, and organizational.[21] While studying the operation of a state police unit, I watched the post commander distribute each morning the log of events from the night before and then conduct a dialogue with the news media on what had happened. The dialogue would deal not only with the items on the log but also with a personal experience the post commander had had with a similar case. Frequently, he would begin by saying, "I remember when I was a rookie. . . ." Thus, the commander's early morning discussion with the news media was a *personal ritual.*

A *task ritual* is associated with one's work duties. The same state police unit had a radio operator who handled after-hours calls from the news media. In every telephone call the script was always the same. The radio operator gave the reporter the information but also gave a friendly warning about the competition. The conversation would go much like this:

RADIO OPERATOR:	"State police, may I help you?"
REPORTER:	"Anything going tonight?"
RADIO OPERATOR:	"Sure is."
REPORTER:	"Well what is it?"
RADIO OPERATOR:	"Don't you know?"
REPORTER:	"You're the expert."
RADIO OPERATOR:	"I get everything I know from you."
REPORTER:	"OK, let's quit the B.S.; what have you got?"
RADIO OPERATOR:	(would read the log then say) "But your competition called two hours ago."

Night after night the same exchange would take place. Eventually, the reporter got the information he or she wanted.

Our example of the Friday afternoon party in the cafeteria is an example of a *social ritual*. The executive roast is an example of an *organizational ritual*.

Language as Culture

Organizations may foster a certain vocabulary and language that reinforce certain beliefs and perceptions, not only about the organization itself but also about other organizations with which it may compete. For example, one company refers to its competition as the "rocks." The title is meant to be negative, much like having "rocks in your head." Not only is it a negative way of expressing feelings about the other company but it also serves to protect the organization from having its employees lured away to the competition. After all, when one spends a few years joining in conversations that frequently refer to the "rocks," it takes some readjustment to accept an offer to go work for the "rocks," even if the "rocks" offers more money.

Organizational Myths

Myths also help to perpetuate organizational culture. One organization is famous for portraying an image of a president who began as a door-to-door salesperson. Sales managers are quick to perpetuate that image. They communicate effectively to motivate their sales force by announcing the impending visit of the president. One of the myths includes a story that the president always inspects the sales representatives' briefcases to see if they carry a flashlight. After all, if you are going to work long past 5:00 P.M. and locate addresses, you will need a flashlight. Not having a flashlight means you are tagged with the image of being a nine-to-fiver and cannot possibly make much of yourself in the company.

Initiations

In many cultures, individuals must undergo intiation rites before they can be considered part of the organization.[22] In a fraternity or sorority, an initiation and/or formal ceremony usually precedes the formal acceptance of the "pledge" into the organization.

Culture is an important aspect of any organization. Understanding the culture is relevant to understanding the total communicative atmosphere of the organization. Rituals, myths, and formal and informal symbols all determine how the members of the organization will interact with each other.

NONVERBAL COMMUNICATION IN ORGANIZATIONS

Our discussion of organizational culture used the example of the office decorated in the same color scheme as the corporate logo. Both the color scheme and the corporate logo are examples of nonverbal communication in organizations. However, much of the nonverbal communication in organizations is that which takes place between individuals, and it involves all of the factors of nonverbal communication we discussed earlier in the text. Other nonverbal factors are related to the physical structure that makes up the work spaces people occupy. Elaborate research designs have studied the spatial characteristics of work places, examining such things as the openness of office areas, the density of employees, the accessibility of employee work areas, and the amount of light entering an office area.

Research has shown some interesting but predictable results when studying the characteristics of office space and its relationships on human interaction.[23] Crowded offices can (but do not always) produce more friendships because people are closer together and interact more. Conflicts, however, become exaggerated in cramped spaces. Crowded spaces also cause a lack of privacy, impacting on both personal and territorial space. Workers who perceive their work environment as being unpleasant are more likely to leave the work area during coffee breaks and not to place personal items in the work area. Interior architects are working to alleviate these problems; modern office complexes are being designed with an understanding of the relationship between human and environmental factors.

NEGOTIATION

Although not as sophisticated as it is today, negotiation has been present ever since our ancestors fought over scraps of meat, firewood, and water. Much of organizational communication is negotiation.

Negotiation occurs in every walk of life. A prison riot is negotiated between the authorities and the prisoners. A labor contract is hammered out between the union and the company with a mediator handling the negotiations. A secretary gets a pay raise after negotiating with a supervisor. Teenagers negotiate with their parents over driving the family car. All of these examples involve some form of conflict resolution: resolution between the conflicting needs and goals of the negotiating parties.[24]

The Role of Argument

A good negotiator understands the fine points of arguing. In its most effective form, argumentation means that parties in a negotiation will offer each other alternatives and then argue about the basic merits of each. Knowing how to handle interpersonal communication under argumentative conditions is a prerequisite in determining what both parties will eventually agree to. The key is to be *critical* of each other's positions but at the same time to be *cooperative*.[25] Being too critical may be construed as being uncooperative. When that happens, negotiations may break off.

The give-and-take of argument has its foundation in human communication. Both parties, through interaction, explore all of the possible alternatives to a negotiated settlement. Through this exploration, they gradually move toward a mutually agreed-upon settlement.

The Role of Power

Each party in the negotiation process has power, despite what might be inferred by their respective titles. Professional negotiator Herbert A. Cohen states succinctly: "Power is based on perception. If you think you've got power, you've got it. If you think you don't have it, even if you've got it, you don't have it."[26]

A secretary negotiating for a raise has power over the boss, who realizes that if the secretary is dissatisfied, the office work will suffer, which will in turn reflect negatively on the boss. Conversely, if the secretary allows the work to suffer too much, the boss will fire the employee; thus, the balance of power is reinstated. Yet although the boss may have the power to fire the secretary, the secretary has the power to quit. Finding a new secretary may be much more costly than giving the secretary a raise. The negotiation can go on and on.

Although we tend to think in terms of dollars and cents as the object of the negotiation, our example points out other factors as well. Satisfaction with the outcome of the agreement is one of the things being negotiated, even though it may not be stated. Even communication itself is a commodity, both in amount and content. The manner and content of one party's reaction to the other party's offer will determine subsequent communication patterns.

The Role of Prediction

Negotiators operate in an atmosphere of prediction.[27] Each statement and offer, each reply and counteroffer, is made with the prediction and expectation of what the other party's reaction will be.

If you plan to talk to your manager about a raise, you will first consider the possible reaction of the manager to your request. You ask yourself: "What will my manager think of me for asking for a raise? Will asking for a raise reflect positively on my future evaluations?" These questions indicate that you're trying to predict the reaction of the manager.

The manager, in turn, listens to you and predicts your reactions. The manager may be asking such questions as: "Will this employee be discouraged from working if I do not grant the pay request? Will the employee leave our company for another job?"

Each party predicts the reaction of the other. The communication pattern that follows reflects these predictive qualities.

As the negotiations continue, each party plays a cat-and-mouse game of self-disclosure, telling the other party just enough to get a reaction to try to predict with accuracy what the next reaction will be to the next proposal. At the same time, each party is careful "not to lay all the cards on the table." Most of us do not walk into a car dealer and say, "This is my best offer." We negotiate; we do not tell the salesperson what our best offer is until we know more about what the salesperson's best offer is. Then we gently give-and-take our positions using such information as the cost of options, the wholesale price, dealer-preparation charges, and so forth. We explore and probe for more information to try to determine profit margins and how far the salesperson will go before we look at each other and say, "This is the best offer I can make," even if, in reality, that may not be the case.

The Role of Compromise

We have learned how fields of experience between individuals must overlap in order for effective communication to take place. Nowhere is this truer and nowhere is it more readily applied to communication than in negotiation.

In negotiation, the fields of experience between the two parties become each side's respective alternative to resolving the issue. Before an agreement is reached, be it a labor negotiation or a family feud, each party will explore the other's alternatives. Somewhere between the point beyond which each cannot go, and the position each would most like to have, is a host of alternatives. These alternatives are the fields of experience each party shares. Using power, prediction, and argument, the parties reach a final compromise.

COMMUNICATION SKILLS IN ORGANIZATIONS

In many small businesses, the entire image of a company rests with the person who answers the phone. This individual must be able to listen carefully, take messages, and be courteous. If the person cannot listen and makes mistakes, customers will go elsewhere.

The communication skills of employees can greatly affect an organization's ability to reach goals and motivate people. One study by researcher Michael Hanna identified 11 troublesome communication situations faced in business: (1) listening, (2) motivating people, (3) giving directions, (4) delegating authority, (5) group problem solving, (6) handling grievances, (7) private one-to-one conferences, (8) using the grapevine, (9) formal presentation, (10) conference leadership, (11) negotiation and bargaining.[28]

In short, the ability to be successful and advance in any organization depends on the ability to communicate effectively. Even responsibilities for bottom-line profits fall back on someone's ability to convince others to purchase the goods or services of the company. Staying alert to communication situations and possessing the communication skills to interact with others are first steps in being a responsible, effective member of an organization.

SUMMARY

Four approaches to management and organizational communication were discussed in this chapter. The classical approach is most closely tied to the organization chart and "chain of command." The human-relations approach places a priority on people interacting with each other and on high morale. A pitfall of this approach can be low productivity, whereas a pitfall of the classical approach can be low morale. The human-resources approach seeks to develop the individual's full potential within the organization as a means of achieving high productivity. The systems approach assumes all the different divisions of a company function as an interrelationship.

Within any organization are different communication networks, which we classified as formal, informal, internal, and external. Each can interrelate to the other. Formal networks closely follow assigned channels of communication, whereas informal networks develop among individuals. Networks operating within an organization are called internal, while those operating outside the organization are called external.

Communication also flows in different directions within organizations. Downward communication from supervisor to subordinate can include job instructions, general information, rules and regulations, performance appraisal, and management philosophy. Upward communication from subordinate to supervisor includes self-appraisal, appraisal of others, and organizational policy. Horizontal communication between employees of equal stature often involves task sharing. All involve internal communication. Yet external communication flow is also present and leaves and enters the organization as an interchange with the public.

In some cases, this external communication is uncontrolled, producing what is called whistle blowing. Whistle blowing is unauthorized communication in which the employee complains outside the organization to the public or press. Although whistle blowing may call attention to the problem, the whistle-blower usually is shunned by peers and often is fired without recourse.

Rumors are difficult-to-confirm information passed through informal channels of communication. Grapevines are the informal communication channels through which rumors flow.

Regardless of what positions we hold in an organization, we fulfill certain roles in our relationships with other people. These relationships are often based on a power structure that can affect interpersonal interaction. While learning the bases of power—knowledge, reward, identification, coercion, and agreement—we also learned that power is a shared process among individuals.

Power structures are also part of organizations. Surface structures involve themselves with everyday solutions to problems and practical concerns affecting the organization. Deeper structures concentrate on the inner power working of the organization. We use communication to identify these power structures.

As with other societies, organizations have their own cultural identities that are reflected through both verbal and nonverbal communication. From rituals to corporate logos, organizational culture is reflected through the communication patterns of the organization's members. Nonverbal communication in organizations is reflected both in the logos and the physical characteristics of the work place.

Much of organizational communication involves negotiation. We negotiate raises, prices, and conflict, among other issues. Skilled negotiators understand the roles that argument, power, prediction, and compromise contribute to the final solution.

Specific communication skills are necessary to function effectively within an organization. Some of the most troublesome areas identified by research include listening, motivating people, giving directions, delegating authority, group problem solving, handling grievances, private one-to-one conferences, using the grapevine, formal presentations, conference leadership, and negotiation and bargaining.

QUESTIONS FOR REVIEW AND DISCUSSION

1. What different styles of management were reflected in the way professors handled the student's registration problems discussed in the beginning of the chapter?

2. What differences exist between the classical, human-relations, human-resources, and systems approaches to management communication?

3. What are the advantages and disadvantages of both internal and external networks?

4. Why does horizontal communication often result in some of the strongest relationships among members of an organization?

5. List some of the preconditions for whistle blowing and the characteristics of participants in whistle-blowing incidents.

6. What are the different communication roles between group members, liaisons, bridges, nonliaisons, and isolates?

7. How do the power of knowledge, reward, identification, coercion, and agreement differ?

8. What are the similarities and differences between surface and deep structures in an organization?

9. How is culture expressed within an organization?

10. In what ways do argument, power, prediction, and compromise operate in the negotiation process?

LEARNING EXERCISES

1. Interview someone who works for either a small company or larger corporation and ask that person to identify bases of power that exist in his or her work environment.

2. Interview that same person or another individual about the different communication networks that exist in the person's organization.

ADDITIONAL READINGS

Asman, D. and A. Meyerson eds. *The Wall Street Journal on Management*. Homewood, IL: Dow Jones-Irwin, 1985.

Bower, J. L. *The Two Faces of Management*. Boston: Houghton Mifflin, 1983.

Dellinger, S., and B. Deane *Communicating Effectively: A Complete Guide for Better Management*. Radnor, PA: Chilton, 1982.

Fisher, R., and W. Ury *Getting to Yes: Negotiating Agreement Without Giving In*. Boston: Houghton-Mifflin Co., 1981.

Frank, A. D. *Communicating on the Job*. Glenview, IL: Scott, Foresman, 1982.

Hamilton, C. R., C. Parker, and D. D. Smith *Communicating for Results: A Guide for Business and the Professions*. Belmont, CA: Wadsworth, 1982.

Kennedy, M. M. *Office Warfare*. New York: Macmillan, 1985.

Myers, G. E., and M. T. Myers *Managing by Communication: An Organizational Approach*. New York: McGraw-Hill, 1982.

Peters, T. J. and R. H. Waterman Jr. *In Search of Excellence*. New York: Harper & Row, 1982.

15

INTERVIEWING

OBJECTIVES

After completing this chapter, you should be able to

- Discuss the communication environment of interviewing
- Describe counseling interviews
- Explain the communication processes necessary to have a successful performance review and appraisal interview
- Tell how you would perform a survey interview
- Identify and discuss some basic "rules" of the journalism interview
- Define and discuss a compliance interview
- Talk about a grievance interview
- Prepare for an employment interview
- Be aware of who you are in order to truly assess what you want from the employment interview
- Prepare a résumé
- Write an introductory letter asking for the employment interview
- Successfully apply communication skills in an employment interview
- Discuss the legal issues involved with employment interviewing.

In few settings are communication skills more important than during an interview. These settings include more than job seeking, although the employment interview will be one of the more important interviews in which we participate. Other interview settings include grievance hearings, performance review and appraisal, medical, legal, political, and journalistic interviews, and a host of others. In a journalistic interview, for example, the reporter interviewing a politician must gather the facts to ask intelligent questions, must know what questions to ask, and must sort through the politician's answers to write or broadcast a news report that can affect millions of people.

In another setting, a question by a member of a congressional fact-finding committee can lead to disclosures having international repercussions.

Employers who can sift through the formalities of a job interview to identify in an applicant the qualities that will make a future corporate president are rewarded well for their efforts. The guidance counselor handling the difficult and sensitive issue of a student's grades or behavior must be trained to walk a thin line between criticism and encouragement.

INTERVIEWING AND THE COMMUNICATION PROCESS

Although examining other interviewing settings will serve us equally well, because the job interview is so important in our lives, let us explore the interviewing process from that setting. In a job interview, the interviewer and interviewee communicate with all of the variables present that exist in any other type of interpersonal interaction.

Communication Variables

Homophily already exists between the employer and the interviewee. Both are interested in working for the same company, and both have most likely done their homework on each other. For example, the employer will have already perused the interviewee's résumé or other supporting documents in order to ascertain the interviewee's goals and aspirations to see how they might fit into the needs of the company. Similarly, the interviewee will have studied the firm's annual report or other documents to see how the company's activities fit in with the individual's personal goals. Assume in the résumé there is a subheading titled "Professional Experience." There the applicant will have listed previous job experiences and some of the responsibilities associated with these experiences. The resume might state: "Designed a new recreation program including summer instruction in swimming, tennis, and track." The employer may not be looking for someone to design a recreation program but the statement does indicate initiative, drive, and the ability to accept responsibility, the same qualities that are being sought by the employer.

Both parties will also bring to the interview certain attitudes and opinions that will affect the outcome of the interview. For example, the interviewer may have a preference toward applicants from a given school. Perhaps the company has had good results from hiring previous graduates from that same school and wants to continue with that pipeline of graduates. Or perhaps the interviewee has internship experience and the interviewer already feels positively toward such on-the-job experience.

The Communicative Atmosphere

Other factors play a part in what is called the *communicative atmosphere* of the interview. For example, some interviews are called *screening interviews.* These determine who will be asked back for a second interview. Consequently, screening interviews play only a partial role in determining who will eventually be hired. As a result, the atmosphere can be more informal in a screening interview. On the other hand, if there is only one interview in the selection process, then the atmosphere will be enhanced, the level of tension will be elevated, and the stakes will be much higher. The higher degree of importance will affect not only how both parties deal with the interview but also the role that the verbal and nonverbal factors will play in the communication process. The number of people vying for the job, the deadline for the decision to be made, and the number of positions available all affect the communicative atmosphere.

The number of interviewers also contributes to this atmosphere. If one person conducts the interview, then that person's perceptions, evaluations, and judgments will be paramount in determining who is hired. When more than one person is conducting the interview, other factors come into play, such as the status or position of each interviewer. Multiple-person interviews, which are common, stress the importance of an applicant being able to communicate with many different types of individuals, something that takes practice and training in communication skills.

FACTORS INFLUENCING INTERVIEWER CHOICE

Research has examined more closely some of the factors affecting the outcome of interviews. Although every interview is different and differing methodologies influence the outcome of research, some findings from employment situations prove interesting. One study examined how a physical handicap of the interviewee affected an interview. It found that people prefer to work with individuals who acknowledge their handicap rather than who try to hide it.[1] Another study used male and female personnel officers who were classified according to whether they were low-, moderate-, or high-authoritarian personality types. The study found that high-authoritarian personnel officers of both sexes made more job offers to male applicants than to female applicants.[2] Still another study examined the effect that the presence of a strong fair-employment policy had on hiring practices. The research found no difference in the number of males or females offered positions in firms having either a strong or a weak fair-employment policy.[3]

One study examined if interviewers selected candidates on the basis of their qualifications, *prior to seeing the applicants,* whether sex and physical attractiveness would be less potent indicators. Despite interviewers making prior decisions based on applicant qualifications, the study found that sex and physical attractiveness were still significant.[4] Researchers also examined how accents affected employment interviews. In a study of English, Canadian, Italian, Greek, Portuguese, West African, and Slavic people, researchers found that people who spoke with accents were rated higher for low-status jobs and lower for high-status jobs.[5] The influence of nonverbal communication in interviewing has been examined in other research.[6] One study, which examined eye contact, discovered that applicants were more likely to be hired if they looked straight ahead as opposed to down.[7] In another study, applicants who exhibited more nonverbal behavior such as smiling and eye contact, were more likely to be hired.[8] Still another study asked personnel officers to view videotapes of applicants and determine if they would ask the applicants back for a second interview. Those who exhibited more active nonverbal behavior, such as high eye contact, good voice qualities, and fluent speech, were more apt to be invited back for a second interview.[9]

While the results of these studies should not be applied to all interviews, they do point out that: (1) our perceptions, sometimes stereotyped, affect the way we react to people, and (2) both an understanding of and an ability to practice good communication skills are necessary to be an effective participant in the interview process.

As we said earlier, the employment interview is just one of several types of interviews. We will now turn our attention to the communication forces at work in other interviewing settings, beginning with the counseling interview.

COUNSELING INTERVIEWS

Counseling interviews take place in schools, corporations, churches, hospitals—anywhere an individual needs assistance and comforting. The need involved may be minor, such as advice on what class to enroll in or what graduation requirement to complete. Or the interviewer may need to offer comfort to a grief-stricken person. What communication factors are involved?

Interviewer Training

Most counseling interviews are conducted by trained professionals who are experienced in dealing with individual problems in a variety of situations. For example, most school counselors have been through special training to help them deal with the concerns of students. This may involve everything from guidance on selecting the correct college, to advice on personal problems. Similarly, members of the clergy may be called upon to counsel people who have experienced the loss of a loved one, injury to a close relative, or a personal illness or hospitalization. Their training as divinity students often involves an internship with a hospital or related institution. During that internship they may serve as part of a trauma team that treats critically injured people. As a member of the team, the chaplain can provide personal and spiritual comfort to the anguished families of those being treated.

The Person-Centered Interview

Another feature of the counseling interview is that it is strongly directed toward the interviewee. The person being counseled is the center of the interview process, and the counselor spends a great deal of time empathizing with the individual, trying to identify and assist in the solving of a problem, clarifying an issue, and being of professional assistance to the individual. The ability to listen is paramount because the counselor is receiving and reacting to information that is of deep personal concern to the other person.

PERFORMANCE REVIEW AND APPRAISAL INTERVIEWS

In school, your progress is evaluated on a report card. When you enter the work force, many organizations also issue "report cards," which are systematically administered through a performance review and appraisal (PR&A) system.

Administration and Philosophy

Performance review and appraisal varies across different organizations. In some companies, supervisors hold lengthy interviews with their subordinates every six months. These interviews culminate in the completion of a performance review and appraisal form on each subordinate which, after the subordinate responds to the form, is sent to a central depository where it becomes part of the subordinate's file. In other organizations, the supervisor may hold an annual conference with each subordinate. Here the supervisor is briefed on any specific concerns the subordinate may have, and some mutually understood goals are established for the upcoming year. In both cases, the appraisal can be either a rewarding experience for both subordinate and supervisor or it can be a psychological disaster. The latter situation arises primarily because the organization has instituted a performance review and appraisal system without understanding the importance of coupling it with good organizational and interpersonal communication skills training. This oversight can trigger distrust, dissension, lack of respect for the administering body, and a host of other ills that can lead to resentment, strikes, or other forms of internal organizational unrest.

One of the critical keys to success of a PR&A system is the interview that takes place between the supervisor and the subordinate. This interview can be at both the upper levels of the company—between a president and a vice-president—or it can operate at a lower level—between a supervisor and a janitor. Wherever the PR&A interview takes place, interpersonal skills are put to their biggest test. In organizations that have instituted PR&A programs but have not provided training for supervisors to administer those programs, the PR&A can destroy a good working relationship that may take months or years to repair. In some cases, the relationship may never be repaired. Where good interpersonal communication skills are employed, the experience can be a growing and positive experience for the subordinate as well as for the supervisor.

Because most of us, at one time or another, will be involved in some type of organization and will participate in some evaluation of our own success, a closer look at PR&A is warranted.

The Role of the Supervisor

Central to the understanding the functioning of a PR&A interview is understanding the role of the supervisor. A good supervisor fulfills many different roles, all affecting his or her relationship with the subordinate. When these roles are fulfilled properly, a positive relationship exists, and this is reflected in the PR&A interview. A good supervisor is available to assist subordinates in developing their talents to their maximum potential. A supervisor also functions as a resource person for subordinates. Even though the PR&A interview takes place at a specific time, a good supervisor serves as a *continuous* evaluator upon which a subordinate can build self-confidence as well as a career. Most importantly, the supervisor must function as a good communicator in order to provide subordinates with this continuous evaluation.

Interview Atmosphere

Good supervisors are sensitive to the importance not only of the PR&A interview but also of the atmosphere surrounding the interview. The interview should be conducted at a time when the supervisor is not rushed or preoccupied. By thinking about something else or trying to jam a large amount of work into a small amount of time, the supervisor may inadvertently cause the subordinate to be defensive about the meeting, something that can communicate dissatisfaction about the subordinate's performance. A good supervisor will remind the subordinate of the upcoming meeting and offer any assistance in preparing for the meeting. The supervisor will also check back periodically to make sure the subordinate is thinking about the meeting and is preparing some goals that can be part of the focus of the PR&A interview.

Planning

Proper planning for a PR&A interview is essential, and a competent supervisor will start by examining the employee's accomplishments, strengths, and weaknesses. In addition, the supervisor will look for areas in which the subordinate can be complimented and praised. A PR&A interview laced with negative reinforcement, as we have learned earlier, can damage an employee's self-concept. Such negative comments, phrased as constructive criticism, are handled much better during the day-to-day working association. The PR&A

interview assumes a level of importance that can cause negative criticism to balloon way out of proportion to its real size. In short, positive communication that stresses maximum performance is better than negative communication that stresses minimum performance.

Proper planning also involves being sensitive to the interviewing agenda and the elimination of emotional stress. For example, a supervisor's agenda, or the topics he or she wants to cover, may be somewhat different from the subordinate's. The supervisor who is only concerned about completing his or her own agenda, without regard to the subordinate's agenda, will accomplish little. The subordinate will leave the PR&A interview feeling cheated, will lack any understanding of what is expected, what improvements to make, and will be confused over the criteria for evaluation.

Communication Skills

As we have already discussed, good interpersonal interaction is primary to an effective PR&A interview. Consider the following consultant's recommendations on communication for inclusion in a supervisor's manual for PR&A interviews:

1. Communication is a two-way process between you and your subordinate. In any normal conversation, much of your time should be spent listening. In this context, where the subordinate assumes much of the responsibility for the thrust of the meeting, your listening time will undoubtedly be considerable.
2. Communication is a process of sharing and shared interaction. Goals are mutually agreed upon and discussed. Avoid getting off on tangents unrelated to the purpose of the meeting. Be concerned about identifying and achieving goals as they relate to job performance. Stated succinctly, keep the discussion on course and on issues that are mutually and simultaneously shared by each of you.
3. Communication includes feedback. Respond accurately (but without interrupting) to what the subordinate is saying by constantly listening (not just hearing) to what is being said.
4. Communication is verbal. Be alert not only to what you say but how you say it. Be alert to the tone and pitch of your voice. The tone and pitch of your voice can communicate something entirely different from the words you use. When this happens, you appear insincere, your credibility is lessened, and your ability to function as a supervisor is hampered.
5. Communication is nonverbal. Research has taught us that we can monitor as many as 1,000 nonverbal cues every second. Be alert to your nonverbal messages. Facial expression, posture, and other nonverbal factors can both contradict and reinforce what you are saying.[10]

We can see that good communication skills are what holds a PR&A interview together. The process of appraising the performance of another individual can result in a growing relationship, increased self-worth, and improved productivity for both supervisor and subordinate. Handled properly, it can improve morale and provide a positive direction for an organization. Handled improperly—mostly the result of a supervisor's inability to practice good organizational and interpersonal communication skills—it can be a negative force that sooner or later will be recognized as such and either changed or eliminated.

SURVEY INTERVIEWS

Survey interviews are used to collect large amounts of data through person-to-person contact. For example, many of us have been to a shopping mall where someone with a clipboard approaches us and asks us questions about our shopping habits. That person is participating in a survey interview. A telephone survey, in which interviewers select a group of people to call and ask questions about a specific topic, is a similar kind of survey. Political preference surveys, buying habits, and radio and television listening and viewing habits, are typical of telephone surveys. Some surveys combine information obtained through direct mail with information gained through face-to-face interviews.

Using Multiple Interviewers

Survey interviews frequently involve many different interviewers all working on the same project. Each interviewer has been trained to ask questions in a similar way so as not to make their appearance and questioning techniques influence the respondents' answers. This training of interviewers is a critical step in the survey. An interviewer who hurries over questions, adds words that are not part of the questionnaire, or who doesn't know how to record and interpret longer answers can ruin the survey. For example, if an interviewer asks, "What is your favorite brand of soap?" while another interviewer asks, "What is your favorite brand of detergent?," the answers will be different. Moreover, when a shopper answers either question by saying, "What do you mean by soap?" or "What do you mean by detergent?," the interviewer must know how to respond.

Structuring Questions

Suppose a survey seeks sensitive information from the interviewees. How do the interviewers obtain this information without offending or silencing the interviewees? They do so in the way they structure their questions, usually starting with general information-related questions first. For instance, personal income is sensitive information to most people. To obtain this information, the interviewer's first question might deal with brand preferences for a product. Then the questions might turn to personal buying habits. A final question might relate to the range of personal income. By first answering the questions about brand preference, the interviewee is given the opportunity to feel comfortable with the interview. When the question about income appears, it will seem to be a natural part of the interview process, and the interviewee will probably answer the question. On the other hand, if the survey interviewer first approaches a person and asks, "How much money do you make?," that person may respond, "That's none of your business" and walk the other way.

In some surveys, the interview is preceded by a telephone request for the face-to-face meeting. For example, the telephone interview could include the following script, which applies to a chamber of commerce survey:

> Hello, my name is ———— of the Elmville Chamber of Commerce. As part of our program to bring new business to Elmville, we are attempting to identify the major issues and problems that face our community. We are asking the help of business leaders with special knowledge of these issues to help us. Could we arrange a time when I might speak with you for about 30 minutes to discuss these issues?

The actual interview will consist of asking the person questions about Elmville. Open-ended questions that seek broad, encompassing answers might include: "What do you feel are some of the problems facing Elmville?" A close-ended question, restricting the respondent's answer, might be: "Is there a problem with pollution in Elmville?" The first answer would be longer and expanded. The answer to the second question would be "yes" or "no."

Face-to-face interviews eliminate many of the pitfalls that occur with questionnaires sent through the mail. In a direct-mail survey, a returned questionnaire may be filled out improperly and, consequently, cannot be used when drawing survey conclusions. In a face-to-face interview, the trained interviewer can make sure that the information is recorded correctly and that information is not omitted. Longer questionnaires are sometimes better administered in person. It is easy to discard a long questionnaire when it arrives in the mail but more awkward to walk away from another individual who may be asking you the same questions. Sometimes the face-to-face interviewer is also able to obtain sensitive information that cannot be obtained through other means.

JOURNALISM INTERVIEWING

In the United States, the First Amendment to the Constitution gives the journalist certain rights to seek out information. In many cases, that information can influence the careers of politicians and other public officials. Thus, partially because of our system of free press and partially because many public officials must manage their image, an adversary relationship exists between the press and the government. This adversary relationship can carry over into other arenas as well. Many business people feel threatened by the press and sense that an adversary relationship exists for them much in the same way it does for government officials. To some extent, this assumption is correct. The journalist does not set aside his or her inquisitive probing nature when leaving the capitol building and walking into the corporate office.

Interviewing: A Way of Life

For journalists, interviewing is a way of life. The day usually begins by contacting various sources from government, education, law enforcement, and other elements of the "news beat." The local sheriff, the police radio operator, and the hospital emergency room nurse are all interviewed by the reporter. In most cases, the interviews are natural conversations, lacking the adversary relationship that may come later in the day when the reporter squares off with a politician. On days in which a crisis has occurred, the interview may be hurried. The reporter may become frustrated over not being able to get the information needed to meet a deadline. The emergency room nurse or the police dispatcher is equally frustrated over too many phone calls seeking the same information. When a reporter knows how to exercise good interpersonal skills, he or she can cut through the hurried pace of the moment and still meet the deadline.

Different media produce different interviewing situations. A newspaper reporter will write down information in shorthand or record it on tape. This later becomes the headlines, leads, and stories we read in the next edition. A radio reporter will not only record the words of the person being interviewed but also will later incorporate those words into a newscast as an "audio actuality." The same applies to television, except that pictures are added. In such cases, the reporter is not only looking for information but also a smooth sequence of words and sentences that will be both accurate and appropriate for on-air use.

Crisis interviews are particularly difficult. Interviewing a tornado victim who has just lost his or her home is not easy. The best rule of thumb is to try to make the person feel as much at ease as possible and then ask only the necessary questions. Similarly, police and other public safety officials may be equally harried during a crisis. Seasoned reporters ask only questions that are necessary; they are composed; they remain professional.

Rules of Questioning

Structuring questions is one of the most important skills to learn as a journalist. You know an exchange of information is going to take place. The key is to develop quickly an ongoing dialogue so you can obtain the maximum amount of information in the minimum amount of time.

Some helpful hints are to: (1) be direct and to the point, (2) phrase questions properly, (3) do not ask double questions, and (4) don't ask the same question twice.[11]

For example, at the scene of a fire don't ask fire officials, "What's happening?" Along with a general answer, you may be told to ask someone else for more specific information. You have wasted a question and valuable time. "How many people were injured?" or "Do you have an estimate of damages?" are questions that will result in more specific and useful information.

Phrasing questions properly is equally important. Consider a business executive who is asked, "What are your workers' reactions in relation to this product?" The executive may wonder if the reporter wants to know how employees will react to more workers being hired to produce the product. Even worse, the executive will not have any idea what the reporter wants but will try to answer the question to avoid seeming inept.

Double questions can be equally troublesome. Consider the question asked of a politician: "Why do you think Congress voted the way it did on this legislation, and what political forces will act upon local officials responsible for administering the funds?" The question draws a relationship—one that may not exist—between members of Congress and local officials. A better way would have been to ask two questions. The first might have been phrased: "What forces acted upon Congress to influence the outcome of the vote on this legislation?" The second could be phrased: "Do you think local officials will have difficulty administering the program?"

Don't ask the same question twice. "Senator, could you explain how the Senate will consider the impeachment issue, and in what way will the Senate handle the case?" The question sounds a bit ridiculous, but many an enterprising local reporter unskilled in interviewing techniques makes similar mistakes every day. Keep questions concise. It leaves much less room for misunderstanding, confusion, and embarrassment.

COMPLIANCE INTERVIEWS

The telephone rings. The voice in somber tones says, "I'm calling about the unpaid parking ticket you received last year." A bit shocked, you reply, "What ticket? I don't know what you are talking about." The voice tells you the time and date you received the ticket and the license number of your car. Now it sinks in. There is no use denying it, and you can only reply, "Oh, that ticket." As the conversation continues, you learn the city has turned your unpaid ticket over to a collection agency, which now intends to make sure you pay up. Moreover, if you do not pay up, you could find yourself in jail. You quickly agree to pay the fine plus the interest plus the collection charges. You have just been interviewed by a trained collector conducting a compliance interview.

Presenting the Demand

Compliance interviews start with the interviewer requesting immediate compliance. An example from a tax collection setting shows that an effective method is to ask for compliance but not to close the door on concessions. For instance, this principle is expressed in the following statement reported by researcher James Gilchrist who examined the way tax collectors gain compliance:

> "Can you bring your check today, or would you rather mail it?"
> "Do you want to send a check or pay in cash?"[12]

Each statement offers a limited set of alternatives while still asking that payment be made. Notice that the statements are not overly demanding and do contain an expectation of payment. By repeating the same statement again, usually after some response and discussion from the taxpayer, it is possible to increase the forcefulness of the demand by not letting the taxpayer feel he or she is up against a brick wall. If, after continued discussion, the collector still does not feel the money will be sent, more demanding language can be instituted. Yet even in this short conversation, a relationship has been established between the interviewer and the interviewee using dialogue rather than demands.

Consider how much less effective the following statements would be:

"This payment *must* be made today."
"The full payment *must* be paid this afternoon or we'll seize your business."[13]

It may be difficult for the person to make the payment. It may be equally difficult for the collector to make the necessary arrangements to seize the business, even if the law permits it. When the payment isn't made and the business is not seized, the collector has lost credibility. Similarly, an intelligent taxpayer can make similar demands on the collector, such as indicating any future calls can be made to the taxpayer's attorney. When the collector finds it necessary to back down from the demand, credibility is lost and compliance is much more difficult.

The Art of Making Concessions

Most compliance interviews result in the interviewer making concessions rather slowly.[14] Attorneys who are skilled in negotiation know how long it takes to come to an agreement because neither side wants to give in any more than is absolutely necessary. Thus, during a compliance interview, no concessions are made until the interviewee acts first. An attorney asking for a settlement from an insurance company will not agree to accept less money until the insurance company offers less money. Similarly, the taxpayer might offer to make the payment the following week; if so, the collector and the taxpayer will negotiate a time between then and the following week.

Once an interviewee makes an alternative offer, such as a taxpayer agreeing to pay the money next week, it becomes a commitment. We can draw another example from real estate. If you are selling a house for $100,000 and someone offers you $85,000, you may reject the offer. If the person offers you $90,000, you may counter with a request for $95,000. The potential buyer may then offer you $94,000. You agree to that price but with the stipulation that the buyer close the deal within 30 days. The buyer agrees to close the deal within 30 days but will only settle for $93,500. You realize now that, psychologically, the other person has bought the house. You counter by saying you are tired of all of this bargaining. The buyer can pay the $94,000 or forget it. The buyer will probably forget it. Why? Because although you feel the person will not back out of the deal over $500, you are forgetting that your credibility as a bargainer has been lost. Not only is the buyer not sure about what you will do next but, more importantly, he or she will look like a fool to accept your latest offer because it will to some degree admit a position of weakness. Saving face may be worth much more than $500, so the person will look elsewhere. You made your mistake when you tried to return to a position already relinquished.

GRIEVANCE INTERVIEWS

Many large organizations have grievance procedures where employees who feel they have been treated unfairly have the opportunity to discuss their problem with an impartial hearing officer.

The observer, someone within the organization, listens while the employee explains the grievance. The other person involved in the grievance, often a supervisor, will then tell his or her side of the story. After sorting through the emotional feelings and reaching the heart of the problem, the hearing officer rules in favor of one party or the other or negotiates a settlement agreeable to both. For example, assume an employee with the AAA Electric Company feels he has been denied sick leave by his supervisor and is having the leave time deducted from his pay. He files a grievance, which is heard by the hearing officer. The hearing officer, after interviewing the employee, then interviews the employee's supervisor who denied the sick leave. After hearing both sides of the issue, the hearing officer may decide either that pay should be reinstated or the decision to deny sick leave should stand.

The interviewer's skill in a grievance interview cannot be overemphasized. The employee who returns to the job unsatisfied will not be a productive worker. If the feelings are serious and deep enough, the employee may resign or take the grievance to some other forum, such as the courts.[15] Although grievance procedures are an important part of most organizations, better training of supervisors, especially in the area of communication skills, would prevent many grievances from surfacing in the first place.

EMPLOYMENT INTERVIEWS

You have spent time and effort going to college. You have taken courses in your major, perhaps had on-the-job experience, have worked during the summers, and have even spent time developing a résumé. But how much time have you spent preparing for your employment interview? How much time have you spent learning about what the interviewer might ask, about the company you are applying to, and about what sources are available for you to seek out more information?

Employment interviews require preparation. For many people, this preparation starts much too late. Stop and consider what year you are in school. If you are a sophomore in college, you only have two more summer vacations until you graduate. If you are already employed or are studying communication in an advanced adult-learning curriculum, you may be planning to change jobs or find a better job at the conclusion of your studies. In any case, the time to begin planning for your next employment interview is now.

An employment interview differs from other types of interviews in several ways. First, the interview itself is usually preceded by some formal communication between the applicant and interviewer. As we will see later in this chapter, the type of information communicated in the cover letter and the résumé is instrumental in determining if the applicant is invited for an interview. This communication process, as we have already learned, allows homophily to be present prior to the interview.

With all of this information available to the interviewer, why is the interview itself still so important? It is important because how the person appears in person and the impression he or she makes with the interviewer will determine what kind of an impression the applicant will make on other employees as well as people outside the organization, namely clients and business associates. Because the interviewer has already determined to some degree that the applicant may be qualified for the position, it is the interview that determines whether the person is given further consideration or is eliminated from the organization's recruitment effort.

PLANNING FOR AN EMPLOYMENT INTERVIEW

One of the shortcoming of higher education is that many colleges and universities ask students to spend thousands of dollars in tuition and living expenses over a four-year period, yet never teach them a few critical skills about what they should do when they leave school and head into job interviews (Fig. 15–1). Career placement and planning services are valuable, but students must usually seek out these services on their own initiative.

Thousands of students are intelligent, have good grades, have good communication skills yet still make ignorant mistakes that cost them choice jobs after graduation. In some cases, entire careers falter because the first job creates a battered self-concept and unfulfilled dreams. The language used here may seem harsh. It is meant to be. Always coming in second is no fun, especially since you weren't aware of some of the basic skills necessary to get off to the right start.

We can only scratch the surface of what you should learn about a job

Figure 15-1
In many instances the recruiter and job seeker will have done some prior research on each other. Good communication skills along with attitude and appearance are necessary for success in a job interview. Also important is the ability to answer questions, some of which may be personal, thought provoking, and difficult.

interview. Do not be foolish enough to stop here. Learn all you can from career-placement services, books, and other sources. Take advantage of seminars. Read, practice, and learn everything about what may be the most important interview of your life, your job interview.

KNOWING WHAT YOU WANT

People entering the job market often forget to ask the all-important question, "Who am I?" Think about that question. You'll probably ask it often in your lifetime, but preparing for a job interview is one of the most important times to ask it. A first career can have a direct effect on a lifelong vocation. Getting into a profession in which you are unhappy and unsettled can burn up energies that could be directed much more productively to another kind of work.

Consider some specific personal qualities that are found in suggestions made to students by the University Placement Service at the University of North Carolina at Chapel Hill.

> *Transferable skills.* What skills do you have and like to use? These skills may or may not be ones used in your major. How might such skills be used in a work situation? Consider skills such as communication skills, mechanical skills, organizational skills, technical skills, or talents.
>
> *People.* All jobs involve people. What kinds of people do you enjoy being with most? Young, old, mixed ages? What do you like to do when working with people? Teach, supervise, motivate, organize?
>
> *Place.* What kinds of institutions interest you? Large, small, medium-sized? Prestigious, growing, innovative, established, conservative? What geographical limits can you set?
>
> *Role models.* What three or four people do you know whose jobs you admire, envy? Role models can be very helpful in visualizing where you want to be right now or in five years. Role models may be able to give you basic information or even help you get started.
>
> *Work values.* What kind of time schedule fits you? Regular eight-to-five or flexible time schedule? What gives you personal satisfaction in a job? How important is money? Prestige? Freedom? What other interests do you have that need to be taken into account when choosing a job (family, travel, continued education)?
>
> *Awareness.* How much do you know about the field you plan to enter? What are the starting salaries, products, services, problems in the field? What is the future outlook for the field?
>
> *Targets.* Do you know names and addresses of organizations in your area of interest?[16]

THE RÉSUMÉ

Every résumé is different (Fig. 15–2). Résumés reflect a person's individuality, and how that individuality is expressed varies greatly. Becoming too tied to a hard-and-fast rule can force you into artificiality. For example, I remember a placement director who consistently stressed that a résumé should be limited to a

---

JANE A. DOE

PRESENT ADDRESS   PERMANENT ADDRESS

    600 Anderson Avenue   1 Hilltop Drive
    Laramie, Wyoming 82070   Vernal, Utah 84078
    (307) 766-0000   (801) 789-0000

PERSONAL DATA

    Born April 7, 1965, in Vernal, Utah.
    Attended the public schools of Vernal, Utah.

EDUCATION

    University of Wyoming, Laramie, Wyoming 82070
    B.A. in Communication, 1988.

PROFESSIONAL EXPERIENCE

    WAZY, Lafayette, Indiana—January 1986. Internship in the news
        department. Involved in writing and on-air announcing.
    KBOI, Boise, Idaho—January, 1985. Internship in the news department.
        Assigned as a police beat reporter.
    KUWR—FM, University of Wyoming—1984 to 1985. Responsible for
        supervising news department personnel and reporting local news.

ORGANIZATIONAL MEMBERSHIP AND ACTIVITY

    Society of Professional Journalists, Sigma Delta Chi—1986—Women
        in Communication, Inc.—1985—

HONORS AND AWARDS

        Wyoming UPI Broadcasters—Best Radio Documentary—1985.

5/87

Figure 15-2 Résumé styles vary considerably. Shown is a chronological résumé. Another style is the functional résumé. There are variations of both types. Consult a college placement service for advice on preparing a résumé. After it is complete but before printing, have it proofread by others. Always include references along with their business, and if possible, home telephone numbers.

single page. It was bad advice. Because of a strong work-study program at the college, many students graduated with two or three different job experiences listed on their résumés. This, along with the stress on awards and activities in the school, resulted in résumés that more appropriately filled two pages. References could neatly be placed at the bottom of the second page. Yet instead of being flexible and realizing that their own abilities filled two pages much better than one, students remembered the placement director's advice and tried to jam everything onto one page, using the smallest typeface they could find. Everything was single spaced, and margins were one-eighth inch on all sides. The end result was a messy jumble, which left the impression that the applicants were lacking not only in neatness but also in common sense.

Appearance

Make sure your résumé has adequate margins. One inch is usually appropriate, although larger margins can work effectively if you are centering a smaller amount of material on a page. Also, choose a good typewriter. Don't type your résumé on an antique ribbon typewriter that looks like it's on its last legs. It communicates to an employer that you may not care enough to take the time to find a good typewriter. Consider having your résumé set in type at a professional printing house. Many companies use typewriters that automatically adjust margins. Thus, in the future a résumé with uneven margins may look as though it has been typed on outdated equipment.

Show your résumé to as many people as possible and *no less than four*. Have the people reading the résumé check it for spelling and content. If they don't understand something, by all means change it. If your roommate or guidance counselor cannot understand something on your résumé, there is a good chance management will not be able to either. In addition, you may never land an interview to explain it. Belonging to a Greek organization on campus is one example. The Zeta Chi Zeta might be a highly trained group of after-dinner speakers. On the other hand, it might be the dormitory clean-up crew. If the content of your résumé is confusing, consider how you could reword it to better explain what you are trying to say.

Functions

The résumé itself has many different functions. Most importantly, it serves as a general introduction. Everything about you must be communicated in a résumé. The résumé is a first impression, and you only have *one* chance to make a first impression.

Second, your résumé may become part of a permanent file, and it will not only be looked at on the day you are considered for hiring, but also may be looked at on the day you are considered for promotion. This time, your credentials may be competing in a completely different league.

Third, and most pertinent to our discussion, a résumé can help you land an interview. Few people are hired because of their résumés alone. They need to meet their prospective employers in person and talk about their qualifications. Putting your best foot forward on a résumé is the first step to putting your best foot forward in an interview. The résumé must make the employer want to meet you in person. Think about that when you are writing your résumé. While reading your résumé, the employer should be able to say, "I think this person would be a positive asset to our organization, and I would like to talk with the person further." That kind of reaction must jump from the pages before you will be invited to meet management on a personal basis.

Strategy

How do you make statements on your résumé "jump from the pages"? First, plan a strategy for your résumé. Do not start writing without thinking. Ask, "What are the important qualities I want to communicate? What kind of experiences have I had in school? Did I take advantage of certain work opportunities? What type of awards have I won?" In other words, what will communicate you as being a professional person to a prospective employer?

Don't forget to include your personal qualities. What are your hobbies? What are your interests? What are those things that will make the employer stop and say, "I'd like to meet this individual in person"?

Consider whether you want to use a *functional* résumé or a *chronological* résumé. Both have advantages, although some people feel the chronological résumé is better for recent graduates. Functional résumés are especially appropriate when you have had good experience but the titles of your jobs have not accurately reflected your abilities. A chronological résumé lists, usually in order of the most recent first, the various activities and professional experiences you have accumulated. A functional résumé lists the talents or abilities you possess without any reference to job titles or chronology.

THE INTRODUCTORY LETTER

Do not forget to include an introductory letter with your résumé. As with the résumé, it also must be perfect, well phrased, and neat. Never send an introductory letter or a résumé to a "Dear Sir." Find out who will make the hiring decision and type the letter to that person. Talk about some of your personal qualities. Explain why you're interested in the company. It's easy to spot a form letter, and you need to make your letter stand out from the crowd. Show some enthusiasm and interest. Do not make it sound like a dry business letter, but at the same time keep it professional. Remember, it's the first impression management will have of you. A résumé is a source of information, but an introductory letter must converse on an interpersonal basis. Will management enjoy talking with you, or will you be just another person taking up valuable time? Without being overbearing, sell yourself and express your unique qualities to management.

Be sure to *ask* for a personal interview in your introductory letter. To do this, close your letter with a statement that calls for a response. "I'll look forward to hearing from you" is all right, but even better is a statement that you will be in the area and will be in contact with the person to set up an interview, or to simply request an interview and indicate that you will call on a given date to set up a time.

Always follow through with a telephone call. Just because a person does not write back or telephone you confirming an opportunity to hold an interview does not mean the person is not interested in hiring you.

PARTICIPATING IN THE INTERVIEW

Be persistent in your quest for an interview. Even though you may not be considered for an immediate opening, other jobs will open up later. If you have had an interview and are thus in the forefront of management's mind, you will be in line to be considered much quicker than if your résumé and cover letter are merely placed in a file.

It is now your responsibility to put your best foot forward, including being prompt and prepared. This also includes being well dressed. Remember, you are being viewed not only as the person who will do the job but also someone who will represent the company. Pay close attention to the important details of nonverbal communication, especially your appearance.

This may seem like common sense, but you only need to spend an afternoon walking the halls of a placement bureau or talking with a corporate recruiter to see how many people have never learned even the basic lessons of presenting themselves.

When you meet the recruiter, or whoever is conducting the interview, greet the person by *name* but make sure you pronounce it correctly. If there is any question, check with a receptionist or someone who is sure of the correct pronunciation. Avoid being chummy. Nicknames and first names are absolutely out unless someone requests to be called by his or her first name or nickname or you have known the person for a long time. If the interviewer moves to shake hands, return the action as if you mean it. A limp handshake is not appropriate. Shaking hands communicates a positive attitude for women as well as for men.

Applying Communication Skills

Practice your good communication skills during the interview. When serving as assistant director of the Career Planning and Placement Center at Eastern Illinois University, Robert Jones summarized nine skills important to an employment interview:

1. Follow the cues given by the interviewer. Let the interviewer take the initiative. Usually you can tell what the interviewer expects very early in the interview. You may need to be a talker, but also may find you need to be a listener.
2. No two interviews will be exactly alike.

3. The interview is a two-way process; do your share of talking if allowed. Remember, you must sell yourself just as a business sells its product to the consumer.
4. Avoid too many "yes" or "no" answers.
5. Try to be friendly and relaxed.
6. Be frank and sincere.
7. Think about the interview from the interviewer's point of view.
8. Be concise and prompt with your answers and questions. Don't be a compulsive talker.
9. Terminating the interview may be as important as making a good first impression. Thank the interviewer for his or her time and consideration.[17]

Responding to Questions

Be prepared for all sorts of questions. Answer honestly, but be on your toes. Some of the questions may become personal. What are some of the typical questions asked during interviews? Frank S. Endicott, director of placement at Northwestern University, surveyed companies and asked them to list frequent questions asked by corporate recruiters. Here are just some of the more than 90 questions Endicott found in his research.[18]

1. What are your future vocational plans?
2. In what school activities have you participated? Why? Which did you enjoy the most?
3. How do you spend your spare time? What are your hobbies?
4. In what type of position are you most interested?
5. Why do you think you might like to work for our company?
6. What courses did you like best? Least? Why?
7. Why did you choose your particular field of work?
8. What percentage of your college expenses did you earn? How?
9. How did you spend your vacations while in school?
10. What do you know about our company?
11. What qualifications do you have that make you feel that you will be successful in your field?
12. What extracurricular offices have you held?
13. What are your ideas on salary?
14. How interested are you in sports?
15. If you were starting college all over again, what courses would you take?
16. Do you prefer any specific geographic location? Why?
17. How much money do you hope to earn at age 30? At age 35?
18. What do you think determines a person's progress in a good company?
19. Why do you think you would like this particular type of job?
20. Tell me about your home life during the time you were growing up.
21. Are you looking for a permanent or temporary job?
22. Do you prefer working with others or by yourself?
23. What kind of boss do you prefer?

24. Are you primarily interested in making money or do you feel that service to other people is a satisfactory accomplishment?
25. What have you learned from some of the jobs you have held?
26. Do you feel you have done the best scholastic work of which you are capable?
27. Have you ever had any difficulty getting along with fellow students and faculty?
28. Which of your college years was the most difficult?
29. What is the source of your spending money?
30. Do you like routine work?
31. Do you like regular hours?
32. What size city do you prefer?
33. What is your major weakness?
34. Do you have an analytical mind?
35. Are you eager to please?
36. What do you do to keep in good physical condition?
37. Have you had any serious illness or injury?
38. Are you willing to go where the company sends you?
39. What job in our company would you choose if you were entirely free to do so?
40. Is it an effort for you to be tolerant of persons with a background and interests different from your own?
41. What type of books have you read?
42. What types of people seem to rub you the wrong way?
43. What are your own special abilities?
44. What job in our company do you want to work toward?
45. Do you like to travel?
46. What kind of work interests you?
47. Do you think that grades should be considered by employers? Why or why not?
48. What have you done that shows initiative and willingness to work?

How would you answer some of these questions? Obviously, many have no right or wrong answer, but if you are asked the question, you must respond. It's a good idea to practice your answers to these questions and any others you can think of. Sit down with a friend and role-play. You may even want to videotape your answers, then play them back and see how you would look to an employer.

Endicott also looked at some of the negative factors evaluated during an employment interview that lead to the rejection of an applicant.[19] Consider some of the following negative characteristics that some people communicate in an interview. Examine closely the ones that could be corrected by the use of good communication skills:

1. Poor personal appearance
2. Overbearing, overaggressive, conceited, superiority complex, know-it-all
3. Inability to express oneself clearly—poor voice, diction, grammar

4. Lack of planning for career—no purpose and goals
5. Lack of interest and enthusiasm—passive, indifferent
6. Lack of confidence and poise—nervousness—ill-at-ease
7. Failure to participate in activities
8. Overemphasis on money; interest only in best dollar offer
9. Poor scholastic record—just got by
10. Unwilling to start at the bottom; expects too much too soon
11. Makes excuses—evasiveness—hedges on unfavorable factors in record
12. Lack of tact
13. Lack of maturity
14. Lack of courtesy; ill-mannered
15. Condemnation of past employers
16. Lack of social understanding
17. Marked dislike for school work
18. Lack of vitality
19. Failure to look interviewer in the eye
20. Limp, fish handshake
21. Indecision
22. Loafs during vacations—lakeside pleasures
23. Unhappy married life
24. Friction with parents
25. Sloppy application form
26. Merely shopping around
27. Wants job only for short time
28. Little sense of humor
29. Lack of knowledge of field of specialization
30. Parents make decisions for the individual
31. No interest in company or industry
32. Emphasis on who one knows
33. Unwillingness to go where company sends him/her
34. Cynical
35. Low moral standards
36. Lazy
37. Intolerant—strong prejudices
38. Narrow interests
39. Spends much time in movies
40. Poor handling of personal finances
41. No interest in community services
42. Inability to take criticism
43. Lack of appreciation of the value of experience
44. Radical ideas
45. Late to interview without good reason
46. Never heard of company
47. Failure to express appreciation for interviewer's time
48. Asks no questions about the job

49. High-pressure type
50. Indefinite response to questions

After you have had a personal interview with a prospective employer, if you have not heard anything from the employer within a week (unless he or she has indicated it will be longer), follow up with a telephone call. Management may have been out of town, or something may have developed that postponed the hiring decision. Be persistent. Do not give up. Yet do not be pushy. The difference between the two can be an extremely fine line, and if you cross over it, you'll be perceived as being aggressive and abrasive. The best advice is to use common sense and judge each situation individually.

EQUAL EMPLOYMENT OPPORTUNITY: INTERVIEWING AND THE LAW

Whether you are planning to be interviewed or are in a supervisory position where you interview others, the law is clear. In most cases it is unlawful to make a hiring decision based on sex, age, race, religion, country of national origin or handicap. As a result, certain questions asked in an employment interview can cross the line between being appropriate and being illegal. Although it may not be unlawful to ask a particular question, doing so may open an employer up to a discrimination complaint. That employer then faces the task of proving that the hiring decision was made on the basis of qualifications and not prejudice. Other areas of questioning may also be inadvisable because they still have the potential to infringe on the rights of the prospective employee. The following section describes areas in which sensitivity is called for when interviewing job applicants. Warning: The discussion here is for educational purposes and not a verbatim statement of the law.[20] If you are involved in conducting employment interviews or believe you have been the victim of discrimination, consult either an attorney skilled in such matters or an appropriate governmental equal-employment or civil rights commission office.

Primary Areas of Questioning

Questions about an applicant's age are not acceptable, either in preliminary interviews, on applications, or in final job interviews. Only when an employer can *prove* that age is one of the qualifications necessary to be able to do the job, can age enter into a hiring decision. Notice the word *prove* is emphasized. Many employers who felt justified in making such a determination found out later that they could not prove their reasoning before a court of law. Even roundabout questions, which, when answered, reflect on a person's age, are in most hiring settings not acceptable.

Questions about ability based on sex are also off limits. Few jobs today can claim exclusion of employees on the basis of sex. A single employee in a similar job anywhere can disprove a claim that sex is one of the criteria for holding a particular job.

Questions about a person's race or color are also inadvisable. The exception is when the organization, with specific approval from legal counsel or as part of an agreement with the government to try to correct racial inequality, is granted permission to state in job advertisements that minorities are free to identify themselves.

Asking about an applicant's religion or creed should be avoided. Again, it is difficult to prove, with the exception of applying for a minister's position in a specific church, that membership in a specific denomination or even believing in God is a qualification for a specific line of work.

An applicant's national origin, per se, cannot be a reason for making a hiring decision. However, it is acceptable to determine if an applicant has the ability to read, write, and speak English or a foreign language when these skills are specific qualifications for the job. On dangerous ground are questions that seek information about an applicant's ancestry, descent, the national origin of the applicant's parents or relatives, or the national origin of the applicant's spouse. Also inadvisable are questions about how an applicant acquired the ability to read or write. These are not appropriate because some individuals obtain such training through schools designed to teach English as a second language, and attending such a school indicates a national origin other than American.

Secondary Areas of Questioning

In addition to these primary question areas, other lines of questioning are also risky. Questions about an applicant's family can be risky, especially when such questions touch on marital status, number and ages of children, spouse's job, and the spouse's or applicant's family responsibilities. Any question asked of one sex in these areas must be asked of the other sex. For example, it is not advisable to ask only females about child-care arrangements. These questions can indirectly be used to identify and judge an individual on the basis of sex and age and as such cannot be used in a hiring situation.

Some questions are, however, more acceptable than others. For instance, it is permissible to ask questions that determine if any family activities or commitments might prevent the applicant from fulfilling the responsibilities of the job. Again, such questions must also be asked of applicants of both sexes. Asking direct questions about whether a person is married, single, divorced, separated, engaged, or widowed is inadvisable because such questions can suggest sex discrimination and take into consideration child-care arrangements only for mothers.

An applicant's citizenship can be discussed, but only to the extent that the interviewer is free to determine if the applicant would be prevented from legally working because of immigration status. Other questions such as asking the applicant to present birth or naturalization papers or a baptismal certificate are not advisable for such questions can reflect on an applicant's national origin. An interviewer can ask *if* the applicant can provide proof of citizenship, an alien registration number, or a visa *after* that person is hired.

Although we may feel that no one wants a criminal working for them, keep in mind that under the American system of justice, an individual is innocent until proven guilty. Thus, arrest without conviction should not be a factor in a hiring decision. For example, for security reasons (and you must be able to prove security is an issue), questions about past criminal convictions can be acceptable. On the other hand, questions about a prior conviction when that conviction is unrelated to the job are not advisable. In other words, someone arrested and convicted for drunk driving may still be able to hold down a job as a receptionist.

An interviewer who asks a question about availability for weekend work and disqualifies applicants because they can't work on either Saturday or Sunday because of a religious preference may run the risk of religious discrimination. Employers are required to make a reasonable accommodation for religious observance. However, specific questions about religious observance are not advised as they may indicate a preference for one religion over another. Questions about general availability for weekend and evening work are acceptable as long as they are asked of both sexes.

Questions about an applicant's financial status are not appropriate unless the applicant is seeking to buy equity in a business, such as purchasing a franchise. Questions about charge accounts, payment records, banks, and other financial matters are questionable because they tend to discriminate against the poor and therefore certain racial and ethnic populations.

Although an interviewer may feel that questions about educational level are within the law, unless an employer can show that a specific degree is a requirement to perform the necessary work, such questions also should be avoided. Related to questions about education are questions about military training. Inquiries into training and work experience in the military are perfectly acceptable, but questions about military discharge should be avoided unless a dishonorable discharge prohibits an individual from performing on the job.

Physical conditions such as handicaps, height and weight, and pregnancy are areas of concern to employment interviewers. It is acceptable to inquire whether a particular mental or physical handicap will prevent the applicant from performing the duties of the job. However, simply asking whether a person has a handicap and then rejecting the person for that handicap, which happens to be unrelated to the job performance, is not acceptable. Similarly, unless a specific height and weight requirement can be proven necessary for satisfactory job performance, questions about height and weight are not acceptable. Women on the average are shorter and weigh less, and people of a particular race are, overall, shorter than others. Thus, such requirements can result in charges of sex or race discrimination. Similarly, being pregnant is not of itself a reason for rejecting an applicant. Eliminating an applicant exclusively because she is pregnant amounts to sex discrimination.

Many of us belong to clubs, organizations, societies, and other social and professional groups, but job-interview questions should avoid discussing such subjects. Too many of these organizations concentrate their membership on a specific type of individual, which may take into consideration such things as sex (college sorority) or national origin. Asking questions about such memberships can be interpreted as a preference for or against a certain group of individuals.

The employment interview is a difficult time for both interviewer and interviewee. Not only must a decision be made on the ability of the applicant to fill the job but also a host of legal issues emerge. It would be difficult to find an interview, especially one of considerable length, that did not at some point contain questions that came close to violating one of the areas we have just discussed. The natural flow of a conversation, information volunteered by the applicant to which an interviewer responds, and the complexity of equal employment and affirmative action guidelines make an employment interview a delicate interchange. But the guidelines are there for a purpose—to prevent discrimination and to be fair to all applicants. What makes it work is a well-trained interviewer who understands the spirit and the letter of the law and makes hiring decisions without prejudice.

Finally, it is important to point out that if you are applying for a job, it is all right to volunteer information about yourself if you feel such information can give you an advantage. If you are applying for a modeling job, a portfolio and pictures may be necessary. There is nothing stopping you from submitting a photograph for any other job. Similarly, while the interviewer may be prohibited from asking specific questions, volunteering such information is not. For example, if you are available for evening and weekend work and you sense it would improve your chances of being hired, you have the choice of volunteering this information.

SUMMARY

The same communication variables that affect any communicative encounter affect the interview. Especially important is the atmosphere in which the interview is conducted. For example, in an employment interview the number of applicants, the number of interviews before the final selection, and the number of different interviewers all affect the atmosphere in which the interview is conducted. Although we chose to examine the interview process in general from the setting of an employment interview, counseling interviews, performance review and appraisal interviews, survey interviews, journalistic interviews, compliance interviews, and grievance interviews were also examined in this chapter.

Research shows that certain factors affect the outcome of interviews. Handicapped individuals who acknowledge their handicap are preferred over those who conceal it; a strong fair-employment policy has little effect on interview decisions; sex and physical characteristics can affect the outcome of interviews; and people with certain accents are rated higher for low-status jobs.

Counseling interviews generally involve an interviewee who needs help with a problem. Frequently, a trained counselor is the interviewer.

The periodic review of an individual's performance in an organization is accomplished through a performance review and appraisal (PR&A) interview. Traditionally, the interview is part of an organization-wide assessment program where supervisors evaluate subordinates. The key to success in such a program is the ability of the supervisor to exercise good communication skills. Without this ability, the PR&A programs can become less than effective, where employees participate as part of an organizational ritual not as an opportunity for improved productivity.

Survey interviews are used to collect large amounts of data through face-to-face contact. Frequently, more than one interviewer is involved.

A journalistic interview sometimes involves an adversary relationship between the interviewer and the interviewee. Being direct and to the point, phrasing questions properly, not asking double questions, and not asking questions with repetitive clauses are important tips in journalistic interviews.

Compliance interviews involve gaining the cooperation of an interviewee. This can begin by offering narrow alternatives to meet specific demands and then negotiating other alternatives.

Grievance interviews are designed to give members of an organization a means to state their grievance to an impartial observer. Frequently, the grievance issue is resolved through a negotiated understanding between the supervisor and the aggrieved party.

To most people, an employment interview is the most important interview in which they will participate. Employment interviews, depending on the size of the organization, can be conducted by anyone from the owner of the company to a lower-echelon staff member. In some larger organizations, personnel officers refer applicants to supervisors, but they can also screen applicants so that applicants never see the supervisor.

Preparation for an employment interview involves planning. One of the first steps is to understand yourself. What type of work do you enjoy and what talents do you bring to the marketplace? Your general and specific personal qualities must also be taken into consideration.

Part of the preparation includes developing a résumé. A résumé should not only reflect your skills and work experience but also should have an attractive, professional appearance, function as an introduction, and help you obtain an interview. A well-worded introductory letter should accompany the résumé.

Under the law, hiring decisions are to be made without regard to sex, age, race, religion, handicap or national origin of the applicant. Employment interviewers must understand and practice the spirit of equal opportunity before administering employment interviews.

QUESTIONS FOR REVIEW AND DISCUSSION

1. What are the results of research into interviewer choice?

2. How can performance review and appraisal interviews endanger relationships between supervisors and subordinates?

3. Why are good communication skills necessary in a performance-review and appraisal interview?

4. Why are the training of the interviewer and the structuring of questions important to survey interviews?

5. What are the rules of questioning in journalism interviewing?

6. Why is gaining concessions in compliance interviews considered an art?

7. What are some of the personal qualities interviewers look for?

8. What are the nine rules of interpersonal skills required for success in an interview?

9. What questioning areas must one avoid to comply with the letter and the spirit of affirmative action?

LEARNING EXERCISES

1. Prepare a résumé and then role-play an interview where the other person asks questions based on your résumé, using some of the sample interview questions found in this chapter. Reverse roles and repeat the exercise.

2. Talk to a corporate recruiter and ask that person what he or she looks for when interviewing a candidate for a job. Ask the recruiter to distinguish between traits looked for in a first interview as opposed to traits examined when interviewing the same person a second or third time.

ADDITIONAL READINGS

Cox, K., and J. Higginbotham, eds. *Focus Group Interviews: A Reader*. Chicago: American Marketing Association, 1979.

Douglas, J. D. *Creative Interviewing*. Beverly Hills: Sage, 1985.

Drake, J. D. *Effective Interviewing*. New York: AMACOM, 1983.

Drake, J. D. *Interviewing for Managers: A Complete Guide to Employment Interviewing*. New York: AMACON, 1982.

Maple, F. F. *Dynamic Interviewing: An Introduction to Counseling*. Beverly Hills: Sage, 1985.

McLaughlin, P. *Asking Questions: Professional Interviewing Techniques*. Blue Ridge Summit, PA: TAB Books, 1985.

Reinsch, N. L., Jr., and M. E. Stano *Communication in Interviews*. Englewood Cliffs, NJ: Prentice-Hall, 1982.

Riches, C. *Developing Interviewing Skills in Education*. Wolfeboro, NH: Longwood Publishing Group, 1986.

Richetto, G. M. and J. P. Zima *Interviewing*. Chicago: Science Research Associates, 1982.

Stewart, C. J., and W. B. Cash, Jr. *Interviewing: Principles and Practices* (4th ed.). Dubuque, IA: W. C. Brown Co., 1985.

16

COMMUNICATION IN THE FAMILY

OBJECTIVES

After completing this chapter, you should be able to

- Discuss the autonomy of individual family members and the need for interdependence as a unit
- Compare and contrast the firm, open, and orderless communication patterns
- Realize that there is no ideal communication pattern within a family
- Explain power in family communication
- List and describe the five interactions of power within a family
- Discuss the family as a small group
- Describe the four communication networks of families
- Understand that different family members fulfill different communication roles
- Discuss the barriers to family communication
- Discuss ways to improve communication with senior citizens
- Explain what happens to family communication during a separation, divorce, and remarriage.

Tim Woodward, whom we met delivering a speech in Chapter 12, is a talented writer for the *Idaho Statesman*. Woodward has a knack for capturing the human emotions that occur during life's tender moments. In a feature about his own family, he talks about the relationships that exist between a mother and a daughter, children and grandparents, and a husband and wife. Many of us in our own families have experienced similar feelings to those expressed by Woodward. His account is a good place to begin our chapter on communication in the family.

Amtrak's morning train from Seattle is on time to the minute. It stops at the station in East Olympia, where five people—two women, a man and two little girls—are exchanging goodbyes. The women hug each other. Another chance will not come again for months. It is no casual hug.

The station at East Olympia is a monument to the decline of rail travel. There was a depot once, but it died of neglect. In its place is a three-sided shelter in the pines, a sort of glorified lean-to. The town is several miles distant by way of a dirt road through the forest. There are no taxis, no ticket windows, not even a telephone. A stranger arriving in the middle of the night could be forgiven for thinking he had been left to die in the wilderness.

The stop is of the half-minute variety. The luggage isn't completely aboard when the porter says it's time to go and the wheels begin to move. The man, the girls and the younger woman lean from the doorway with last goodbyes. The other woman stands on the platform, waving. She smiles, but doesn't fool anyone. Her eyes betray her best attempt at bravery.

The train stops again in about 20 minutes. The man and woman are surprised by the number of passengers that file from the ornate brick station and aboard the train at Centralia. The children, for the most part, are quiet. The oldest, who is nearly 7, says she wishes she could stay at her grandmother's house for a million years.

The subject of her wistful thoughts is in downtown Olympia by now. It is her first day on a new job, after 16 years on the old one. It doesn't seem fair. Starting over is tough enough all by itself.

Centralia behind, the man and woman begin the inevitable conversation. Perhaps they could visit sooner next time. Perhaps in the spring. The woman says six months between visits is too long. Her husband agrees, but the old obstacles waste no time presenting themselves. Not enough time, too many miles. It helps to talk about next time, but not very much. Next time is always so far away.

They talk some more, and then no one feels like talking. The children begin to play with their dolls. Western Washington glides by, white in the windows of Amtrak's Superliner. It is snowing, not just in western Washington, but throughout the Northwest.

On the trip over, the train had to back up and make three runs at a snowdrift in the Blue Mountains. Then it pulled onto a siding and waited for a three-diesel snowplow. Nothing could have been more reassuring to the holiday-minded passengers than the sight of that churning snowplow. It was a happy trip. Now the thought of getting stuck doesn't seem so bad.

More towns. Kelso–Longview, Vancouver, Portland. The Columbia River Gorge is lovely, even under a foot of snow, but the scenery is lost on the parents of the little girls. Unlike their daughters, they have found no suitable distractions. Their thoughts remain with the woman they left on the platform at East Olympia.

The man is thinking about something that happened at her house that morning. He was in the living room, searching for things that might have been overlooked in packing. She was in the kitchen, preparing a hot breakfast to brace her granddaughters for the rigors of train travel. He overheard her talking to them, and suddenly he realized she was crying. It wasn't surprising really. He half expected it.

She is not the sort who would manufacture tears to make them stay longer—or move closer—and that made it worse. She didn't know anyone else could hear, and would have been upset if she had known. The conversation was meant to be private, between her and her only grandchildren. She was telling them how she felt about them. Her voice sounded terrible, all shaky and broken. The man stayed in the living room longer than necessary, pretending to look for things he knew were already in the suitcases. Another man might have known what to do, but he was not another man, and he felt clumsy and helpless. And a little guilty.

It was he, after all, who had taken her daughter to live and raise children in another state. She was happy there, but sometimes she got a certain look in her eyes, and he knew she was thinking about her mother, and he would wonder for the hundredth time if he had done right by them. There had been chances to move. Perhaps he was wrong to love Idaho so much.

When it was quiet in the kitchen, he sneaked down the hallway, opened his suitcase, and made a show of being busy.

More stops. Hinkel, Pendleton, LaGrande. This time the train crosses the Blue Mountains without incident, putting yet another barrier between people who want to be together. How many other families are aboard, leaving behind the people and places they know best?

The train arrives in Boise early in the morning. The man and woman carry their sleeping daughters to the car, load the luggage and drive home. It is cold inside. The man stays up a long time, fussing with the wood stove and wishing it were a heat pump. When he does come to bed, he lies awake for a long time.

He wonders if she knows that her daughter isn't the only one who misses her, and if she has any idea how bad he feels about the separations. He wishes he had told her how much he wished that it didn't have to be the way it was. Most of all, he wishes he had gone into the kitchen that morning and given her a hug.

He hopes she'll read this someday, and that she'll understand.[1]

Woodward's description of the emotional warmth spiced with sadness reflects on the changing communication patterns that a family faces. As we will learn, family communication is a developmental process. The communication networks that were formed in Woodward's wife's childhood were broken and changed by the necessity for the family to move away. The mother and daughter do not have the frequency of communication that existed when she lived at home. Yet at the same time, the network has grown with the addition of grandchildren. As the grandchildren grow older, their ability to relate to different things in their world will alter the way they interact with other members of the family. Although their grandmother's house is their favorite place today, the future will change that pattern of interaction for the children. Their parents' home or their own homes will become their center of family interaction. To some degree, this process will be a balance between autonomy and interdependence.

FAMILY STRUCTURE AND CHANGE

Earlier in this text we talked about the need to have control over our own lives and how this need shows up in our communicative interactions. Just as it affects our social and working relationships, the need for control also affects the communication relationships with our family members.

Our personalities begin to develop while we're infants.[2] While we're generating new ideas and exploring new experiences, those caring for us balance our explorations with a need for order, even for our safety. If we want to walk out onto a busy street, we will be stopped. If we try to put our fingers into an electrical socket, we will be stopped. But our desire to search out new experiences, to be independent, and to achieve identities continue into adulthood.[3]

The Need for Autonomy

Within the family, this desire for autonomy and identity influences our communication patterns. We seek to be recognized among other members of the family. Sometimes this desire for autonomy results in sibling rivalries, sometimes in strained relations between parents and offspring. We only need to think back to our own childhood and adolescence to remember those first assertions of our autonomies. The first time we made choices of what to wear, what food to order in a restaurant, or what clothes to buy were big occasions.

This need for identity remains throughout our lives. Even after two people have reached a "bonding" stage, the necessity to retain an identity continues to play a part in the relationship.

The Need for Interdependence

While each family member strives for autonomy, the family as a unit must hold together. The family by its very nature is *interdependent*. At times this means sharing the rent or sharing the bathroom. At other times it means emotional interdependence, the need to turn to someone else who immediately understands us and can empathize with our joys and problems. Some people view the family as a source of strength. Achievements are accentuated and failures are minimized because of strong family ties and the family-support system.

Tim Woodward's passage at the beginning of this chapter feflects this interdependence. While each member of the family is autonomous, all of them are emotionally interdependent. It was this emotional interdependence that resulted in the grandmother's tears and the youngster wanting to stay at her grandmother's house for a "million years."

In family interaction, the individual's need for autonomy is balanced against the family unit's interdependence on one another.

Balancing

Recognizing the forces that operate between autonomy and interdependence is a first step in avoiding and resolving conflicts. The next time a family argument develops, pause long enough to consider how autonomy and interdependence are colliding. Ask yourself if your own desire for autonomy conflicts with your family's need to be interdependent. If it does, can you avoid the conflict by recognizing the force and dealing with it in a positive way? When you find yourself in a family dialogue bordering on conflict, ask yourself if you can negotiate a compromise. See if you can recognize the forces at work and communicate clearly what you feel or if you can help someone else to see the problem in a broader perspective. Although you may not be totally successful, understanding what each family member has at stake is a start in the right direction.

PATTERNS OF FAMILY INTERACTION

We can become even more sensitive to family interaction by viewing it as different patterns of communication.[4] Research has not suggested that any one pattern is more successful or creates any greater happiness than any other. Therefore, we must be careful not to place a particular value on a given communication pattern. While viewing these patterns, keep in mind that individuals, families, and situations differ.

Firm Communication Patterns

The terms *downward communication* or *tough-minded* might apply to a family member who has control over other family members—whether the control was earned or taken—and on whose shoulders much of the decision making falls. Families operate in different ways than organizations do. The tough-minded classical manager who rules through strong downward communication is not the same as the tough-minded parent who rules with love. At the same time, however, the family authority figure who keeps order through one-way communication directives could be said to perpetuating a *firm communication pattern*.

Where problems exist is in the interpretation of varying *degrees of firmness*. Consider that we are given the freedom to make decisions on our own. We are permitted to leave home and go to college, make decisions about schedules, and handle relationships with peers. We also handle our own finances. Yet when vacation time arrives, we may return home to family-communication patterns more firm than those to which we have become accustomed.

Many times we rebel against firm patterns of family communication. Often these patterns can be part of the natural evolutionary process of families and generations. When parents are much older and unable to care for themselves, the children may instill a reverse firm pattern of communication with their parents.

Open Communication Patterns

Open patterns of communication evolve because the family has found it can function effectively in an open atmosphere of discussion, with each member working toward his or her individual autonomy and needs while not sacrificing the interdependence of cohesiveness of the family unit. Open patterns should not be confused with a lack of caring or with sloppy communication skills. Rather, they are characterized by *two-way* communication in which the family unit retains its stability but is receptive to individual messages.

The key to a truly open pattern of communication is the ability of family members to understand and accept continual change. As members of the family grow older, and as new people are brought into the family unit through birth or bonding, the patterns are necessarily altered. Involving all members of the family in two-way communication is a difficult process and requires flexibility and understanding. Such "ideals" are not easily achieved. But when members of a family understand good human communication skills, *open patterns* have the best chance for success.

Orderless Communication Patterns

The least stable communication pattern is an *orderless pattern.* Orderless communication patterns are similar to brainstorming where all ideas are considered and encouraged, sometimes regardless of the consequences. The price for this free expression is a lack of stability. Again, this does not mean that an orderless pattern is bad, just that it is unpredictable.

In an orderless pattern, each individual member of the family is given as much freedom as possible to seek out his or her strengths and communicate feelings to other family members. Other members, in turn, accept this free exploration of thoughts and ideas, and support such interaction. Orderless patterns are indicative of considerable self-disclosure in which each member of the family explains and tests feelings and opinions.

Recurring Patterns

Once the family has a workable communication formula, it encourages the continuation of that formula. Thus, even though communication within families is a developing process, communication patterns do become recurring.

By their very nature, these recurring patterns are difficult to change. This can create problems, especially when some family members don't get along with each other. Suppose two children have a rivalry and disagree with each other whenever they interact. Each sees the other as a threat to personal credibility, as a competitor for the love of a parent, and as a generator of other conflicts that can occur in close family relationships. They fight over territorial space, clothes, or other possessions. Because the family has worked to develop recurring patterns of communication, changing the pattern either to resolve the sibling conflict or to prevent it requires a strong commitment and a knowledge of communication skills.

The Phantom: An Ideal Pattern

After reading about these various patterns, it is easy to make value judgments about our own family's communication and whether we would like a more firm, open, or even orderless pattern. Sometimes we equate more happiness with a certain pattern. Perhaps we feel that other family members should be more open to our ideas. Or we might desire more firmness and one-way communication in our quest for more direction in our lives.

As the saying goes, the grass always looks greener on the other side of the fence. Because we are not part of another family, we naturally see the positive sides of other people's interactions. A guest for dinner or the weekend often sees families on good behavior and fails to realize that everything isn't always polite and ordered in the day-to-day interaction. Some scholars even suggest that families have much more disagreement than agreement.[5] The very fact that a family creates bonds unlike those elsewhere in society can make disagreement less threatening to family members than it would be to people involved in interactions outside the family.

THE FAMILY AS A SMALL GROUP

The family is essentially a small group of individuals. Thus, the skills of small-group interaction play an important role in family communication. We can apply those small-group skills to the family setting, mindful, of course, of some variations.

Applying Small-Group Skills

If we are asked to take part in a corporate board meeting, we would pay close attention to the way in which we interacted with other group members. After all, the profits of the company might be at stake, we would be evaluated by peers, and our future relationships with our co-workers would depend on our use of good communication skills.

When we get back home and interact with our family, we often neglect those skills. For some reason, we may feel it's not as important to use them in our own home. We may even feel that we can get away with *not* using those skills with our family. In other words, we sometimes take our family members for granted. Arguments, conflict, and hurt feelings are just some of the consequences of such neglect. We tend to live in our own worlds, and recognizing other people's perceptions of the world sometimes takes practice. To fail to recognize these perceptions means that homophily is absent, communication is one-way, and people hear but do not listen.

Every person in a group has a responsibility for group cohesiveness. Apply that same principle to family communication. Remember that the content of small-group interaction can include supportive statements, statements of unity, and solutions to problems as well as arguments against solutions, expressions of disunity, and messages that show superficial interest. Be alert to these different messages found in all small-group communication, and be constantly aware of which statements support group cohesiveness, which promote positive relationships; work toward solutions to problems that each member understands, appreciates, and accepts.

Leadership Behavior

Small-group communication in the family is usually spontaneous and without an appointed leader. This does not mean that leadership can be discounted. If a group discussion has a recurring theme, a leader may emerge. Many times the leader will be the person who initiated the communication. Yet if the topic changes, which it often does within a relatively short period of time, the leadership may also change.

Assume that three members of a family are driving in a car together on their way to the ski slopes. Within a period of 15 minutes, three topics are discussed. The father initiates a discussion about the Winter Olympics. Brother John initiates a discussion about the latest ski boots. His sister Lisa initiates a discussion about skiing a particularly difficult run. We assume that Lisa is younger than John. During the discussion about the Olympics, the father listens most of the time, and Lisa offers some opinions. When Lisa initiates the discussion about the difficult ski run, John tends to monopolize the conversation. He tells Lisa about his own experience and explains to her exactly how the run should be skied. When Lisa makes a suggestion, John disagrees, then asks their father for his opinion. John assumes he has a right to lead the discussion because he is older and has already skied that difficult run. But John fails to see that not only has Lisa initiated the discussion but also that she is the one personally involved. Sometimes the differences in age, experience, and perceived status within the family cause people to assume leadership positions at a time when they actually might improve family relations by deferring to the person who initiated the discussion and who has the most at stake in its outcome.

Small-Group Permanence

Earlier, we said that the family represents variations from other small groups. One of the most distinct is its *permanence*. The board of directors of a company changes, sometimes quite rapidly. In a family, however, the group will last for the members' lifetimes. Even though some members may come and go, such as by birth, marriage, divorce, or death, that extended group is still the only family to which you will belong (Fig. 16–1).

This permanence has both assets and liabilities. It does retain a relative stability over time. Members know how other members react and have adjusted their communication patterns accordingly. On the other hand, the security and permanence may mean that more members may be prone to risking disagreement, which can cause strained relationships.

Be alert to these characteristics in your own family interaction. Ask yourself how much the permanence and consistency of the family as a small

Figure 16-1   A family is an emotionally bonded unit which, although affected by changes in lifestyles, endures over most of one's lifetime. The recurring patterns of communication are a product of the permanence of the family unit which, although not constant, remains intact for longer periods of time than most other personal associations. As a result, communication patterns are also more permanent, even though the roles and ages of family members experience transition. (Ken Karp)

group permits members to disagree, and what are the consequences of this disagreement.

COMMUNICATION NETWORKS

More complex than the small-group perspective of a family is the view that it is part of a larger communication network.[6] Here we take into consideration not only communication patterns within the family but also communication patterns beyond the family. The "extrafamily" relationships become important when they influence patterns of communication among family members. A family is seen by others not only by how members relate to each other but also by how they relate to those outside the family.

To understand families as communication networks, we will break families down into (1) formal, (2) informal, (3) closely knit, and (4) loosely knit networks. These four divisions are *interrelated*, but to help us understand them, we will discuss them separately.

Formal Communication Networks

Formal communication networks are lines of communication that are understood and accepted by all members of the family. Many times these formal networks are keys to family decision making and problem solving. The family banker, lawyer, doctor, minister, or rabbi are members of a family's formal communication network. These professionals and their decisions, the accuracy of their communications, their opinions, and their credibility all influence the family. Suppose family members sit down to discuss the financial ramifications of expanding the family business. Even though the banker might not be present, the communication that has taken place between the banker and the family becomes part of the discussion and the decision making. The perceptions other people have of the family may also be determined by the capability of the banker: "The Smiths retain Sam Curtis as their lawyer. Therefore, the Smiths must be a fine family." The same can be said for the family's other formal networks.

Informal Communication Networks

Informal communication networks also play a role in family interaction. Some of the Smiths' valued customers can be part of their informal communication network. The customers do not have the same relationship with the family as does the lawyer, but their advice still may be sought about the decision to expand the business. The interaction with the customers may not be as formal as that with the banker—meetings may be by chance instead of by appointment—and the credibility may not be the same. Nevertheless, the customers, many of whom the Smiths know on a personal basis, are important links in the network.

Friends, neighbors, club members, and other social acquaintances may all be part of a family's informal communication network. Susan plays with Randy. Susan gets in a fight with Randy. Susan's mother gets in an argument with Randy's mother. Susan's mother tells her problems to Susan's father, who happens to be Randy's father's best friend.

Closely Knit Communication Networks

Closely knit communication networks consist of people outside of the family unit with whom at least one member of the family is related. In many cases, relatives not living with the family, such as grandparents, aunts, uncles, and cousins, are part of closely knit networks. Frequent communication takes place within the network, and a close emotional bond may exist among the members. Closely knit networks are nurtured through frequent visits, telephone calls, family reunions, and similar reaffirmations.

Loosely Knit Communication Networks

Those people who have limited emotional involvement and contact with family members make up a family's loosely knit communication network. These casual acquaintances do not readily or profoundly affect the relationships or communication among members of the family unit. Unlike the members of closely knit networks, members of a family's loosely knit networks usually do not know one another.

COMMUNICATION ROLES

Different family members have different roles within family-communication networks. One member of the family may have the role of maintaining the networks. A parent who frequently exchanges letters with relatives may fill this role. Other family members may act as liaisons between two different networks. For instance, suppose Julio is a member of the Valencia family. He is thus part of the Valencia family communication networks. When Julio marries into the Feliciano family, he also functions as part of the Feliciano family networks. In addition, he serves a third role being the liaison or the *link* between the two networks. The next time you attend a wedding reception at which two families meet for the first time, notice how the initial greetings center around the "links" in the network. "Oh, I see, you're Julio's uncle. Well, then, who is Juanita? Ah, she's Julio's aunt. How nice."

BARRIERS

In order for communication to flow freely within communication patterns and networks, it must overcome various barriers. By analyzing your own family-interaction patterns, you will undoubtedly come up with many more barriers than we can treat here. A few of the more common ones, however, include generation differences, nonverbal barriers, stress, and stereotyping.

Generation Differences

If the "generation gap" were responsible for everything it is blamed for, most of the communication problems people face could be solved by concentrating our research efforts on this single phenomenon.[7] Yet although the generation gap is often a scapegoat, in some cases it is a very definite block to human communication. It becomes particularly troublesome when emotional and social distances develop between different family members.

Let's look at a situation in which a family is dealing with financial matters. For parents who have lived through hard economic times, their primary goal in life may be to earn a good living. In fact, a lack of happiness for them is associated with the trauma and stress of not being able to make ends meet. Sons and daughters, on the other hand, who may not have shouldered the responsibilities of a family or weathered tough economic times, may be more concerned about the quality of life as opposed to income. This does not mean that they are not concerned about earning a living, only that money is considered a secondary goal to the quality of life.

The way in which different generations feel about earning a living and living a life can be illustrated by what happened at a chemical company. When reprimanding employees, the company forced them to take days off without pay. Management found that ordering employees who were 40 years old and older to take days off without pay was effective; it hurt their economic security. Yet when the company told employees aged 25 to 35 to take days off without pay, the response was, "Hell, we'll take the whole week!" The younger workers took economic security for granted and did not see the threat. Thus, the company changed its policy and made younger employees who made mistakes work overtime.[8]

Families confront many issues. An acceptable dating partner, appropriate clothes to wear, and satisfactory living arrangements with peers can all be areas about which different and deep-seated generation-related opinions can create barriers to communication.

Nonverbal Barriers

The size and architecture of houses and the size of families can create some awkward situations that result in barriers to communication. As we learned earlier, different people require different amounts of territorial and personal space. Rooms on different floors and seating arrangements that do not allow face-to-face communication can produce artificial barriers. Similarly, when adequate territorial space is unavailable for all family members, such as separate bedrooms for all of the children, friction can surface. The future may not hold a solution for such problems. Because of high energy costs, unpredictable interest rates, and inflation, much smaller houses will be the norm for the future, some experts predict.

For children between the ages of 6 and 12, conflicts between verbal and nonverbal cues can be troublesome. For children older than 12, when the verbal and nonverbal cues are in conflict, the nonverbal cues will be read as correct. To better understand these nonverbal barriers, consider the use of satire. Because adults are more adept at understanding figurative meanings of words, they will be able to understand the point of a satirical story much more than will young children, who take words at their literal meaning.[9]

Stress

Traditionally, the family has been looked upon as a sanctuary from the stress of a job and the outside world. Yet the family environment sometimes can be more stressful than the world from which we are supposed to escape.

People react to stress in different ways. Some people return home after a stressful day and want to talk out their problems and frustrations. They desire to be with other people to whom they can relate and explain how rough the day was. Other people want to be alone. They may want to collect their thoughts and ponder the day's activities. Not wanting to talk to other members of the family, doing exercise routines alone, and going upstairs to lie down for an hour may be some of their reactions. When these two opposite types of people happen to meet at the end of the day, such as husband and wife, additional stress is almost unavoidable. The wife may feel that her husband doesn't care about her because he's avoiding her. The husband may perceive his wife's need for attention as a continuation of the stress he left behind. The resulting communication, if it takes place at all, may be explosive.

To be able to communicate under stress, it is important to understand these different reactions to stress. Try to determine how the person with whom you're communicating handles stress and then adapt to that style. If the person wants to unload his or her problems, try to be a good listener. If he or she wants to be alone, try to give the person that freedom.

Stereotyping

Stereotyping can create as many barriers to effective family communication as it can to other communication. One of the stereotypes we discussed when learning about listening skills was the assumption that people from a given class or background possess certain traits. When the family network stretches to include such people, the same unjustified stereotypes can be imposed. What friends we should associate with and who is the right person to date can be some of the barrier-filled discussions that ensue. As family members associate with individuals outside the family and as networks expand to include new friends and associates, open communication without prejudice, although sometimes difficult, is a step toward understanding.

COMMUNICATING WITH SENIOR CITIZENS

As part of our continuing research efforts into communication skills, we are becoming more sensitive to the needs of the elderly and ways to bring them into meaningful interaction with each other and with the younger generation.[10] Much of the adjustment to growing older has a foundation in human communication, beginning with self-concept.

Challenges to Self-Concept

We have learned that one of the first prerequisites of positive and satisfying human communication is a positive self-concept. Self-concept has its roots in our value system, our past, our perceptions of the future, and the answer to the question "Who am I?"

The elderly face constant challenges to their self-concept, which can make human communication difficult.[11] For many elderly people the work place was the source of self-esteem. Colleagues and co-workers were present to provide the positive reinforcement for jobs well done, to reaffirm competence, to praise, and to mold.[12] People's perceptions of themselves were closely tied to this network of positive reinforcers. Upon retirement, the source of this reinforcement disappeared. Not only were there no people to offer praise but there was no setting in which praise could take place. Thus, one of the main sources of self-concept disappeared.

A vision of the future, personal ambitions, and aspirations that were a vital and vibrant part of our younger years now become less helpful to self-esteem because of the limited opportunities to make a valuable contribution to society through employment. Corporate retirement programs, some lucrative enough to force individuals into early retirement without consideration for their emotional health, compound the problem.

The well-being of our mental and physical health, as well as perceptions of the future, can also influence self-concept.[13] If a person is less than active and ailing, the ability to interact positively with others deteriorates. Sometimes this becomes a self-fulfilling prophecy: The worse we feel, the worse we perceive ourselves; the worse we perceive ourselves, the worse we feel.

Improving Self-Concept and Communication

When we communicate with older people, positive steps can be taken to make human communication more fulfilling. By no means are we doing these to be condescending or to pamper. On the contrary, we have much to learn from older people and can do so by communicating with them.[14]

For example, homophily means sharing. Look for common communication ground with the elderly. At first, the common ground may not seem important and may even seem superficial. Discussion about television programs, sports, and the latest books are openers to any conversation, and they can lead to a deeper understanding of the background and experiences of the elderly. Even if you cannot share the same experiences, asking about and sharing new perspectives is meaningful and important.

Avoid Stereotyping

What we hear and read conditions how we respond to the elderly. But that must be balanced by what we actually experience. Do not fall into the trap of assuming that just because a person is old, he or she is less active, less alert or intelligent, less sensitive, or less able to relate to those of a younger generation. Case after case proves those assumptions false. When we set stereotypes aside, we can interact with another person through appreciation and mutual respect as opposed to pity.

Communicate as an Equal, Not to a Subordinate

We sometimes treat an elderly person more as a subordinate than as an equal, even when pity is not involved. Our communication habits, from nonverbal cues to language, fall into patterns somewhat similar to those we use when communicating with a child. Respect an elderly person as an equal and work to communicate on this basis.

Participate in Positive Stroking

Your own "positive stroking" can replace the reinforcement no longer provided to the elderly by the workplace. Compliments freely yet honestly given about abilities and contributions can help supplement the lack of positive reinforcement from other sources.

Take the opportunity to improve your communication skills with the elderly. Be responsible for initiating communication, and be alert to the pitfalls that prevent effective and meaningful communication. The role of senior citizens in our society is changing. We're all recognizing that contributions to society, levels of mental and physical health, accomplishments, and potential are not always related to chronological age.

DIVORCE, SEPARATION, AND THE EXTENDED FAMILY

The breaking up of a marriage occurs with much less stigma today, a contrast from a few years ago when divorced people were generally shunned by society. Today, although prejudices sometimes still exist, most people view divorce and separation as a better alternative than the continuation of a destructive relationship. That does, however, mean divorce is more common today than ever before. Statistics abound, but it is safe to say that of the readers of this book, approximately 25 percent were raised by a single divorced parent, and a higher percentage live with a divorced parent who may have remarried (Fig. 16–2).

Because the high rate of divorce is a relatively new phenomenon, we

Figure 16-2
Today, because of more permissible attitudes toward divorce, many children grow up with single parents. Communication patterns in the extended family can be considerably different from patterns which exist in households where the child's natural family unit has remained intact. (Laimute Druskis photo)

cannot draw on long-term research as we can in other areas of psychology and communication. Thus, much of what we know about communication in situations of divorce and separation comes not from large-scale surveys but from the clinical files of marriage counselors. Even then, a large body of unreported experiences exists where parties have not the background, finances, or wherewithal to seek counseling before a separation or divorce takes place. Add to this the fact that every divorce and separation is unique, and we can see why analyzing the phenomenon is still risky.

Attacks on Self-Concept: The Spouses

To understand what happens to human communication during divorce or separation, we will begin by examining what happens to the self-concept of the parties involved—spouses as well as children.[15] The breaking up of a relationship is a force that can significantly lower a person's self-concept. Remembering that self-concept is one of the key components of good human communication, we can see immediately that such communication is affected when a person experiences an "uncoupling," either legally or emotionally.

A sense of failure can grip both individuals. The best-intended plans have not succeeded, and both parties, whether admitting it or not, may feel responsible for the failure. If nothing else, each has incorrectly judged the other, or they would not have joined together in the first place. The inability to successfully judge the qualities or characteristics of one's mate is a very personal kind of failure.

Emotional Battles

The dissolving of the relationship is particularly unpleasant and drags out over a long period of time; the fatigue of these emotional battles can take its toll. Small victories and put-downs, either through interpersonal interaction or through legal sparring of attorneys, can be somewhat hollow vindications. Destroying one's mate may outwardly signal a form of satisfying revenge, but it takes little time to look in the mirror and ask, "What kind of a person have I become that I should need to enter into these battles?" It takes maturity to keep self-concept intact in the face of threats to our judgments about love and relationships.

Moreover, communication between the two parties lessens or becomes "only for the sake of the children." Yet during the time of the relationship, the parties may have come to rely heavily on each other as a communication partner.

Rebuilding the "I"

In the chapter on relationships we discussed how, at a certain stage of a relationship, the "I" is replaced with "we." Now the "we," which makes up the whole person, is sliced off. Each individual temporarily becomes only half a person, and each person's identity is in limbo. Such occurrences may result in temporary, even intimate, reconciliations as each party seeks out the "lost" emotional partner. Some people are so shaken by the experience that they go through life emotionally dragging along past relationsips as a form of security blanket which seriously interferes with their ability to build new bonds. In other cases, another person or lover may enter the scene. When this occurs too soon after the divorce, the new relationship may be superficial or awkward, for the newly divorced party may still be identifying with the "we" part of the other party. It will take time before the new self-concept can function independently of the "we."

Acquiring a new self-concept may be further complicated by the couple's children, who desire for parents to get back together again. Children may have a difficult time understanding why two people they love so much should not love each other. Even unintentional attempts at bringing the parents together, such as arranging lunches or times when the old family structure can be re-created, may inadvertently retain the "we" when the "I" is striving to rebuild itself.

Diminishing Friendships

Friends who want to remain neutral during marital discord avoid both parties, not wanting to play favorites or offend either side. Thus, the friendships and interaction that used to reinforce each person's self-concept are absent and loneliness sets in. Withdrawal then occurs, which can create more loneliness.

Changes in residence can be another threat. Familiar surroundings that once were the "security of home" abruptly change. Because one party must usually move out, the need to adapt to a new residence, even a new town or a new part of the city, presents another challenge. Many times we overlook the fact that divorce and separation are synonymous with a physical move, with all of the challenges to the self-concept a move can bring, except that those challenges are operating when the emotional well-being of the parties is simultaneously under fire.

Diminishing Possessions

Personal possessions usually enhance a person's self-esteem and become part of his or her identity. To some, success may be defined by owning a nice home or driving a nice car. Yet divorce usually involves a splitting up of property, and one party may lose some of these possessions, in addition to losing part of his or her self-esteem in the process. Instead of returning to the well-furnished house in the suburbs, one party may drive a "clunker" to an empty apartment. All that the individual has worked for, perhaps measured by what he or she was able to purchase by working hard and moving up the ladder, is gone. The person is abruptly back to square one, forced to start all over again. The blow to self-concept is very real.

Self-Concept and the Children of Divorce

No matter what their age, children of divorced parents can experience attacks on their self-concept. Because children's identities are made up of both themselves and parents, the child, depending on how custody is awarded, now finds himself or herself developing an identity with only one parent. The structure in which he or she is viewed by friends is also shattered. If the child has friends who are also the children of divorced parents, the sharing of feelings and experiences may help to rebuild self-concept more rapidly. Until that time, however, interactions with others may be awkward. This is particularly true if friends of the children were friends of both parents. Youngsters may be haunted by such questions as, "How can I explain my parents' divorce? What will my friends think of me now that I come from a single-parent family?"

Guilt can be particularly strong if a child has been forced to take the side of one parent. The inhumanity of some of our courts of law and the antiquated ideas and incompetence of some judges still leave their marks on children. When a child sits in a courtroom and hears his or her parents attacking each other, when the child is forced to testify against a parent, or when the child is caught as a pawn between two parents because a judge or the attorneys find the child the only ammunition to win the case or settle the dispute, that child may be consumed with guilt. It takes a very mature youngster to realize that the sometimes artificially induced conflict of a legal confrontation should not be the image of a parent that the child carries from that day forward. When these legal skirmishes can be set aside and the relationship between parents and children moved forward, then the rebuilding of self-concept of all parties can begin.

Changing Communication Networks During Separation and Divorce

Examine for a moment how divorce and separation alter the networks and channels of human communication. Most immediate is the disruption of the channels of communication among family members, especially between the separated or divorced parties. Direct communication may be replaced by indirect communication through intermediaries. One party communicates with an attorney, who in turn communicates with another attorney, who in turn communicates with the second party. Distortion of messages naturally increases with this new, more complex network. When A talks directly to B, the message may be slightly different from the message that passes from A through A's attorney to B's attorney to B. Party B, who now may receive conflicting information, may not know whom to believe. Tensions increase, the parties become suspicious of each other, and breakdowns in communication occur.

Outside of the immediate family, communication is also disrupted. Whenever two people join together in a relationship, they also join together their respective families. Over a span of time, the networks between these two families may become very active and intertwined. The breaking up of the relationship disrupts these communication networks. Such breakups can be especially difficult for children and their grandparents. When the child becomes the custody of one parent, maintaining communication with the other parent's side of the family can be difficult. New networks may develop when one of the parties finds another mate, and children find themselves building relationships with the new family.

The communication networks between the children and the divorced or separated parents may even change. One parent may become possessive of the child as a means of hurting the ex-partner or reducing the communication that takes place between the child and the ex-partner. Even though a custody agreement may stipulate that a child is to spend six weeks each summer with the noncustodial parent, the custodial parent may sabotage that arrangement. Vacations, Little League baseball, riding lessons, and summer camp may be scheduled in conflict with the six-week visitation period. The child is faced with choosing between these fun activities and seeing the other parent. The other parent, in the meantime, is faced with the guilt of either denying the child the pleasure of these activities or the agony of not seeing the child during the legitimate visitation.

Under such circumstances, many children, especially young ones, do not perceive what is happening. They want to enjoy the activities, not realizing the hurt being inflicted on the other parent. The custodial parent rationalizes the activities as something good for the child and something he or she is providing, which the noncustodial parent is not. But the end result is a lessening of the communication ties between the noncustodial parent and the child.

When a child is older and understands the responsibility to keep the channels of communication open, extra efforts can be made to lessen the severity of the absence. If the child must participate in activities that interfere with visitation, perhaps he or she can visit the noncustodial parent at another time, making several shorter visits. More frequent phone calls and letters are also vital communication links. Ideally, each parent is mature enough to assume the responsibility for arranging for the child to spend time with the other parent. Unfortunately, the ideal is not always achieved.

Merging Families: New Communication Challenges

Few communication situations can be more challenging than when two families merge. Here, understanding as well as skill in human communication is necessary to negotiate the relationships that will develop when one parent becomes "bonded" to a different parent.

Most basic when two families merge is the fact that the number of people with which communication takes place increases. In the chapter on small groups, we learned how rapidly the number of possible relationships increases when just one additional person is added to a group. When families merge, those possibilities jump dramatically.

Second, some relationships are more developed than others. Rarely does everyone start out equally. The children from one family have had a longer relationship in that family than they have had with members of the newly merged family. Thus, time is necessary to let relationships develop at their own pace. Unfortunately, the mere logistics of living together prevent this. Two families find themselves eating together, watching television together, even sharing each other's clothes. Brothers may verbally spar with each other, neither taking the other too seriously, but the same sparring with a new member of the family would seem rude and insensitive.

Available territorial space is subdivided, and this adds to the tension. A child who once enjoyed his or her own bedroom now finds the space shared with new "brothers" or "sisters." Adjusting to reduced territorial space can be frustrating and conflict-producing. Added to this is the fact that one of the merged families is adjusting to a new environment, having moved in with the other family. Familiar surroundings and neighborhoods are gone, and self-concept is a little shaky.

Children who do not have the maturity to cope with the "merged" situation force parents to negotiate crisis after crisis. Not only does the negotiation put a tension-filled, time-consuming drain on the parents, but in the eyes of the children, no negotiated settlement is satisfactory unless their side wins. This may place an additional burden on the parents' ability to develop effectively their own new relationship. They may not have time to communicate with each other because they are too busy communicating with the fighting children.

Applying Communication Skills to the Extended Family

How do we cope with the new demands of the extended family? First, we can understand that divorce and separation challenge the self-concept of all parties involved. In understanding these challenges, we can be more sensitive to the feelings and actions of others. Realize that low self-esteem can create unnatural communication. Thus, during these times, both parents and children can help to reassure each other that they are still respected, loved, and that they want to communicate and spend time with each other.

Second, realize the changes that will alter traditional family communication networks. Evaluate these changes and determine if you can play a role in keeping the channels of communication open.

Third, the time when it may seem natural to withdraw from a parent or an individual who is going through a divorce may be the very time that increased communication is necessary. The ability to empathize and listen will be especially appreciated.

Fourth, when families do merge, understand the new parents' need to develop their own relationship. Also understand that any good relationship, be it step-family or friend, needs time to develop. Time and "breathing room" may mean less communication now but more enjoyable and meaningful communication in the future.

SUMMARY

Communication patterns in families are developed in an atmosphere that balances the individual's need for self-identity with the family's need for interdependence. We labeled these patterns as "firm," which reflects one-way communication from an authority figure; "open," in which each individual's self-identity is retained along with the interdependence of the family unit; and "orderless," in which individual autonomy is supported to the point that family stability is sacrificed. Once they are workable, communication patterns in families seem to be recurring and operate to retain the autonomous-interdependence balance. However, no ideal pattern exists, because families determine their criteria for satisfying family structures.

We found that power in families and the interaction of that power can affect family communication just as it does organizational communication. Because a family is a small group, we can and should apply small-group communication skills to the family setting.

Families can also be viewed as communication networks. The formal network consists of individuals who provide services to the family. Informal networks also provide valuable information and relationships but are less structured than formal networks. Closely knit networks usually are composed of kin closely attached to the family through emotional bonding. Loosely knit networks are made up of casual acquaintances, many of whom have no contact with each other. Much like networks in organizations, people in family networks fulfill specific roles.

Communication in families must frequently conquer barriers. Some of these include generation differences, nonverbal barriers, stress and stereotyping. Communication with senior citizens may also be challenging. Yet with a little sensitivity to the elderly's self-concepts and the encouragement of positive and meaningful discussions, this aspect of family communication can be delightfully rewarding.

Special sensitivity to human communication must prevail during a separation or divorce. During such times, challenges to self-concept abound for all parties involved, including children. Communication networks within and among families also change when a relationship dissolves. The role of intermediaries, the custody of children, and the feelings held for the other party all alter the traditional patterns of communication. Merging two families creates new interpersonal relationships, changes in territorial space, and the need for the parents to have the time and privacy to develop their own relationship.

QUESTIONS FOR REVIEW AND DISCUSSION

1. What is the definition of a family?
2. Why do family members need both autonomy and interdependence?

3. What are the differences that characterize firm, open, and orderless patterns of family communication?

4. Why do family members sometimes perceive the illusion of an ideal pattern?

5. How is power applied to family interaction?

6. How are small-group skills and leadership applied to family communication?

7. What are the different networks that exist in family communication, and what are the differences and similarities among these networks?

8. What are the obstacles that exist in family communication, and how do they influence family communication patterns?

9. What are important considerations when communicating with the elderly?

10. How does communication function in extended families where separation or divorce has occurred?

LEARNING EXERCISES

1. Interview someone who at one time was divorced. Ask the person to explain how he or she went about rebuilding the "I" quality in his or her life after becoming single again. An alternative exercise is to interview a marriage counselor and ask that person to describe the most common types of communication problems that exist in a marriage.

2. Visit a nursing home and talk to the staff who work there. Ask them to discuss the ways in which different families who visit the nursing home interact with the residents and with each other. What activities take place at the nursing home to reinforce the self-concept of the residents?

ADDITIONAL READINGS

ATLAS, S. L. *Single Parenting*. Englewood Cliffs, NJ: Prentice-Hall, 1981.
CAPLOW, T. ET AL *Middletown Families*. Minneapolis, MN: U. of Minn. Press, 1982.
GILBERT, S. *How to Live with a Single Parent*. New York: Lothrop, Lee and Shepard Books, 1982.
GILBERT, S. *Trouble at Home*. New York: Lothrop, Lee and Shepard Books, 1981.
GREYWOLF, E. S. *The Single Mother's Handbook*. New York: William Morrow, 1984.
KORNHABER, A., and K. L. WOODWARD *Grandparents, Grandchildren: The Vital Connection*. New York: Doubleday, 1981.
POGREBIN, L. C. *Family Politics*. New York: McGraw Hill, 1983.
RHODES, S. and J. WILSON *Surviving Family Life*. New York: G. P. Putnam's Sons, 1981.
VISHER, E. and J. VISHER *How to Win as a Stepfamily*. New York: Dembner Books, 1982.

17

MASS COMMUNICATION

OBJECTIVES

After completing this chapter, you should be able to

- Understand what distinguishes mass communication from other types of communication
- List and discuss the factors affecting the choices that gatekeepers make
- Explain how mass media reach specialized audiences
- Explain what is meant by "personalized" media
- List and compare new technologies affecting mass communication
- Be more alert to the presence of newspapers, magazines, books, radio, television, and motion pictures
- Explain the role that advertising and public relations play in mass communication.

When Abraham Lincoln ran for President, he considered it a good day of campaigning if he could reach a crowd of people gathered in a small town auditorium, around a tree in a city park, or alongside the tracks of a campaign train. Today, when the candidates for the Presidency step before a television camera they can reach tens of millions of people. With satellite communication linking international television networks, that audience is increased to the hundreds of millions. In Lincoln's time, the Associated Press could telegraph a short wire-service dispatch across state lines in a matter of minutes. Today, the entire edition of the *Wall Street Journal,* already composed in pages, can be transmitted across the United States or around the world in the same amount of time. New technologies permitting two-way electronic communication, such as that used in teleconferencing, can link people thousands of miles apart in a small-group discussion where each participant has audio and video access to all other participants.

Mass communication has changed drastically since the time of Lincoln. It affects our lives from the time we are children, and it has a profound effect on the way we view our world as adults. No longer do we sit at home and confine ourselves to reading newspaper copy about a war thousands of miles away. We turn on the television and witness live reports of the death and destruction. The pictures of a newborn heir to the British throne are flashed across continents in seconds as dozens of communication satellites positioned in space form an international web of communication links bringing us correspondent reports from Rome or Roanoke.

To most of us, television is our most familiar form of mass communication. But mass communication is much more. It is the morning radio disc jockey who brings us news, weather, sports, and the latest recordings. It is the evening newspaper that gives us an in-depth look at the world around us. It is the advertising executive preparing the latest campaign. It is book publishing bringing us the textbook you are now reading.

DISTINGUISHING CHARACTERISTICS OF MASS COMMUNICATION

Mass communication (Fig. 17–1) can be distinguished from other types of communication by (1) a mass medium, (2) limited sensory channels, (3) impersonal vs. personal characteristics, (4) delayed feedback, and (5) a gatekeeper.[1]

A Mass Medium

The mass medium of television, for example, makes it possible for the political candidate to reach millions of people. Interpersonal communication limits us to the people in range of the speaker's voice. Newspapers, magazines, books, radio, and television are all examples of mass media.

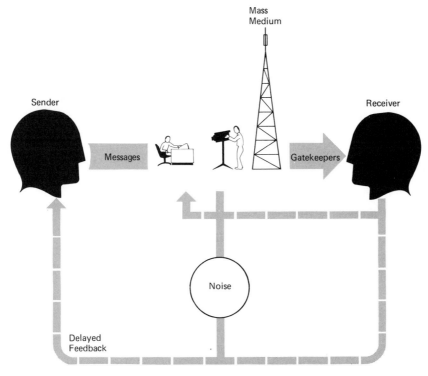

Figure 17-1   Expanding our model of communication first introduced in Chapter 1, we can see the addition of a medium of communication which includes newspapers, magazines, books, radio, television, motion pictures, and other more specialized media such as cable television. A gatekeeper, mass medium, and delayed feedback are three concepts which distinguish mass communication from other types of communication. Other distinguishing characteristics include limited sensory channels and impersonal communication.

Limited Sensory Channels

With interpersonal communication, we see, hear, smell, and can many times reach out and physically touch the other person. In most instances, all of our senses are operating. The use of nonverbal communication is also much more intense because we can read many subtle nonverbal cues when we are in the presence of another person. Media severely restrict our sensory use, for not only are we physically separated from the other person but we also may be interpreting that person's thoughts, comments, and ideas from a printed page. Radio and television improves on our ability to receive communication, but even then we may only be able to hear the other person or that individual's presence may be restricted by the size of the television screen.

Impersonal vs. Personal Communication

These limited sensory channels make mass communication much more impersonal. When we first meet another person it takes place in an atmosphere of anticipation. Our interpersonal sending and receiving mechanisms are working at a conscious level. If we meet that same person through television, for example, we may pay little attention to the individual. We cannot talk to the person and we know he or she cannot hear or see us. We therefore are connected through an impersonal, not an interpersonal, link.

Delayed Feedback

In earlier chapters we learned about the importance of feedback to the communication process. Feedback exists and is no less important in mass communication, but it is delayed, not immediate. For example, the reporter who covers the politician's speech may write a story and the story is published. A few days later the newspaper receives a letter from a politician of the opposing party. The letter strongly criticizes the speech. The letter, which could have also been sent to the person who delivered the speech, represented delayed feedback.

Other characteristics common to all communication can occur in mass communication. For instance, noise can enter the process. Your radio may contain static. The printing press at the newspaper may have malfunctioned, resulting in blurred pages. Both are examples of noise.

The Gatekeeper

A gatekeeper is anyone controlling the flow of information via a mass medium. A reporter covering the politician's speech is a gatekeeper. The television network news organization, which is made up of reporters, directors, producers, and writers, is a gatekeeper organization. The film director who edits the latest release, the person who designed the cover of this textbook, the television network censor who cuts a sexually explicit scene from a prime-time program, the newspaper editor who writes an editorial, the paper carrier who delivers the newspaper (Fig. 17–2)—all are gatekeepers. These people operate between the senders of communication and the audience.

Gatekeepers have the ability to both limit and expand our knowledge of events and people. They limit our knowledge by selecting only some of the information available to them. A reporter who covers a speech has only so much space in the newspaper or so much time on radio or television. As a result, some of the speech will not be reported. The gatekeeper also limits the amount of information being sent to us. Because we are not able to be present at the speech, the gatekeeper is also in a position to expand our knowledge by providing us with information we would not normally be able to receive.

Figure 17-2
The gatekeeper includes anyone who
controls the flow of information via
the mass medium, including those
who work in the distribution area. At
the heart of newspaper distribution is
the paper carrier, a concept that has
not changed much since the turn of
the century. (Library of Congress)

The gatekeeper must also reinterpret the information being sent via the mass medium. In a newspaper story, for example, the reporter will add his or her own comments between the quotes. Whereas objectivity is an ideal, it is not always achieved. The factors of selective retention, perception, and exposure we discussed in the chapter on listening will come to bear on the gatekeeper's decision making and, consequently, on what we learn about the speech.

FACTORS AFFECTING GATEKEEPER CHOICE

Why does some information reach the public and other information get stopped at the gatekeeper? What are the forces that act upon gatekeepers to select or reject information? The answers to these questions add another dimension to our understanding of how the process of mass communication works.

Economics

One force acting on the selection process is economics. In the United States, most mass media are profit-making enterprises. Even those that are not, such as public broadcasting stations, some campus newspapers, and literary magazines, must be concerned about finances. As such, the sponsors, advertisers, and contributors impact on what gets disseminated to the public. For example, if a newspaper is highly profitable it has the money and the staff to support investigative reporters. Thus, the readers of the newspaper will be served by watchdog reporters who are paid to expose corruption in government, scandal, or injustices of one kind or another.

In smaller communities a tiny number of advertisers may have a major impact on the profit-and-loss column of the local newspaper or radio station. News unfavorable to the advertiser can result in pressure on the media for a more favorable editorial line.

Legal Restrictions

The media in the United States are relatively free, but there are still laws and regulations that can be invoked to protect the interests of the public. For example, while publishers in a free society can print virtually anything they want, it is not done without risk. A poorly prepared story attacking the character or integrity of another person can quickly open up the publisher to a libel suit where damages can be substantial. This does not mean that anyone who is criticized is able to collect damages. Truth is always a powerful and effective defense. It does, however, mean that libel law forces publishers to think twice before making personal attacks without all the facts.

In broadcasting, the rules and regulations enforced by the Federal Communications Commission (FCC) help determine who will or will not own broadcasting stations. For example, because there are only so many broadcast frequencies available in which stations can operate, not everyone who wants to be on the air can start a radio or television station. If that were the case (and at one point in our history it was), so many stations would be on the air they would interfere with each other to the point where no single station could be clearly heard. Other FCC rules and regulations affect technical operations, hiring practices, and other station operations.

Cable television is governed mostly by local government, which has considerable latitude over the franchise requirements of the cable system. Backed by Supreme Court decisions, local government can determine what type of programming will be offered on the cable system. Thus, if the local government decides to deny a franchise to a cable system that wants to air X-rated movies, the local government has some latitude and support from the courts.

The Presence of Deadlines

The deadline can determine if a reporter is "scooped" by the competition or gets credit for an exclusive. Both have their risks. The ability to beat the deadline may look good to a reporter's boss, but beating the competition by sacrificing accuracy will have its own repercussions. The story may have to be retracted. A libel suit may be filed and the reporter will have to prove in court that every effort was made to check the facts.

Deadlines are present in every reporting situation. In radio, deadlines can occur every hour. A newspaper reporter faces similar pressure. If a story is not acceptable, a blank space is not acceptable. Filler material will need to be added where a good local news story should have appeared. In television, film or videotape not ready at air time can cause a story to be bumped. When two stories of equal value are available and one has video, the video story will take precedence.

Ethics

Ethics, both personal and professional, enter into a gatekeeper's decision making. Assume you are working as a radio journalist and one morning the station's largest sponsor is arrested on a drunk-driving charge. At about the time the story is to run the manager of the station walks in and tells you to stop the story. What do you do? If you agree with the manager, who has a perfect right to demand you stop the story and can fire you if you refuse, you compromise your professional ethics. On the other hand, if you air the story you run the risk of losing your job. What decision would you make?

Competition

The number of competing media in a community determine what the public receives. In small communities where there are only one or two media outlets, complacency can result. There is a tendency to fall in line with the local political and economic forces. A larger, more competitive market makes it possible for different media to compete with each other and bring everyone associated with the media to a higher level of professionalism.

The negative aspects of too much competition are reflected in our previous examples of trying to obtain exclusives at the cost of accuracy. But this is usually a lesser price to pay than the cost of a one-media town where only the voice of a single publisher or broadcaster is heard.

News Value and News Hole

Two interrelated factors, the news value of an event and the news hole, affect gatekeeper selection. *New value* is a relative term and refers to the value or intensity of a news item in comparison to all other news items. *News hole* refers to a theoretical amount of time or space available to air or print the story. An example will help us understand these terms more clearly. Assume a newspaper editor has the opportunity to select from two stories. One story is of a plane crash 10 miles from town. The other story is about an equally serious plane crash 1,000 miles away. The editor will choose the story about the plane crash close to home because it is of more interest to local readers. To that particular editor, the local plane crash had more news value and intensity than the plane crash 1,000 miles away. Now let's suppose that it is what reporters call a slow news day. Nothing much is happening. Few stories exist to fill the paper. In the slang of the newsroom, "it's dead." It also means there is a large news hole. The hole is big because there is little competition among stories for placement in the paper, and both plane crash stories can fit.

Attention Factors

Earlier we learned that when two television news stories of equal value are available the one with video will be chosen. The video adds another attention factor to the story. Stories that would normally be of low news value can be selected for the newspaper or a newscast because of their attention factor. We could argue that this attention factor actually increases the news value of an event, and to some extent we would be correct, for attention factors go beyond news value. Drug busts are a frequent occurrence in many cities. When one occurs it may or may not get media attention; this is mostly determined by the size of the news hole on that particular day. Now consider what happens when someone is arrested on drug charges in a hospital emergency room where the person is being treated for an overdose. A radio reporter happens to be at the emergency room and records the patient's words as he explains to the police officer how he feels. The recording adds an attention factor to the story, makes it more appealing, and improves its chances of getting on the air.

Peer Pressure

In some areas, "journalism reviews" serve as watchdogs for local media. In some cases where intense competition exists and where one reporter reflects negatively on all media, one media outlet may openly criticize its competition. While such tactics may prove beneficial from the public's standpoint, they can quickly degenerate into mudslinging.

Reacting to Feedback

We know that one of the qualities that makes communication a dynamic, circular process is feedback. Although in mass media the feedback is delayed, it still provides an opportunity for the public to react to what it reads or hears and to influence the work of reporters, editors, television producers, and others. The most familiar form of feedback is the letter to the editor. Letters to the editor have been a traditional part of journalism wherever the press operates in a free society.

Some newspapers employ ombudsmen, whose sole responsibility is to review feedback from the public. In some media organizations these individuals may be given their own column, with great latitude for criticism. In other organizations they work internally to help solve problems, answer the public's questions, and provide internal feedback about the public's criticism and concerns.

CHANGING DEFINITIONS OF MASS COMMUNICATION

The term *mass media* makes us think of millions of television viewers spread over the country, thousands of newspaper readers of every age, sex, national origin, religion, and other statistical characteristics. To some extent these images are correct. However, we need to understand that the mass media, while still reaching large numbers of people, are becoming more and more specialized.

Media and Specialized Audiences

Different media offer examples of this trend. For instance, newspapers publish suburban editions, foreign-language editions (Fig. 17–3), regional editions, and special sections to reach specialized audiences. City magazines have grown over the years until today most large metropolitan centers have their own city or regional magazine. Some areas have more than one magazine. For example, if you want to reach business people who work in Seattle you could advertise in *People*. But you would also waste a great deal of money because many people besides business people living in Seattle read *People*. A much smarter, economical, and more effective choice would be to advertise in a magazine titled *Seattle Business*. If you want to reach people living in Dallas, you can advertise in a magazine called *Dallas*. A city magazine reaching readers in Denver is titled, appropriately, *Denver*. In Oregon you can read *Oregon Coast* (Fig. 17–4).

Radio is another example of a specialized medium. In the 1930s, when network radio was in its prime, the audience for network radio was a national

Figure 17-3 Newspapers, once a mass medium, are becoming more specialized with regional, suburban and foreign-language editions. Special Zipcode sorting systems make it possible to reach specific neighborhoods. Below is an editorial cartoon from the Spanish-language edition of the *Miami Herald*. (Courtesy *El Miami Herald*)

audience. The same program heard in New York was listened to in Los Angeles, San Francisco, and most other cities and towns in the United States. The majority of what people heard on radio came from the networks. Gradually, under the competition of television, radio adopted more and more local programming until today it primarily reaches local specialized audiences. Rarely, except in the coverage of catastrophic events, does radio become a mass medium. Take any major city and tune across the radio dial. Programming can be heard that appeals to the teenage listener, the middle-aged listener, the highly educated listener, the listener who speaks a foreign language, and so on. Similarly, an advertiser picks and chooses which radio stations to advertise on based on what specialized audience that station reaches.

Personalized Media

Two examples of personalized media are videotape and videodisc. These media are personalized because it is an individual's "personal" decision that determines which media to purchase, rent, and when and where to use the media. If we aren't satisfied with the time that our favorite television program appears, we can preset our videotape recorder, automatically record the program, and play it back at our convenience. We can use a personal computer and access data banks containing much the same information available through traditional media. For example, electronic editions—called "on-line" editions—of newspapers, magazines, and encyclopedias are available. By keying-in the correct information on our personal computer we can access these on-line editions and read much the same information that appears in the print edition.

NEW TECHNOLOGIES AFFECTING MASS COMMUNICATION

The on-line editions of newspapers, magazines, and encyclopedias are examples of the many new technologies that are changing our media environment. For example, in the 1940s, enterprising business people in Pennsylvania and Oregon discovered that they could install a television antenna on a mountain top and run a line from the antenna to a nearby community. There, people would pay to hook up and receive better television reception than was possible from their rooftop antennas. Thus cable television was born. Cable television still operates on the same principle, but today some sophisticated systems also offer two-way capabilities. Among other things, the interfacing makes it possible for the home cable subscriber to vote in public-opinion polls, to shop, and to rent first-run movies.

High-frequency microwave transmission systems permit new links, including satellite links, to transmit television pictures and data through rough terrain, over skyscrapers, and across oceans to bring us live news reports from around the globe. A local television station in Chicago can switch to its own correspondent at a European summit meeting or cover a sporting event a continent away. Smaller, land-based microwave systems can send television signals to an apartment complex where tenants can subscribe to programming services much like those provided by cable systems. The dirigible flying over a football field during a game and the local television reporter on the other side of town both employ microwave technology to transmit signals back to a television station or other distribution point where the signals are retransmitted directly to home television sets or to a television network control center.

Teletext and *videotex* are two alternative transmission systems that provide "textual" information to subscribers. Teletext is an unwired system that uses the same signal that carries the television program. Different "frames" of textual material are sent in sequence and subscribers are able to capture the frame they want to retain and read. Videotex is a wired system that uses two-way cable television or telephone lines. Subscribers can interact with the central computer and select textual information from a video index. Combinations of the teletext and videotex systems are used in corporate settings where businesses share information among offices, or companies subscribe to a central information service.

New technologies are also affecting television transmission and receiving systems. Low-power television stations serve small geographic areas with localized programming. Digital television uses computer technology in the camera and receiving systems to greatly enhance picture quality. Stereo television is providing enhanced sound accompaniment to programming.

As already discussed earlier in this chapter, the increased use of videotape technology—the VCR—has made television much more of a personalized medium and provides wider and more convenient selection of programming. Compact discs are replacing tapes and records and bringing new levels of quality to sound reproduction. All of these new technologies are changing the way we use media and the traditional definitions of mass communication.

THE MASS MEDIA

To some extent, the earliest forms of human communication—pictographs on the inside of caves and stone tablets—were forms of mass communication. Someone—an ancient gatekeeper—placed the messages on stone for others to see, and the audience used and reacted to those messages much in the way we use media today.

Newspapers

Newspapers, called posted bulletins, were in use as early as 59 B.C. where they were placed on public places for display. During the American Revolution, bulletins were printed and sold by Paul Revere. In 1690, a newspaper titled *Public Occurrences, Both Forreign and Domestick* was published in Boston. The telegraph and improved printing processes made publishing a newspaper more popular and profitable. The thirst for news increased, sometimes through conflict such as the Civil War and also through westward expansion. Today, truly international newspapers have emerged such as the *Wall Street Journal,* which publishes both U.S. regional and foreign editions. Newspaper chains are becoming the new national publishing empires, and many of the larger newspaper conglomerates are plowing profits into diversified holdings, such as radio, television, and other media.

Magazines

Magazines were an important part of early colonial America. Benjamin Franklin published the *Pennsylvania Gazette* and the *General Magazine.* In 1776 Thomas Paine's *Common Sense* polarized public opinion to support independence from England. Louis Godey founded an American magazine for women that carried the title *Godey's Lady's Book.* Edited by Sarah Joseph Hale, a Boston feminist, it dealt with such topics as women's fashions, manners, and homemaking. Photography and printing increased magazine circulation in the 1800s and by the 1900s *The Saturday Evening Post, Life, Look,* and other magazines were reaching a truly mass audience. Prosperity followed circulation. *The Saturday Evening Post* issue of December 7, 1929, gave the reader almost two pounds of magazine and 272 pages. It kept the average reader occupied for 20 hours.

But the era of the mass-circulation magazine was already coming to an end. Television was able to reach more people for less money. The increased postage, printing, and paper costs gradually made it more and more difficult to reach the large audience and still charge a reasonable fee for the magazine. Some magazines, such as *Colliers,* went out of business and did not return. Others, such as *The Saturday Evening Post,* went out of business but were later repurchased and directed at much narrower and specialized audiences, thus making the titles once again profitable but on a smaller scale. Other magazines managed to survive the transition and became specialized themselves.

Today, specialized magazines abound. Some of these, such as the city magazines discussed earlier, reach a very particular audience and are concentrated in a specific geographical locale. Others are national in scope but still reach a specialized audience. *Business Week* is an example of the latter. Many national magazines publish regional editions. A restaurant owner in San Francisco needs only buy the western edition of a national magazine and pay only for the limited circulation of the regional edition.

Books

More than any other media, books have stood the test of time. They have a longevity, a substance, an ability to be possessed and cherished, and an ability to communicate knowledge. Books have also been feared for their ability to incite protest and have been suppressed for their ability to be champions of liberty. Newspapers are rarely saved by the average reader; radio and television programs are fleeting; but books survive.

The earliest books were rolls of papyrus attached to two rods that could be unwound from either end. Each roll contained a tag to identify it, and the rolls were placed in cubicle storage compartments much like a wine rack. Sometimes entire books were contained on a single roll. Early libraries, such as those in Rome about the time of Christ, are reported to have contained thousands of volumes. Caesar commanded the building of libraries, some of which contained hundreds of thousands of volumes.

In colonial America, "bookbinders" spent much of their time binding publications for private citizens who possessed the only available copy of a work. Some authors had their own books bound, others wanted Bibles repaired, while still others wanted to buy ledgers and other books in which to record business and financial transactions. With the Industrial Revolution, book publishing advanced and gradually became the mass publishing medium that it is today. The book you are now reading is only part of a long history of textbook publishing that included such distinguished authors as William Holmes McGuffey and his McGuffey *Eclectic Readers.*

Gradually, more and more paperback publishers emerged. Paperback books were cheap to produce, were easy to ship, were portable, and could be purchased at places other than bookstores.

The popularity and the profitability of paperback book publishing have been aided by more aggressive and sophisticated marketing techniques. Television advertising has combined with special events and the novelty manufacturers to develop new promotional themes. Today, a new book may be released with fanfare that includes a press conference and reception, television advertising campaign, author's tour, in-store displays, and novelties ranging from imprinted shirts to balloons and bookbags.

Radio

As early as 1909, Charles David Herrold began to transmit music and voice from his experimental radio station in San Jose, California. It operated as part of Dr. Herrold's School of Radio; the station later evolved into KCBS, licensed in San Francisco. Station WHA at the University of Wisconsin became the first major noncommercial broadcasting station, and regularly scheduled programming began in 1919. Today, the University of Wisconsin system is one of the most developed educational radio systems in the United States.

Commercial stations also signed on the air as radio began to develop in the early 1920s. While KDKA in Pittsburgh is one of the most famous, it does not hold the undisputed title of being first. In Detroit, WWJ, the *Detroit News* station, began intermittent broadcasting on August 20, 1920, by playing two records on an Edison phonograph. KDKA signed on in November, 1920, and has remained on the air ever since. The promotional campaign behind KDKA's sign-on, combined with continuous programming, has managed to give it a firm grip on the public's perception of being the nation's first radio station.

Radio began as a mass medium. Gradually, however, especially in the late 1940s and early 1950s, television began to cut into radio's national audience. The local audience remained, but it needed something other than the radio drama, which had been radio's mainstay. Although some predicted the end of radio, the medium instead reorganized and prospered. National programming was replaced by local programming. The skill and ability of a program director to compete against the growing number of radio stations became the key to success. Today, it is this ability to find the specialized niche among competing stations that gives radio its competitive edge.

Radio programming is dependent on the external and internal factors that affect a station's competitive environment. External factors include news events, new music, other stations in the market, employment, sports events, other media. Stations have little control over many of these external factors. For example, a program director has little control over news events.

A station's internal factors are somewhat easier to control. For example, the station playlist is determined by the program director. If he or she chooses to play the top-ten songs or integrate the songs with news coverage, the choice is an internal management decision. How often the records rotate within the playlist is also an internal decision. The talents of the program director can be crucial, and finding a good program director is always a challenge to management. Similarly, good news directors are difficult to find. Both of these individuals cooperate to provide the best programming possible, and their talents are reflected in all areas of on-air production.

Radio's ability to operate inexpensively and its ability to offer local programming, especially in news, make it an attractive media buy for advertisers and a popular and portable medium for the public.

Television

The television of today, bringing picture-perfect signals into our homes from around the world, began as a crude mechanical contraption of wires and lights that would hardly be recognized next to a modern receiving set. A German scientist, Paul Nipkow, invented a scanning disc system that used photoelectric cells and a rotating disc with holes in it to transmit pictures over short distances—as far as the wires could stretch. Gradually, mechanical television gave way to electronic television. Two men, V. K. Zworykin and Philo Farnsworth, developed separate electronic television systems in the 1920s. Part of each system makes up the components of today's television camera and receiver.

The first programs reflected programming developed by radio. Thus, studio drama became popular by the early 1950s. A pioneer star was Milton Berle on the *Texaco Star Theatre*. New York restaurant owners watched as Tuesday nights brought vacant tables because most of the clientele stayed home to watch "Uncle Milty." *I Love Lucy*, and *The Life of Riley* were two comedy favorites. For children, *Kukla, Fran, and Ollie* and Jack Barry's *Juvenile Jury* and *Mr. Wizard* were favorites.

By the 1960s, television had become a political and social force. The televised debate between Presidential candidates John F. Kennedy and Richard Nixon showed the power of the medium to reach the masses. It also forever changed political campaigning. At the same time that television was becoming a political medium, it was bringing the horror of the Vietnam War into the living rooms of America. For the first time, Americans being slaughtered on the battlefields of a tiny Asian nation spilled into the daily evening news, and the criticism of American foreign policy erupted into civil protest.

Television of the 1970s opened with the situation comedy. Special-interest groups, partially supported by a sympathetic FCC, heard calls for legislation to govern the content of children's television, to place curbs on violent shows, and to give financial support for public broadcasting. Public broadcasting received its financial support, but the First Amendment and its guarantee of free speech prevented wholesale control over television programming. A report by the staff of the U.S. Surgeon General's Office examined the effects of television violence but left as many questions unanswered as answered.

Today, television continues to adapt to new video technologies such as cable. The public in many areas has access to programming other than that offered by the major networks. Music television, all-news and all-sports networks, and local public-access has opened up new possibilities and new competition for traditional television programming.

Motion Pictures

From the inventive mind of Thomas Edison came a workable motion picture camera called the *kinetograph* in 1889. With the assistance of his associate, William Dickson, the two men produced short films in a tarpaper shack at their laboratory in West Orange, New Jersey. The films were shown on a large contraption called the *kinetoscope*.

While the technical aspects of motion picture production continued to be important, more and more attention was paid to the content of the film. A Frenchman, Georges Méliès, added special effects and produced the first science-fiction film, *A Trip to the Moon,* which showed a group of scientists and chorus girls launching a rocket to the moon. Edwin S. Porter, one of Edison's employees, produced *The Great Train Robbery.*

Along with the films came the reputation of the directors. Among them was D. W. Griffith. He had intended to be a serious playwright, but when he was unsuccessful in selling some of his work to the Edison studio, Edwin S. Porter encouraged him to try his hand at acting. More importantly, he was always available as an assistant to the director when an extra hand was needed. After a chance to direct proved successful and impressed the studio heads, other opportunities occurred. He graduated from single-reel films and moved to long epics. Two of his most famous works were *The Birth of a Nation* and *Intolerance,* produced at the pinnacle of his career. An understudy of Griffith named Mack Sennett also went on to fame as a producer and director. With a desire to produce comedies, he developed the comical style of the Keystone Kops. One of his stars, Charlie Chaplin, went on to become the king of silent-film comedy.

As the 1930s arrived, so did color, improved animation, and an industry that was growing to meet the public's insatiable appetite for the silver screen. What started out as *Steamboat Willie* resulted in the introduction of a new star named Mickey Mouse. From Mickey came the film and amusement park empire of Walt Disney. Drama and romance also filled the era. Considered by some to be the greatest American motion picture, *Citizen Kane* (Fig. 17–5) was the brilliant handiwork of director Orson Welles, who also starred in the film. Also critically acclaimed, and much more profitable, was *Gone With the Wind.*

The decades that followed continued to impact the industry. When the 1950s arrived, motion pictures tried a short stint at gimmicks such as 3-D. Gradually the novelty of television wore off. The 1960s, with its accent on youth, saw such films as *The Graduate,* with Dustin Hoffman and Katherine Ross. *Billy Jack* became a cult film that starred Tom Laughlin as an Indian veteran who is rejected by people living near the reservation. Directors, such as Stanley Kubrick, left their mark with films such as *2001: A Space Odyssey.* The 1970s produced its share of science-fiction and disaster epics represented in such works as *The Poseidon Adventure, The Towering Inferno,* and *Earthquake.* But the science-fiction film that ushered in the era of the computerized special effects was *Star Wars.* Its sequels, *The Empire Strikes Back* and *The Revenge of the Jedi,* proved equally popular.

Figure 17-5   As the motion picture industry began to mature in the 1930s, it spawned a number of major films, such as *Citizen Kane*, which remain classics. (National Film Information Service, Academy of Motion Picture Arts and Sciences)

The 1980s saw a readjustment of the motion picture industry after the decade began with the threat of pay-TV eating into studio profits. Some lean years had occurred before the *Star Wars* blockbuster, and many of the larger movie houses closed. Moviegoers found themselves in small-screen theaters in shopping malls, and sale of films to nontheatrical outlets such as videotape outpaced theater revenues.

ADVERTISING AND PUBLIC RELATIONS

Advertising is responsible for much of the commercial content of mass media. But if you are marketing a product or service and are sensitive to the total role played by both media and interpersonal communication, you will include public relations as part of your marketing strategy.

Advertising Agencies

Advertising agencies appeared in the late nineteenth century when newspapers became more and more independent of government printing subsidies and began to rely on advertising for their revenue. Creative talents of the newspaper people were used to design and place ads for merchants, manufacturers, and others with goods and services to sell. Soon, the most talented employees found their skills as valuable in the open marketplace as behind the desk at the newspaper. Independently, these creative people began to form their own organizations, which were the forerunner of today's advertising agencies. As magazines became more and more popular and featured improved graphics and photography, the agencies grew more important.

Advertising agencies have four functions: talent, research, distribution, and monitoring feedback. Talent is the commodity a retailer or manufacturer thinks of first when considering an ad agency. Knowing how to research both the product and the market are also important. For example, if you are going to be responsible for the advertising campaign for a new product, you need to know as much about the product as you can to be able to communicate its strong selling points to the public. But you must also know what segment of the public will use the new product and how to reach that segment. Distribution refers to the message you will design and what media will best distribute the message. If you are advertising something that moves, such as automobiles, you may want to consider television to show off the key features of the product. If the product is intangible, such as financial services, then a different medium might be a more cost-effective buy.

Monitoring feedback means reading key indicators to see if your ad campaign and the products are receiving public acceptance. Knowing basic sales figures is one important part of this monitoring process, but gauging public opinion is equally important. By knowing what people like or dislike about a product or service, and combining this with knowledge about how the public is reacting to the advertising campaign, you can restructure the campaign if necessary.

Public Relations and the PR Campaign

A person involved in public relations can be called by many different titles. "Director of Public Relations," "Public Information Officer," "Coordinator of Public Relations," "Vice-President, Public Relations" are some of the titles held by those whose responsibilities encompass public relations.

Whereas advertising is designed to sell a product or service, public relations is designed to inform the public and create goodwill toward that product or service. A byproduct of that public awareness and goodwill may very well be sales.

Public relations frequently deals directly with gatekeepers who control the flow of information to the public. A new product release is called to the attention of the editor of a trade magazine reaching the audience that will buy the product. Less expense is also a reason why many firms are quick to point out the value of public relations in a complete marketing strategy. Guarding against bad publicity and creating a positive impression of a product or service before bad publicity occurs are two parts of this publicity function.

A well-designed public relations campaign can be as valuable as hundreds of thousands of dollars in advertising. It can create an awareness for a product or service in ways that advertising cannot. A series of commercials might tell the public how community-minded a company is, but having that company sponsor a charitable fund drive, hold a ski tournament for handicapped children, or organize a city clean-up program will do something that advertising cannot.

A public relations campaign begins by analyzing a need. For example, if you are designing a public relations campaign around a theme of carpooling, you would first determine that the need for carpooling exists. Perhaps there's an energy crisis. Perhaps the traffic arteries are overloaded and parking has become a problem. Once the need is established you establish the objectives of the campaign. What do you want to accomplish? Perhaps you want to establish a goal of a certain number of participants in the carpooling program. Or maybe you want to enlist the cooperation of 50 percent of the businesses in your community to join the carpooling effort.

After analyzing the need and establishing objectives it is necessary to develop a plan and pretest the plan. Perhaps the plan includes a series of billboards on key roads leading in and out of the community. After you design the billboards you want to check if the message is effective. Pretesting the plan can range from asking a few people in the office to a complete survey of the public to determine if they can identify the theme of the campaign. With the data obtained in this pretest, the plan is revised and implemented. When the plan is fully operational, evaluation begins. Usually this occurs as early into the execution of the plan as possible. The earlier a problem can be spotted and changed, the better the chance the campaign has of being successful. After the campaign has ended, it is necessary to review the campaign to determine how future campaigns can be improved.

With the increasing number of media, such as cable television, city magazines, and other specialized media, the talent of creative and competent people in advertising and public relations will continue to be in demand. Knowing about the fundamentals of communication, as practiced in a setting of interpersonal communication or mass communication, is necessary in order to function as a responsible practitioner or consumer of media messages.

SUMMARY

Mass communication continues to have an increasingly important impact on our lives. From politics to entertainment, mass media permit us to reach millions of people worldwide with instant information, which less than 100 years ago would have taken weeks and even then would have been confined in many ways to live audiences.

The presence of a mass medium, limited sensory channels, impersonal vs. personal communication, delayed feedback, and the presence of a gatekeeper distinguish mass communication from other forms of communication.

Gatekeepers process information individually and as a group. A gatekeeper can consist of entire organizations, such as a network news division. A number of factors affect the reason gatekeepers choose the information that will eventually reach the public. These factors include economics, such as how profitable a medium may be; legal restrictions, such as libel laws; the presence of deadlines; ethics of gatekeepers and codes of ethics; the competition among media; the value of a news event and the size of the news hole; attention factors affecting a story; peer pressure; and how gatekeepers react to feedback.

The traditional definition of mass communication is changing. Media are becoming more specialized and reach more specialized audiences. Personalized media, such as personal computers, are adding new definitions to the term "mass communication." New technologies are contributing to these new definitions.

Mass media historically represent a wide variety of technologies and issues. Print media, such as newspapers, have had an impact in the United States since colonial times. Magazines also played a part. Books were once hand-copied and stored on large rolls. Later, bindings were added and an accordion-fold replaced the rolls. Paperback books have changed the book publishing industry.

Radio is a highly specialized electronic medium. Television began with a mechanical scanning disc system, and today is a portable medium of entertainment and education. The motion picture camera was perfected at about the same time as the scanning disc television. With the improvements in cameras and projection systems and the talent of directors such as D. W. Griffith, and stars such as Charlie Chaplin, motion pictures matured into a major industry.

Advertising and public relations are responsible for much of the content of media messages. Advertising agencies began to develop in the late nineteenth century as creative individuals working for newspapers began to free-lance and eventually to start their own businesses. Complementing many marketing strategies is a public relations campaign designed to increase public awareness and goodwill toward a product or service. Public relations campaigns involve analyzing a need, establishing objectives, developing a plan, pretesting it, revising and implementing the plan, evaluating effectiveness, and reviewing procedures.

QUESTIONS FOR REVIEW AND DISCUSSION

1. What is meant by the *social context* of mass communication?

2. Describe the difference between a gatekeeper group and a gatekeeper chain.

3. What is the theory of the two-step flow?

4. How can economics affect a gatekeeper's decision making?

5. How can deadlines and competition influence the selection and presentation of news?

6. What is the difference between personal and professional ethics, and how do both affect people working in media?

7. What is the relationship between news value and news hole?

8. How do stories with high attention factors affect gatekeeper decisions?

9. How does peer pressure and the ability to react to feedback influence a gatekeeper?

10. What are some of the highlights in the history of media development?

11. What are the functions of advertising agencies?

12. What is the developmental process used in evaluating a public relations campaign?

LEARNING EXERCISES

1. Along with a small group of your classmates, attend a speech, visit the city council, or witness some other public function at your school or in your community. Write a news story about what you saw and heard. Compare your stories with each other and discuss.

2. Along with a group of other people, discuss what products you use or *why* you chose to see a film at a local theater. In each example, isolate and identify the role that interpersonal communication played in your decision to purchase the product or to attend the motion picture.

ADDITIONAL READINGS

BITTNER, J. R. *Mass Communication: An Introduction* 4th ed. Englewood Cliffs, NJ: Prentice-Hall, 1986.

CHANEY, L., and M. CIEPLY *The Hearsts: Family and Empire-The Later Years.* New York: Simon and Schuster, 1981.

EISENSTEIN, E. L. *The Printing Press as an Agent of Change.* New York: Cambridge University Press, 1980.

EMERY, E., and M. EMERY *The Press and America,* 6th ed. Englewood Cliffs, NJ: Prentice-Hall, 1988.

FORNATALE, P., and J. E. MILES *Radio in the Television Age.* Woodstock, N.Y.: Overlook Press, 1980.

KAPLAN, D. *Video in the Classroom: A Guide to Creative Television.* White Plains, NY: Knowledge Industry Publications, 1980.

KERNS, R. L. *Photojournalism: Photography with a Purpose.* Englewood Cliffs, NJ: Prentice-Hall, 1980.

MARZOLF, M. *Up from the Footnote: A History of Women Journalists.* New York: Hastings House, 1977.

MAY, M. *Screening Out the Past: The Birth of Mass Culture and the Motion Picture Industry.* New York: Oxford University Press, 1980.

MAYES, H. R. *The Magazine Maze.* Garden City, NY: Doubleday, 1980.

STRANG, R. A. *The Promotional Planning Process.* New York: Praeger, 1980.

WADEMAN, V. *Money-Making Advertising: A Guide to Advertising That Sells.* New York: John Wiley, 1981.

GLOSSARY

Abdicrat: A submissive person. His or her control need is best fulfilled by being controlled, not controlling others.

Abstract: Words and sentences that are more complex.

Accenting: Nonverbal messages that highlight certain words or phrases we express verbally.

Adaptors: Body movements that help us to orient ourselves or to adapt to our environment; used more when we are alone.

Adult state: The ego state of the well-adjusted person, the rational thinker.

Advertising agencies: Intermediary businesses that design and place advertising in the mass media.

Affection: An interpersonal need that is much more emotional than *inclusion* or *control* and may include love, infatuation, and intimacy.

Analogy: A form of inference between two different things that are perceived as being alike.

Anchoring: The need for touching behavior later in life.

Argumentative analyses: Messages that, through argument, insight, or presentation of information, dispute a solution.

Assertive: Asking for what you want, telling people how you feel.

Attitudes: Subparts and support mechanisms for values; more narrowly defined than values. See also values.

Attribution: The source to which a quote, fact, or other information is credited.

Audience expectations: What an audience expects from a speech and a speaker.

Authoritarian: Style of a dominant leader in a group discussion.

Autocrat: A person whose decisions may be dogmatic, based on that person's insecurity to maintain control.

Avoiding: The fourth stage in the coming-apart process of a relationship, during which the two people avoid the unpleasantness and pain of seeing each other.

Balance theory: A theory that suggests we seek a balanced psychological state in our relationships with other people. Consists of three elements, a perceiver, a second person, and an object.

Batons: Movements which account for or emphasize a particular word or phrase.

Beliefs: Our personal feelings; can be either basic beliefs, those which are not easily changed, have been positively reinforced over time, and of which we do not seek continual confirmation; or peripheral beliefs, which are not absolute.

Bogeys: Untrue rumors that create fear or lower morale in an organization.

Bonding: The last stage in the coming-together process of a relationship; signifies that commitments have been formally contracted.

Brainstorming: Interpersonal interaction, usually in small groups, with the objective of generating as many ideas into the discussion as possible.

Breadth: The number of different topics of information exchanged between individuals. See also *depth*.

Bridges: Persons responsible for linking the gap between groups.

Bullet theory: Outdated theory of mass communication which posited that people become aware and are persuaded by information from the media. Discounts the role of other people in media persuasion and knowledge acquisition.

Bypass statements: Statements that do not say what we mean; we do not verbalize desired behavior.

Cable television: Television programming delivered from a master antenna to a central cable system, which in turn is fed directly by smaller cable to individual subscribers' homes.

Child state: The ego state in which we act silly, "let ourselves go," and react much as a child would react.

Circles of experience: A way to examine relationships by which we view our different levels of information, from our innermost thoughts and feelings to thoughts we don't mind revealing, such as our favorite colors.

Circumscribing: The second stage in the coming-apart process of a relationship, during which time two people avoid interaction that discusses the relationship.

Clarification: Positive feedback that says, "What you are saying is important to me, and I want to be able to understand it."

Classical approach: An orientation to management in which the emphasis is placed on an "orientation chart"; strong emphasis on downward communication.

Closely knit network: In family communication, those people outside of the family unit with whom at least one member of the family is related.

Cohabitant relationship: Both in verbal and nonverbal communication, a relationship in which interaction plays a small role; there is little commitment from both partners to the relationship itself.

Communication model: A stop-action picture of the communicative process that enables us to look at communication from different perspectives.

Concrete: Words and sentences that are simple and direct.

Conflict: The simultaneous presence of two incompatible goals.

Connotation: The meaning of a word that is less precise and explicit than its denotation.

Consistency theory: A theory that suggests individuals seek a psychological balance. Consistency theory is a common thread running through many theories of persuasion.

Contractive: A mode of speech that we frequently use when we are attempting to initiate "contact" or gain the attention of another person.

Control: An interpersonal need that encompasses a range of behavior that varies from strong or total control of others to no control.

Conversative: A mode of speech in which our language styles approach human interaction.

Corporate culture: The values, beliefs, customs, rituals, life style patterns, and symbols of an organization.

Deep structure: The power structure of an organization where the roles and functions of organizational members are clearly defined. Compare with surface structure, where verbal interaction occurs in small groups and other organizational settings.

Deictic movements: Pointing to an object, place, or event.

Delayed feedback: Feedback received by gatekeepers in the media or by senders of mass communication. Compare with "feedback," which is not delayed in a face-to-face interpersonal encounter.

Democrat: An individual with the ability to understand the feelings and desires of others and, whenever possible, to make decisions that take those feelings into consideration.

Demographics: The vital statistics of an audience dealing with basic characteristics such as sex, age, race, national origin, education, income, group membership, year in school, and similar information.

Denotation: A precise or explicit meaning of a word.

Depth: The degree of intimacy and information exchanged between individuals.

Descriptive: A mode of speech in which words appear in a definite sequence that tells a story or directs someone to do something; same as *directive.*

Differentiating: The first stage in the coming-apart process of a relationship, during which the people involved talk more about what they do not share than what they do share.

Directive: A mode of speech in which words appear in a definite sequence that tells a story or directs someone to do something; same as *descriptive.*

Dissonance theory: A theory that suggests that dissonance produces stress and that individuals experiencing dissonance will move to reduce the stress and avoid additional dissonance.

Downward communication: Formal communication that flows from management down to employees.

Dynamism: The dynamic qualities of a speaker associated with the way he or she delivers a speech.

Dysfunction: A disorder of a bodily system, often produced by the inadequate resolution of conflict or by not overcoming frustration between what we want and what we can obtain.

Ectomorph: A body type best described as tall and skinny.

Ego-defense mechanism: The means we use to keep our self-concept, guard our self-confidence, and protect our ego.

Elaborative: A mode of speech in which language tackles the task of moving from one concept to another, much in the way paragraphs are used in a book.

Emblems: Movements that can be substitutes for words.

Empathize: To enter mentally and with emotion into the feelings of another person; a form of positive feedback.

Endomorph: A body type characterized as being short and fat.

Ethos: The character of the speaker and a central governing principle that separates the speaker from other speakers. See *pathos, logos.*

Evaluation: Positive feedback that is normally objective and free from personal emotion or biased opinion, and is separated from the person with whom we are talking.

Ever-ready expressor: A person whose face "says it first"—that is, a person very expressive at the slightest reaction to emotion or any other stimulus.

Exit phase: The third and final phase of the developmental process of interpersonal interaction, during which the people involved might make a decision as to whether or not to continue their relationship.

Experimenting: The second stage in the coming-together process of a relationship, during which people exchange basic information about each other.

Expressions of disunity: Messages showing disagreement or rejection.

Expressions of personal involvement: Messages relating personal experience, affection, commitment, or personal dilemma.

Expressions of unity: Messages showing agreement or acceptance.

External networks: Communication networks that carry information beyond the confines of the employees or people who make up the organization (that is, communication channels with the news media).

Fallacy: In logic an incorrect assumption based on an error in the major or minor premise.

Family: An organized system of interaction based on changing relationships between people who may live together.

Federal Communications Commission: Federal regulatory agency controlling electronic communication.

Feedback: Information received back in response to information verbally or nonverbally imparted.

Feeler: An emotional, sensitive person who likes emotional involvement with people and may lead a more carefree life than the thinker.

Fields of experience: Personal experiences

which are common references that aid in processing both intrapersonal and interpersonal communication.

Firm pattern: Communication within a family designed to keep order and stability; one member of the family has control over other family members.

Formal networks: Communication networks operationally defined by organization charts, appointed committees, and other identifiable characteristics known by management and employees.

Frustration: An obstacle to achieving a goal.

Gatekeeper: Anyone controlling the flow of information via a mass medium. A gatekeeper can expand or shrink our informational environment.

Goal listening: Beginning to establish listening goals for ourselves.

Grapevines: Informal communication networks that have become synonymous with carrying rumors.

Heterophily: Dissimilarities between two people that play a role in communication patterns; the individuals' fields of experience do not overlap.

Homestretchers: Rumors which anticipate something.

Homophily: That point at which two people communicating have things in common with each other; their fields of experience overlap.

Horizontal communication: Communication between people at similar levels of responsibility within an organization.

Human-relations approach: In organizational theory, running a company in a democratic way, putting the stress on everyone's being satisfied.

Human-resources approach: An organizational theory which recognizes that individuals within the company have talents which can be nurtured to increase their productivity and improve their effectiveness.

Ideographs: Movements that sketch the path or direction of thought.

Illustrators: Movements, such as hand gestures, which complement what we say.

Impression management: Choosing to present ourselves in a certain way to another person, either verbally or nonverbally.

Impulsive: A mode of speech that is characterized by short utterances without the need for complex language structure.

Inclusion: An interpersonal need to belong, to participate, to be acknowledged.

Informal networks: Communication networks operating outside established and identifiable channels in organizations.

Information diffusion: The flow of information, usually from the mass media to other people, who then tell others and relay the information through a social system. See *two-step flow.*

Initiating: The beginning stage of any relationship, whether it lasts a lifetime or a few minutes; the first contact with another.

Inoculation theory: We can become psychologically conditioned to resist certain persuasive messages that are not openly debated or overly controversial.

Integrating: The fourth stage in the coming-together process of a relationship, when the people involved and those around them begin to view them more as partners than as individuals; they have a commitment to interaction.

Intensifying: The third stage in the coming-together process of a relationship, during which more personal information is exchanged and nonverbal information plays a larger role.

Internal networks: Communication, either formal or informal, that operates within an organization.

Interpersonal communication: Encoding information, communicating it verbally or nonverbally to another person, and receiving information back in return.

Intrapersonal communication: Communication within ourselves.

Intuitor: An imaginative individual, but one who can also be impatient with people who do not immediately see the value or lack of it in something or someone.

Isolates: People most removed from the decision-making process.

Job instruction: Directives from management that are part of an organization's downward communication.

Journalism reviews: Publications serving a watch-dog role over the news media.

Kinetographs: Movements depicting bodily action or some nonhuman physical action.

Laissez-faire: A "hands-off" style of leadership in group discussion.

Language intensity: Expressing strong opinions and emotional involvement with an issue.

Language style: The use of different words and the respective arrangement of those words.

Leadership: Influential behavior accepted by group members; it moves a group toward its recognized goal and/or maintains the cohesiveness of the group.

Leaking: Unauthorized communication in which an employee takes a grievance or complaint to the public or the press. See also *whistle blowing.*

Liaisons: The "linkers" of information in a communication network, both in transmitting and receiving information between groups.

Logos: Appeal to logic and reasoning. See *ethos, pathos.*

Loosely knit network: In family communication, those people who have limited emotional involvement and contact with family members.

Management philosophy: Directives and other downward communication in an organization that describe the philosophy of management. Frequently transmitted in executive speeches, memoranda, and in-house newsletters.

Mass communication: Communication in which the presence of a mass medium helps carry the message between a sender and a receiver; the message is controlled by a gatekeeper; the sender and receiver are not in close proximity to each other; the sender and receiver are limited in the number of sensory channels they can use to process the information, and feedback is delayed.

Memory: A form of intrapersonal communication that retrieves and encodes information stored in our brains.

Mesomorph: A body type best described as muscular and athletic and physically fit.

Minus-minus conflicts: Serious conflicts that require us to face two conflicting goals, both of which are undesirable.

Modes of speech: The way words are joined together in particular patterns to accomplish different communication goals.

Mutual gaze: The action and contact of two people's eyes, usually in an intense conversation.

Negative stroking: Verbal or nonverbal com-

munication that makes us feel intimidated, hurt, and uncomfortable.

News hole: An imaginary hole represented by the amount of time and space that is available to news stories in competition with other news stories of varying importance.

News value: The value of a news event in relation to other news events.

Nonliaisons: Group members who do not have contact with other groups.

Open pattern: Communication within a family that allows the family to function in an open atmosphere of discussion, working toward each individual's autonomy and needs, while not sacrificing the interdependence or cohesiveness of the family unit.

Opinion leader: A person who influences another person's decisions, attitudes, and behavior; a person whose judgment we trust and whom we seek for advice.

Orderless pattern: Communication within a family in which each member of the family is given as much freedom as possible to seek out his or her strengths and communicate feelings to other family members.

Organizational plan: How a speech is organized around its main points and subheadings. Spatial, chronological, problem-solving, cause-effect, and related topics and combinations of plans are used.

Organizational policy: As discussed in this text, a form of upward communication where employees voice their opinions about how an organization should operate. Can also be communicated downward by management as rules and regulations.

Orthodox relationship: The traditional relationship in which each partner functions in the "we" state with little individuality.

Overpersonal: A person who may be overbearing in social relationships.

Paraconflict: Conflict that is conceived, whether or not it actually exists.

Paralanguage: The way we use the sound of our voice to utter words; includes voice quality, resonance, and tempo.

Parent state: The ego state in which we tend to be very directive in our communication and behavior, much as a parent reacting to a young child.

Participant style: High-involvement leadership style in group discussion.

Pathos: Appeal to one's emotion. See also *logos, ethos.*

Performance appraisal: Downward communication in an organization in which an employee is evaluated by a supervisor.

Personal: A person who has satisfactory relationships centering around affection.

Personal phase: The second phase of the developmental process of interpersonal interaction, during which discussion might stress more personal issues, such as our attitudes and beliefs.

Personal space: The area surrounding us that is concerned with psychological traits rather than the physical structures of territorial space; influences the way we communicate with others.

Phatic communications: Messages showing superficial interest; often joking or accommodating.

Physical noise: Sounds which may interrupt the communication process.

Physiognomy: The mostly unscientific study of the face as an indicator of personality types.

Pictographs: Early wall etchings on the insides of caves and temples. Also movements that draw a picture in the air of the shape of the referent.

Pipe dreams: Rumors that are best described as wishful thinking.

Plus-minus conflicts: Conflicts that require us to approach a positive goal but simultaneously acquire something negative.

Plus-plus conflicts: Those conflicts that are the easiest to resolve and produce the least strain; resolving them will not seriously affect our self-concept.

Primary source: The original or first-reported source of information. See also *secondary source.*

Problem-solving groups: Small groups which seek solutions to problems, either by implementing those solutions or recommending them.

Procedural communications: Messages dealing with problem-solving methods, criteria for making decisions, clarity of wording, or comments on the experimental situation.

Psychographics: The psychological makeup of an audience, such as values, beliefs, opinions, attitudes, mental images, perceptions, and similar information.

Ratios: One unit of analysis divided by another.

Referent: An image in our minds to which we

refer when we encounter a word or symbol (flower = symbol; rose = referent).

Revealers: People whose emotions show readily on their faces.

Rhythmic movements: Movements which depict the rhythm or pacing of an event.

Rumors: Sometimes difficult-to-confirm information passed through informal channels of communication.

Secondary source: A report of information that has been first reported elsewhere. See also *primary source.*

Selective disclosure: Choosing which information we tell others about ourselves, dependent on how well we know the person.

Selective exposure: Choosing to come in contact with communication from others we perceive to possess certain beliefs, frequently similar to our own.

Selective perception: Hearing and consequently perceiving what is many times determined by our preconceived notions about someone or something.

Selective retention: Retaining or remembering only that communication which we perceive as important to us or with which we agree.

Self-appraisal: Upward communication in an organization where employees describe their performance with supervisors.

Self-concept: The way we feel about ourselves.

Self-disclosure: Divulging information about ourselves, our values, our attitudes, and our beliefs to see how other people are reacting to our self-concept.

Semantic noise: A misunderstanding of the meanings of words, which may interrupt the communication process.

Semantics: The science of meanings, originating from the Greek words for *significant* and *sign.*

Sensing: Using all of our senses to absorb everything we can about the person talking to us.

Sensor: An individual who likes to absorb the things around him or her using all of the senses.

Sequential structure: The independence of messages in sequence to one another.

Sharing relationship: A relationship in which sharing takes place between individuals, but in which each partner retains a great deal of autonomy in his or her life.

Social judgment theory: A theory that suggests our attitudes are situational and anchored in our initial perceptions to the world around us.

Source credibility: How the audience perceives the speaker's dynamism, character, and authoritativeness.

Spatial movements: Movements depicting spatial relationships.

Specialized media: Mass media reaching specialized audiences. Radio and magazines are examples of specialized media.

Specific purpose: A statement that clearly identifies the purpose and content of a speech.

Stagnating: The third stage in the coming-apart process of a relationship, during which the partners begin to feel uncomfortable with each other and conversations are most likely unpleasant.

Statistics: Numerical data usually grouped in summary form.

Stereotyping: Prejudging a person on the basis of prejudices attributed to groups or individuals.

Stroking: The supportive process for our egos, which can consist of both verbal and nonverbal communication; something many of us seek in everyday life to confirm what we say and do; can be in the form of negative stroking.

Substitute expressors: People who show a different facial expression from what they are feeling.

Supportive analyses: Messages that, through argument, insight, or presentation of information, confirm a solution.

Surface structure: Dialogue that takes place in small groups and other interaction settings in organizations. Compare with *deep structure*, where the power of an organization operates in the roles and functions of the organization's members.

Switching listening styles: Changes in the way we process messages by using four basic cognitive or mental switches: agree, disagree, think, or question.

Syllogism: The three parts of deductive reasoning consisting of a major premise, minor premise, and conclusion.

Systems approach: An organizational theory that states that people and divisions within organizations are functionally dependent and interrelated to each other.

Task-oriented groups: Small groups which set out to accomplish specific goals.

Terminating: The last stage in the coming-apart process of a relationship, during which the verbal and nonverbal rituals signal the end of the relationship.

Territorial space: The area around us that is defined by physical boundaries and which affects the way we communicate with others.

T-groups: Encounter groups that engage in primarily intensive communicative experiences; generally consist of well-functioning individuals who are seeking greater competence in their ability to experience life.

Therapeutic groups: Groups that bring people together for the purpose of enhancing their abilities to deal with others, and with life in general.

Thinker: A person who is deliberate in thought and action, is businesslike, and lives a highly structured life.

Transaction: The sending, receiving, and sending back of information to the sender as a form of feedback.

Two-step flow: Information travelling from the mass media to another person, who then tells someone else. Step one is the media, step two is the person who communicates the information to another person.

Underpersonal: A person who relates very superficially to others.

Upward communication: Formal communication that flows from employee upward to management.

Value hierarchy: The ranking of one's individual values.

Values: Broad-based qualities of the individual that are held as important and which affect behavior.

Verbal immediacy: The degree with which we associate ourselves with a message.

Visual aid: Photographs, charts, and other illustrations used to add a visual dimension to a speech.

Wedge-drivers: Rumors that divide or relay untrue and damaging information.

Whistle blowing: External communication that management does not control.

Withholders: People who keep their feelings from appearing on their faces.

APPENDIX A
SAMPLE SPEECH
WITH QUESTIONS
FOR ANALYSIS
AND DISCUSSION

THE FUTURE OF SPORTS IN AMERICAN SOCIETY*

By Larry Gerlach, Professor of History, University of Utah

1. Before I begin my remarks, I would like to let you know where I am coming from in terms of interest in sports. I was on my way to Cooperstown by way of the New York Yankees when I discovered as a freshman at the University of Nebraska that I could no longer throw or hit a curve ball. I then bent upon a career in football and I was going to play, believe it or not, with the Detroit Lions. Except as a freshman at the University of Nebraska, I got hurt. I was not injured; I was only hurt. People kept beating the hell out of me, and I decided that what I would then do is turn to history.

2. I always had an interest in sport but it was not considered to be academically respectable in those days. When I got to the University of Utah, intent on staying a year or two—that was 15 years ago—I got involved with the athletic program, was a member of the athletic board for some eight years and

* Speech to the Warren P. Williamson Symposium, Youngstown State University, Youngstown, Ohio, October 25, 1983. Published in Larry Gerlach, "Telecommunications and Sports," *Vital Speeches*, March 15, 1984.

began at that time to very seriously cultivate an interest in understanding sport as a social, political, and economic phenomenon in our society.

3. My remarks today will constitute remarks, not a paper. I wrote a paper three weeks ago on television and intercollegiate sports and then when the program for this symposium arrived I realized that there was a session devoted to that so I tore it up and wrote another paper. A couple of days ago I had a fight with my son about sports and I wrote another paper. What I did this weekend is take parts of the three papers and put them together, the idea being that I would not try to present any kind of definitive statement about sport but rather throw out a number of ideas that we might discuss.

4. Each spring I teach a course entitled "The History of Sport in America." The course draws extremely well with 300 or 400 students. It is the only course I teach where the students come convinced of the importance of the subject at hand and are deeply interested in exploring the topic at great length.

5. The first day of class I ask two questions: What is sport? What is athletics? I am not especially bothered when most students respond to my questions by casting their eyes downward in the unmistakable, "please don't call on me" message of body language. But I am perplexed that without exception my students who cover sports for the local campus newspaper have no idea as to the nature of that about which they write. And I am absolutely amazed that the 40 or 50 varsity athletes in class have no intellectual comprehension of the activity which brought them to the university in the first place and which constitutes the driving force of their collegiate lives.

6. Sport, I am convinced, is the best known yet least understood phenomenon in American society. Much of our misunderstanding and misconceptions about sports stems from our failure to make meaningful distinctions among the various components of the sport world. And I don't want to get into a long definitional discussion here, except to highlight the difference between our two major sport phenomenon.

7. One is sport. Sport is an extension of play involving two or more persons. Sport turns on games and contests which are highly organized, competitive, characterized by the established rules, but like play, sport has as its primary purpose fun for the participant.

8. Athletics, on the other hand, derives not from play at all, but from work. Athletics, as they have been referred to from the ancient Greeks on, refers to intensely competitive confrontation between specially trained performers whose primary objectives are: (a) spectator entertainment and (b) victory. Although the game involved in sport and athletics may be the same as, for example, basketball, the two activities are worlds apart in terms of purpose and attitude. And to make this very complicated thing exceedingly simple, I would simply call your attention to the obvious difference that we understand between intramural sport and intercollegiate athletics.

9. My reason for raising the definitional issue is not to confuse but to clarify. The fundamental truth is that modern American society is preoccupied not with sport but with athletics. This symposium is in fact misnamed; the telecommunications industry is interested in athletic contests not sporting events. However, today I will defer to convention and use sport and athletics interchangeably.

10. Two fundamental and basically irreconcilable philosophical conflicts color our involvement with sport. First of these is while we extol the amateur sportsman we insist that our performers be professional athletes. Second, we want sport to be fun and to be purposeful. Now the amateur/professional dichotomy we can talk about later if you'd like. Today, in trying to determine the sort of role or why the emphasis on sport in American Society, I would like to look at that second phenomenon.

11. Purposeful sport; although we persist in paying lip service to the fun or the recreational dimension of sport, the historical record clearly shows that Americans have always considered sports to be primarily a serious, that is, a purposeful activity. The roots for purposeful play extend deep into our past to the inability of New England Puritans to distinguish between work and play, to the efforts of pre-Civil War reformers and child-guidance writers to promote sport as a means of developing ethical values and character traits, discipline, courage, teamwork necessary for success in a modernizing society, to the attempts of the late nineteenth century to utilize sport as a means of Americanizing immigrants, controlling the frustrations of industrial laborers, and ensuring the physical fitness of a virile nation on the global make, and to the recent systematic efforts of the government to employ sport as the mechanism of chauvinism, military preparedness, and international diplomacy.

12. Surely our emphasis on sport in modern America stems in large measure from the basic fact that Americans view sport as a serious, purposeful enterprise related to the fundamental well-being of society at large. We still hear, and this is why I had a fight with my son, ad nauseam, such mindless prattling as "sports builds character" when the very actions of the lords of sport give lie to that simple-minded rhetoric.

What is the large significance of our insistence on purposeful sport? I would like to quote to you and then comment on two observations, one from a student of American culture and another from a sports writer. The first, the student of American culture, Christopher Lash, who wrote an issue entitled, "The Corruption of Sport." And Chris Lash made this observation:

> The degradation of sports consists in its subjugation to some ulterior purpose, such as profit making, patriotism, moral training or the pursuit of health. Sport may give rise to these things in abundance but ideally it produces them only as by-products having no essential connection with the game.

And second is Robert Lipsyte, former sports writer for *The New York Times:*

> For the past 100 years most Americans believe that playing and watching competitive games are not only healthful activities but represent a positive force on our national psyche. This faith in sport has been vigorously promoted by industry, the military government, and the media. The values of the arena and the locker room have been imposed on our national life. Even for ball games these

values with their implicit definitions of manhood, courage, and success are not necessarily in the individual's best interest, but for daily life they tend to create a dangerous and grotesque web of ethics and attitudes. The sport experience has been perverted into a sport world state of mind in which the winner was good because he won and the loser, if not actually bad, was at least reduced and had to prove himself over again through competition (i.e., Roberto Duran). Sport World is a grotesque distortion of sport, it limits the pleasure of play for most Americans while concentrating on turning our best athletes into clowns. It makes the finish more important than the race.

Well, among modern students of sport and society, terms like corruption, distortion, grotesque, and degradation are watchwords. Surely these are among the by-products of purposeful sport in America today.

13. The problems associated with purposeful sport have always been with us, but as we move during the past three centuries from informal folk games and recreations before the Civil War to organized commercial sport after the Civil War to the era of national sport industries today, those problems have been increasingly troublesome. . . . Just as television is responsible for the creation of the modern sport industry, television has contributed fundamentally to the problem of modern sport. The impact of television is manyfold.

14. First of all, promotional. The enormous capacity of television to reach people has sold sport. If TV moguls devote so much programming time to sport it must be important. If television devotes virtually an entire day to covering the Super Bowl, then that contest must be important. And by extension, sport itself must be very important. I would suggest that sport is regarded as being much more influential in our society than it really is because of the attention that television pays to it.

15. The second is financial. Television, with its national marketing capabilities, has brought unbelievable wealth to the world of sport and created nothing short of a sport industry. The result has been an extraordinary proliferation of sport franchises and leagues—the major leagues, baseball, the National Football League, the NBA. When I was a kid, that is in the 1950s, there was no resemblance to these institutions today. The result is greatly expanded playing schedules and the domination of sport not by the gentlemen sportsmen of the pre-WWII era, but by corporate executives. Once there was a Tom Yawkey and now there is a George Steinbrenner. It is often said—it is a cliche—that money is the root of all evil and so it is with the world of sport.

16. Television, third, has fundamentally intruded on sport by directly affecting the contests themselves. Baseball's league championship series and nighttime World Series, football's absurd playoffs, and the hyperbolic Super Bowl, even NCAA's utterly reprehensible mass postseason basketball tournament, are due to television payoffs. Contests start at times that conflict fundamentally with common sense and the interest of performers because of television payoffs. My friend Bear Bryant says, "I'll play any time, anywhere, if the price is right." Basketball now incorporates TV timeouts in a way that fundamentally affects the strategy and execution of the game. The New York Jets defeated the San Diego Chargers earlier this season thanks in part to a referee's concern about a TV commercial. Two-minute warnings in professional football games are there simply to provide one more commercial opportunity. The point is that television does not merely broadcast games; television manipulates the games.

17. Fourth, television broadcasts a distorted image of sport. Television promotes an illusion of sport, its values, its importance, its role in society, that is at odds, I think, with reality. Television is not concerned with sport but with professional athletics. Television made the National Football League. Television made the National Basketball Association. Television made the golf and professional tours. At the time of WWII, there was no stable NFL, there was no systematic professional basketball in this country, there was no golf tour, there was no tennis tour. And today when most Americans think of sport they think of professional televised sport. And it is not surprising, I think, that the sports that are televised are the ones that televise best. The coverage of sport in your local newspaper is a far more accurate view of American's interest in sport than the broadcast schedules of the national networks. Although I keep complaining about the coverage in my local paper, the sports editors know the real world of sport.

18. Fifth, television promotes a perverse concept of athletism as the norm in sport world. The pros have become the models, and the value of the pro game becomes the values of the sport generally. I think that is obvious to anyone who has watched youth or high school sports and those youngsters slavishly imitating the pros. The athlete is a conspicuous minority among the inhabitants of sport world, yet the athlete sets the tone due to television. Moreover, the incredible hype of television promotes a larger-than-life concept of sport in which winning triumphs over participation.

19. Do not underestimate sport think, which has fundamentally and, I think, cruelly defined my son's self-image and his world view. Now, as to the future of this, the pro games will go on albeit in somewhat diminished form. I think we can put up with only so much shock, so much pimping, so much hype, and frankly so much bulla. Ratings are down for Monday night football whether it is Monday Night Football on Monday, Monday Night Football on Wednesday, Monday Night Football on Thursday, Monday Night Football on Friday, Monday Night Football on Saturday, or Monday Night Football on Sunday. Television has made sport almost a caricature, a grotesqueness of cheap commercialism where the broadcast all to often overshadows the contest. Monday Night Football is only the most gross offender. The likelihood is that network coverage will diminish in favor of cable broadcasting, which focuses more closely on the contest per se.

20. The greatest impact of television has been on intercollegiate athletics. Television in the next decade promises to accomplish what university presidents, athletic directors, and coaches have been trying to do for the last 100 years, namely, destroy intercollegiate athletics as an academic amateur sports enterprise. The open professionalism of intercollegiate athletics will, if nothing else, end the rampant corruption and blatant hypocrisy that currently afflict the collegiate sport establishment.

21. In 1873, Andrew D. White, president of Cornell University, responded thusly to a request by Cornell footballers to travel to Michigan for a game. "I will not permit 30 men to travel 400 miles merely to agitate a bag of wind." Three years later John Bascom, president of the University of Wisconsin, responding to student and alumni pressure for increased athletic programs as entertainment, said, "If athletics is needed for amusement, we should hire a few persons as we do clowns to set themselves apart to do this work."

22. Well, in the intervening years, university presidents learned about the money to be made from intercollegiate sport if not directly then indirectly through alumni donations and so on, and 100 years later, my friend Bear Bryant made the following statement, "I used to go along with the idea that football players on scholarships were student athletes, which is what the NCAA calls them, meaning a student first, an athlete second." We are, of course, kidding ourselves, trying to make it more palatable to the academician. We don't have to say that anymore and we shouldn't. At the level we play, the boy is really an athlete first and a student second. When men like Joe Paterno of Penn State and Tom Osborn of Nebraska agree to play a kickoff classic in August in East Rutherford, New Jersey, after publicly arguing that game was against the best interest of the program and their players, the collegiate sport scene is in sad shape.

23. Well, I ducked the basic issue here, which is the great appeal of sport today and I wrote some remarks which are intended to be provocative. And I wrote them after watching a Lite Beer commercial, which kind of puts the whole thing together. Mr. Butkus and Mr. Smith, trying to achieve a modicum of class and culture, have gone to the opera. Well, I wonder why the great appeal of sports today. I think it is very simple. Sport accurately reflects American society, its frustrations, its fantasies, its cultural values. The arena is at once apart from and a part of everyday life. But, of course, the same thing is true for a variety of other activities, i.e., the opera, so what is the special appeal of sport? My son asked me about the comment he hears always that sport is simply children's games played by adults. He said, "Is that right?" And I think that is right and I think that is why sport plays such a very important role in our society.

24. Four reasons: Sport is pure. That is, sport is the only nonideological cultural activity in our society, or any society. Literature, art, music, dance, all of these activities are value laden. Sport is only a kinetic enterprise. There is no value represented as two athletes line up to run 100 meters. It is pure. It is innocent. It is basic.

25. Second, sport is elemental and elementary. It involves confrontation between obvious good guys—my team, and obvious bad guys—your team. That conflict is cleanly, finely, and clearly resolved through the use of physical force. The more physical the game, the more popular the game. One defeats opponents literally by beating them, and that is the basic mechanism of conflict resolution. It is, in a word, a kind of Star Wars mentality.

26. Third, sport is simple and simplistic. It is the cultural activity in our society that is wholly intelligible to the lowest common denominators in society. My 13-year-old can discuss basketball on an equal basis with me. It is the ideal cultural activity in a democracy rather like the public school system. It is intelligible, too, and embraceable by all elements in the culture.

27. And fourth, sport, to continue the childhood metaphor, is fantastic. That is, sport turns on illusion, on fantasy, on dreams whether dreams of future glory of nostalgic remembrances of glories that once were or might have been. I think it symbolic that the relationship between journalism, particularly broadcast journalism, and sport is so evident and that the majority of TV addicts, Star Wars freaks, fairy tale fanatics, and sports fans in this country are children. Sport represents in large part the maintenance of childlike innocence and values in a harsh, cynical adult world.

28. Speaking of kids, to wind up my formal remarks, whatever the reality of sport and sport personalities, in my youth there were perceived heroes, perceived exalted values to sport participation. That's why I ate and slept and breathed sport. As a youth, I viewed sport as a blissful refuge from everyday life. Today my son views sports as a component of the cheapness, tackiness, selfishness, corruption of everyday life. The tragedy is that where I once believed, my son and his friends have never believed. Fantasy has always been an essential, perhaps the essential, element in sport. If sport loses its illusions and becomes part and parcel of reality, I fear very much about the future of sport in American society.

Thank you.

QUESTIONS FOR ANALYSIS

1. How does the speaker's introduction appeal to the audience, and does it contribute to homophily?

2. How does it contribute to the speaker's credibility?

3. When is humor first used in the speech?

4. Do you think it was effective?

5. What appeal is employed in paragraph 5—logos, pathos, or ethos?

6. How does the distinction between sport and athletics in paragraphs 7 and 8 contribute to the speech? To holding the audience's attention?

7. In paragraph 10, what purpose does the use of the term "we" serve, such as in: "First of these is while we extol the amateur . . ."?

8. What organizational plan is employed in paragraph 11?

9. Are the quotations employed in paragraph 12 appropriate for the point the speaker is trying to make?

10. What organizational plan did the speaker choose in paragraph 13?

11. In paragraph 14, what organizational plan(s) did the speaker use?

12. In paragraph 14, to what syllogism does the speaker allude? How sound is the reasoning?

13. Read the last sentence of paragraph 10. If this were a main point how would you organize paragraphs 11, 12, and 13?

14. What organizational plan is employed in paragraphs 14 through 18?

15. What organizational plan does the speaker use in the first two sentences of paragraph 15?

16. In paragraph 19, how does the more intense use of language affect the speech? At this point in the speech, if a member of the audience were agreeing with the speaker, how do you feel that person would respond to paragraph 19? If the person were disagreeing?

17. What organizational plan does the speaker use in paragraphs 24 through 27?

18. Evaluate the effectiveness of the speaker's conclusion.

19. If you had been in the audience, do you think you would have enjoyed the speech?

APPENDIX B
CLASSROOM ACTIVITY
NEGOTIATING A LABOR CONTRACT

Objective: To better understand the communication process by participating in collective bargaining.

INTRODUCTION

Perhaps the most publicized form of negotiation in our society is the labor negotiation. Although we read about labor negotiations and hear a great deal about them on radio and television, few of us have ever participated in collective bargaining. This exercise permits part of the class to play the role of both union and management negotiators. The remainder of the class consists of groups of six students each, with each group functioning as an arbitration board.

CLASS STRUCTURE

Two groups of six students each play the role of union and management negotiators. The remainder of the class is divided into groups of approximately six students per group, with each group functioning as an arbitration board. The instructor serves as a "parliamentarian" between the union and management negotiating groups.

DIRECTIONS

Six participants will serve as the union representatives and six will serve as the management representatives. Arrange a long table so six students from one team can face-off with the participants of the other team. The remainder of the class, also divided into groups which serve as arbitration boards, remain in their seats and observe the negotiations. Individually, the following roles are assumed by the students in the union and the students in the management negotiation groups: lawyer, accountant, union/management president (one president per negotiating group), and three chief negotiators per group.

In a class period prior to the exercise, the negotiation teams and the arbitration boards should study the following information:

Specter Corporation, a manufacturer of high-technology guidance systems, has three months remaining on a contract with the Microchip Installers Union. The current contract provides for an hourly wage of $12, two weeks' vacation per year, one week sick leave, and company-paid medical and dental coverage with a $100 deductible clause.

Last year, Specter had a break-even year because of another company infringing on its trademark and dumping Specterlike chips on the market. The case is still pending. Imports also threaten Specter's share of the market.

Specter's latest annual report shows the following information pertinent to the negotiations:

Gross income before taxes:	$500,000,000
Amount paid out in compensation:	$300,000,000
Taxes: Local, State, Federal	$100,000,000
Research and development	$50,000,000
First year of a 15-year depreciation schedule on a new assembly plant	$50,000,000

The union is asking for an increase in wages to $15 an hour, equal to Specter's nearest competitor, located in the same community. In addition, the union is asking three weeks' vacation per year for workers with ten years of service, and four weeks' vacation per year for workers over 60 years of age. The union wants Specter to absorb the $100 deductible from medical/dental coverage. A tuition credit plan is also being requested, which would mean that Specter would provide scholarships of $100 per year for four years for employees' children who maintain a C average while carrying a full academic load at an accredited college.

After the information about the negotiations and the financial data has been made available to the class, the negotiating teams *and* the arbitration boards meet and plan their strategies before the class meeting when the negotiations are to take place. (Note: The arbitration boards should propose the terms of a settlement but keep it secret until called upon by the instructor.)

The negotiations begin with a statement (no more than 30 seconds) by each of the respective negotiators (have each student stand). First, the president of Specter, then the president of the union, addresses the group, then the accountants address the group, followed by the lawyers, and then negotiators 1, 2, and 3 for the management and union teams, respectively.

The instructor should be positioned at the head of the table as a parliamentarian and should only recognize one participant at a time during the negotiations.

A settlement must be reached by the end of the class period or the arbitration board will be forced to decide at the next class meeting what the terms of the settlement should be.

If a settlement is not reached, at the next class meeting the arbitration boards discuss their proposed settlement. If a settlement is reached, each board reports what its strategy might have been if it had been asked to intervene.

NOTES

CHAPTER 1

1. J.D. Robinson, "The Paradox of Communications in an Information Society." Speech delivered before the American Advertising Federation, Washington, D.C., June 11, 1979.

2. J.W. Carey, "High-Speed Communication in an Unstable World," *The Chronicle of Higher Education,* (July 27, 1983), 48.

3. See J. Curley, "Some Firms Switch From Bathing Beauties to Savvy New Sales Forces at Trade Shows," *The Wall Street Journal,* (September 1, 1982), 17.

4. J.C. Hafer and C.C. Hoth, "Selection Characteristics: Your Priorities and How Students Perceive Them," *Personnel Administrator,* (March, 1983), 26.

5. J. Muchmore and K. Galvin, "A Report of the Task Force on Career Competencies in Oral Communication Skills for Community College Students Seeking Immediate Entry into the Work Force," *Communication Education,* 32 (April 1983), 207–20.

6. "Text of the College Board's Outline of the Basic Academic Subjects," *The Chronicle of Higher Education,* (May 18, 1983), 14.

7. One of the earliest models is discussed in C.E. Shannon and W. Weaver, *The Mathematical Theory of Communication* (Urbana: University of Illinois Press, 1949) p. 98.

8. The psychological basis for intrapersonal communication can be found in a number of sources. Helpful to my discussion of this material was: S. Worchel, and W. Schebilske, *Psychology* (Englewood Cliffs, N.J.: Prentice-Hall, 1983). Material on the basic nervous system can be found on pages 35–38; material on perception can be found on pages 65–87.

9. See *The Chronicle of Higher Education,* reporting the research by F.C. Volkmann, L.A. Riggs, and R.K. Moore and reference to the original report, which appeared in the February 22, 1981 issue of *Science.*

10. *Indianapolis Star,* July 6, 1980, reporting the work of University of California scientists J. Ruesch

and A.R. Priestwood, reported by J. Gibson, "Understanding People: Biggest Worries Vary with Worrier's Age, Finances, and Health."

11. See also the section on selective perception in Chapter 5.

12. Various explanations of the mass communication process have been advanced over the years. G.R. Miller compared it to interpersonal communication in "The Current Status of Research in Interpersonal Communication," *Human Communication Research,* (Winter 1978), 164–78.

13. For example, R.K. Avery and T.A. McCain, "Interpersonal and Mediated Encounters: A Reorientation to the Mass Communication Process," in *Inter/Media: Interpersonal Communication in a Media World,* 2nd ed., eds. G. Gumpert and R. Cathcart, p. 30. For a perspective on the relationship of interpersonal and mass communication see also R. Cathcart and G. Gumpert, "Mediated Interpersonal Communication: Toward A New Typology," *Quarterly Journal of Speech,* 69 (1983), 267–77. A perspective on the concept of "feedback" in public speaking instruction can be found in C.L. Book, "Providing Feedback: The Research on Effective Oral and Written Feedback Strategies," *Central States Speech Journal,* 36 (Spring/Summer 1985), 14–23.

CHAPTER 2

1. C. Rogers, *On Becoming a Person: A Therapist's View of Psychotherapy* (Boston: Houghton Mifflin, 1970).

2. A.H. Maslow, *Motivation and Personality,* 2nd ed. (New York: Harper & Row, 1970).

3. Adapted from, among others, L. Thomas, *A Manual for the Differential Value Profile* (Ann Arbor: Educational Service Company, 1966), p. 6. All the authors recognize the contributions of Rokeach to the development of theoretical constructs associated with values, attitudes, and beliefs as they affect the individual's self-concept. See M. Rokeach, *Beliefs, Attitudes, and Values: A Theory of Organization and Change* (San Francisco: Jossey-Bass, 1969); M. Rokeach, *The Nature of Human Values* (New York: The Free Press, 1973); J.R. Bittner, "A Comparison and Analysis of the Value Profiles of a State vs. State Supported College" (unpublished honor's thesis, Dakota Wesleyan University, 1967).

4. Thomas, *Differential Value Profile.* Test instructions.

5. Thomas' approach, espoused by others under different terms, is to look at values as existing at various distances from the person's "self." In short, some values are more important than others.

6. See, for example, J. McGuire, "The Nature of Attitudes and Attitude Change," in *The Handbook of Social Psychology,* Vol. 3, eds. G. Lindzey and E. Aronson (Reading, Mass.: Addison-Wesley, 1969), pp. 136–314.

7. In an effort to make the concept of beliefs meaningful to the student taking his or her first course in communication, beliefs are grouped into broader categories than advanced courses in other disciplines might apply. For example, Rokeach breaks beliefs into various belief structures upon which there are varying degrees of consensus. Primitive beliefs with unanimous consensus are the first order, followed by primitive beliefs with zero consensus, authority beliefs, derived beliefs, and inconsequential beliefs. Rokeach, *Beliefs, Attitudes, and Values,* pp. 26–29.

8. The account is from the Economics Press, Inc., Fairfield, N.J.

9. Rokeach's approach is to see the belief system (which includes beliefs, attitudes, and values) as central to the self-concept. The individual is faced with numerous opportunities for incongruity to exist.

10. Stroking is based on a number of concepts related to transactional analysis. Eric Berne's work in this area and the more popularized works of Thomas Harris are most familiar to communication scholars. Sources include T. Harris, *I'm OK–You're OK* (New York: Harper & Row, 1969); E. Berne, *Games People Play* (New York: Grove Press, 1964).

11. See, for example, P.H. Wright, "Toward a Theory of Friendship Based on a Conception of Self," *Human Communication Research,* 4 (1974), 196–207.

12. See E. Berne, *Transactional Analysis in Psychotherapy* (New York: Grove Press, 1974); E. Berne, *The Structure and Dynamics of Organizations and Groups* (Philadelphia: Lippincott, 1963).

13. See R.A. Bell, "Conversational Involvement and Loneliness," *Communication Monographs,* 52 (September 1985), 218–35.

14. See E. Goffman, *Encounters: Two Studies in the Sociology of Interaction* (Indianapolis: Bobbs Merrill, 1961). Goffman has devised a complex analysis scheme to explain his approach to human interaction. It includes breaking down human interaction into *frame analysis:* the basic element of interpersonal communication is a frame, and a series of frames is a *strip.* An initial encounter is a *face engagement.* Goffman places considerable importance on the "storytelling" aspect of a relationship in which self-disclosure (discussed in this chapter) is a form of storytelling. This process is what actually determines the self in the context of a given relationship.

15. M. Snyder, "The Many Me's of the Self-Monitor," *Psychology Today,* (March 1980), 33–34. See also W. Douglas, "Scripts and Self-Monitoring: When Does Being a High Self-Monitor Really Make a Difference?," *Human Communication Research,* 10 (Fall 1983), 81–96.

16. J.C. Horn, "Measuring Shyness, The 12-inch Difference," *Psychology Today,* 13 (1979), 102; reporting the work of B. Carducci and A. Webber (*Psychological Reports,* Vol. 44). The shyness test is Philip Zimbardo's "Stanford Survey of Shyness."

17. *Chapel Hill Newspaper* (September 4, 1976).

18. Ibid.

19. For general background on self-disclosure see P.C. Cozby, "Self-Disclosure: A Literature Review," *Psychological Bulletin,* 79 (1973), 73–91; G. Egan, *Encounter: Group Processes for Interpersonal Growth* (Belmont, Calif.: Brooks/Cole, 1970), pp. 234–38; L.B. Rosenfeld, "Self-Disclosure Avoidance: Why Am I Afraid to Tell You Who I Am?" *Communication Monographs,* 46 (1979), 63–74; S.J. Gilbert and G.G. Whiteneck, "Toward a Multidimensional Approach to the Study of Self-Disclosure," *Human Communication Research,* 2 (1976), 347–55; S.M. Jourard and P.E. Jaffe, "Influence of an Interviewer's Behavior on the Self-Disclosure Behavior of Interviewees," *Journal of Counseling Psychology,* 17 (1970), 252–57; W.B. Pearce and S.M. Sharp, "Self-Disclosing Communication," *Journal of Communication,* 23 (1973), 409–25; M. Worthy, A.L. Gary, and G.M. Kahn, "Self-Disclosure as an Exchange Process," *Journal of Personality and Social Psychology,* 13, (1969), 59–63.

20. C. Rogers, *On Becoming a Person* (Boston: Houghton Mifflin, 1961), p. 344. Cited in S. W. Littlejohn, *Theories of Human Communication* (Columbus, Ohio: Chas. E. Merrill, 1978), p. 224.

21. J. Powell, *Why Am I Afraid to Tell You Who I Am?* (Niles, Ill.: Argus Communications, 1969).

22. Rosenfeld, "Self-Disclosure Avoidance," pp. 63–74.

23. Ibid.

24. Gilbert and Whiteneck, "Multidimensional Approach to the Study of Self-Disclosure," pp. 347–55.

25. See, for example, S.J. Gilbert and D. Horenstein, "The Communication of Self-Disclosure: Level Versus Valence," *Human Communication Research,* 1 (1975), 316–22. Also citing: P.M. Blau, *Exchange and Power in Social Life* (New York: John Wiley & Sons, 1964); S.J. Gilbert, "A Study of the Effects of Self-Disclosure on Interpersonal Attraction and Trust as a Function of Situational Appropriateness and the Self-Esteem of the Recipient" (unpublished doctoral dissertation, Department of Speech Communication, The University of Kansas, 1972). Other related sources to a multidimensional approach to self-disclosure include: L.R. Wheeless and J. Grotz, "Conceptualization and Measurement of Reported Self-Disclosure," *Human Communication Research,* 2 (1976), 338–46; J.C. McCroskey, V. Richmond, J.R. Daly, and R.L. Falcione, "Studies of the Relationship Between Communication Apprehension and Self-Esteem," *Human Communication Research,* 2 (1977), 270–77; W.B. Pearce, S.M. Sharp, P.H. Wright, and K.M. Slama, "Affection and Reciprocity in Self-Disclosing Communication," *Human Communication Research,* 1 (1974), 5–14; L.R. Wheeless, "Self-Disclosure and Interpersonal Solidarity: Measurement, Validation, and Relationships," *Human Communication Research,* 3 (Fall 1976), 47–61; S.J. Gilbert, "Effects of Unanticipated Self-Disclosure on Recipients of Varying Levels of Self-Esteem: A Research Note," *Human Communication Research,* 3 (Summer 1977), 368–70; L.R. Wheeless and J. Grotz, "The Measurement of Trust and Its Relationship to Self-Disclosure," *Human Communication Research,* 3 (1977), 250–56.

26. L.B. Rosenfeld and W.L. Kendrick, "Choosing to Be Open: An Empirical Investigation of Subjective Reasons for Self-Disclosing," *The Western Journal of Speech Communication,* 48 (Fall 1984), 326–43.

27. Wheeless, "Self-Disclosure and Interpersonal Solidarity," pp. 47–61; Wheeless and Grotz, "Conceptualization and Measurement of Reported Self-Disclosure," pp. 338–46. And research based on the test instrument the Revised Self-Disclosure Scales (RSDS). The dimensions of the RSDS are the basis for this discussion in the text.

CHAPTER 3

1. "Pigeon Talk," *Time,* February 11, 1980, p. 53.

2. "Apes Use No Language," *Newsweek,* December 31, 1979, p. 66.

3. U. Bellugi, "Learning the Language," in *Language Concepts and Processes,* ed. Joseph A. DeVito (Englewood Cliffs, N.J.: Prentice-Hall, 1973), pp. 110–20. Also see *The Western Journal of Speech Communication,* 48 (Spring 1984), a special issue devoted to children's communicative development; B. Haslett, "Acquiring Conversational Competence," 107–24; E.S. Andersen, "the Acquisition of Sociolinguistic Knowledge: Some Evidence from Children's Verbal Role-Play," 125–44; M. Rice, "A Cognition Account of Differences Between Children's Comprehension and Production of Language," 145–54; B.R. Burleson, "Role-Taking and Communication Skills in Childhood: Why They *Aren't* Related and What Can Be Done About It," 155–70; E. Wartella, "Cognitive and Affective Factors of TV Advertising's Influence on Children," 171–83; N. Elliott, "Communicative Development from Birth," 184–86 (N. Elliott also served as editor for the special issue).

4. F.L. Johnson, "Communicative Purpose in Children's Referential Language," *Communication Monographs,* 47 (1980), 46–55.

5. D. Atkinson Gorcyca, W.R. Kennan, and M.G. Stitch, "Discrimination of the Language Behavior of College and Middle-Aged Encoders," *Communication Quarterly,* 27 (1979), 38–43.

6. J. Tough, *The Development of Meaning,* (New York: John Wiley & Sons, 1977).

7. See also: B. Haslet, "Communicative Functions and Strategies in Children's Conversations." *Human Communication Research,* 9 (Winter 1983), 130–45.

8. Ibid., 130–45.

9. See J.B. Bavelas, "Situations That Lead to Disqualification," *Human Communication Research,* 9 (Winter 1983), 130–45.

10. Ibid.

11. Ibid., p. 140.

12. Ibid., P. 140.

13. See E.F. Dulaney, Jr., "Changes in Language Behavior as a Function of Veracity," *Human Communication Research,* 9 (Fall 1982), 75–82.

14. Ibid., pp. 80–81. See also C.L. Camden, M.T. Motley, and A. Wilson, "White Lies in Interpersonal Communication: A taxonomy and Preliminary Investigation of Social Motivations," *The Western Journal of Speech Communication,* 48 (Fall 1984), 309–25.

15. Especially helpful in researching material on language variables were: A. Bochner, "On Taking Ourselves Seriously: An Analysis of Some Persistent Problems and Promising Directions in Interpersonal Research," *Human Communication Research,* 4 (1978), 179–91; J.J. Bradac, J.A. Courtright, and J.W. Bowers, "Three Language Variables in Communication Research: Intensity, Immediacy, and Diversity," *Human Communication Research,* 5 (1979), 257–69; B.S. Greenberg, "The Effects of Language Intensity Modification on Perceived Verbal Aggressiveness," *Communication Monographs,* 43 (1976), 130–40; H. T. Hurt, M.D. Scott, and J.C. McCroskey, *Communication in the Classroom* (Reading, Mass.: Addison-Wesley, 1978); S.T. Jones, M. Burgoon, and D. Stewart, "Toward a Message-Centered Theory of Persuasion: Three Empirical Investigations of Language Intensity," *Human Communication Research,* 3 (1975), 240–56; W.J. McEwen and B.S. Greenberg, "The Effects of Message Intensity on Receiver Evaluations of Source, Message and Topic," *Journal of Communication,* 20 (1970), 340–50; A. Mulac, "Effects of Obscene Language Upon Three Dimensions of Listener Attitude." *Communication Monographs,* 43 (1976), 300–307; R.E. Nofsinger, Jr., "On Answering Questions Indirectly: Some Rules in the Grammar of Doing Conversation," *Human Communication Research,* 2 (1976), 170–80; N.L. Reinsch, "Figurative Language and Source Credibility: A Preliminary Investigation and Reconceptualization," *Human Communication Research,* 2 (1974), 75–80; K.A. Andersen, *Introduction to Communication Theory and Practice* (Menlo Park, Calif.: Cummings Publishing, 1972).

16. See M. Burgoon and L.J. Chase, "The Effects of Differential Linguistic Patterns in Messages Attempting to Induce Resistance to Persuasion," *Speech Monographs,* 40 (1973), 1–7; M. Burgoon and G.R. Miller, "Prior Attitude and Language Intensity as Predictors of Message Style and Attitude Change Following Counterattitudinal Advocacy," *Journal of Personality and Social Psychology,* 20 (1971), 240–53; C.W. Carmichael and G.L. Cronkhite, "Frustration and Language Intensity," *Speech Monographs,* 32 (1965), 107–11; see also sources cited in footnote 15.

17. C.E. Osgood and E.G. Walker, "Motivation and Language Behavior: A Content Analysis of Suicide Notes," *Journal of Abnormal and Social Psychology,* 59 (1959), 58–67.

18. For example, G.R. Miller and J. Basehart, "Source Trustworthiness, Opinionated Statements and Responses to Persuasive Communications," *Speech Monographs,* 36 (1969), 1–7.

19. The arena for research in the area of language intensity is defined by Bradac, Courtright, and Bowers, "Three Language Variables," pp. 258–62.

20. Bradac, Courtright, and Bowers, "Three Language Variables," p. 262.

21. Ibid., p. 262.

22. Ibid. Citing as an example: R. Conville, "Linguistic Nonimmediacy and Communicators' Anxiety," *Journal of Psychology,* 35 (1974), 1107–14.

23. Bardac, Courtright, and Bowers, "Three Language Variables," p. 262.

24. R.P. Hart, "Absolutism and Situation: Prolegomena to a Rhetorical Biography of Richard M. Nixon," *Communication Monographs,* 43 (1976), 204–28.

25. Bradac, Courtright, and Bowers list the following generalizations associated with results of research in verbal immediacy: (1) positive affect on the part of a source toward the topics of a message is directly related to verbal immediacy; (2) cognitive stress on the part of a source is inversely related to verbal immediacy; (3) verbal immediacy is directly related to receiver attributions of positiveness of source affect; (4) verbal immediacy is directly related to receiver judgments of source competence; (5) verbal immediacy is directly related to receiver judgments of source character; (6) verbal immediacy interacts with initial receiver agreement with the proposition of the message in the production of receiver attributions in such a way that immediacy in congruent messages enhances but in discrepant messages inhibits attributions of source similarity.

26. Hurt, Scott, and McCroskey, *Communication in the Classroom,* pp. 76–77. See also W.G. Shamo and J.R. Bittner, "Information Recall as a Function of Language Style" (paper presented at the annual meeting of the International Communication Association, Phoenix, Arizona, April 1971).

27. When viewed as the degree of lexical diversity an individual employs. Lexical diversity is defined as the "manifest range of a source's vocabulary." (Bradac, Courtright, and Bowers, "Three Language Variables," p. 262.)

28. K. Andersen, *Introduction to Communication Theory and Practice* (Menlo Park, Calif.: Cummings Publishing, 1972), pp. 141–42. Andersen approaches humor as a "strategy of interpersonal style."

29. Ibid.

30. Ibid.

31. Ibid.

32. Refer especially to generalizations 3, 4, and 5 discussed by Bradac, Courtright, and Bowers as cited previously in note 25.

33. Adapted from F. Williams and R.C. Naremore, "On the Functional Analysis of Social Class Difference in Modes of Speech," *Speech Monographs,* 36 (1969), 77–102. Also discussed in F. Williams, "Language and Communication," in *Communication and Behavior,* eds. G.J. Hanneman and W.J. McEwen (Reading, Mass.: Addison-Wesley, 1975).

34. B. Bernstein, *Class Codes and Control* (London: Routledge & Kegan Paul, 1971). As discussed by Williams in *Communication and Behavior,* p. 73.

35. Ibid.

36. The author is indebted to the editorial and production divisions of Prentice-Hall for providing the booklet "Prentice-Hall College Division Guidelines on Sexism," which was the basis for this section of the chapter. Material found in this section was either quoted directly or adapted from the "Guidelines." Also helpful was P.R. Randall, "Sexist Language and Speech Communication Texts: Another Case of Benign Neglect," *Communication Education,* 34 (April 1985), 128–34.

CHAPTER 4

1. S.J. Ramsey, "Prison Codes," *Journal of Communication,* 26 (1976), 39. Additional perspectives can be found in: J.K. Heston and P.A. Gardner, "A Study of Personal Spacing and Desk Arrangement in a Learning Environment" (paper presented at the annual meeting of the International

Communication Association, Atlanta, April 1972); A. Hare and R. Bales, "Seating Position and Small-Group Interaction," *Sociometry*, 26 (1963), 480–86; G. McBride, "Theories of Animal Spacing: The Role of Flight, Fight, and Social Distance," in *Behavior and Environment*, ed. A.H. Esser (New York: Plenum Press, 1971), pp. 53–68; M.L. Patterson, S. Mullens, and J. Ramano, "Compensatory Reactions to Spatial Intrusion," *Sociometry*, 34 (1971), 114–21.

2. For a review of research on personal space and a discussion of the developing theory of personal space and violations, see J.K. Burgoon and S.B. Jones, "Toward a Theory of Personal Space Expectations and Their Violations," *Human Communication Research*, 2 (1976), 131–46.

3. See D.M. Pedersen, "Developmental Trends in Personal Space," *Journal of Psychology*, 83 (1973), 3–9; R.F. Priest and J. Sawyer, "Proximity and Peership: Bases of Balance in Interpersonal Attraction," *The American Journal of Sociology*, 72 (1967), 633–49.

4. See, for example, D.F. Lott and R. Sommer, "Seating Arrangements and Status," *Journal of Personality and Social Psychology*, 7 (1967), 90–94; A. Mehrabian and M. Williams, "Nonverbal Concomitants of Perceived and Intended Persuasiveness," *Journal of Personality and Social Psychology*, 13 (1969), 37–58; G.A. Norum, N.J. Russo, and R. Sommer, "Seating Patterns and Group Tasks," *Psychology in the Schools*, 4 (1967), 3.

5. As with evaluations: R. Sommer, "Spatial Parameters in Naturalistic Social Research," in *Behavior and Environment*, ed. A.H. Esser (New York: Plenum Press, 1971); W. Leipold, "Psychological Distance in a Dyadic Interview" (unpublished doctoral dissertation, University of North Dakota, 1963).

6. K.B. Little, "Personal Space," *Journal of Experimental Social Psychology*, 1 (1965), 237–47; F.N. Willis, "Initial Speaking Distance as a Function of the Speaker's Relationship," *Psychonomic Science*, 5 (1966), 221–22; G.W. Evans and R.B. Howard, "Personal Space," *Psychological Bulletin*, 80 (1973), 334–44; J. Gullahorn, "Distance and Friendship as Factors in the Gross Interaction Matrix," *Sociometry*, 5 (1952), 123–34.

7. N. Russo, "Connotation of Seating Arrangements," *Cornell Journal of Social Relations*, 2 (1967), 37–44.

8. E.T. Hall, *The Hidden Dimension* (New York: Doubleday, 1966); S.A. Jones, "Comparative Proxemics Analysis of Dyadic Interaction in Selected Subcultures of New York City," *Journal of Social Psychology*, 84 (1971), 35–44; O.M. Watson and T.D. Graves, "Quantitative Research in Proxemic Behavior," *American Anthropologist*, 68 (1968), 971–85; O.M. Watson, *Proxemic Behavior: A Cross-Cultural Study* (The Hague: Mouton, 1970); R.F. Forston and C.U. Larson, "The Dynamics of Space: An Experimental Study in Proxemic Behavior Among Latin Americans and North Americans," *Journal of Communication*, 18 (1968), 109–16; H.G. Triandis, E. Davis, and S. Takezawa, "Some Determinants of Social Distance Among American, German and Japanese Students," *Journal of Personality and Social Psychology*, (1965), 540–51.

9. Results of research are less clear when the sex variable is involved. Also, research is scant on the effects of the women's movement and the presence of additional women in the professional work force. See also G.W. Evans and R.B. Howard, "Personal Space," *Psychological Bulletin*, 80 (1973), 334–44; T. Rosegrant, "The Relationship of Race and Sex on Proxemic Behavior and Source Credibility" (paper presented at the International Communication Association Convention, Montreal, April 1973).

10. See D. Byrne and J.A. Buehler, "A Note on the Influence of Propinquity upon Acquaintanceships," *Journal of Abnormal and Social Psychology*, 51 (1955) 147–48; R. Sommer, *Personal Space: The Behavioral Basis of Design* (Englewood Cliffs, N.J.: Prentice-Hall, 1969); H. Rosenfeld, "Effect of Approval-Seeking Induction on Interpersonal Proximity," *Psychological Reports*, 17 (1965), 120–22.

11. E.T. Hall, *The Silent Language* (New York: Doubleday, 1959).

12. See J. Fast, *Body Language* (New York: M. Evans and Company, 1970); R. Sommer, "Studies in Personal Space," *Sociometry*, 22 (1959), 247–60.

13. Knapp classifies the functions as: repeating, contradicting, substituting, complementing, accenting, and regulating. Source: M.L. Knapp, *Nonverbal Communication in Human Interaction* (New York: Holt, Rinehart & Winston, 1978), pp. 20–25. Barker uses the terms *repeating, substituting, complementing, deceiving, revealing,* and *regulating*. Source: L. Barker, *Communication*.

14. See F.S. Haiman, "Nonverbal Communication and the First Amendment: The Rhetoric of the Streets Revisited," *Quarterly Journal of Speech*, 68 (1972), 371–83.

15. As reported in *The Chronicle of Higher Education*, (October 10, 1980), 14.

16. P. Eckman, "Movements with Precise Meanings," *Journal of Communication,* 26 (Summer 1976), 14–26; P. Eckman, R. Sorenson, and W.V. Friesen, "Hand Movements," *Journal of Communication,* 22 (Summer 1972), 353–74.

17. Eckman, "Precise Meanings," p. 19. Other discussions of emblems can be found in P. Eckman and W.V. Friesen, *Unmasking the Face* (Englewood Cliffs, N.J.: Prentice-Hall, 1974); P. Eckman and W.V. Friesen, "Constants Across Cultures in the Face and Emotion," *Journal of Personality and Social Psychology,* 17 (1971), 124–29; P. Eckman and W.V. Friesen, "The Repertoire of Nonverbal Behavior; Categories, Origin, Usage, and Coding," *Semiotica,* 1 (1969), 49–98.

18. See, for example, Eckman, Sorenson, and Friesen, "Hand Movements," pp. 358–59, and 367–69.

19. Eckman, Sorenson, and Friesen, "Hand Movements," p. 360. Also D. Efron, *Gesture and Environment,* current ed. (New York: King's Crown, 1941).

20. See Efron, *Gesture and Environment.*

21. Knapp, *Nonverbal Communication,* p. 399.

22. See, for example, A. Brandt, "Face Reading: The Persistence of Physiognomy," *Psychology Today,* 14 (December 1980), 90–96.

23. Knapp, *Nonverbal Communication,* p. 265.

24. Adapted from Eckman and Friesen, *Unmasking the Face.* Cited in Knapp, *Nonverbal Communication,* pp. 267–68.

25. See, for example, J.D. Boucher and P. Eckman, "Facial Areas and Emotional Information," *Journal of Communication,* 25 (Spring 1975), 21–28.

26. As discussed in H.T. Hurt, M.D. Scott, and J.C. McCroskey, *Communication in the Classroom* (Reading, Mass.: Addison-Wesley, 1978), p. 10.

27. Discussion of research on visual behavior and social interaction can be found in P.C. Ellsworth and L.M. Ludwig, "Visual Behavior in Social Interaction," *Journal of Communication,* 22 (December, 1972), 375–403. See also M. Argyle and M. Cook, *Gaze and Mutual Gaze* (Cambridge, U.K.: Cambridge University Press, 1976); D.J. Cegala, A.F. Alexander, and S. Sokuvitz, "An Investigation of Eye Gaze and Its Relation to Selected Verbal Behavior," *Human Communication Research,* 5 (Winter 1979), 99–108; A. Kendon, "Some Functions of Gaze Direction in Social Interaction," 26 (1967), 22–63; M. Argyle, R. Ingham, F. Alkema, and M. McCallin, "The Different Functions of Gaze," *Semiotica,* 7 (1973), 19–32.

28. As reported in the *British Journal of Social and Clinical Psychology* and cited in *Psychology Today,* 13 (October 1979), 40, 115.

29. See J.K. Burgoon and L. Aho, "Three Field Experiments of the Effects of Violations of Conversational Distance," *Communication Monographs,* 49 (June 1982), 71–88.

30. See J.K. Burgoon, "Attributes of the Newscaster's Voice as Predictors of His Credibility," *Journalism Quarterly,* 55 (1978), 276–81, 300; W. Addington, "The Effect of Vocal Variations on Ratings of Source Credibility," *Speech Monographs,* 38 (1971), 235–41.

31. See A.L. Sillars, D. Parry, S.F. Coletti, and M.A. Rogers, "Coding Verbal Conflict Tactics: Nonverbal and Perceptual Correlates of the 'Avoidance-Distributive-Integrative' Distinction," *Human Communication Research,* 9 (Fall 1982), 83–95.

32. An interesting popular discussion of the subject is found in S. Isaaca, "The Living Touch," *Parents,* (February 1980), 58–62.

33. For a discussion of the changing patterns of nonverbal behavior between children and teachers, see Hurt, Scott, and McCroskey, *Communication in the Classroom,* pp. 99–100.

34. T. Nguyen, R. Heslin, and M.L. Nguyen, "The Meanings of Touch: Sex Differences," *Journal of Communication,* 25 (Fall 1975), 92–103.

35. See, for example, L.B. Rosenfeld, S. Kartus, and C. Ray, "Body Accessibility Revisited," *Journal of Communication,* 26 (Summer 1976), 27–30.; S.E. Jones, "Sex Difference in Touch Communication, *The Western Journal of Speech Communication,* 50 (Summer 1986), 227–41.

36. See S.E. Jones and E. Yarbrough, "A Naturalistic Study of the Meanings of Touch," *Communication Monographs,* 52 (March 1985), 20–56.

37. S.M. Jourard, *Disclosing Man to Himself* (New York: Van Nostrand Reinhold, 1968); see also R. Shuter, "A Field Study of Nonverbal Communication in Germany, Italy, and the United States," *Communication Monographs,* 44 (November 1977), 298–305.

38. R. Heslin and D. Boss, "Nonverbal Boundary Behavior at Airports" (unpublished paper, Purdue University, 1976). Cited in C.M. Rinck, F.N. Willis, Jr., and L.M. Dean, "Interpersonal Touch Among Residents of Homes for the Elderly," *Journal of Communication*, 30 (Spring 1980), 44–47.

39. *American Bar Association Journal*, 66 (January 1980), 21.

40. L.D. Schmidt and S.R. Strong, " 'Expert' and 'Inexpert' Counselors," *Journal of Counseling Psychology*, 23 (1976), 553–56.

41. J.J. Thompson, *Beyond Words: Nonverbal Communication in the Classroom* (New York: Citation Press, 1973), 69.

42. A Mehrabian, *Public Places and Private Spaces* (New York: Basic Books, 1976).

43. Thompson, *Beyond Words*, p. 69.

44. M. Busniakova, "Preference of Colors and Colored Stimulus Structures Depending on Age," *Phychologia a Paloksychologia*, 12 (1977), 401–10.

45. For a perspective on time (pauses) in regulating conversation see O. Robbins, S. Devoe, and M. Wiener, "Social Patterns of Turn-Taking: Nonverbal Regulators," *Journal of Communication*, 28 (Summer 1978), 38–46. In comparisons between children or working-class and middle-class workers, Robbins, Devoe, and Wiener found (pp. 42–43):

   1. Working-class speakers emit unfilled pauses, . . . in significantly greater absolute numbers than do middle-class speakers.

   2. Middle-class speakers emit filled pauses significantly more often and in signficantly greater absolute numbers than do working-class speakers.

46. G.G. Luce, *Body Time: Physiological Rhythms and Social Stress* (New York: Random House, 1971), p. 16.

CHAPTER 5

1. *Advertising Age*, June 29, 1981.

2. From a report by M. Knight in *Pro Com*, newsletter of Women in Communication, Inc. See also G. Hunt and L.P. Cusella, "A Field Study of Listening Needs in Organizations," *Communication Education*, 32 (October 1983), 398, which identifies listening needs perceived by corporate training and education managers.

3. Copyright 1981 United Technologies Corporation.

4. Perhaps because of the difficulty in measuring some of those skills: R.A. Palmatier and George McNinch, "Source of Gains in Listening Skill: Experimental or Pre-Test Experience?" *The Journal of Communication*, 22 (March 1972), 70–76.

5. The author acknowledges the work of Ralph Nichols, "Do We Know How to Listen? Practical Helps in a Modern Age," *Speech Teacher*, 10 (1961), 118–24, in formulating this section of the chapter. Nichols' writings have been adapted and discussed in other texts and articles. An assessment of research in listening is found in S.C. Rhodes, "What the Communication Journals Tell Us About Listening," *Central States Speech Journal* 36 (Spring/Summer 1985), 24–32. Also M.J. Beatty and S. Payne, "Listening Comprehension as a Function of Cognitive Complexity: A Research Note," *Communication Monographs*, 51 (March 1984), 85–89; P. Backlund et al., "A National Survey of State Practices in Speaking and Listening Skill Assessment," *Communication Education*, 31 (April 1982), 125–30; L. Barker, K. Watson, and R. Kibler, "An Investigation of the Effect of Presentations by Effective and Ineffective Speakers on Listening Test Scores," *Southern Speech Communication Journal*, 49 (Spring 1984), 309–18.

6. As discussed by R.C. Arnett and G. Nakagawa in "The Assumptive Roots of Empathetic Listening: A Critique," *Communication Education*, 32 (October 1983). 368–78 (citing page 369). See also R.E. Norton and L.S. Pettegrew, "Attentiveness as a Style of Communication: A Structural Analysis," *Communication Monographs*, 46 (1979), 13–26.

7. See, for example, A. Mulac and M.J. Rudde, "Effects of Selected American Regional Dialects upon Regional Audience Members." *Communication Monographs*, 44 (1977), 185–95.

8. The concept has been widely researched by J.C. McCroskey and others. See in particular J.C. McCroskey, "Scales for the Measurement of Ethos," *Speech Monographs*, 33 (1966), 65–72; D.K. Berlo, J.B. Lemert, and R. Mertz, "Dimensions for Evaluating the Acceptability of Message Sources," *Public Opinion Quarterly*, 22 (1969), 563–76.

9. L.D. Lovrien, "Navajo and Caucasian Mother's Differing Perceptions of Behavior," *Psychology Today*, 13 (1979), 40.

10. Ibid.

11. See, for example, T.A. McCain and M.G. Ross, "Cognitive Switching: A Behavioral Trace of Human Information Processing for Television Newscasts," *Human Communication Research*, 5 (1979), 121–29.

12. A more general perspective of Mok's adaptation is found in D. Lynch, "Getting 'In Sync' with the Customer," *Sales and Marketing Management*, 124 (1980), 42–46.

13. See J.G. Delia, R.A. Clark, and D.E. Switzer, "The Context of Informal Conversations as a Function of Interactants' Interpersonal Cognitive Complexity," *Communication Monographs*, 46 (1979), 272–81.

14. For a perspective on the measurement of perceived effectiveness of an interpersonal encounter see M.L. Hecht, "The Conceptualization and Measurement of Interpersonal Communication Satisfaction," *Human Communication Research*, 4 (1978), 253–58.

CHAPTER 6

1. See, for example, J.C. McCroskey, V.P. Richmond, and J.A. Daly, "The Development of a Measure of Perceived Homophily in Interpersonal Communication, *Human Communication Research*, 1 (1975), 324–32.

2. Ibid.

3. Ibid.

4. Ibid.

5. Ibid.

6. G.R. Miller, "The Current Status of Theory and Research in Interpersonal Communication," *Human Communication Research*, 4, (1978), 164–78. See also J. Ayres, "Four Approaches to Interpersonal Communication: Review, Observation, Prognosis," *The Western Journal of Speech Communication*, 48 (Fall 1984) 408–40.

7. See, for example, C.R. Berger and R.J. Calabrese, "Some Explorations in Initial Interaction and Beyond: Toward a Developmental Theory of Interpersonal Communication," *Human Communication Research*, 1 (Winter 1975), 99–112.

8. W. Schultz's theories, specifically FIRO (Fundamental Interpersonal Relations Orientation) theory, can be found in W. Schultz, *FIRO: A Three Dimensional Theory of Interpersonal Behavior* (New York: Holt, Rinehart & Winston, 1958); *The Three-Dimensional Underworld* (Palo Alto, Calif.: Science and Behavior Books, 1966); *Here Comes Everybody* (New York: Harper & Row, 1973); *Elements of Encounter* (New York: Bantam, 1975); *Leaders of Schools* (LaJolla, Calif.: University Associates, 1977). See also Stephen W. Littlejohn, *Theories of Human Communication* (Columbus, Ohio: Chas. E. Merrill, 1978), pp. 212–17.

9. Ibid.

10. As reported in *Glamour*, (September 1982), p. 242.

11. Ibid.

12. The literature on compliance-gaining behavior is reviewed by L.R. Wheeless, R. Barraclough, and R. Stewart in their chapter titled, "Compliance-Gaining and Power in Persuasion," in *Communication Yearbook No. 7*, eds. R.N. Bostrom and B.W. Westley (Beverly Hills, Calif.: Sage, 1983), pp. 105–45.

13. Compliance-gaining message strategies are adapted from H. Witteman and M.A. Fitzpatrick, "Compliance-Gaining in Marital Interaction: Power Bases, Processes, and Outcomes," *Communication Monographs*, 53 (June 1986), 130–43, citing page 131. The categories were established by a compilation and review of the Wheeless and others article cited above.

14. M.J. Cody, M.L. Woelfel, and W.J. Jordan, "Dimensions of Compliance-Gaining Situations," *Human Communication Research*, 9 (Winter 1983), 99–113. The above study and the Cody–McLaughlin typology was modified by J.P. Dillard and M. Burgoon, "Situational Influences on the Selection of Compliance-Gaining Messages: Two Tests of the Predictive Utility of the Cody-McLaughlin Typology," *Communication Monographs*, 52 (December 1985), 289–304. Other re-

lated research on compliance-gaining behavior may be found in M.A. deTurck, "A Transactional Analysis of Compliance-Gaining Behavior: Effects of Noncompliance, Relational Contexts, and Actors' Gender," *Human Communication Research*, 12 (Fall 1985), 54–78; J.S. McQuillen, "The Development of Listener-Adapted Compliance-Resisting Strategies," *Human Communication Research*, 12 (Spring 1986), 359–75.

CHAPTER 7

1. T. Levitt, "After the Sale Is Over . . . ," *Harvard Business Review*, (September-October 1983), 87–93.

2. The author gratefully acknowledges the work of such researchers as Altman, Taylor, and Knapp in conceptualizing the organization of this chapter. See, for example, M.L. Knapp, *Social Intercourse* (Boston: Allyn & Bacon, 1978); I. Altman and D.A. Taylor, *Social Penetration: The Development of Interpersonal Relationships* (New York: Holt, Rinehart & Winston, 1973).

3. See, for example, G.R. Miller, "The Current Status of Theory and Research in Interpersonal Communication," *Human Communication Research*, 4 (Winter 1978), 164–76. Representative research on stages in the development of relationships can be seen in such works as C.R. Berger and R.J. Calabrese, "Some Explorations in Initial Interaction and Beyond: Toward a Developmental Theory of Interpersonal Communication," *Human Communication Research*, 1 (1975), 99–112.

4. Both Altman's and Knapp's portrayals of this concept can also be studied. In this text the author chose to deviate from the pictorial representations presented by these authors to reflect the concept of dyadic communication and the growing together of two individuals' personal agendas. See Knapp, *Social Intercourse*, p. 12.

5. P. Kelvin, "Predictability, Power, and Vulnerability in Interpersonal Attraction," in *Theory and Practice in Interpersonal Attraction*, ed. S. Duck (London: Academic Press, 1977), as cited in W.K. Rawlins, "Openness as Problematic in Ongoing Friendships: Two Conversational Dilemmas," *Communication Monographs*, 50 (March 1983), 1–13.

6. Rawlins, "Openness," p. 8.

7. Ibid., pp. 10–12.

8. Ibid., p. 11.

9. J.C. McCroskey and T.A. McCain, "The Measurement of Interpersonal Attraction," *Speech Monographs*, 41 (August 1974), 261–66.

10. An example of the "goodbye" stage is found in M.L. Knapp, R.P. Hart, G.W. Friedrich, and G.M. Shulman, "The Rhetoric of Goodbye: Verbal and Nonverbal Correlates of Human Leave-Taking," *Speech Monographs*, 40 (August 1973), 182–98.

11. See Knapp, *Social Intercourse*, pp. 13, 17–28. The author has used Knapp's interaction stages as a means of analyzing the hypothetical relationship discussed in the text. Other scholars have used different terms and even different stages of interaction than those discussed by Knapp. Also, the application of the hypothetical example is arbitrary and makes no pretense of classifying the various stages of interaction in the same way that Knapp or others might choose.

12. The example is from W. Boroson and R. Boroson, "First Meetings," *Glamour*, 78 (1980), p. 96.

13. Knapp, *Social Intercourse*, p. 21.

14. M.C. Cody, "A Typology of Disengagement Strategies and an Examination of the Role Intimacy, Reactions to Inequity and Relational Problems Play in Strategy Selection," *Communication Monographs*, 49 (September 1982), 148–70.

15. Ibid., methodologies discussed on pp. 151, 160–61.

16. Ibid., p. 163.

17. Ibid., p. 169.

18. Ibid., p. 162 (based on factor analysis).

19. Ibid., p. 162.

20. Ibid., p. 168.

21. Ibid., p. 169.

22. Another perspective can be seen in F.L. Johnson and E. Aries, "Close Friendship in Adulthood: Conversational Content between Same-Sex Friends" (paper presented at the annual meeting of the Speech Communication Association, New York, 1980). See also W.F. Owen, "Thematic Metaphors in Relational Communication: A Conceptual Framework," *The Western Journal of Speech Communication*, 49 (Winter 1985), 1–13; J.K. Burgoon, D.B. Buller, J.L. Hale, M.A. deTurck, "Relational Messages Associated with Nonverbal Behaviors," *Human Communication Research*, 10 (Spring 1984), 351–78; M.L. Hecht, "Satisfying Communication and Relationship Labels: Intimacy and Length of Relationship as Perceptual Frames of Naturalistic Conversations," *The Western Journal of Speech Communication*, 48 (Summer 1984), 201–16.

23. Johnson and Aries, "Close Friendship in Adulthood."

24. See, for example, D.S. Prentice, "The Effects of Trust-Destroying Communication on Verbal Fluency in the Small Group," *Speech Monographs*, 42 (November 1975), 262–70. Applied to group communication, see D.G. Leathers, "The Process Effects of Trust-Destroying Behavior in the Small Group," *Speech Monographs*, 37 (1970), 180–87. See also L.R. Wheeless, V.E. Wheeless, and R. Baus, "Sexual Communication, Communication Satisfaction, and Solidarity in the Developmental Stages of Intimate Relationships," *The Western Journal of Speech Communication*, 48 (Summer 1984), 217–30.

25. See, for example, J.J. Bradac, L.A. Hosman, and C.H. Tardy, "Reciprocal Disclosures and Language Intensity: Attributional Consequences," *Communication Monographs*, 45 (March 1978), 1–17; L.A. Baxter, "Self-Disclosure as a Relationship Disengagement Strategy," *Human Communication Research*, 5 (1970), 215–22; M. Prisbell and J.F. Andersen, "The Importance of Perceived Homophily, Uncertainty Reduction, Feeling Good, Safety, and Self-Disclosure in Interpersonal Relationships" (paper presented at the annual meeting of the Speech Communication Association, San Antonio, Texas, 1979).

26. A perspective on the psychological and clinical foundations of the unwritten contract in a relationship is offered by Dr. Kenneth R. Mitchell, a former Menninger Foundation staff member, and is reported in K.R. Mitchell, "Secret Marriage Contract," *Cosmopolitan*, 187 (August 1979), p. 263.

27. T. Mochizuki, "Changing Patterns of Mate Selection," *Journal of Comparative Family Studies*, 12 (1981), 317–28, as reported in W.B. Gudykunst and T. Nishida "Social Penetration in Japanese and American Close Friendships," (paper presented at the annual meeting of the International Communication Association, Dallas, Texas, May 1983).

28. C. Nakane, *Japanese Society* (Berkeley: University of California Press, 1970), as cited in Gudykunst and Nishida, "Social Penetration."

29. A.R. Lanier, "The Chinese, The Arabs: What Makes Them Buy," *Sales and Marketing Management*, (March 1979), 41.

30. L. Baxter and W.M. Wilmot, "Communication Characteristics of Relationships With Differential Growth Rates," *Communication Monographs*, 50 (September 1983), 264–72, citing p. 270.

31. A perspective on relational types can be seen in M.A. Fitzpatrick and J. Indvik, "What You See May Not Be What You Have" (unpublished paper, Communication Research Center, Department of Communication Arts, University of Wisconsin, Madison, 1980). This paper was an important source for developing the conceptual framework for this section of the chapter.

32. The relationship may have begun as orthodox.

CHAPTER 8

1. Group size and its effects on discussion are treated in L. Barker, D.J. Cegala, R.J. Kibler, and K.J. Wahlers, *Groups in Process: An Introduction to Small Group Communication*, 2nd ed. (Englewood Cliffs, N.J.: Prentice-Hall., 1983), pp. 72–75.

2. For agendas in task-oriented research see, for example, E.A. Mabry, "Exploratory Analysis of a Development Model for Task-Oriented Small Groups," *Human Communication Research*, 2 (1975), 66–74. Early work by Bales addressed the foundations of the problem many researchers have drawn upon: R.F. Bales, "Interaction Process Analysis," (Reading, Mass: Addison-Wesley, 1950); R.F. Bales, "The Equilibrium Problem in Small Groups," in *Working Paper in the Theory of Action*, eds. T. Parsons, R.F. Bales, and E. Shils (New York: The Free Press, 1953), pp. 111–61.

3. For a detailed look at the phenomenon of brainstorming, see F.M. Jablin and L. Sussman, "An Exploration of Communication and Productivity in Real Brainstorming Groups," *Human Communication Research,* 4 (1978), 329–36.

4. An important source for this section of the book is B.A. Fisher and W.S. Werbel, "Communication in the T-Group and the Therapy Group: An Interaction Analysis of the Group Process" (paper presented at the annual meeting of the Speech Communication Association, San Antonio, Texas, 1979).

5. W.S. Werbel, D.G. Ellis, and B.A. Fisher, "A Comparative Morphology of Groups: A Systems Perspective" (paper presented to the annual meeting of the International Communication Association, New Orleans, 1974). Cited in Fisher and Werbel, "Communication in the T-Group and the Therapy Group," pp. 3–4.

6. Fisher and Werbel. "Communication in the T-Group and the Therapy Group," p. 4.

7. E. Polster and M. Polster, *Gestalt Therapy Integrated: Contours of Theory and Practice* (New York: Vintage Press, 1974). Also see J.B. Clark and S.A. Culbert, "Mutually Therapeutic Perception and Self-Awareness in a T-Group," *Journal of Applied Behavioral Science,* 1 (1965), 180–94.

8. Fisher and Werbel, "Communication in the T-Group and the Therapy Group," p. 5. Also see I. Yalom, *The Theory and Practice of Group Psychotherapy* (New York: Basic Books, 1975). Cited in Fisher and Werbel.

9. Fisher and Werbel, "Communication in the T-Group and the Therapy Group," p. 6.

10. Ibid.

11. Adapted from T.S. Saine, L.S. Schulman, and L.C. Emerson, "The Effects of Group Size on the Structure of Interaction in Problem-Solving Groups," *The Southern Speech Communication Journal,* 39 (1974), 337.

12. Research on sequential interaction has been conducted in a variety of settings, many employing Markov chain models. See D.G. Ellis, "Relational Control in Two Group Systems," *Communication Monographs,* 46 (August 1979), 154–66; L.C. Hawes and J.M. Foley, "A Markov Analysis of Interview Communication," *Speech Monographs,* 40 (1973), 208–19; D.G. Ellis and B. Aubrey Fisher, "Phases of Conflict in Small Group Development: A Markov Analysis," *Human Communication Research,* 1 (1975), 195–212; D.E. Hewes, "Finite Stochastic Modeling of Communication Process: An Introduction and Some Basic Readings," *Human Communication Research,* 1 (1975), 271–83.

13. Jablin and Sussman, "An Exploration of Communication and Productivity," p. 329.

14. P. Hayes Bradley, "Power, Status, and Upward Communication in Small Decision-Making Groups," *Communication Monographs,* 45 (March 1978), 34.

15. Ibid. See also D. Cartwright and A. Zander, "The Structural Properties of Groups: Introduction," in *Group Dynamics,* 3rd ed., eds. D. Cartwright and A. Zander (New York: Harper & Row, 1968) (as cited in Bradley, "Power, Status, and Upward Communication," p. 34).

16. A.R. Cohen, "Upward Communication in Experimentally Created Hierarchies," *Human Relations,* 11 (1958), 41–43 (as cited in Bradley, "Power, Status, and Upward Communication," pp. 33–34).

17. Ibid. See also the work of W.H. Read, "Upward Communication in Industrial Hierarchies," *Human Relations,* 15 (1962), 3–15.

18. R. Lippit, N. Polansky, F. Redl, and S. Rosen, "The Dynamics of Power," *Human Relations,* 5 (1952), 37–64; cited by Bradley, "Power, Status, and Upward Communication."

19. T.R. Sarbin and V.L. Allen, "Role Theory," in *The Handbook of Social Psychology,* 2nd ed., eds. G. Lindzey and E. Aronson (Reading, Mass.: Addison-Wesley, 1969); also discussed in Barker and others, *Groups in Progress.*

20. See, for example, D.S. Prentice, "The Effects of Trust-Destroying Communication on Verbal Fluency in the Small Group," *Speech Monographs,* 42 (1975), 262–70.

21. See W.T. Rogers and S.E. Jones, "Effects of Dominance Tendencies on Floor Holding and Interruption Behavior in Dyadic Interaction," *Human Communication Research,* 1 (Winter 1975), 113–22; L.B. Rosenfeld and G.D. Fowler, "Personality, Sex, and Leadership Style," *Communication Monographs,* 43 (November 1976), 318–24.

22. J.T. Wood, "Leading in Purposive Discussions: A Study of Adaptive Behavior," *Communication Monographs,* 44 (June 1977), 152–65.

23. Saine, Schulman, and Emerson, "The Effects of Group Size on the Structure of Interaction in Problem-Solving Groups," pp. 335–36. The quotation states a confirmed hypothesis as reflected in the results of research reported in the article. See also J.E. Baird, Jr., "A Comparison of Distributional and Sequential Structure in Cooperative and Competitive Group Discussions," *Speech Monographs,* 41 (August 1974), 226–32. Time can also play a part. See for example: G. Sorensen and J.C. McCroskey, "The Prediction of Interaction Behavior in Small Groups: Zero History vs. Intact Groups," *Communication Monographs,* 44 (March 1977), 73–80; M.S. Poole, "Decision Development in Small Groups, II: A Study of Multiple Sequences in Decision Making," *Communication Monographs,* 50 (September 1983), 206–32; P.H. Andrews, "Ego-Involvement, Self-Monitoring, and Conformity in Small Groups: A Communicative Analysis," *Central States Speech Journal,* 36 (Spring/Summer 1985), 51–61.

CHAPTER 9

1. From M.H. Bright, "The Ten Commandments of Oral Argument," *American Bar Association Journal,* 67 (September 1981), 1136–39.

CHAPTER 10

1. Early studies reporting source credibility research include D. Berlo, J. Lemert, and R. Mertz, "A Factor Analytic Study of the Dimensions of Source Credibility" (paper presented at the annual meeting of the Speech Communication Association, 1961); J. McCroskey, "Scales for the Measurement of Ethos," *Speech Monographs,* 33 (1966), 65–72.
2. M. McCombs, D.L. Shaw, and D. Grey, *Handbook of Reporting Methods* (Boston: Houghton Mifflin, 1976), p. 56.
3. Ibid., p. 63; citing J. Berendt, "The Worst American State," *Lifestyle,* (November 1972).
4. McCombs, Shaw, and Grey, *Handbook of Reporting Methods,* pp. 64–65; citing F. Mosteller, "A Resistant Adjusted Analysis of the 1971 and 1972 Regular Professional Football Season," Memorandum EX-5, Department of Statistics, Harvard University, Cambridge, Mass., January 1973.

CHAPTER 12

1. From Tim Woodward's column in *The Idaho Statesman,* October 10, 1980.
2. Ibid.
3. Among many works on communication see: J.C. McCroskey, *Oral Communication Apprehension: A Reconceptualization.* In M. Burgoon, Ed., *Communication Yearbook 6* (Beverly Hills, Calif.: Sage, 1982).
4. Helpful in the development of this section of the text was C. Van Riper, *Speech Correction,* 6th ed. (Englewood Cliffs, N.J.: Prentice-Hall, 1978), p. 78.
5. Ibid., pp. 60–61.
6. Ibid., p. 50.

CHAPTER 13

1. For example: E. Black, "The Second Persona," *Quarterly Journal of Speech,* 56 (1970), 109–19. An analysis of approaches to rhetorical criticism and a section dealing with different orientations for the analysis of rhetoric can be found in H. Simons, *Persuasion: Understanding, Practice, and Analysis.* (Reading, Mass.: Addison-Wesley, 1976), pp. 300–305.
2. I.P. Pavlov, *Conditioned Reflexes.* (New York: Oxford University Press, 1927).

3. As set forth in J.W. Kling, "Learning: Introductory Survey," in *Woodward and Schlosberg's Experimental Psychology,* J.W. Kling and L. Riggs, eds. (New York: Holt, Rinehart & Winston, 1971), pp. 551–613, as cited in S.W. Littlejohn, *Theories of Human Communication* (Columbus, Ohio: Chas. E. Merrill, 1978) p. 170.

4. Originally advanced by F. Heider, "Attitudes and Cognitive Organization," *Journal of Psychology,* 21 (1946), 107–12.

5. See Leon Festinger, *A Theory of Cognitive Dissonance* (Stanford, Calif.: Stanford University Press, 1957).

6. M. Sherif, C. Sherif, and R. Nebergall, *Attitude and Attitude Change: The Social Judgement-Involvement Approach* (Philadelphia: Saunders, 1956).

7. W.J. McGuire, "Including Resistance to Persuasion: Some Contemporary Approaches," in *Advances in Experimental Social Psychology,* L. Berkowitz, ed. (New York: Academic Press, 1964), pp. 191–229.

CHAPTER 14

1. "Corporate Communications," *Wichita Business,* (1981), 31–35.

2. Adapted from D. Katz and R. Kahn, *The Social Psychology of Organizations* (New York: John Wiley & Sons, 1966), pp. 239–43.

3. Ibid., p. 245.

4. J.W. Koehler and G. Huber, "Effects of Upward Communication on Managerial Decision Making" (paper presented at the annual meeting of the International Communication Association, New Orleans, 1974).

5. "Corporate Communications," *Wichita Business,* pp. 31–35

6. Ibid.

7. J.D. Robinson, III, "The Paradox of Communication in an Information Society" (speech delivered before the American Advertising Federation, Washington, D.C., June 11, 1979).

8. See, for example, L.P. Stewart, " 'Whistle Blowing': Implications for Organizational Communication," *Journal of Communication,* 30 (Autumn 1980), 90–101; J.E. Grunig, "Accuracy of Communication from an External Public to Employees in a Formal Organization," *Human Communication Research,* 5 (Fall 1978), 40–53.

9. R. Perrucci, R.M. Anderson, D.E. Schendel, and L.E. Trachtman, "Whistle-Blowing; Professionals' Resistance to Organizational Authority," *Social Problems* 28 (December 1980), 149–64 (reporting research at the San Francisco BART system).

10. Ibid., p. 153.

11. Ibid., p. 154.

12. Ibid., p. 156.

13. Ibid., p. 157.

14. Especially helpful in the section on rumor and grapevine was R. Rowan, "Where Did That Rumor Come From?" *Fortune,* (August 13, 1979), 130–31.

15. Ibid.

16. K. Davis, "Care and Cultivation of the Corporate Grapevine," *Dun's Review,* 102, (July 1973), 46.

17. D. MacDonald, "Communication Roles and Communication Networks in a Formal Organization," *Human Communication Research,* 2 (Summer 1976), 365–75. See also K.H. Roberts and C.A. O'Reilly, Ill, "Organizations as Communication Structures: An Empirical Approach," *Human Communication Research,* 4 (Summer 1978), 283–93.

18. A good basis for discussion of the variable can be found in R.A. Emerson, "Power-Dependence Relations," *American Sociological Review,* 27 (1962), 31–41; D. Cartwright, ed., *Studies in Social Power* (Ann Arbor: University of Michigan, 1959).

19. Adapted from J. French and B. Raven, "The Bases of Social Power," in *Studies in Social Power,* ed. D. Cartwright (Ann Arbor: University of Michigan, 1959), pp. 118–49.

20. The author gratefully acknowledges the work of Charles Conrad in interpreting power in an organizational context based on different structures and the importance of communication in

identifying power within those structures. See, specifically, C. Conrad, "Toward a Symbology of Organizational Power" (paper presented at the annual meeting of the Speech Communication Association, 1982).

21. M.E. Pacanowsky and N. O'Donnell-Trujillo, "Organizational Communication as Cultural Performance," *Communication Monographs*, 50 (June 1983), 126–47.

22. Ibid., p. 144–45.

23. G.R. Oldham and N.L. Rotchford, "Relationships Between Office Characteristics and Employee Reactions: A study of the Physical Environment," *Administrative Science Quarterly*, 28 (1983), 542–56.

24. Adapted from a communication-argumentation orientation as presented in N.A. Reiches and H.B. Harral, "Argument in Negotiation: A Theoretical and Empirical Approach," *Speech Monographs*, 41 (March 1974), 36–48. Reiches and Harral point out (quoting Patchen) that "most theories of bargaining do not give direct and explicit attention to the process of interaction between the parties." Citing M. Patchen, "Models of Cooperation and Conflict: A Critical Review," *Journal of Conflict Resolution*, 14 (1970), 392. Using an extension of Sawyer and Guetzkow's work, Reiches and Harral see "negotiation interaction most usefully recognized as argumentation . . ." (Ibid., p. 36). Citing J. Sawyer and H. Guetzkow, "Bargaining and Negotiation in International Relations," in *International Behavior: A Social Psychological Analysis*, ed. Herbert C. Kelman (New York: Holt, Rinehart & Winston, 1965), p. 479.

25. Ibid., p. 39, and pointing to: Douglas Ehninger, "Argumentation as Method: Its Nature, Its Limitations and Its Uses," *Speech Monographs*, 37 (1970), 101–10. Reiches and Harral, "Argumentation in Negotiation," p. 39, note:

> In Douglas Ehninger's terms, they are engaged in a critical and cooperative investigation. Particularly fitting this view of negotiation, Ehninger claims that argument encompasses those situations in which mutually exclusive, or noncontenable, positions present themselves. Both arguers present their perspectives on the issue, and both may examine, probe, and correct the other's viewpoints. Hence they produce a dialectic, moving toward mutually acceptable conclusions.

26. R. Zemke, "Using Power to Negotiate: Everyone Can Do It—Successfully," *Training/HRD*, (February 1980), 29–30. (Quoting Herbert A. Cohen)

27. Reiches and Harral, "Argumentation in Negotiation, p. 39. An additional perspective can be found in W.A. Donohue, "An Empirical Framework for Examining Negotiation Processes and Outcomes," *Communication Monographs*, 45 (August 1978), 247–57.

28. M.S. Hanna, "Speech Communication Training Needs in the Business Community," *Central States Speech Journal*, 28 (Fall 1978), 163–72.

CHAPTER 15

1. The review of research on interviewing variables is drawn from R.D. Arvey and J.E. Campion, "The Employment Interview: A Summary and Review of Recent Research," *Personnel Psychology*, 35 (1982), 281–318.

2. Ibid., pp. 301–304.

3. Ibid.

4. Ibid.

5. Ibid.

6. Ibid., pp. 304–306.

7. Ibid.

8. Ibid.

9. Ibid.

10. J.R. Bittner, Consultant's report to the Personnel Department of Jefferson Pilot Broadcasting Company, Chapel Hill, N.C., July 1980.

11. Adapted from J.R. Bittner and D.A. Bittner, *Radio Journalism* (Englewood Cliffs, N.J.: Prentice-Hall, 1977), pp. 54–55.

12. J.A. Gilchrist, "The Compliance Interview: Negotiating Across Organizational Boundaries" (paper presented at the annual meeting of the International Communication Association, Boston 1982), p. 13.

13. Ibid., p. 14.

14. Ibid., p. 14.

15. S.A. Hellweg and C.A. Sullivan, "An Examination of Current Grievance Interviewing Practices in Major American Corporations" (paper presented at the annual meeting of the International Communication Association, Dallas, Texas, 1983), pp. 7–8.

16. *Job-Seeking, Resumes, Interviewing.* (Chapel Hill, N.C.: University Placement Services), p. 1. (n.d.)

17. R.E. Jones, "Your Interview—Be Prepared!" *ASCUS 80* (Madison, Wis.: ASCUS, 1980), 23. (No. 9 changed by author of this text to read his "or her.")

18. F.S. Endicott, as reported in "Making the Most of Your Job Interview," *ASCUS 80* (Madison, Wis.: ASCUS, 1980). The questions that recruiters frequently ask and the reasons that candidates for positions are frequently rejected are found in *The Northwestern Endicott Report*, published by the Placement Center, Northwestern University, Evanston, Illinois 60201.

19. Ibid.

20. Information on EEO guidelines and interviewing procedures can be found in many government and trade association sources. Especially helpful in the preparation of this section of the chapter was E.G. Aird, *A Broadcaster's Guide to Designing and Implementing an Effective EEO Program.* (Washington, D.C.: National Association of Broadcasters, 1980), 30–34.

CHAPTER 16

1. Tim Woodward, *The Idaho Statesman,*

2. A sociological framework for this approach can be found in the work of Hill. See, for example, R. Hill and D.A. Hansen, "The Identification of Conceptual Frameworks Utilized in Family Study," *Marriage and Family Living,* 22 (1960), 299–311; G. Miller, "The Current Status of Theory and Research in Interpersonal Communication," *Human Communication Research,* 4 (Winter 1978), 164–78.

3. As conceptualized by Bochner, in A.P. Bochner, "Conceptual Frontiers in the Study of Communication in Families: An Introduction of the Literature," *Human Communication Research,* 2 (Summer 1976), 381–97. Citing: E. Bott, *Family and Social Network: Roles, Norms, and External Relationships in Ordinary Urban Families* (New York: The Free Press, 1971); R.D. Hess and G. Handel, *Family Worlds: A Psychological Approach to Family Life* (Chicago: University of Chicago Press, 1959); D. Kantor and W. Lehr, *Inside the Family: Toward a Theory of Family Process* (San Francisco: Jossey-Bass, 1975); A. Koestler, *The Act of Creation* (New York: Macmillan, 1964); S. Minuchin, *Families and Family Therapy* (Cambridge, Mass: Harvard University Press, 1974); L. Wynne, I. Rychkoff, J. Day, and S. Hirsch, "Pseudo-Mutuality in the Family Relations of Schizophrenia," *Psychiatry,* 21 (1958), 205–20.

4. The work of Kantor and Lehr (*Inside the Family*) applies here, as does the research originating in the organizational literature. C. Barnard, *The Functions of the Executive* (Cambridge, Mass: Harvard University Press, 1938); F. Herzberg, "One More Time: How Do You Motivate Employees?" *Harvard Business Review,* 46 (January-February 1968); 53–62; R. Miles, "Keeping Informed—Human Relations or Human Resources?" *Harvard Business Review,* 43 (July-August 1965), 148–63.

5. H.L. Lennard and A. Bernstein, *Patterns in Human Interaction* (San Francisco: Jossey-Bass, 1969).

6. As reflected in E. Bett, *Family and Social Networks: Roles, Norms and External Relationships in Ordinary Urban Families* (New York: The Free Press, 1971); R.V. Speck and C.L. Attneave, *Family Networks* (New York: Random House, 1973).

7. Interesting popular perspectives on the generation gap are found in: T.I. Rubin, "Bring Back the Generation Gap," *Ladies' Home Journal,* (September 1974), 33; T. Griffith, "Party of One: The Generation That Won," *Atlantic,* 243 (May 1979), pp. 22, 26.

8. As reported in "Morris Massey: Values and the Workplace," *The New York Times,* October 12, 1980.

9. H.T. Hurt, J.D. Scott, and J.C. McCroskey, *Communication in the Classroom* (Reading, Mass: Addison-Wesley, 1978), p. 105.

10. Examples include B.S. Monfils, "The Aged as Subculture: A Pilot Study of Verbal Interaction Patterns" (paper presented at the annual meeting of the Speech Communication Association, San Antonio, Texas, 1979); A.J. de Long, "Environments for the Elderly," *Journal of Communication,* 24 (1974), 101–11; M.J. Graney and E.E. Graney, "Communications Activity Substitutions in Aging," *Journal of Communication,* 24 (1974), 88–95; H.J. Oyer and E.J. Oyer, "Communication with Older People: Basic Considerations," in *Aging and Communication,* eds. H.J. Oyer and E.J. Oyer (Baltimore: University Park Press, 1976), pp. 10–12.

11. E.R. Mahoney, "The Processual Characteristics of Self-Conception," *The Sociological Quarterly,* 14 (Autumn 1973), 517–33.

12. R. Cohn, "The Effect of Employment Status Change on Self-Attitudes," *Social Psychology,* 41 (1978), 81–93; J. Champoux, "Work, Central Life Interests, and Self-Concept," *Pacific Sociological Review,* 21 (1978), 209–20.

13. E. Palmore and C. Luikart, "Health and Social Factors Related to Life Satisfaction," *Journal of Health and Social Behavior,* 13 (1972), 68–80.

14. K. Connor, E. Powers, and G. Bultena, "Social Interaction and Life Satisfaction: An Empirical Assessment of Late-Life Patterns," *Journal of Gerontology,* 34 (1979), 116–21.

15. The following sources were especially helpful in preparing this section of the chapter: S. Kalter, *Instant Parent* (New York: A & W Publishers, 1979); C. Berman, *Making It as a Stepparent* (New York: Doubleday, 1980); L.A. Westoff, *The Second Time Around* (New York: Harper & Row, 1966); J. Noble and W. Noble, *How to Live with Other People's Children* (New York: Hawthorn Books, 1977); S. Gettleman and J. Markowitz, *The Courage to Divorce* (New York: Simon & Schuster, 1974).

CHAPTER 17

1. Expanded discussion of the subjects and issues treated in this chapter can be found in the author's texts: J.R. Bittner, *Mass Communication: An Introduction,* 4th ed. (Englewood Cliffs, N.J.: Prentice-Hall, 1983); J.R. Bittner, *Broadcasting and Telecommunication,* 2nd ed. (Englewood Cliffs, N.J.: Prentice-Hall, 1985).

Index

Positive tone, 152–55
Possessions, separation/divorce and, 329
Posted bulletins, 346
Post hoc, ergo propter hoc fallacy, 214
Postreinforcement, 251–52
Posture, 44, 237
  language of, 92–93
Power
  balance of, 275
  messages, 134
  negotiations and, 280
  in organizations, 273–74
    sharing of, 275
    structures of, 275–77
  in small groups, 172–73
  status vs., 172
  values, 191
Praise, personal space and, 82
Predicasts Basebook, 225
Predicasts Forecast, 225
Prediction, negotiations and, 280–81
Pregnancy, 309
Prejudice, listening and, 114
Presence of speaker, speech delivery and, 236–39
Presentation of self, 41–43
Press, government and, 293
Primal therapy, 49
Principles of Psychology, The (James), 41
Problem-solution plan for speech organization, 205–6
Problem-solving groups, 167
Procedural bonding, 165
Procedural statements, 170
Product distribution, 352
Programming
  radio, 348–49
  television, 349
Projective function of child language, 58
Proximity, law of, 14
Psychographics, audience, 189–92
Psychological Abstracts, 225
Psychological makeup, personal space and, 83
Psychological traits, 81
Public Affairs Information Services, 224
Publications, trade, 226–27
Public relations, 351–53
Public speaking, 5, 20–22. *See also* Speeches
Purpose, specific, 200–201

Questions and questioning
  fear of, 112–13
  primary areas of, 307–8
  responding to, 304–7
  rules of, 294–95
  secondary areas of, 308–10
  structuring, 292–93

Race of job applicant, 308
Radio, 336, 343–44, 348–49

Ratios, 216–17
Rawlins, Williams, 144–46
Reader's Guide to Periodical Literature, 224
Reasoning, 212
  speech making and, 213
Receiver styles, switching, 58, 116–17
Reciprocity, 50
Recruiters, company, 6. *See also* Interviews
Recurring communication patterns, 318
Reference sources, 222–23
Referent, 63–65
Regulations, organizational, 267–68
Reinforcement, 49
  through touch, 97–98
Rejection, latitude of, 255–56
Related-topics plan for speech organization, 206–7
Relational consequences, 135
Relational function of child language, 58
Relationship(s), 139–62
  breadth of, 142
  candor in, 145–46
  commonality and, 141–43
  contracts of, 157
  depth of, 141–42
  development of, 128
  ending, 152–55
  enhancement of, 50
  "extrafamily," 321
  flexibility in, 143
  helping, 48–49, 50
  "I'm OK, you're OK," 34–35
  inside, 147–49
  interpersonal attraction and, 146–47
    changes in, 150–52
  interpersonal bonding and, 140
  maintenance of, 50
  management of, 140–41
  messages, 134
  micro, 152
  press-government, 293
  rules of behavior and, 128
  shyness and, 43–44
  types of, 158–60
    societal values and, 160–61
  variables influencing, 155–58
  vulnerability and, 143–45
  See also Interpersonal communication
Relaxation
  adapting to stress through, 16
  strategies for, 232
Religious discrimination, 308, 309
Remembering, 107
  selective, 141
Repeating function of nonverbal communication, 84
Rephrasing, 110
Research, 219–28, 352
  abstracting services and, 224-25
  card catalogue and, 221–22
  compiling information for, 227
  indexes, 223–24

Speeches (*cont.*)
  statistics use in, 216–17
  support for, 210
  topic choice, 199–201
Speech sounds, producing, 233–34. *See also* Language
Stagnating stage of coming-apart, 151
Standard & Poor's Statistical Service, 225
Statements
  biased, 71–73, 74
  bypass, 45–47
  personal-involvement, 170, 171
  procedural, 170
  solution, 170–71
  superficial, 170, 171
  unity, 170, 171
  See also Language
Statistical abstracts, 225–26
Statistical Abstracts of the United States, 225
Statistical indexes, 225–26
Statistical Reference Index, 225
Statistics used in speeches, 216–17
Status
  personal space and, 81
  power vs., 172
  professional, of women, 44–45
  in small groups, 172–73
Stereotypes
  of elderly, 326
  facial, 93
  as family barrier, 325
  listening and, 115
  nonverbal, 86–87
  of self, 49
  of women, 73
Stimulus, unconditioned and conditioned, 251
Strategy(ies)
  compliance-gaining, 134
  in ending relationships, 152–55
  persuasive, 256
  for relaxation, 232
  for researching speech, 220–21
  for résumé, 302
Stress, 324–25
  adapting to, 15–16
  verbal immediacy and, 67–68
Stroking, 34–35, 327
  negative, 47
Structure(s)
  of discussion, 172
  of family, 316–17
  power, 275–77
Style(s)
  communication, 116–17
  language, 69
  leadership, 180
  receiver, 117
  sender, 117
  situational, 69
Subject-heading cards, 221

Substitute expressers, 94
Substituting function of nonverbal communication, 84, 90–91
Substitution of sound, 236
Summarizing, 110
Superficial statements, 170, 171
Supervisor, PR&A interview and, 290
Survey interviews, 292–93
Survey of Current Business, 225
Swain, Cynthia, 104
Switching of receiver styles, 58, 116–17
Syllogism, 212
Symbolic interaction, 129–30
Symbols, 10, 63–65. *See also* Language
Systems approach approach to management, 263–64

Task
  attraction, 147
  bonding, 165
  -oriented groups, 167–68
  ritual, 277
Technologies affecting mass communication, 345–46
Teletext, 345
Television, 336, 345–46, 349
  cable, 340, 345
  violence on, 214
Terminal branches, 12
Terminating stage of coming-apart, 152
Territorial space, 79–81
Tests, achievement, 39
T-groups (training groups), 169
Theory of Cognitive Dissonance, A (Festinger), 253
Therapeutic groups, 168–69
Therapy, primal, 49
Thinker, 117
Thinking interpersonally, 135–36
Time, 100–101
  interpersonal communication developing over, 127–28
  small-group meeting over, 166–67
Timing, 107–8
Title card, 221
Titles, 74
  sexist language and, 71–72
Tolerance of vulnerability, 144–45
Tone of voice, 106
  positive, 152–55
Topics
  personal space and, 82–83
  for speech, 199–201
Touch, 55, 97–99, 157
Trade publications, 226–27
Training, interviewer, 288–89
Training (T-) groups, 169
Traits, psychological, 81
Transaction, 8, 9, 10
Transfer, 8, 9